COLONIAL WEST AFRICA

COLONIAL WEST AFRICA

Collected Essays

MICHAEL CROWDER

First published 1978 in Great Britain by
FRANK CASS AND COMPANY LIMITED

This edition published 2012 by Routledge

Taylor & Francis Group, 711 Third Avenue, New York, NY 10017
Taylor & Francis Group, 2 Park Square, Milton Park, Abingdon, Oxon OX14 4RN

Copyright © 1978 Michael Crowder

ISBN13: 978-0-71462-943-8

All Rights Reserved. No part of this publication may be reproduced in any form or by any means, electronic, mechanical, photocopying, recording or otherwise, without the prior permission of Frank Cass and Company Limited in writing.

For my Father

CONTENTS

Preface

I. West Africa and the Europeans: Five Hundred Years of Direct Contact   1

II. Background to the Scramble   26

III. West African Resistance   45

IV. Bai Bureh and the Sierra Leone Hut Tax War of 1898 (*with LaRay Denzer*)   61

V. Blaise Diagne and the Recruitment of African Troops for the 1914-18 War   104

VI. The White Chiefs of Tropical Africa   122

VII. The Imposition of the Native Authority System in Bussa: the Rebellion of 1915   151

VIII. The French Suppression of the 1916-1917 Revolt in Dahomeyan Borgu   179

IX. Indirect Rule: French and British Style   198

X. West African Chiefs (*with Obaro Ikime*)   209

XI. West Africa 1919-1939: The Colonial Situation (*with J. F. Ade Ajayi*)   231

XII. Colonial Backwater   259
    (a) *Problems of the Gambia*
    (b) *Rice Revolution in the Gambia*

XIII. The Vichy Régime and Free France in West Africa during the Second World War   268

XIV. Independence as a Goal in French-speaking West African Politics: 1944-60   283

XV. Colonial Rule in West Africa: Factor for Division or Unity?   314

Index   331

PREFACE

For the past twenty years, since flying across the desert in a rickety military aircraft to join the Nigeria Regiment for fifteen months of National Service, I have been fascinated by the impact of colonial rule on West Africa. This fascination has been committed to print in a number of books and articles, including a travel book and a number of contributions to newspapers and magazines. Since many of my ideas on colonial rule in West Africa have been expressed in *West Africa under Colonial Rule,* when Messrs Frank Cass asked me whether they could publish a collection of my articles, I was at first hesitant to permit them to go ahead with the project. I did, however, finally agree in the hope that a series of my articles on the colonial period in West Africa scattered in different journals and symposia, might supplement rather than duplicate *West Africa under Colonial Rule.* In selecting the articles for publication I have tried to group them together so that they form as coherent a story as is possible for a series of papers which were never written with an eye to publication as a collection. To show colonial rule in West Africa from its inception to its end I have included a modified version of a section of a chapter in *West Africa under Colonial Rule* on the partition of West Africa. Though in some ways it is cheating to put a section of a book in a collection of essays, I hope that it will be accepted as necessary. Where I have changed my views, say, on the nature of the differences between French and British local administration in West Africa as between 'Indirect Rule – French and British Style' published in 1964, on the one hand, and 'West African Chiefs' published in 1970, on the other, I have made no attempt to reconcile them. Nor, when an interpretation has proved wrong, as that of the Niger election of 1958 in 'Independence as a Goal in French-speaking West African Politics, 1944-60' published in 1965 which has been effectively challenged by Finn Fugelstad's 'Djibo Bakary, the French and the Referendum of 1958 in Niger' in the *Journal of African History,* XIV, 2, 1973, have I altered it. I felt that the business of up-dating essays, some written more than a decade ago, would involve in some cases complete rewrites and change the character of the series in which this collection appears. I have, however, made minor changes to 'West African Resistance' and 'West African Chiefs' which were originally published as introductions to symposia. Their character as introductions has been altered to make them suitable for publication as independent essays. The only paper that has been substantially revised is

PREFACE

'Colonial Rule in West Africa: Factor for Division or Unity', since before being invited to publish this collection of essays I had already revised it for a public lecture at Makerere University. Inevitably in a collection such as this there is some repetition of explanation in the various essays since they were not written with an eye to publication in a single volume. In order not to destroy the original character of the essays in question, these have not been edited out, except in one case.

These essays treat a number of themes. The first is the contact between the varied cultures of Europe and the equally varied cultures of West Africa which began five hundred years ago. This theme, particularly as it relates to the colonial phase, runs through this volume of essays. The second theme is the scramble by the new, nationalistic powers of Europe to occupy Africa and the way in which Africans resisted them. After considering generally why West African resistance to European occupation was unsuccessful, a case study is presented of the Temne Hut Tax War against the British led by Bai Bureh of Kasseh. This is followed by a study of the widespread rebellions in French West Africa against colonial rule provoked by forced recruitment of Africans for service in the First World War. The role of Blaise Diagne, Deputy of Senegal, as an archetype of the men who accepted the European system in order to win concessions from it, is examined in the context of these rebellions, many of whose leaders hoped to regain their lost independence. This theme is re-echoed in a later essay on the movement for independence in French West Africa, which discusses the debate between those politicians who were prepared to work within the colonial framework provided, like Diagne, they could gain concessions thereby, and those who wanted independence.

The problems faced by the colonial powers in imposing new political, social and economic systems on West Africans is next examined, first from the point of view of the colonial rulers, in particular their representatives in the field – the White Chiefs of Tropical Africa. This is followed by two case studies of an African polity, Borgu, which was brought under two different types of colonial rule. The varying reactions of the Borgawa to British and French attempts to press their traditional administrative systems into new, alien forms of government are examined in relation to the revolts provoked by these attempts.

The short-term similarities and longer term differences between French and British administration of their West African colonies, which emerge so clearly in the Borgu case studies, are a recurring theme in this collection of essays and are drawn out in a more general study of Indirect Rule, French and British Style. Closely related to this is the fate of the chiefs, still a live issue in West African politics,

PREFACE

which raises wider questions concerning historical continuity in the political sphere.

The essay on the colonial situation provides a wider perspective on the total impact of European rule on West African society in the colonial phase, while the brief studies of the Gambia, made while it was still under British administration, provide a glimpse of that impact on a microcosm of colonial society to which the first concessions of eventual independence had not yet been made but when the historical movement towards that goal was already perfectly clear from what was taking place elsewhere in West Africa.

The concluding studies show how Francophone Africa moved towards independence: how French thinking on the relationship of their colonies to the motherland evolved during the Second World War and then how African thinking on this relationship moved from one of integration with profits to independence, if necessary without any dividends, that is from an assimilationist to an increasingly nationalist outlook on this relationship.

Finally, the West African experience of contact with Europe is summed up in an essay reflecting on the differences in political culture that French and British rule had produced and attempting to assess how deep the impact of colonial rule was both within individual colonies and as a factor inhibiting closer integration whether at the political or economic level between independent states that experienced different systems of colonial rule.

To Hutchinsons I am grateful for permission to publish the section of *West Africa under Colonial Rule* as well as the introduction to *West African Resistance*. I must also thank Oxford University Press, Cambridge University Press, Ife University Press, Longman and Walker of New York, as well as the editors of *Africa, Afro-Asia, Civilisations,* and *The Times* (for the now defunct *Times British Colonies Review*) for permission to include material which they first published. I am particularly grateful to Professor Adu Boahen for permitting me to print 'West Africa and the Europeans: Five Hundred Years of Direct Contact' which was specially commissioned by the Historical Society of Ghana. I must thank Professor Lalage Bown and, especially, Professor R. J. Gavin for advice and criticisms. I am very grateful to Professor J. F. Ade Ajayi, Professor Obaro Ikime and Miss LaRay Denzer for permitting me to publish articles which we jointly authored. Finally, I must thank Malam Rafiu Ibrahim for his patience in typing out the manuscript.

Lagos 1977   MICHAEL CROWDER

I

WEST AFRICA AND THE EUROPEANS: FIVE HUNDRED YEARS OF DIRECT CONTACT* (1971)

A BARREN THREE CENTURIES

When the Portuguese sea captains, João de Santarem and Pedro de Escobar, landed near Cape Coast in January 1471, five hundred years of direct contact between Europe and what is now Ghana began. Significantly in the context of Portuguese motives for undertaking the hazardous task of exploring the West African coast, the stretch of it on which these two captains landed was rich in supplies of gold and gold dust. Accordingly they named it El Mina, or the mine, though later it came to be known by the Europeans as the Gold Coast, the name it bore until 1957.

Apart from the desire of Christian Europe to break the Muslim monopoly of trade with the Far East by opening a sea route to India, Europeans wanted to gain access to West African gold supplies, which were also a monopoly of the Muslims. Their voyages of exploration were in addition partly motivated by missionary zeal: any African Kingdoms which they might convert to the Christian faith could be used to provide a counterbalance to Muslim power.

The discovery of the availability of ready gold supplies on the West African Coast was for Europe as significant as would be today the discovery of a new, major source of oil not under the control of the Arabs and their allies. Since gold, along with silver, formed the basis of the currency of Europe, and supplies of both came largely through the Muslim World at that time, the discovery of gold on the coast of modern Ghana broke the Muslim monopoly of this vital metal. Once the sea passage to India was opened, Europe now had an alternative means of access to Far Eastern goods, as well as plentiful supplies of

*This paper was written specially for the Conference of the Historical Society of Ghana held in 1971 to mark the 500th anniversary of the first arrival of Europeans on the coast of Ghana.

gold to use as foreign exchange for the purchase of these goods which it had previously had to purchase at much higher prices from the Arabs. The latter had also charged higher prices for West African gold than the Europeans now had to pay as a result of having direct access to it. Even after the mines of the Americas had been opened, West African gold remained important for European nations, since for long Spain alone controlled the output of the Transatlantic mines. Thus a number of European nations established themselves on the coast of modern Ghana, vying with each other for gold supplies, and in the process building a series of impressive forts which are among the few visible legacies of the first three hundred years of European contact with West Africa.

Although small quantities of gold had previously been purchased by the Portuguese explorers from Muslim merchants on the West Atlantic Coast, it was not until the coast of modern Ghana was reached that one of the three main objectives of the Portuguese exploration of Africa had been achieved: direct access to its gold supplies. Even before reaching the Gold Coast, Portuguese had shipped back some Negro-Africans as proof of the fact that they had rounded Cape Bojador. And, although the Americas had not yet been opened up by the Europeans, the potential use of Africa as a source of slaves had already been realised. One idea was to use them as labour in the thinly populated areas of Southern Portugal, from which the Muslim Arabs had recently been expelled, another was to put them to work on the plantations of the uninhabited but fertile lands of the island of São Thomé.

Early on then, the basic nature of the next three hundred years of contact between West Africa and Europe had been established: commerce in gold and slaves. True, before the sea-route to India had been opened, trade in ivory and peppers also interested other Europeans who followed in the wake of the Portuguese. But these were subsequently found to be more readily obtained direct from the Far East. The Portuguese, and the other European nations whose ships followed them, also indulged in the carrying trade along the coast. Indeed it could be argued that one of the most important results of the arrival of the tiny Portuguese caravels on the West Coast of Africa was to open up coastal trade. But it has been suggested elsewhere that African seamen themselves conducted long-distance trade along the coast, in sea-going canoes, so that the significance of the arrival of the Portuguese for coastal trade was not so great as has often been thought.[1]

Until the opening-up of the Americas in the sixteenth century, gold was the more important of the two principal items of trade with Europe. And supplies of gold were concentrated on the 'Gold Coast' since the gold fields of the interior were still inextricably tied up with the Arab-controlled trans-Saharan trade. Sixty years after the European arrival on the coast of modern Ghana, however, slaves began to surpass gold as West Africa's most important export to the European traders. On other stretches of the West African Coast, slaves were almost the only 'commodity' in which the Europeans were interested.[2] In the 'Gold Coast', gold continued to compete with humans as a source of foreign exchange for African traders interested in purchasing European goods.

For the three centuries between the start of the Atlantic Slave Trade and Britain's legislation against participation in it by its nationals in 1807, Europe's impact on West Africa was for the most part negative. The principal items exchanged for gold and slaves were cheap liquor, salt, cloth, dried fish, iron bars, copper, brass, cowrie shells and guns. With the exception of copper, brass, cowries and guns, all these items were locally obtainable in one form or another on the African coast.

Only copper, brass and salt were really scarce, while Africans could have learnt the technology of gun manufacture, as the Almami Samori was to prove in the nineteenth century. African life was not substantially enriched by the European trade.[3] The only technological advantage to Africans of the trade was the acquisition of guns, which were used as the principal instrument of prosecuting the wars by which slaves were secured as exchange for yet more guns and the other commodities Europe provided, which as we have said Africans could for the most part have produced themselves. The price: the sale of some twelve million or more Africans to the Americas, and the death of many more killed in the process of obtaining those who were sold into slavery. As a result, many societies were deprived of their man-power, since the slave traders were only interested in physically fit men, women and children.[4]

During the first three and a half centuries of West Africa's contact with Europe, few West Africans learnt how to read or write, let alone avail themselves of the education that was available to the upper classes of Europe.[5] A notable exception was, of course, the Reverend Philip Quaque of Cape Coast.[6] The Europeans gave them little inkling of the technological and cultural changes that were taking place in their own continent in those years.

After a few desultory attempts at conversion to Christianity, little attempt was made to evangelise West Africans.[7] Nor were European ideas on government and law borrowed by West Africans. The most that can be said culturally to have resulted from Europe's contact with West Africa was the development of crude pidgins, which, judging by the Diary of the Calabar trader, Antera Duke, could hardly be said to have enriched the English language.[8]

This very limited cultural influence of Europe on West Africa contrasts dramatically with the much more extensive impact of Arab culture. Take, for example, the three centuries of contact between the Hausa States of Kano and Katsina and the Arabs during the same period. It seems that trade across the desert between North Africa and the Hausa states did not really open up until the fifteenth century.[9] Islam had percolated through to both Kano and Katsina as a result of trade with Wangara merchants from Mali and with Kanem-Borno, both already deeply involved in the trans-Saharan trade. By the time the trans-Saharan trade had become an important factor for Kano and Katsina, both their Kings, Mohammed Rumfa and Mohammed Korau, had become Muslims. Not only did they adopt the religion of the Arab traders but they sought advice from a distinguished Muslim jurist, Al-Maghili, as to how they should run their governments according to Muslim law. For them, he wrote a treatise, subsequently translated into English as *The Obligations of Princes*.[10] Mohammed Rumfa himself is remembered as a great *Mujaddid* or Muslim reformer.

Islam had, of course, long since become an important factor in some other states of the Western and Central Sudan with which the Arabs had already opened up trade: Ghana, its successor Mali, and Kanem-Borno. The reason for here singling out Kano and Katsina is that Arab trade with these two states began at roughly the same time as European trade began with West Africa. And yet the cultural impact of the two sets of traders was of a totally different order. Despite the proximity of the European ports to the capital of the Asante Empire, the Asantahene Osei Kojo (1764-77) employed literate Muslim Africans in his chancery, not literate Christian Africans for there were none available.[11] While Africans adopted the religion of the Arab traders and its adjuncts of literacy, a legal system and system of government, the Europeans made negligible cultural impact. In the Hausa states, the Islamic religion had been sufficiently implanted in these same three hundred years to provoke a *jihad* or holy war by Muslims against rulers whom they accused of not governing their people according to the *sharia*. The extent of the learning that backed up this attempt at reform is amply demonstrated by the writings of its leader, the Shehu Usman dan Fodio, his brother Abdullahi, and his son, the Caliph Muhammad Bello.

Initially of course the Portuguese had intended that they both trade with Black Africans and convert them to their religion. In their confrontation with the Muslim world, a Christian Black Africa might be used as an effective counter balance. Hence the search for Prester John. In Benin the Portuguese tried to convert the king, and De Barros, Commander of the Fort of São Jorge da Mina (El Mina) from

WEST AFRICA AND THE EUROPEANS

1522 to 1515, was to write:

> Though the Christianising of these people of the Congo progressed greatly to the glory of God, through conversion of their King, little profit accrued from what the King (of Portugal) did in the matter of the request of the King of Beny, whose kingdom lay between that of Congo and the Castle of S. Jorge da Mina. For at the time of Diogo Cam's first return from Congo, in the year fourteen hundred and eighty six, this King of Beny also sent to solicit the King (of Portugal) to dispatch thither priests who might instruct him in the Faith. . . . But, as the King of Beny was very much under the influence of his idolatories, and sought the priests rather to make himself powerful against his neighbours with our favour than from a desire for baptism, he profited little from the ministrations of those sent thither. On this account they were recalled. . . .[12]

Where the Portuguese were disheartened by such attitudes,[13] the Arabs and their converts persevered, for the number of 'mixers' in the Western Sudan were legion. But the end product was the establishment of Muslim polities ruled according to the *sharia*, as in the case of Usman dan Fodio's establishment of the Sokoto Caliphate.

The story of the Portuguese experiment in the Kongo Kingdom is instructive about the nature of the European-African contact in these three centuries. When the Portuguese reached the Kongo in 1483, they found a well-organised kingdom whose ruler agreed readily to trade with Portugal. He received missionaries and by 1506 had became a practising Christian. The Portuguese persuaded his successor, King Affonso, to adopt European titles so that his vassal kings became Dukes, and in 1595 a Portuguese report on the organisation of the kingdom described it as having under the King 'six Christian dukes, who may either be called little kings . . . and as well as these, there are catholic counts and marquises who obey the King's orders . . .'[14] Here a parallel may be drawn with the Caliphates that were established in West Africa where the titles Amir al Mumunin was taken by the Caliph and Amir by his provincial governors in the case of Sokoto.

The Portuguese, indeed, gave technical aid to the kingdom, sending Congolese to Europe for education, helping rebuild in stone its capital, now called San Salvador, sending out carpenters and other skilled artisans. The Portuguese, not unlike Al-Maghili, tried to instruct their converted King Affonso (1507-1543) in how to run a Christian State. An ardent Christian, he was perhaps the parallel of Muhammed Rumfa of Kano of whom it was written in *The Kano Chronicle:* 'He was a good man, just and learned; he can have no equal in might from the time of the founding of Kano until it shall end'.[15]

What then went wrong with the Portuguese experiment in the Kongo? Though Affonso was a Christian, he indulged in some slave trading as the only means of securing the foreign exchange to develop his state. But Portuguese demands for slaves for their new colony of Brazil, established in 1500, proved insatiable and in 1526 Affonso complained to his brother the King of Portugal about the effects of these demands. 'We cannot reckon how great the damage is... and so great, Sire, is the corruption and licentiousness that our country is being completely depopulated'.[16] In short, when it came to a choice between creating a Christian State in Africa and securing slaves for the development of Brazil, the latter was paramount as far as the Portuguese were concerned.

'Technical assistance' was withdrawn, and by 1575, to ensure regular supplies of slaves from the area, Paulo Dias de Novais was sent as *conquistador* to give Portugal a firm base at Luanda, south of the Kingdom of Kongo, for her slave supplies. Appeals were made by the Christian Kings of the Kongo whose southern provinces were being raided by the Portuguese for slaves, to the Holy Father in Rome to stop the depredations. But despite the Pope's letters to the Kings of Portugal, nothing was done and the once-mighty Christian Kingdom of the Kongo soon disintegrated as a result of Portuguese slave-raiding.

For the Europeans, then, before 1800, slave supplies from Africa were far more important than imparting their religion and their technology to its inhabitants. Africa gained little of Europe's developing technology, but lost her manpower to assist in its development.

It may, however, be argued that the Arab contact with West Africa also depended on the slave trade. The main difference was that Arab demands were of a much lesser dimension, since they did not have plantations to run. So in their relations with Western Sudanese States the issue of slavery never loomed so large.[17]

The slave trade made the relationship between West Africans and Europeans a culturally barren one. But the contact between the two had profound effects, beyond the direct one of removing the able-bodied. The coast, which hitherto had been of little importance, now became an area of great prosperity. External trade, instead of being exclusively directed northwards to the Sahara 'sea', was now also directed southwards to the Atlantic. New states arose to take advantage of the trade with the Europeans; others, already established, developed into more powerful polities. The Atlantic Coast assumed much of its importance in West African history because of the arrival of the Europeans. We must, however, be careful in our attributions of the development of states exclusively to the slave trade. Benin and Ife certainly existed as major states near the coast long before the European arrival; and the case has been made by Alagoa (contrary to Horton) that the Niger Delta states owed their origin to Lagoon trade *prior* to the European arrival and not to the opportunities offered by the slave trade, though he accepts that this speeded up their growth.[18] The slave trade, too, had the effect of creating a diaspora of the Negro race into the Americas and the Caribbean so that it now forms one-tenth of their population, and in countries like Brazil, Cuba and Haiti it has heavily influenced cultural life.

While the contact between Europe and West Africa before 1800 can legitimately be described as a culturally barren one, there was one enclave where Europe had left a legacy of its culture – in Saint Louis de Sénégal, whose significance we shall discuss below.

Three final points should be made with regard to these first three centuries of contact between West Africa and Europe. First, the slave trade, as Christopher Fyfe has pointed out, clearly exacerbated distinctions between those rulers who indulged in it and their subjects, by concentrating considerable wealth in their hands.[19] Secondly, as Walter Rodney has convincingly argued, the European slave trade, as the Arab slave trade before it, introduced a new concept of slavery to West African society: that is of slaves who were not just a servile group in society, but merchandise for sale and purchase.[20] Finally, in contrast with what happened on the Angolan coast, the Europeans traded with Africans at the latter's pleasure as commercial and, let it be said, moral equals.

NINETEENTH CENTURY ESSAYS IN ASSIMILATION

The nineteenth century history of West Africa is dominated by the movements for Islamic reform, starting with the *Jihad* of Usman dan Fodio. The attacks on lax Muslim Kings or on 'pagan' states by the Jihadists had some repercussion on almost every African state; only a few corners like the Niger Delta and its Ibo-Ibibio hinterland were not affected. By comparison with the impact of these jihads, which sought to establish societies in West Africa ruled according to the *sharia* and were the logical outcome of long years of Muslim proselytism, the European impact on West Africa in the nineteenth century can at a casual glance appear to have been negligible. After all, before 1880 Europe had only tentative footholds on the coastline of West Africa: Senegal, Gambia, the Gold Coast and Lagos.

In terms of the lands occupied by reformist Muslim rulers, the square mileage of European-controlled territory stood in the same contrast as Albania to the Warsaw Pact Powers. But whereas we have argued that contact with Europe during the first three centuries had had negligible positive results for West Africans, now it must be asserted that in the nineteenth century Europeans were to sow the seeds of a revolution that was to affect West African societies more profoundly than even the Jihads.

When in 1807 the British Parliament forbade slave-trading by its nationals few foresaw that this act would have as great an impact on West Africa as the *jihads* which were sweeping the Western Sudan.[21] On the face of it, the Act of Abolition merely stopped slave traders of one European nation trading in slaves with Africans; there were plenty of other nations still prepared to continue with the trade. The economic motives for the British Abolition have been the subject of considerable debate, and need not concern us here. What was important is that Britain, whether for economic or humanitarian reasons, was determined to see that the slave trade was brought to a halt altogether. To achieve this, not only did she persuade other nations to abolish the trade, but she also established a patrol of her Navy to intercept slave-ships, free the slaves and settle them in the Christian Community for Freed Blacks established in Sierra Leone by Granville Sharp. For the first time, the government of a slave-trading European nation had questioned the morality of the slave trade, though of course there had been many individuals who had done so before the British Parliament made its decision. There were, too, economic arguments in favour of the abolition for Industrial Britain, in that trade in the 'legitimate' goods of West Africa now became of greater importance to her economy than the import of slaves into her few West Indian possessions. But a number of the advocates of abolition passionately believed that the slave-trade and indeed slavery itself was a sin against God, and were determined to see its end. These humanitarians, as they came to be known, were, like the Jihadists, inspired by the desire to convert Africans to their own religion. Where for three and a half centuries Europeans had shown little interest in proselytising West Africans, and where what they had done had met with little success, *now* great plans were made to evangelise West Africa.

These plans coincided with the interests of industrialists in Britain, anxious to find new markets for their goods and to ensure regular supplies of palm-oil and other West African products needed for their factories. If missionaries could evangelise the interior and persuade African rulers to abandon trade in slaves, so that the manpower thus released could be used for the production of palm-oil and cotton, or the felling of timber, this would be to their advantage. *The humanitarians, for their part, saw that while the Anti-Slavery Squadron of the British Navy could stop some export of the slaves, the coastline was too great, and the patrol too small, for it to eradicate it; and indeed the first half of the nineteenth century was to be the heyday of the Atlantic

Slave Trade. What was needed, as they saw it, was to persuade African rulers that there were means of gaining foreign exchange other than the sale of Africa's manpower to European traders. Hence the early close alliance between industrialists and the humanitarians in the attempt to open up the interior of West Africa to Europe. The list of the patrons of the African Association, which financed most of the major British exploring voyages of the early nineteenth century, bears witness to this.[22] The expeditions up the Niger, the supposed highway into the interior of West Africa, were also joint missionary-industrialist enterprises.

The British, and later other Europeans, were now concerned with reforming West African society to conform with its norms, just as Muslims had been for centuries before. The British, and subsequently other European nations, underwent a radical change in their attitudes to Africans. From being moral equals with Africans with whom they traded, they now posed as moral superiors. Commercially, as Christopher Fyfe has put it, they now wanted to deal with Africans as customers rather than merchandise.[23] Further, they wanted to convert them to their own way of life and this implied, at least for most of the nineteenth century that, like the Muslim Arabs, they were prepared to treat Africans as equals once they had accepted their religion. Though at the same time these same humanitarians demoted Africa in the European mind by describing it not as the continent of the noble savage but one of 'slavery and sin'.[24] Nevertheless Europeans before the 1860s largely held to universalist values which transcended the bounds of race.[25] It was only in the latter half of the nineteenth century that racist theories which placed Africans at the bottom of the ladder of achievement and Europeans at the top took hold. The story of Sierra Leone, the Gold Coast, Senegal, and the little British Colony of Lagos before the Scramble for Africa are instructive to this end, as we shall see. In the government of these colonies, Africans or Mulattoes attained high administrative posts, which after the invasion of Africa by the European powers at the end of the century they were not to achieve again until independence.

Until the Scramble for Africa the European nations were for the most part prepared to spread their trading influence and their religion by peaceful means, though where life seemed in danger, or where coastal kings were unwilling to abandon the slave trade, force was called on. But, with the notable exception of Faidherbe's conquest of the Senegal river valley, until the late 1870s European nations preferred to trade and evangelise without control of their home government being extended over the areas in which they worked.

The European missionaries, like their Muslim counterparts,

wished to impose on Africans their ideas of the way life should be lived. They wanted not only to abolish the Transatlantic Slave Trade, but all forms of slavery. They wished to stop all practices that were repugnant to their religion: human sacrifice, twin murder and cannibalism where they existed. But above all they wanted to persuade Africans to abandon their own gods for the Christian God, and to live the Christian way of life (as they, the missionaries, understood it). In a sense, they were taking up the experiment started and then abandoned by the Portuguese in Kongo three centuries before. Alongside instruction in the Christian way of life they also taught Africans elements of European technology, such as carpentry, masonry and printing. Commerce and Christianity would go hand in hand: the Bible and the Plough. For the nineteenth century humanitarians the two were not separate, but interdependent variables, so that the promotion of trade could in turn lead to conversion and vice versa. Above all, to teach Africans to read their Holy Book, the Bible, they had to provide them with education. Thus, like the Muslims long before them, they introduced literacy to Africans, this time in European languages or their own languages in Roman script. But their education did not stop just there. They also wanted to train priests, so that some Africans were sent, like Samuel Ajayi Crowther, to England for training. Others were trained in local institutions, notably Fourah Bay College, which was founded in 1814 and in 1876 achieved University College status. Such education had a second and just as important purpose, to train clerks and officials for the commercial companies and for the administration of the colonial enclaves of West Africa. One of the first things Faidherbe did when he became Governor of Senegal was to establish additional schools in Saint Louis.

Where European governments were established in West Africa, they attempted to introduce European systems of law and order, a notable example being the informal administration of George Maclean and his successors in the Fante States where, by the 1860s, British law had largely replaced African law, that is even before the Fante States were finally made a colony of the British Empire.

In all these activities the nineteenth century Europeans can be seen as not very different from the Muslim reformers. They wished to introduce the concept of one God to Africans, to make their Holy Book available to them and through education to establish their norms of behaviour in African societies: in government, justice and commercial practice. Like the Arabs earlier, the Europeans had the conviction that Africans could achieve the same levels of education as themselves, and could do jobs that they themselves did as equals. The only difference before 1870 was that, unlike the Jihadists, they did not seek to impose their ideas by force but, as the early Muslim Arabs had, by preaching. In general, it was only after the 1870s that the Europeans tried armed might to press their notions of good government on West Africans.[26] As we shall see, resort was to be made later to military conquest, and once having conquered West Africa, they did not continue in the early spirit of the nineteenth century. Africans, from being treated as potential equals of Europeans, were to be treated as a subject and inferior race, second-class citizens in their own lands.

It is easy to forget, with the memory of the colonial era so vivid in African minds, that during the nineteenth century, Europeans whether French or British had accepted Africans as men of equal capabilities once they had accepted the European way of life. In this context it is instructive to examine nineteenth century French and British experiments in cultural assimilation on the West African Coast.

But before we do so, it is also important to appreciate the extent of the economic revolution that the trade in the products of Africa as distinct from its manpower brought about. While trade in gold continued, and the trade in slaves progressively diminished, new items for foreign exchange were developed during the nineteenth century: groundnuts, palm-oil, cotton and later cocoa and coffee. It is important to note that these were produced by Africans on their own initiative once their value as export items was realised. Palm-oil plantations were established in Old Calabar and Dahomey; groundnuts were produced in the Senegambian region outside Faidherbe's riverain colony of the Senegal. Indeed French and British traders preferred to trade outside areas controlled by their governments, for the obvious reason that they did not then have to pay taxes to them. Even when colonial rule was imposed, the cocoa revolution in Ghana owed very little to government assistance but was largely generated by Africans themselves.[27] The essential point here is that African states, once they had become aware of new commercial possibilities, were able to undertake the necessary social reorganisation to take advantage of them. After all, the gold trade across the Sahara had been undertaken without Arab occupation,[28] as had the gold and slave trade on the Coast without European occupation.

During the nineteenth century, European demands for the legitimate products of Africa, and the abandonment of the slave trade produced a profound economic revolution in West Africa. Some states like Old Calabar were able easily to switch from slaves to palm-oil. Some societies, in which the slave trade had not been of great importance, became rich because they had products which the Europeans now wanted. Other societies, which had depended on the slave trade, but now had no substitute to offer the Europeans, languished. But perhaps the most profound effect of the opening up of legitimate trade with the Coast, was to re-orient the West African economy increasingly away from the Sahara 'sea' to the Atlantic ocean so that after the 1870s the Trans-Saharan trade began to decline.

From the cultural point of view, the nineteenth century experiments in assimilation of West Africans by the European powers in their coastal enclaves were, though on a small-scale, of enduring importance for West Africa. For once colonial rule had been imposed on West Africa, and Africans reduced to the status of second-class citizens, excluded from the senior service of their governments, the memory of their past achievements in the European cultural ambit remained as an inspiration for future generations.

Both the French in Senegal and the British in their enclaves in the Gambia, Sierra Leone, the Gold Coast and Lagos, practised a policy of assimilation. That is, they considered not only that Africans, given appropriate educational opportunities, could be their equals, but that they could operate metropolitan models of government. Thus, in the Senegal, French law and French representative councils were introduced, while in the British Colonies of the Gambia, Gold Coast and Lagos, Legislative Councils and Executive Councils, similar to those devised for the white colonies, were established with Africans as well as Europeans as members.

The French had begun their assimilationist experiment much earlier than the British: France had occupied Saint Louis de Sénégal since 1659 with rude interruptions by Britain during the Seven Years and Napoleonic Wars. A mixed community of French, Mulattoes and Negro-Africans had sent their *Cahier des Doléances* to the Estates-General, and after the Napoleonic wars the French government made it clear in a despatch to Governor Schmaltz that the coloured population of Saint Louis and Gorée enjoyed 'the same status as the whites do. A mulatto is now mayor of the capital of our possessions, and a black could become so too'.[29] Schmaltz's successor, Baron Roger, was informed that the free population of Saint Louis was 'composed in great part of free Negroes and Mulattoes who have enjoyed up till now equal rights with the Europeans and who have the same privilege of having mayors chosen from among them, (and) it is very important not to let the same discriminations and prejudices such as exist in other colonies be introduced among them'.[30] That French attitudes in these respects were genuine was given ample witness by the fact that the first Deputy to be elected by Senegal in 1848 to the French Chamber of Deputies was a Mulatto, Durand Valentin. Al-Hajj Omar's siege of the French fort of Medina was lifted by the Mulatto Paul Holle, while the French conquistador of Dahomey was a Saint-Louisien, General Dodds.⁽³¹⁾ The small *colony* of Senegal by the time of the Scramble was endowed with the same representative institutions as a Department of Metropolitan France: Communes de Pleine Exercice, a Conseil-Général, and a seat in the Chamber of Deputies. Mulattoes and Africans served in the senior échelons of the Administration. It was an African officer, Yaro Coumba, who successfully defended the French post at Sénédoubou against Mahmadou L amine.

This legacy of equality lingered on into the twentieth century, when Blaise Diagne, having been elected Deputy for Senegal, was made High Commissioner for the Recruitment of Troops in 1918 with equal status to the Governor-General of French West Africa, and later became Under-Secretary for Colonies. By this time, France had long abandoned her policy of assimilating her African population; and, apart from the inhabitants of the *colony* as distinct from the *protectorate* of Senegal, the great mass of West Africans were *sujets* with no legal rights. But the point was that France had shown that she could accept Africans as equals, and they for their part had proved that they could take as full advantage of the educational opportunities offered them as white men.

While in the British colonies, with the exception of Sierra Leone, the British never went as far as the French in endowing them with metropolitan institutions, it was accepted that Africans could undertake the work of Europeans on equal terms. In Sierra Leone, the re-captives were settled in communities modelled on English villages, with jolly names like Regent, Hastings and Waterloo. Each had its village church and school. In the capital, Freetown, an institution of higher learning was established. When the Executive and Legislative Councils were established in 1863, Africans were represented on both. In 1893 Freetown was created a municipality with an elected Mayor. Samuel Lewis, the first to hold this office, was also made the first African knight.

By the 1870s Africans held half the posts in the civil service and Sir John Pope-Hennessy, admittedly a somewhat idiosyncratic Governor,⁽³²⁾ declared that there were enough qualified Africans to man the whole Senior Service of the Colony.⁽³³⁾ The educated re-captives and settlers of Sierra Leone, who by the mid-century had become known as Creoles, provided an African elite who staffed not only the administration of their own colony but also the Gambia, the Gold Coast and Lagos. A short list of the offices they and other educated West Africans held shows that in the nineteenth century the British were prepared to accept and use Africans in the highest offices of state. Samuel Ajayi Crowther, a re-captive Yoruba, became Bishop of the Queen's Dominions in West Africa; J.A.B. Horton became the first West African doctor, with a commission in the British Army; J.N. Parkes became Secretary of Native Affairs at the time Britain was expanding into the future Sierra Leone Protectorate. A Creole acted as Chief Justice, and another as Colonial Secretary of Sierra Leone. In 1875 in Lagos the head of police, the head of posts and telegraphs, the head of customs and the Registrar of the Supreme Court were all Nigerians.[34] They also contributed to the study of the history, languages and even medicine of West Africa.[35]

In the Gold Coast, the story was not dissimilar. But it had an unusual twist, for Africans, having benefited from European education, tried to establish a government of their own based partly on a European model. The story of the Fante Confederacy need not be discussed in detail here: an educated African, James Africanus Beale Horton, wrote its constitution, educated Africans took the chief administrative and executive offices of the new state under the presidency of a 'traditional' ruler. An army was formed, taxes levied and courts operating both British and customary law established. But the Confederation was short-lived, largely because the British were not prepared to have Africans, over whom they had an informal protectorate, establish a government *independent* of their control. And this despite the recommendation of the Parliamentary Select Committee of 1865 that it should be British policy in West Africa 'to encourage in the natives the exercise of those qualities which may render it possible for us more and more to transfer to them the administration of all the Governments (British), with a view to our ultimate withdrawal from all except, probably, Sierra Leone'.[36]

Despite apparent French and British willingness to accept Africans as equals in the nineteenth century, two factors militated against any ultimate transfer of power to them. The undermining of the Fante Confederation by the British shows that, whatever British policy at *home* may have been, the administrators *on the spot* were expansionists. However much the French Parliament or the British Treasury at home may have railed against colonial ventures, governors and soldiers on the spot were to press increasingly, and sometimes contrary to express orders from home, for expansion of their colonies.[37] Africans could serve under European Governments in the highest posts: but education and the training they received in the civil service and professions were not designed in the eyes of local governors – Pope-Hennessy excepted – to equip them for self-government. Secondly there was throughout the nineteenth century an underlying current of racism amongst the Europeans who may have accepted Africans as professional colleagues, but could not accept subordination to them. Thus though Henry Venn, Secretary of the Church

Missionary Society in England, could conceive of an African of Crowther's qualities being Bishop over all his society's missions in West Africa, the English missionary Henry Townsend in Abeokuta could not.[38] And Abeokuta, where Crowther himself had laboured as a missionary, was therefore excluded from his jurisdiction.

In Senegal, when a committee of French officials, naval officers and parliamentarians and one trader considered the future of French trade and settlements in Africa, while accepting that Bambara soldiers were 'as good as white soldiers' it recommended 'that these (native) troops should be completely assimilated to troops sent from Europe in regard to pay and rations, though care should be taken that they are organised in separate units...'[39]

By the end of the nineteenth century, though a substantial French- and English-speaking educated African class had developed, they were now to find themselves disinherited. Two factors account for this. First, in both Britain and France, racist theories proclaiming the natural inferiority of the Black Race had gained wide currency by that time.[40] Secondly, while it was relatively easy to assimilate a small group of Africans in coastal enclaves, the problems of pursuing such a policy in the vast areas invaded and occupied by the Europeans between 1880 and 1904 were insurmountable. For one thing, the sheer cost of introducing education to so large and scattered a population was prohibitive; and in many Muslim areas open hostility was shown to attempts to introduce missionary education.[41] For another, when confronted by the diversity of societies, in many different stages of technological development, the Europeans — French and British — could claim to have confirmed for themselves the current theories about the 'inferiority' of the African. At best, they held that the African was separate but equal,[42] and that European education would destroy his natural dignity.[43] But more generally they had come to believe with Sir Harry Johnston that it was 'the white-skinned sub-species which alone had evolved the beauty of facial features and originality of invention in thought and deed'.[44]

So Africans, from having participated in the governments established by the Europeans before 1880, were now subjected to them. The educated elite no longer had a say in how they and their fellow citizens were to be governed. But throughout the next sixty years of colonial rule it was they, and those few who were fortunate to gain higher education during the colonial period, who were to voice the demand that once more they participate in the governments set over them. They had proved to themselves that they could do so effectively and efficiently in the nineteenth century; and all the oppressions of the colonial rulers in the twentieth century and what Professor Ajayi has called their quaint racist theories[45] did not shake their belief in their own capacities. Thus in the nineteenth century Europe had sown the seeds of her own demise as a colonial power in West Africa not only by educating Africans but by employing them in the highest posts in their colonies' governments, thereby showing these very same Africans that Europeans, even though they had now adopted racist policies, had once believed in their abilities.

WEST AFRICA SUBJECTED TO EUROPE

This is no place to examine in detail either the motives for Europe's invasion of West Africa or the reasons for Africa's resistance. Superior weaponry and military drill enabled European officers and sergeants leading African soldiers to overcome the mightiest empires of West Africa.[46] This superiority had only been established by the latter half of the nineteenth century with the invention of rapid-firing guns like the Gatling and Maxim and the discovery that quinine acted as a prophylactic against the West African 'fever'. Asante had shown before then that a European army could be defeated, while Samori demonstrated that with a modest supply of rapid-firing rifles and an understanding of European military tactics, he could give the invading French more than a good run for their money. But by and large the comparative ease with which Europe conquered her African territories had a traumatic effect on African societies. The empires and states of nineteenth century West Africa were now dismembered or integrated into a new state system determined by the British, French, Germans and Portuguese. As far as the world of nineteenth century Africa was concerned things had apparently fallen apart. As the Yoruba say, *Aiye d'aiye Oyinbo*: 'the world has become a white man's world'. Today, the extent to which this view of the colonial period is true is being increasingly questioned. During the sixty years of colonial occupation Africans retained much more initiative in the colonial situation than has been generally supposed. The European invasion did not mean a rude break with the past for most African societies: sovereignty was lost, but in most societies pre-colonial rulers, culture and law survived, either covertly or with the approval of the colonial rulers, as in the British Native Authority system. When Europeans were seen to be at a disadvantage, as the French were during the First World War,[47] Africans did not hesitate to rebel and seek once more their independence;[48] though of course they found that ultimately the Europeans had the power to re-conquer them. But generally lack of sufficient force at their disposal, and lack of sufficient numbers of European administrators and technicians, meant that both French and British had to design their administrative systems so as to achieve their exploitative aims without provoking the African into open resistance. And the fact that French rule was more generally reckoned by Africans in the colonial period to have been harsher than that of the British provoked mass migrations from French-controlled to British-controlled territories, particularly during the French compulsory recruitments during the First World War.[49] So West Africans at least retained the negative initiative of being able to opt out of a system of rule they did not like, though of course their choice was severely limited.

We are not concerned here to examine in depth African initiatives in the face of colonial rule — whether in the field of politics, culture or religion. Rather we wish to emphasise that in trying to analyse the nature of Europe's impact on West Africa when it was under her full control, we should not forget that there was an African side to the story.

Against this background, our concluding task in this study is to try and assess not only how great the European impact on West Africa was, but in what ways it manifested itself. For all the talk of a *mission civilisatrice*, the overriding motive for the European occupation in Africa was economic, whether it was to avoid a rival European power establishing a monopoly in one trading area, or to reduce an African ruler who was inimical to European trading ambitions. The administrative systems designed by the French and the British were intended to facilitate trade with and the opening up of the resources of their African colonies. For the Europeans successfully to administer and exploit their African colonies, railways, roads, bridges and harbours had to be built and telegraph lines laid. European residential areas with clean water and sanitary facilities had to be constructed. Furthermore offices for government and commerce had to be built and staffed. The alternative to bringing out Europeans to provide these facilities and staff the commercial and governmental administrations even at the most junior levels, was to train Africans to assist them.

While the Europeans may not have permitted Africans, so to speak, to drive the engines, they needed Africans to assist as fitters, sell the tickets and maintain the railway lines. The whole subaltern organisation of the colonial administration and economy required the training of Africans. There simply were not the Europeans available or willing to undertake these tasks. For this African subaltern class to be effective, education, at least at a primary level, was necessary; so the British, French and the Germans, either directly or through missionaries, established schools to provide themselves with these subalterns. The intention was certainly no longer to educate Africans to take over the directorial posts in government, business or even, now, the church.[50] But formal Western-style education once given to intelligent youth, did not necessarily stop where the colonial masters intended it to. In any case there was already an educated elite in the coastal towns of both French and British West Africa who knew the advantages of higher education and were determined to secure it for at least some of their fellow countrymen. Thus the European powers, by providing West Africans with the modicum of education needed to enable those powers to administer and exploit West Africa, initiated Africans into the secrets of their own technological superiority. And it was this apparently overwhelming technological superiority of Europeans to Africans which was the most important factor in the colonial situation.

Education not only provided Africans with the key to understanding Europe's technology; it also revealed that Europeans practised one policy at home, another in the colonies.

Lamine Guèye, who became Mayor of Dakar and sometime Deputy of Senegal, recalls in his memoirs *Itinéraire Africaine* how hollow the words *liberté, egalité* and *fraternité* seemed to him in his youth.[51] Many African leaders were to appeal to European domestic practice of democracy and law in their calls for reform. Some did so bitterly, as I. T. A. Wallace Johnson, the Sierra Leonean nationalist, who on the occasion of the Italian invasion of Ethiopia wrote in the *African Morning Post*: 'Ye "civilised" Europeans, you must "civilise" the "barbarous" Africans with machine guns. Ye Christian Europeans, you must "Christianise" the pagan Africans with bombs, poison gases, etc'.[52]

Much less virulently, Senghor appealed to French metropolitan standards when he told the Second Constituent Assembly 'If the French Union is to endure, and here I am ,.. reiterating the thesis of the Socialist Party, it is essential for it to be founded on liberty and equality, conditions of human brotherhood and of French brotherhood'.[53]

In retrospect the most important single contribution of Europe to West Africa was formal style western education, whatever the motives for which it was given, or however it was obtained. Such education before the end of colonial rule was acquired by only a small elite. For the vast majority of West Africans life was not radically changed by the colonial conquest. Many Africans still live today much as they did before the invasion. Economically, comparatively few were affected by colonial exploitation other than by having to pay taxes. Few became wage-earners in the urban centres. Apart from cocoa and coffee, cash crops brought in only modest revenues for the farmer; certainly not enough to enable him substantially to enrich his way of life. For most West Africans the major change brought about by the European occupation was that a new set of chiefs ruled him: the white Residents and Commandants de Cercle. And in British West Africa, where indirect rule was practised, the white administrator was a high god, whose lesser gods, the traditional chiefs, were perceived by the people still to be the effective authorities. There are areas in Tivland in Nigeria, even today, where no one has ever seen a white man.[54]

One feature of the colonial era was the establishment of peace throughout West Africa, except, of course, during the First World War when the European powers fought their battle on African as well as European soil. Freedom of movement was guaranteed for traders; slave-raiding, slave-trading and ultimately slavery itself were abolished. This is certainly one of the factors that was appreciated by many Africans at the time of the conquest.[55]

But once peace was established, the European administrator saw himself as an agent for law and order, as a symbol of stability rather than as an innovator. Where development-conscious District Officers put forward plans, these got little encouragement from the central government. Sir Hugh Clifford as Governor of the Gold Coast emphasised this when he wrote that it was the Ghanaians themselves who initiated the cocoa revolution in the then Gold Coast.

> This man, reputed to be lazy by the superficial globetrotter or the exponent of the damned nigger, has carved from the virgin forest an enormous clearing, which he has covered with flourishing cocoa farms.... With no means of animal transport, no railways and few roads, he has conveyed his produce to the sea, rolling it down in casks for miles and carrying it on his own sturdy cranium.[56]

And it was cocoa farmers themselves who built roads and commissioned bridges to get their cocoa to the coast.

Some writers on the colonial economy have seen it as revolutionary:[57] but how can this be so when the standards of living of the average peasant did not improve in any substantial way under colonial rule? Many lived outside the cash-crop growing areas and thus were not directly involved in the colonial economy except as tax-payers. Where Africans did have surplus income after feeding and clothing their families and paying their taxes, most of the imported goods available to them, with notable exceptions such as bicycles, sewing machines and pan-roofing, were only substitutes for goods which hitherto had been manufactured locally.

Three major changes took place as a result of European colonial rule. The first was the establishment of a cash-crop economy geared to export to Europe. This export had, as we have seen, preceded colonial occupation; but it was intensified under colonial rule to such an extent that the health of a colony's economy was measured not by its internal trade but by its imports and exports. To ensure that cash crops were produced, taxes were imposed so that the people had either to grow such crops in sufficient quantities to raise the money to pay their taxes, or, if their soil did not produce cash crops, migrate to areas where they could earn enough money as stranger-farmers to pay them. Thus hundreds of thousands of French West Africans migrated to Ghana to work on the cocoa fields or in the gold mines to earn their taxes.

The second major economic revolution brought about by the colonial rulers was the communications revolution. To exploit the resources of West Africa roads, railways, bridges and ports were built. They were, however, built to serve the import/export economy, not to open up internal trade. Thus communications between Lagos and Enugu were by rail via Jos, not by road across the Niger. Eastern and Western Nigeria were only linked effectively after Nigeria became independent, when the Niger bridge was built.

The third major economic revolution was the introduction of an easily portable currency and of banking facilities.

These were positive economic contributions by the Europeans. But the European expansion of the African economy also had profound negative effects. Africans who, in the nineteenth century, had profited from the middleman trade in the products of West Africa and those of Europe now found themselves increasingly excluded from this sector of the economy. Where Europeans did not trade direct with African producers, the Lebanese and Syrians increasingly supplanted the African middleman.[58] African importers and exporters were cut out of their businesses by preferential treatment given by the banks to Europeans and Lebanese. Even the peasant-farmer could not always obtain a fair price for his goods because of the price-rings organised by the European export houses, the most notorious of which was the one established for the purchase of cocoa in the Gold Coast in 1938 which provoked the great 'Hold-Up' of sales by the cocoa-farmers.

By the Second World War, the prelude to decolonisation, the African had, economically speaking, largely been reduced to the role of peasant producer. The benefits of the European-provoked *Economic Revolution in West Africa*,[59] as Alan Mcphee described it, did not accrue in any measure to the African. Capital gains were exported to Europe, not re-invested in Africa. Thus West African palm-oil went to Europe to be made into Palm-Olive Soap for sale in Africa. Factories were only established in Africa where it was not profitable to establish them in Europe.

It was against a background in which Africans were treated as subjects to be exploited without rights, that African nationalism developed. And it was Europe which, as we have suggested, by providing Africans with education, sowed the seeds of the destruction of the colonial system. The course of African nationalism and the achievement of independence belong more to the story of Africa's impact on Europe than Europe's impact on Africa. That African demands for self-government and independence did grow may be attributed to the provision of education and to the basic social and economic injustices of European regimes which prescribed different social and political norms for their African subjects from those for their metropolitan citizens. That western-style education led quickly to African protest against the injustices of the European colonial regimes was given early demonstration by the role of the educated elite in the foundation of the Aborigines Rights Protection Society in Ghana in 1897 to protest the Land Bill.

I have argued elsewhere[60] that colonial rule in West Africa ended in the early 1940s and that the period 1944-1960 was one of decolonisation when Africans once again began to take initiative in the control of their own affairs.

In West Africa, during the fifteen years' struggle for independence, there were no wars between Europeans and African nationalists.[61] There was severe oppression in Ghana and the Ivory Coast. But, with the exception of Guinea, so shoddily treated by the French when she took her option for independence from France in 1958, there is a surprising lack of bitterness in West African-European relations and in particular those with the former metropolitan powers. Apart from the technological and educational acquisitions made by Africans as a result of colonial rule, what can we, today, say, without the advantage of a long historical perspective, are the legacies of those sixty years of domination? I believe them to be fivefold.

In the first place, just as the Muslims before 1900 had integrated much of Africa into the wider world of Islam, so too the Europeans now integrated Africa into the culture and economy of the so-called Western World. Secondly, Europe created a series of new nations in Africa which did not correspond with the pre-colonial political configurations of Africa. With the exception of Cameroun and Eritrea/Ethiopia, these states have not altered the boundaries laid down by the Europeans. Thirdly, as far as West Africa is concerned, the Metropolitan powers left their own languages as the official languages of their former colonies. Fourthly, because the European colonial regimes were almost exclusively interested in exploiting export crops, this led to uneven development within the West African states they created. This unevenness in development was particularly characterised by the dichotomy between poor north and prosperous south, for not only did the products of the forest area command higher prices on the world market, but also the supplanting of the Trans-Saharan by the Atlantic export routes concentrated trade and administration on the coast. And, finally, perhaps the greatest obstacle to eventual Pan-African or regional unity in Africa is the fact that not one European power colonised Africa, but seven, each leaving a different cultural and linguistic influence. It may be noted, though, that in Latin America where, with the exception of Brazil and the Guyanas, all the states were once Spanish colonies, the advantage of having been colonised by a single colonial power in this respect has not proved positive.

The European colonial impact on Africa was undoubtedly a major one. But as we have suggested, West Africa became only in certain senses 'a white man's world'. African culture and values survived even where a policy of determined assimilation was pursued. After five centuries of contact with Europe, West Africa has remained primarily a black man's world. It still remains to be seen how independent West Africa will assimilate the results of this contact with the the white world of Europe.

NOTES

1. Ivor Wilks. A Medieval Trade Route from the Niger to the Gulf of Guinea'. *Journal of African History*, III, no. 2, 1962.
2. Of course the Europeans were interested in other items such as leopard-skins, provisions of food for the trans-Atlantic voyage, and some local products such as striped cotton garments and blue cloths manufactured in Benin which they used for sale on the Gold Coast and the rivers Gabon and Angola respectively. See Olfert Dapper. *Description de l'Afrique*. Amsterdam, 1686, cited in Thomas Hodgkin (ed). *Nigerian Perspectives*. London, 1960, p.128.
3. The trade was of course to the mutual advantage of both African and European participants, otherwise it would not have been carried on. Ghanaian gold enabled local craft industries to purchase cheap supplies of copper, brass and iron. But by and large only the coastal ruling classes benefited. For instance, while clothes were a major item in the trade, they improved the life-style of the ruling classes alone, since from contemporary European accounts it is clear that the majority of coastal peoples continued to go about naked or wear a simple loin-cloth.
4. Here, of course, we have to be careful. In most cases, Africans did not sell members of their own societies to the Europeans, but prisoners taken in war, who often would have been killed if there had been no slave trade. On the other hand, the slave-trade promoted wars with the object of obtaining slaves for foreign exchange. Thus, here, it can be argued, the slave trade did deprive Africa of its manpower. Where societies did sell their own members into slavery, it was usually because they had committed criminal acts which otherwise would have been punishable by death. This practice can be compared to the transportation for life of convicts from Britain to Australia.
5. There were of course exceptions. Captain John Adams in his *Remarks on the Country extending from Cape Palmas to the River Congo*. London, 1823, describing his voyages along the West Coast of Africa between 1786 and 1800, notes that many of the inhabitants of Old Calabar wrote English, 'an art first acquired by some of the traders' sons, who had visited England, and which they have had the sagacity to keep up to the present period. They have established

schools and schoolmasters, for the purpose of instructing in this art the youths belonging to families of consequence'.

But judging from Antera Duke's diary, published in Daryll Forde (ed), *Efik Traders of Old Calabar*. London, 1956, the standard of English was a rudimentary pidgin.

6. Quaque, the son of the 'Cabosheer' of Cape Coast, was sent to London for education by the Society for the Propagation of the Gospel, and returned to his country, unlike other West Africans who, as freed slaves, gained education but never came back to Africa to impart it to their fellow-men.
7. In the mid-eighteenth century, however, the Society for the Propagation of the Gospel was active on the Gold Coast, while in Saint Louis a number of Africans were converted to Catholicism.
8. See footnote 5. We shall show later that Saint Louis was an exception to this generalisation.
9. Abdullahi Smith. 'The Central Sudan to c.1500' in J. F. Ade Ajayi and Michael Crowder (eds). *History of West Africa*, Vol. I.
10. Shaikh Muhammad al-Maghili, *The Obligations of Princes*, trans. from the Arabic by T.H. Baldwin. Beirut, 1932.
11. Ivor Wilks, *The Northern factor in Asante History*, Institute of African Studies, University of Ghana, 1968
12. João de Barros, *Da Asia*, First Decade, book iii, in Hodgkin *Nigerian Perspectives*, pp. 87-88.
13. The Portuguese, it must be said in fairness, did try to back up their early success in converting the King of Warri to Catholicism by sending missionaries from time to time. But by the late eighteenth century Captain Adams found that though there were vestiges of Catholic survivals, 'we could not learn that the Portuguese had been successful in making proselytes', cited by Hodgkin, *Nigerian Perspectives*, pp. 177-8.
14. Cited in Basil Davidson. *Africa in History: Themes and Outlines*. London, 1968. p.136.
15. 'The Kano Chronicle' translated by H.R. Palmer in *Sudanese Memoirs*, Vol. III, Lagos, 1928, p. ?
16. Cited in Basil Davidson, *The African Past*. London, 1964, p. 191.
17. 'Ahmad Bābā, the celebrated Muslim jurist from Songhai, complained that his being taken as a captive in chains across the desert was illegal since a Muslim could not be a slave. See J. O. Hunwick, 'Ahmad Bābā and the Moroccan invasion of the Sudan (1591)', *JHSN*, II, 1962, pp. 311-28.
18. E. A. Alagoa, 'Long Distance Trade and States in the Niger Delta', *Journal of African History*, XI, 3, 1970 and 'The Niger Delta States and their Neighbours' in Ajayi and Crowder, *History of West Africa*, Vol. I; Robin Horton, 'From Fishing Village to City States' in Mary Douglas and Phyllis Kaberry (eds), *Man in Africa*, London, 1969.
19. Christopher Fyfe, 'Reform in West Africa: The Abolition of the Slave Trade' in Ajayi and Crowder (eds), *History of West Africa*, Vol. II.
20. Walter Rodney. 'African Slavery and other forms of social oppression on the Upper Guinea Coast'. *Journal of African History*, VIII, 3, 1966, pp. 431-44.
21. Some of the authors of the act did indeed foresee its vast consequences for Africa, which were not to be realised for a much longer time than they had expected.
22. Robin Hallett (ed), *Records of the African Association 1788-1831*. London, 1964, pp. 289-299.
23. Christopher Fyfe, 'Reform in West Africa', *op. cit.*
24. See Philip D. Curtin, *The Image of Africa*, Madison, 1964.

25. For instance a European like Henry Venn certainly adhered to such values. See J. F. Ade Ajayi 'Henry Venn and The Policy of Development'. *Journal of the Historical Society of Nigeria*, I. 4. 1959.
26. The exception, here in West Africa. is Faidherbe's conquest of the Senegal river valley.
27. Polly Hill. *The Gold Coast Cocoa Farmer*, London. 1956 and David Brokensha. *Social Change at Larteh, Ghana*, Oxford. 1966.
28. The Moroccan invasion of Songhai was designed to gain direct control of the sources of supply of West African gold. But though Songhai was conquered, the Moroccan aim was not realised.
29. Christian Scheffer. *Instructions Générales données de 1763 à 1870 aux Gouverneurs et Ordonnateurs des Etablissements Français en Afrique Occidentale*, Paris. 1921. Vol. I. p. 290.
30. *ibid.*, p. 350.
31. Parallels may be drawn between Dodds' work on behalf of the French to that of George Ekim Ferguson for the British in Northern Ghana and Upper Volta.
32. James Pope-Hennessy. *Verandah*, London. 1964.
33. Cited by J.B. Webster and A.A. Boahen. *The Revolutionary Years: West Africa since 1800*, London. 1967. p. 143.
34. J. F. Ade Ajayi. *Milestones in Nigerian History*, Ibadan. 1962.
35. For instance: J. A. B. Horton. *The Medical Topography of the West Coast of Africa;* Samuel Ajayi Crowther. *Grammar and Vocabulary of the Yoruba Language;* Carl Christian Reindorf. *History of the Gold Coast and Asante;* Samuel Johnson. *The History of the Yorubas*, etc.
36. 'Report of the Select Committee of the House of Commons on British Establishments in West Africa. 26 June. 1865'. *Parliamentary Papers*, 1865. V (412) p. iii §3.
37. See A. S. Kanya-Forstner. *The Conquest of the Western Sudan: A Study in French Military Imperialism*, Cambridge. 1969.
38. J. F. Ade Ajayi. *Christian Missions in Nigeria 1841-1891: The Making of a New Elite*, London. 1965. pp. 206-7.
39. Cited in J. D. Hargreaves (ed). *France and West Africa*, London. 1969. p. 101.
40. Philip D. Curtin. *Image of Africa, op. cit.*
41. E. A. Ayandele. *The Missionary Impact on Modern Nigeria, 1842-1914*, London. 1966.
42. This view is implicit in Lugard's. *The Dual Mandate in British Tropical Africa*, London. 1922. when he considers the question of the status of the Moslem rulers of Northern Nigeria. It must be recalled, too, that it was Lugard who appointed Henry Carr, a Nigerian. as Resident of Lagos Colony.
43. C. L. Temple. *Native Races and their Rulers*, 2nd ed. London. 1966. p. 41.
44. Sir Harry Johnston. *History of the Colonisation of Africa by Alien Races*, 2nd ed. p.450.
45. J. F. Ade Ajayi. 'Colonialism: An Episode in African History' in L. H. Gann and Peter Duignan (eds). *The History and Politics of Colonialism 1870-1914*, Volume I of *Colonialism in Africa 1870-1960*, London. 1969. p. 497.
46. Michael Crowder (ed). *West African Resistance*, London. 1971. 'Introduction'.
47. Michael Crowder. 'West Africa and the 1914-18 War'. *Bulletin de L'IFAN*. T.XXX sér. B. no. 1. 1968. pp. 227-247.
48. National Archives of France. Section Outre-Mer. Mission 1919. Rapport fait par M. Ch. Phérivong (on the Borgou rebellion). See Michael Crowder. *Revolt in Bussa*, London. 1973. ch. VI. note 17.
49. Michael Crowder. 'West Africa and the 1914-18 War'. *op. cit.*
50. After 1891, the year of the death of Bishop Crowther. Africans from having been

leaders in the Church Missionary Society, for instance, became subalterns in the Society's programme of evangelisation. See Ajayi, *Christian Missions op. cit.*
Lamine Guèye in *Itinéraire Africaine*, Paris, 1966, p. 21, records a conversation he had with a senior French official in which he asked him why African subjects could not pursue studies in France just as some African citizens had. The reply was: 'The Administration is not at all favourably disposed towards the despatch to France at great expense of young people who, as soon as they return to their country will interest themselves in nothing but politics and in a way of which we are only too aware'.
51. *Ibid.*
52. Quoted by Kwame Nkrumah, *Ghana: the Autobiography of Kwame Nkrumah*, London, 1959.
53. *Journal Officiel* Debates of the Second Constituent Assembly, 1st Session, 18th September, 1945, p. 3789.
54. Information from Mr. Andre Ter-Sugh, a Tiv student formerly at Abdullahi Bayero College of Ahmadu Bello University, Kano.
55. See Mary Smith, *Baba of Karo: A Woman of the Moslem Hausa*, London, 1954. This is confirmed by the research of one of my students, Sylvester Bature, on the life of Pa Baikie, who was freed from slavery after the British occupation of Borno.
56. Cited in Michael Crowder, *West Africa Under Colonial Rule*, London, 1968.
57. Alan Macphee, *The Economic Revolution in West Africa*, London, 1926. A.G. Hopkins in his masterly *Economic History of West Africa*, London, 1973, also cast doubts on the revolutionary character of change in this period, though the crude quantities of goods exchanged increased enormously, while as we also argue, new communications systems, new currencies, new classes of the community emerged.
58. For a detailed discussion of how the Lebanese supplanted African middlemen see Crowder, *West Africa Under Colonial Rule, op. cit.*, pp. 293-98.
59. Mcphee, *op. cit.*
60. Michael Crowder, *West Africa Under Colonial Rule*, London, 1968.
61. The obvious exception here is Guinea-Bissau where the Portuguese are still fighting the nationalists who have declared their country independent.

II

BACKGROUND TO THE SCRAMBLE*
(1968)

THE LOCATION OF EUROPEAN INTERESTS IN WEST AFRICA, 1850-80

A comparison of a map of European colonial possessions in West Africa in 1850 with one of 1880 shows very little change in their extent, with the notable exception of Senegal where Faidherbe's expansionist policy had brought almost a third of the modern state under French control between 1854 and 1865.

In 1850 Britain's interests were limited to Bathurst on St. Mary's Island at the mouth of the River Gambia; Freetown and its peninsula; and the Gold Coast Forts. Over and above these colonial possessions, Britain had in return for military protection, usually against the Ashanti, contracted special relationships known as 'Bonds' with a number of states on the Gold Coast. Under these Britain could intervene in the administration of justice in these states where capital punishment was involved, but not their government. In 1874 these states were annexed by Britain, creating her first major colony in West Africa. Further down the coast in the Niger Delta region, a Consul for the Bights of Benin and Biafra interfered frequently in the affairs of the palm-oil exporting states in the interests of both British commerce and the suppression of the slave trade, but there was no attempt to acquire a territorial base from which he could operate. The French had, by West African standards in the 1850s, a major colony in Senegal based on Saint Louis at the mouth of the River Senegal along which she maintained a number of trading posts. She was also established on the island of Gorée off the Cape Verde peninsula; Albreda on the Gambia; the Boke region of Guinea, and the posts of Assinie, Grand Bassam and Dabou on the

*Reprinted by permission of Hutchinson Publishing Group Ltd. from *West Africa under Colonial Rule* by Michael Crowder. London. 1968. pp 45-64. and earlier reprinted in Joan G. Roland ed. *Africa: The Heritage and the Challenge - An Anthology of African History*, Fawcett Publications Inc.. Greenwich. Conn.. U.S.A.. 1974.

Ivory Coast. In 1850 the Dutch still owned a number of forts on the Gold Coast, but these were later handed over to the British, and the Netherlands ceased to have colonial interest in West Africa. The Danes had ceded their forts to the British in 1850. Portugal held the tiny fort of Sao João Batista da Ajuda at Ouidah and, more important, forts at Cacheu and Bissau in what is Guinea-Bissau. By 1880, apart from French expansion in Senegal, the situation had changed very little, though in the decade that followed the map of West Africa was to be radically altered.

The thirty years between 1850 and 1880, despite the lack of activity of the colonial powers in West Africa, are of interest because they help to explain why France and Britain obtained their colonies where they did. For though Britain and France in this period had negligible influence on West Africa as a whole in comparison with Al Hajj Umar, his predecessors and contemporaries, there were forces at work for both nations which were extending their influence in many of those parts of West Africa that they were subsequently to occupy What follows, then, will not in any way be an attempt to describe the extremely complex events that preceded the so-called Scramble for West Africa. This has been done brilliantly elsewhere.[1] Rather it will try to highlight certain trends in the growth of French and British involvement in West Africa during this period, whether this was official, commercial or evangelical, that had significant bearing on the future partition of West Africa.

Throughout this period the British Government, and indeed the Parliament to which it was responsible, maintained a deep-seated hostility towards colonial ventures in West Africa. Only Palmerston and Russell actively backed the expansion and protection of British trade in this region. When Palmerston acquired Lagos for the Crown in 1861, it was described by the Colonial Office which had to take charge of it as 'that deadly gift from the Foreign Office'.[2] Ranged beside the Colonial Office in opposition to such enterprise was the increasingly tight-fisted Treasury, which kept an eagle eye on any gubernatorial venture on the West Coast that might involve it in an increase of expenditure, even if the motive were the protection of British trading interests. Palmerston and Russell had been strong in their advocacy of government support for British nationals in West Africa, but as Hargreaves points out, by 1865 both their careers were coming to an end, and that was of course the year when the Parliamentary Select Committee recommended the abandonment of all Britain's West Coast commitments except Sierra Leone. The predominant view at the Colonial Office is summed up in the words of Sir Fredric Rogers, its Permanent Under Secretary from 1860-71: 'expensive and troublesome'.[3] Colonies were seen as useful neither for the prosecution of the abolition of the slave trade nor for the advancement of British trade.

It is essential to point out here that Britain's hostility towards the acquisition of colonies in West Africa did not mean she was unwilling to help advance her trading interests there. Before the Committee of 1865, Government had helped finance the Niger expeditions of 1841 and 1854, and had been responsible for the great exploration of Hausaland and the Western Sudan undertaken by Barth, from which it was hoped to find the means of tapping the supposed vast commercial potential of that area. The 1854 expedition, led by Baikie, on which the use of quinine as a prophylactic and cure for the 'fevers' of Africa proved successful, led to the establishment of a trading settlement at Lokoja. And though this was not officially a British colony, Baikie presided over it with semi-official consular status. Government supported Macgregor Laird's trading expeditions up the Niger from 1857 until his death. However, after 1865 Government was notably more reluctant to take action on behalf of her traders, inclining to the view that high risks brought high profits and that the merchants should look after themselves.[4] Anyway, in the scheme of world diplomacy, in which Britain as the most powerful imperial nation in the world at the time was more involved than any other nation, West Africa did not enjoy great prominence in the thoughts of the Cabinet except with regard to the abolition of the slave trade.

The British traders on the Coast on the whole agreed with Government policy: though they were quick to call for the gunboat, they were reluctant that their activities should be subject to permanent British administration, for this would involve them in paying dues on their exports to maintain such administration. In this attitude they were joined, for different reasons, by the missionaries, who resented government interference and whose guiding principles were to help the Africans to help themselves through conversion to the Christian way of life as it was conceived by Victorian England. They were also seeking the establishment of small self-governing states, for example like Abeokuta, with emphasis on the 'native agent'.[5] Thus the three main arms of British influence in West Africa before the Berlin Conference of 1884-5 — government, trader and evangelist — were agreed on one point: territorial expansion in West Africa was neither desirable nor necessary. The only divergence from this general policy came from the administrator on the spot, who, faced with the realities of the problems of administering a West African colony, often found, like a Glover in Lagos or a Kennedy in Freetown, a policy of non-interference in the affairs of the people surrounding the colony he was meant to govern incompatible with effective administration. And though unauthorised expansion was undertaken by local administrators, this was negligible compared with the increase in the interests of the British traders and missionaries in the West African hinterland in the years preceding the Berlin Conference. And it is to them, particularly the former, that we must look for the basis of Britain's occupation of West Africa outside the small enclaves she already possessed.

Britain, apart from the acquisition of Lagos, had, despite its avowed policy, extended its territorial interests in West Africa, but these were very small in size. A full-scale and successful invasion of Ashanti in 1874 did not result in any imposition of British rule or even informal control over that nation. However, the 'Bond' states were declared part of the new Gold Coast colony, which was separated for administrative purposes from Sierra Leone. As Kimble puts it, 'the Ashanti campaign had forced a general realisation of the extent to which Britain was committed on the coast'.[6] The choice was between 'complete annexation or total abandonment'.[7] Complete annexation, however much it might go against the grain, seemed inevitable if Britain were to continue to trade on that part of the coast: nevertheless in the debate on the question in the House of Commons there was an important minority advocating withdrawal. Further down the coast the island colony of Lagos expanded on to the mainland, westwards to Badagry.

The interests of British traders before 1880 were concentrated mainly in the Niger Delta region and along the River Niger, where the palm-oil trade, which together with groundnuts was the only major produce of West Africa of interest to Europe at that time, was the chief attraction. In these parts, traders had in effect preceded missionaries and were of much greater importance as far as the Africans were concerned. In the Lagos hinterland missionaries had been at the vanguard of British penetration, but trade, which the missionaries themselves sought to encourage, was of considerable size, though it was frequently impeded by the long drawn-out civil wars that had followed on the collapse of the Oyo empire in the early part of the nineteenth century. British customs officials were also interested in the area west of Badagry, particularly Cotonou and Porto Novo, which were rival 'independent' ports to Lagos where traders had to pay irksome duties on imports and exports for the maintenance of colonial administration. But here they came up against French interests, and their conflict was the cause of protracted disputes and negotiations between the British and French governments. The other major area in which Britain had trading interests was the Gold Coast, but beyond the Colony, as we have seen, they were impeded by the powerful Ashanti nation. It has however been argued by Ivor Wilks that British traders were in fact hurt more by their government's policy of supporting the coastal states against Ashanti, which was itself anxious to open up trade, but on its own terms [8] Nevertheless the existence of the colony, and the rich trade of the hinterland, indicated this as a natural sphere for British expansion once the European occupation of Africa became inevitable after the Berlin Conference. In Sierra Leone British or rather Creole traders had been active in opening up commerce with the hinterland of the Colony, and in so doing there had again been differences with the French over the River Mellacourie region. Bathurst had become an important trading town. Here British, French and Gambian traders were handling over 10,000 tons of groundnuts a year for export to Europe.[9] Though French traders were very active in this area — indeed the bulk of the groundnut crop was exported to France — Britain maintained its hold over the colony, gaining treaty rights over Albreda, where France had once been active. British traders were in fact handling a larger bulk of trade than the French, so that the Gambia river became a natural area for British expansion when this became inevitable.

The only area where British traders had penetrated deeply into the African hinterland and had become deeply involved in local politics was in what later became Nigeria: and it is significant that Britain's largest colony on the West Coast should have been the one where her traders were most active and bears out the contention that for Britain at least in the West African case, flag followed trade. Indeed the fact that Britain was able to claim the lands of the Niger Delta and its hinterland at the Berlin Conference was due to the activities of Sir George Taubman Goldie, who, foreseeing the dangers of a future Scramble for Africa, in which he considered the Niger region one of the most valuable prizes, welded together his British competitors into a formidable national monopoly to fight off his French rivals. He further took the initiative of signing treaties with local chiefs giving his company exclusive trading rights with them. These treaties were to involve even the distant Sokoto Caliphate.

To the west of the Niger, missionaries in Yorubaland had claimed for British churches this unhappy area plunged in seemingly interminable civil war. From their bases at Abeokuta and Ibadan, they had proclaimed an evangelical empire that was as important in guiding Britain to territorial acquisition in that region as Goldie's trading in the Niger. Whereas in Yorubaland traders had followed evangelists, and were in turn followed by the flag, in the Niger the traders were followed by the missionaries, the Anglican sect of which established a diocese of the Niger under an African Bishop, Samuel Ajayi Crowther.

By 1880, then, Britain's formal commitments in West Africa were very small with the exception of the Gold Coast. Her informal commitments were large only in the Niger region and Yorubaland, and significantly produced her only large colony in West Africa. Any informal commitments traders and missionaries would have liked to make in the hinterland of the Gold Coast Colony were blocked by the Ashanti. Nevertheless Britain's relationship with that nation, though hostile, was symbiotic, so that when the Scramble came, it was natural that Ashanti should come under her sway, and produce from the small colony of Gold Coast a sizeable unit, which in the event turned out also to be very rich. The restricted trading empires of Gambia and Sierra Leone reflected themselves in the smallness of both colonies. In Sierra Leone, flag followed trade too. In this case it was not British traders, but African traders from the Colony, who were British subjects, who acted as a pressure group on Government to occupy the hinterland.

The consistency of policy towards the question of colonial expansion of nineteenth century British Administrations is not to be found among their French counterparts. Indeed it seems that attitudes were almost as varied as the regimes by which that country was governed. Nevertheless on the eve of the Berlin Conference and at the time when French forces were pushing rapidly into the heart of the Western Sudan, France was as anxious as Britain to limit her colonial commitments in West Africa. Indeed a number of French administrations had shared Britain's monolithic distaste for colonial enterprise on the West Coast.[10] But unlike Britain they did not have a Treasury, backed up by the Colonial Office itself, which speedily put a damp cloth on any new colonial venture. Rather they were subjected to strong contrary pressures, the chief of which was their own Marine, which with the Army had, since the defeat of their country at the hands of the British, been seeking to compensate for their humiliation by extending France's empire overseas. This tendency was exacerbated by the defeat they suffered at the hands of the Prussians in 1870. At times the Marine, whose Ministry had responsibility for the colonies, and Army, served under administrations that were favourable to their colonial ambitions and were able to pursue expansion unchecked. Those administrations that found colonies essentially a nuisance could not abandon those already acquired because of the strength of the interests supporting their maintenance, and often had difficulty in staving off demands for new colonies.

Perhaps too much has been made of the colonies as a compensation for national humiliation, but it certainly serves to explain why France in West Africa acquired tracts of land that were little more than, if not actually, desert, and why even in the early conquest of Senegal Faidherbe took for France the least commercially interesting parts of that region. Whereas for Britain traders largely demarcated her future empire in West Africa, sailors, bizarrely seeking on land the dominion they could not hold over the high seas, traced out the main lines of the future French West Africa. However, so bald an explanation does not take into account the important role of French traders in the acquisition of France's West African empire.

France never had such pressing needs for colonies as Britain did. Her economy was largely self-sufficient. She had no surplus or hungry population to export overseas. She only became an industrial nation in the 1840s, and her need for outlets for her manufactured goods were never as pressing as for Britain. Nor could the acquisition of her West African colonies be explained by surplus capital seeking new fields for operation. Nor, too, was she interested in acquiring bases for the suppression of the slave trade, as Britain did, for France never showed herself an enthusiastic abolitionist. She did however have traders on the Coast who had been established there since the era of the slave trade, and they naturally sought to find alternative commodities in which to trade. Thus along the Senegal river a desultory trade in gum kept St. Louis and the escales in business. It was not until the 1840s, when France's industrial revolution got underway, that her need for vegetable oils became important, and the 1850s a great expansion of trading activity on the West Coast of Africa by the French. Thus as Hargreaves points out it was the Marseilles trader, Régis Ainé, who was largely responsible for the hoisting of the French flag at posts on the Ivory Coast and at Ouidah in Dahomey. Again Régis Ainé persuaded the French to establish a protectorate over Porto Novo in 1863 'with the sole purpose of securing for Régis's substantial imports of spirits an entry into Yorubaland free of the heavy duties levied at Lagos'.[11] And here we begin to see that the role of the French trader vis-a-vis his government was not dissimilar to that of his British counterpart. French protection would be invoked if it could serve the useful purpose of gaining the trader commercial advantage. But for the most part French traders preferred like the British to live outside the direct influence of a French colonial administration, though they were happy to call on French force to help them in dispute with Africans. The expeditions against the Moors of Trarza were designed originally to relieve French traders from the crippling taxes that were being imposed on their gum exports. The subsequent subjugation of the area to French protection was the design of the military. French traders in West Africa were as pragmatic as the British: they sought the political situation that brought them most profits. Thus at times they would trade under British protection, at times French. For the most part they preferred African control. But they were quick to put pressure on France for support if they saw dangers of British official encroachment on their domain, as in the case of Britain's trade expansion westward from Lagos during the 1860s and 1870s. In the period from 1850 and 1880, apart from the area conquered by Faidherbe between 1854 and 1865, French trading interests were concentrated in the region immediately north of the Gambia, to its south as far as Sierra Leone, in the Dahomey region and to a lesser extent along the Ivory Coast. These were all eventually to become French colonies, and to a large degree they owed their existence as such to the fact they had initially been identified as of commercial importance by traders. Another area in which French traders interested themselves in the 1870s was the Niger Delta, which hitherto had been the exclusive preserve of the British. To a certain extent their late arrival in this region is explained by the preference of the French for groundnut oil to palm-oil as a base for the manufacture of soap. But as French demands for oil increased this distinction became less important. More pressing a reason was that in the seventies France could rival Britain in manufactures required by the African, and, like Goldie, the French traders saw the Niger as a highway to commerce with the interior.

If the French coastal colonies were largely the result of longstanding French trading activities in that region, the Western Sudanese colonies of Senegal, Soudan (Mali), Upper Volta and Niger were the result of the desire for imperial expansion for its own sake on the part of the Marine. The precursor of this empire was Faidherbe. This is not of course to say the French military were not as anxious to secure the coastal colonies for France as they were the interior. But it was only in the interior, and in Senegal under Faidherbe, that the soldiers had the initiative. The coastal colonies of Guinea, Ivory Coast and Dahomey were under civilian control and credit for their acquisition must be shared with the traders who were able to give France after the Berlin Conference the necessary claims to established interests in those areas.

Faidherbe was, as we have already pointed out, called in to deal with the threat to French trade on the Senegal by the Moors. He did not content himself with merely demonstrating to them that they could ill afford to risk further military expeditions by the French, but proceeded to establish a French protectorate over this area though not over the Trarzas of the left bank. This too was his method in dealing with Al Hajj Umar so that by the time he left Senegal in 1865 after his second governorship, he had brought a third of modern Senegal under French control, and established a fully-fledged colonial capital at St. Louis and sanctioned the founding of Dakar. Yet then, and today, the greater part of the area of Senegal he brought under control was the least interesting from the commercial point of view. As Suret-Canale has pointed out, more than half of France's groundnuts came from the Rivières du Sud. Most of Gambia's groundnut export found its way to France too. Faidherbe in fact considered that the gum and indigo trade were the more important.[12] He was also convinced that the most important markets lay in the Western Sudan, so that his colony pointed like an arrow in that direction, whilst the French trader's 'empire' went at a right angle to it, south from St. Louis towards Sierra Leone. Faidherbe was Governor at a time when France was ruled by a man who sought the renaissance of France's lost glory in the creation of a new empire. He was not particularly concerned about the expense of creating that empire, so long as he could be Emperor in fact as well as name. This suited the Marine well, and thus a colony was acquired for Senegal whose cost of administration compared with its economic viability would have rendered the British Colonial Office and the Treasury hysterical.

The subsequent defeat of Napoleon III's army by the Prussians, and his replacement by a Republican government which was not inspired by the ideal of imperial conquest, did not fundamentally alter the situation. The new governments, whilst not interested in colonies, had to be permissive in their attitude both to the ones they had inherited and the possibility of the acquisition of new ones, for the motivation of the navy and army for compensation for the loss of national prestige was now greater than ever. Considerable pressure was placed on the government by the Ministry of the Marine to undertake colonial ventures, and the Marine itself was one of the main instruments in rousing jingoism among the French public. It thus acquiesced in these pressures, only trying to restrain activities that might bring it into conflict with the British, for perfidious Albion was now replaced by the Germans as France's major enemy. This attitude was reciprocated by the British. Hence Salisbury's main preoccupation, when Lagos occupied the village of Ketenou, was its possible effect on Anglo-French relationships.[13]

In summary, then, before 1880 Britain was able to maintain a monolithic policy towards colonial enterprise in West Africa, whether the administration was Tory or Liberal, because all were agreed that colonies were in that part of the world economically unrewarding. Even when French administrations were persuaded of the validity of such reasoning, there were powerful forces that made the maintenance of a similar policy impracticable so that where Britain's map of West Africa showed her with few colonial commitments over and above those she already had in 1850, France had expanded her territory and was poised for further expansion that Britain was reluctant to contemplate right up to 1900.

In the perspective of West African history, even France had made little impact on the indigenous peoples before 1880 except through her traders. The situation was radically to change in the next four years which culminated in the Berlin Conference of 1884-5, whereby European powers sought not to divide Africa amongst themselves, but to seek ways in which they could limit colonial acquisitions, because all, including France, saw them as an economic burden they would prefer to forgo. But the Berlin Conference, far from limiting the Scramble, gave international acknowledgement to its actuality.

THE BEGINNINGS OF THE SCRAMBLE 1880-5

In a pithy comment on the dramatic change in European attitudes to Africa in the half decade from 1880 to 1885 Lord Salisbury remarked: 'When I left the Foreign Office in 1880 nobody thought about Africa. When I returned to it in 1885 the nations of Europe were almost quarrelling with each other as to the various portions of Africa they could obtain'.[14] Indeed in 1880 there still seemed no pressing reason why any European government should consider the occupation of any portion of Tropical Africa as either politically desirable or economically profitable. Any increases in trade that might be likely to occur as a result of such occupation still seemed sure to be offset both by political repercussions on the chancelleries of Europe and by the expenses that would be involved in imposing on, and maintaining over, Africans an administration which for the most part they were quite unwilling to accept. Even France, imperially inclined in North Africa and South East Asia, was still diffident in Tropical Africa. As European powers saw it at the time Tropical Africa offered little inducement to occupation. European settlement seemed impossible for health reasons; the products Europe required, which were anyway very limited in range, were exported without the need for more than the occasional despatch of a gunboat to ensure continuation of trade when terms were disputed between Africans and Europeans. Finally, at least in West Africa, the slave trade could not be adduced as an argument in favour of occupation, for the export of slaves had ceased. Nevertheless the question of the widespread existence of domestic slavery caused considerable concern. The abolition of the slave trade and the promotion of legitimate trade had not abolished or even diminished slavery in West Africa. Those who were formerly exported to the New World as slaves were now employed in the production or porterage of the palm-oil and groundnuts European traders now required in place of slaves. Thus the 1865 Parliamentary Report, while it advocated the withdrawal of Britain from her West Coast settlements, called for the elimination of domestic slavery. Even in Angola, the importance of the slave trade had diminished as a result of Portugal's effective as distinct from formal abolition of the slave trade by the middle of the century. Leopold of the Belgians was of course to make great play of the continuation of the Arab slave trade from the Congo to the East of Africa as a justification for his occupation of the former.

How then can we account for the spectacular change of attitude on the part of the European powers between 1880 and 1885, so that within twenty years the whole of Tropical Africa, with the exception of Ethiopia and Liberia, was brought under European rule? The answer to this belongs as much to the history of Europe as of Africa. The Scramble of the European powers for Africa raises two questions of importance for the history of the colonial period in West Africa. The first, why it took place when it did, has been the subject of much scholarship in recent years,[15] and some consensus is being reached as to the question of what triggered it off. But the second question — why it took place at all — is still far from being answered, if we do not accept the Leninist-Hobson thesis of the occupation being a function of Europe's imperative need for an outlet for her surplus capital as the unique explanation. In our present state of knowledge it is impossible to provide a satisfactory overall answer as to why Europe occupied Africa. Beyond such obvious basic considerations already discussed, such as the vastly superior technological and economic position Europe had gained relative to Africa which gave her the potential of occupation if trading interests or national pride in relation either to other European powers or to African states were threatened, it is difficult at this stage to point to more than general patterns in the motives that seem to have lain behind occupation.

Although in 1880 European governments saw little reason for occupying Tropical Africa, there were strong pressures at work in favour of such action. First of all ignorance of West Africa had led traders and non-traders to suppose that it was a far more important market for their goods than it eventually turned out to be. The Congo and the Niger assumed much greater importance in their minds as highways to the interior markets than events subsequently justified. Industrialists and traders in Europe were looking for outlets for their surplus capital. Africa, still the Dark Continent as far as Europe was concerned, held forth promise of rich opportunities. What little was known was highly suggestive of commercial possibilities. Barth's account of his travels in the Western Sudan, for instance, gave confidence to traders that there would be rich rewards in the Sokoto Caliphate. Explorers like Stanley ventured into the Congo basin to assess, among other things, the commercial potential of the region. Capitalists naturally asked themselves whether railways could do for Africa what they were doing for the Americas and Australia. Already in Senegal two railways were being traced out by government, one to connect the Senegal with the Niger, and another to link St. Louis with Dakar, which was strongly supported by commercial interests. But capital investment on the scale of a railway had to be protected whether it was privately or publicly financed, witness the change in relations between the French and the Tokolor empire from one of co-existence to occupation once the railway had been planned to extend into the latter's territory.[16] Finally, though it may have appeared that the necessary raw materials were forthcoming from Africa without the need for intervention over and above the occasional visit of the gunboat, indications on the Niger were that the growing competition for markets between traders of the same nationality, and between French, British and to a lesser extent the Germans, was forcing European merchants to seek new markets inland where prices were more favourable to them, for those on the coast had been forced up by competition. Inland they came up against the African middlemen who naturally resented this intrusion into their hitherto unchallenged monopoly. Resentment led to conflict, and in such cases the European traders were quick to call on their own governments for protection. Such appeals were in themselves a prelude to occupation. Faidherbe had been appointed largely at the suggestion of St. Louis traders who were confident that he would take a strong line with the Moors.[17] In the Niger Delta Taubman Goldie was arguing as yet unsuccessfully with the British Government that they should give his Company a Charter whereby it would assume administrative control on behalf of the British Government of a large area of modern Nigeria.

If administrators on the spot, and in some cases missionaries and traders, were coming round to the view that the occupation of African soil was the only way in which the progress of their trading and evangelising could be ensured, the Governments in Europe were either overtly unsympathetic or not really interested. There were exceptions, like Jules Ferry, who actively supported the expansionist policies advocated by the men on the spot and who asked the French Chamber of Deputies on 12th November 1884: 'Is it not clear that, for all the great powers of modern Europe, since their industrial power commenced, there is posed an immense and difficult problem, which is the basis of industrial life, the very condition of existence — the question of "markets"? Have you not seen the great industrial nations one by one arrive at a colonial policy? And can we say that this colonial policy is a lunacy for modern nations? Not at all, Messieurs, this policy is, for all of us, a necessity like the "market" itself'.[18]

Another spur to occupation was also economic in nature: the fear of Protectionism. If governments were reluctant to occupy Tropical

Africa, they were even more reluctant to see any part of it fall to a power that espoused protectionism. Britain and Germany both feared the protectionist trend in French Colonial as distinct from domestic policy, though as Newbury points out the French in West Africa were just as worried about the protectionist aspects of Britain's 'Free Trade' in her coastal colonies.[19] Both Britain and Germany were determined to ensure that the Congo and Niger remained open to Free Trade, while the French, if they could not gain control of these two rivers, were also anxious that they should remain open to all comers.

Colonies and empire became increasingly popular subjects in European countries.[20] Interest in them was manifested not only among the commercial classes, who were directly concerned with overseas trade, but also among the literate middle classes generally. To commercial motives for the acquisition of colonies, they added those of national glory and 'humanitarianism'. Theories of the racial superiority of the white man coupled with the explorers' and missionaries' tales of the backward condition of Africa, increased support for the occupation of Africa and its subjection to the 'benefit' of European rule. Thus Jules Ferry told the French Chamber: 'It must be said openly that the superior races, in effect, have a right vis-à-vis the inferior races', to which M. Jules Margne replied, 'You dare to say that in a country where the rights of man were declared'.[21] In the Europe of the 1880s the views of Ferry rather than Margne were prevailing, and it was thus easier for governments, even when they were not being demanded to do so, to undertake colonial ventures.

There were, then, substantial pressures on European governments to begin the Scramble for Africa, but they were not strong enough in the early 1880s to force their hand. It is at this point that we have to ask why the Scramble did take place when it did. Here we have to look at the changing political positions and attitudes of the powers which eventually occupied West Africa, and how these influenced each other.

In the 1880s, of the four powers which occupied West Africa, only Portugal was really colonially ambitious in Tropical Africa. France, despite the substantial advances already made in the Senegal region, was still by and large officially hostile to any major extension of her commitments in this area. Britain rejected any prospect of colonial acquisition that would not pay for itself. Germany, under Bismarck, was reluctant to engage in colonial enterprise of any sort, though again there were pressures on the government to change its attitude, in particular from traders.

These powers, with the exception of Portugal, may have been reluctant to undertake colonial ventures in Tropical Africa, and

Portugal anyway was in no position economically or politically to do so at that time. But this was not the view they held of each other. Britain's intentions may have been innocent — from the point of view of her fellow European powers she was the largest imperial power of the day, and there was no reason for them to suppose that, isolated in Europe, she would not seek further expansion abroad, even in Tropical Africa. France, too, may have baulked at such expansion, but a country with a history of colonial ventures such as she had in the past fifty years, and which was already active in Senegal, had to be regarded with suspicion as to any move she might make. Germany was an unknown factor as far as colonial expansion was concerned. But nevertheless so great was her power that she could not be discounted in this field. Only Portugal could be looked on with any degree of confidence, unless of course one of the other powers sought alliance with her to further its ambitions in Africa. Thus whilst both Britain and France were reluctant to expand their commitments in Tropical Africa, they watched any move on the part of the other with suspicion. Germany, interested in maintaining the Balance of Power in Europe, was concerned as to how such moves might affect this balance.

The Scramble for Africa took place when it did because the mutual suspicions of the interested European powers of each other's intentions had reached such a pitch that none of them was willing to stave off the undesirable for fear their own interests might be pre-empted by another. However reluctant France may have been officially to involve herself in this Scramble, once committed, the strong political and economic pressures for occupation became dominant.

In France the political pressures for expansion in Africa were almost as strong as the economic. Such expansion was seen increasingly as a means of compensating for the humiliating defeat she had suffered at the hands of the Germans in 1871. Bismarck, himself, was anxious to encourage such an approach to take the mind of France off the loss of Alsace-Lorraine. In France itself, however, there was division between those who sought expansion elsewhere and those who felt France would be better occupied recovering the 'lost provinces'. This is well illustrated by the exchange between Ferry and Déroulède, an ardent 'continentalist'.

'You will end by making me think you prefer Alsace-Lorraine to France. Must we hypnotise ourselves with the lost provinces, and should we not take compensation elsewhere?' asked Ferry, to which Déroulède replied, 'That is just the point. I have lost two children and you offer me twenty domestics'.[22]

Those in France who favoured colonial expansion were given a great boost by Britain's unilateral occupation of Egypt, where Anglo-

French control had broken down. In the first place British action there weakened the traditional co-operation between the two governments.[23] It also aroused the indignation of the French public, already increasingly coming to see Britain as the enemy presiding over a mighty and expanding empire, rather than Germany. The occupation of Egypt by Britain supplied the climate in which the French government did not have much alternative to accepting the Makoko treaties in 1882 whereby the explorer de Brazza had acquired for France territory on the Congo.[24] These treaties, it is clear, as much as anything else precipitated the Scramble, though they certainly did not cause it. They made the European powers face the realities of a situation that had been developing over the past three years.

Portugal was the power most directly affected by the Makoko treaties, since she laid claim to the whole Congo area. Britain feared that if France were to establish herself on the Congo, she would preclude other powers from 'free trade' on the river. Germany, too, was concerned to maintain freedom of trade there. In the background Leopold of the Belgians, unsupported by his own country, was anxious to establish a colony in the Congo for his country under the guise of his International Association. The French ratification of the Makoko treaties threatened his own projected colony, for the Congo river was to be its lifeline. Thus a series of treaties ratified by a reluctant government under the pressure of public opinion and the Press were to lead inevitably to a conference of European powers at Berlin whereby the conditions of occupation of the African Coasts and maintenance of freedom of trade on the Congo and Niger were to be determined. And yet, as *The Times* wrote, 'Never has a government submitted to parliamentary ratification a treaty of the reality of which it knew so little'.[25]

Britain responded to the French action by negotiating with Portugal a treaty which would acknowledge Portugal's claims over the Congo mouth in return for a guarantee of freedom of trade on the river, which would be assured by an International Commission. Portugal refused to accept an international commission and insisted on a simple commission limited to Britain and herself. The limited nature of this commission helped build the image of Britain as a power with dangerous ambitions in the Congo area. Indeed Portugal was so fearful of her long-standing ally, whose national David Livingstone had after all explored territory to which Portugal laid claim, and had criticised severely her administration, that at one time she tried to conclude this treaty with France.

The other major participant was Germany under its Chancellor, Bismarck, who felt that 'for Germany to acquire colonies would be like a poverty-stricken Polish nobleman providing himself with silks and sables when he needed shirts'.[26] His main concern was preventing any other power in Europe from gaining ascendancy in Africa. The British occupation of Egypt had persuaded him to drop his antagonism to colonial ventures in Africa and to give support to his nationals' expansionist ambitions of German traders in Togo, Cameroun and South West Africa. This change of heart[27] can be seen both as a response to the changing international situation — Bismarck was particularly alarmed by the nature of Anglo-Portuguese negotiations — and to pressures of German traders. But for Bismarck, colonies in Africa were not of interest in themselves, but were pawns in a European game in which some of the players had moved the board to Africa. This intervention on the part of powerful Germany aggravated the situation even more. International opposition to the Anglo-Portuguese treaty increased; it was presented as a sinister conspiracy to keep powers other than Britain and Portugal off the Congo, particularly by Leopold II who became chief lobbyist against it. This, together with British intervention in Egypt, provided a diplomatic situation in which Bismarck was able to call European powers to the conference table in Berlin. There they would discuss the terms by which henceforth they were to acquire territory in Africa and how freedom of trade could be maintained in the Congo basin and freedom of navigation on the Congo and Niger rivers.

That it took place when it did is explained by the Makoko treaties. What is certain is that the economic factors outlined earlier would have 'en tout état de cause, un peu plus tôt, ou un peu plus tard, déclenché le mouvement'.[28] The European countries felt they needed Africa's supposed wealth, and unable to agree among themselves to leave it open to free trade by all, and not trusting their capital investments to African governments, all had to grab their own portions, large or small.

THE BERLIN CONFERENCE

The Berlin West Africa Conference of 1884-5 gave international recognition to a situation that already existed. Rather than initiating the Scramble for Africa, it tried to bring some form of discipline to a situation that looked as though it might rapidly get out of hand. That the Scramble had already begun in earnest was brought out clearly at the Conference when the various powers put forward their claims to territory. France had already begun the eastward march across the Sudan and Bamako had fallen to her forces in 1882. Her territories of the Senegal were now linked with the Niger. At the other end of that river, Goldie, with the assent of Britain, had amassed treaties in the Niger Delta and its hinterland and as far north as Sokoto and

Gwandu, the twin capitals of the Sokoto Caliphate. Germany had laid claim to Cameroun, and Togo, and Joseph Flegel had similarly drawn up treaties with the Fulani rulers. France had undertaken treaty-making in the Niger Delta and had already established herself on the Dahomey Coast.

The Conference, which met from 13 November 1884 to 26 February 1885, included every major power in Europe. Also present were the Ottoman empire, the U.S.A. and Leopold's still shadowy International African Association. The main question for discussion by the Conference was: how to draw up formalities for the effective occupation of the coast of Africa.[29] It is interesting that the purpose of the Conference was to consider only the occupation of the coasts of Africa, though the Act that emanated from the discussions became the basis for the occupation of any part of Africa. It laid down that a power wanting to claim African lands should inform the other signatory powers 'in order to enable them, if need be, to make good any claims of their own.'[30] However, to be valid such claims should be supported by effective occupation. Freedom of navigation was to be maintained on the Niger and the Congo, though no provision was made to secure it: and in the event there was freedom of trade on neither river. There was also to be freedom of trade in the Congo basin: monopoly resulted.

The rules agreed upon, the various participants began to play the game with differing degrees of enthusiasm, and for different stakes. As far as West Africa was concerned, it was rather like a game of Monopoly, with France and Britain the only two serious contestants, Britain relying for her success on Park Lane and Mayfair, Whitechapel and the Old Kent Road, whilst France bought up anything she could lay her hands on that hadn't been taken by Portugal or Germany.

Thus at the conference tables of Berlin, with no African present, the rules for the partition of West Africa into units that were to become the basis of its modern nation states were determined, though the guidelines had already been set by the activities of European traders, missionaries and administrators in the eighty-odd years since abolition. Looking back on the colonial period, we may ponder the fact that probably the most enduring mark left by Europe on Africa has been the creation of new political units, which, though they took much more account of ethnic, religious and geographical factors than is usually supposed, completely changed the map of Africa. In West Africa these units have, almost unaltered, formed the basis of the new independent states.[31]

NOTES

1. J. D. Hargreaves, *Prelude to the Partition of West Africa*, London, 1963.
2. Ronald Robinson and John Gallagher with Alice Denny, *Africa and the Victorians: The Official Mind of Imperialism*, London, 1961, p.36.
3. Hargreaves, *Prelude*, p.39.
4. *Ibid.*, p.33.
5. See J. F. Ade Ajayi, *Christian Missions and the Making of Nigeria*, London, 1965.
6. David Kimble, *A Political History of Ghana 1850-1928*, London, 1963, p.273.
7. *Ibid.*, p.273, citing a minute from the Parliamentary Under-Secretary of the Colonial Office, J. Lowther, dated 20 April 1874.
8. Ivor Wilks, 'The Northern Factor in Ashanti History: Begho and the Mande', *Journal of African History*, II, 1, 1961, pp.25-34.
9. Harry A. Gailey, *A History of the Gambia*, London, 1965, p.72. By 1889, they had reached nearly 20,000 tons.
10. For this account of French colonial policy from 1850-80 I have relied heavily on Hargreaves, *Prelude*, and Henri Brunschwig, *Mythes et Realités de l'Impérialisme Colonial Français 1871-1914*, Paris, 1960.
11. J. D. Hargreaves, 'Towards a History of the Partition of Africa', *Journal of African History*, I, 1, 1960, p.102.
12. J. Suret-Canale, *L'Afrique Noire Occidentale et Centrale*, Paris, 1961, p.182.
13. Hargreaves, *Prelude*, p.99.
14. Quoted by Jan Stengers from Lady G. Cecil, *Life of Robert, Marquis of Salisbury*, Vol. IV, London, 1932, p.310, in 'The Partition of Africa − I: L'Impérialisme colonial de la fin du XIXe siècle: mythe ou realité', *Journal of African History*, III, 3, 1962, p.471.
15. *Ibid.*, pp.469-491; Robinson and Gallagher, *Africa and the Victorians*; Hargreaves, *Prelude*; C. W. Newbury, 'The Scramble for Africa: Victorians, Republicans and the Partition of West Africa', *Journal of African History*, III, 1962, pp.493-501; Henri Brunschwig, 'Les origines du Partage de l'Afrique Occidentale', *Journal of African History*, V, 1, 1964, pp.121-5.
16. J. D. Hargreaves, 'The Tokolor Empire of Segou and its Relations with the French', *Boston University Papers on Africa*, Vol. II, African History, ed. J. Butler (Boston, 1966), pp.138-9.
17. André Villard, *Histoire du Sénégal*, Dakar, 1943, pp.90-4.
18. Quoted by Stephen H. Roberts, *The History of French Colonial Policy, 1870-1925*, 2nd edition, London, 1963, p.15.
19. C. W. Newbury, 'Victorians, Republicans and Africans'. N.B. In 1878 Germany adopted a protectionist tariff, but as Henri Brunschwig points out in *L'Expansion allemande outre-mer du XVème siècle à nos jours*, Paris, 1957, p.99, contrary to the opinion of many this did not concern colonial expansion.
20. See Carlton J. Hayes, *A Generation of Materialism, 1871-1900*, New York, 1941, pp.216-33, for a useful summary of the development of the forces favourable to imperial expansion in Europe before 1885.
21. *Débats parlementaires: séance de la Chambre des Deputés*, 28 Juillet, 1885, p.1062.
22. Quoted by C. P. Gooch in *Franco-German Relations, 1871-1914*, London, 1913, p.21.
23. Hargreaves, *Prelude*, p.283.
24. See Stengers, 'Partition of Africa', and Brunschwig 'Les Origines du Partage'.
25. *The Times*, 30 November 1882, quoted in Stengers, 'Partition of Africa', p.475.
26. Quoted by W. O. Henderson, *Studies in German Colonial History*, London, 1962, p.3.

27. Herbert von Bismarck ascribed his father's change of heart to his fear of the pro-English influence of the Crown Prince's wife, who was a daughter of Queen Victoria: When we entered upon a colonial policy, we had to reckon with a long reign of the Crown Prince. During this reign English influence would have been dominant. To prevent this we had to embark on a colonial policy, because it was popular and conveniently adapted to bring us into conflict with England at any given time'. Quoted by A. J. Hanna, *European Rule in Africa*, London, 1961, p.8.
28. Stengers, 'Partition of Africa', p.490.
29. S. E. Crowe, *The Berlin West Africa Conference, 1884-85*, London, 1942, pt. 1, chap. II.
30. *Ibid.*, p.90.
31. See Saadia Touval, 'Treaties, borders and the partition of Africa', *Journal of African History*, VII, 2, 1966, pp.279-93.

III

WEST AFRICAN RESISTANCE
(1971)

In 1861 the administration of the newly acquired British colony of Lagos commissioned Captain A. T. Jones to make a report on the army of their north-western neighbours, the Egba. Jones summed up their military strategy with the same contempt so many European historians have subsequently shown for pre-colonial African armies, describing it as 'the irregular marching and skirmishing of the barbarous horde'.[1] Because so many European historians of Africa have dismissed African armies as little better than slave-hungry rabbles, easy prey for the disciplined, well-equipped European armies of occupation, very little attention has been paid to the African military response to the European invasion.

Indeed the history of the Scramble for Africa has largely been written with reference to its implications for European history. For the majority of the European historians of the quarter-century of African history from 1880-1905, during which the European conquest was largely completed, the most important events have been European ones. In a widely used history of Africa the chapter on the European Scramble for Africa devotes only one short paragraph to the West African stand against the Europeans, and makes no reference to the military quality of this stand.[2] Yet one of the reasons why the European occupation of West Africa took over twenty-five years was the strength of African resistance. Parts of Ivory Coast, Mali, Niger, Eastern Nigeria, the plateau of Northern Nigeria, and Mauritania were not 'pacified' until the second decade of the twentieth century. Not only was resistance bitter, it was often skilful. It was provided not by a few states with well-developed armies like Dahomey or Ashanti but by a very wide range of peoples. Indeed, it is

*Reprinted by permission of Hutchinson Publishing Group Ltd. from the 'Introduction' to *West African Resistance: The Military Response to Colonial Occupation*, by Michael Crowder, London, 1971, pp. 1-18.

rarely appreciated that a good majority of the states of West Africa, large and small, as well as most of the people living in segmentary societies, opposed European occupation with force.[3]

The conquest has been seen as an unequal contest and, as such, little interest has been shown either in the scale, organisation or effectiveness of resistance. Yet though it was an unequal contest – the Europeans had Maxim guns, for which African military leaders, however brilliant, had no ultimate answer – the Africans in many cases gave their European opponents a much stiffer battle than the latter had anticipated and the cost of conquest in terms of men and money was much higher than has generally been appreciated. Experience of the determination of African resistance, even if easily overcome with superior weapons, slowed down the rate of occupation, since each advance had to be worked out with regard to the scale of opposition likely to be encountered. This is borne out by the journals of the European military commanders, who, though they necessarily saw the battles they fought in terms of their own preconceptions of military strategy, were rather more generous in their assessment of the military capabilities of their opponents than most historians of colonial rule have been.[4]

While many European historians have seen, and still do see, the period 1880-1905 largely in terms of the diplomatic negotiations between European powers and accept that once agreement had been arrived at as to which power should have what part of Africa, effective occupation was only a question of time, the contemporary African historian naturally sees the period through a different optic. He is interested to know why African military resistance was not more effective, why some states defied the invaders and others did not, why some states were able to adapt their armies to deal with the military strategies of their European opponents, why others fought entirely in traditional terms. Where the heroes of the European histories of this period in West Africa are Archinard, Gallieni, Dodds, Lugard, Garnet Wolseley and Texeira Pinto, those of the African are Samori, Bai Bureh, Lat Dior, Nana of Ebrohimi, Behanzin and Attahiru Amadu. Battles are seen not in terms of the success of the conquerors but of the prowess of the defeated leaders in the face of overwhelming odds. And these battles, fought only seven or eight decades ago, are still vivid in oral tradition.

Such an attitude is understandable in purely nationalistic terms, but it is also historically justified. What can be more absurd than to record the history of these twenty-five years almost exclusively in European terms, without looking at the African response to the immense upheaval in African society that was brought about by the European partition? Ranger has shown that in East and Central

Africa there is a definite correlation between the resistance against colonial rule and the development of modern nationalism,[5] though such a correlation has not been demonstrated so clearly for West Africa. The heroes of some West African nations may be the heroes of the resistance, but, as Flint has pointed out, in the West African case historians have tended to see progressive figures such as Samuel Crowther, James Johnson or E.W. Blyden as 'the real pioneers of modern Africa and the builders of nationalism' while Jaja, Ovenramwen or Sultan Attahiru 'retain only the romantic veneration due to noble lost causes'.[6] This no doubt is the status of Bai Bureh in Sierra Leone.[7] But in French West Africa, as Ruth Schachter-Morgenthau has shown, Sekou Toure, a descendant of Samori Toure, consciously emphasised the parallel between his resistance to colonial rule and that of his ancestor to colonial occupation.[8] Indeed the Rassemblement Démocratique Africain (R.D.A.) not only in Guinea, but in French Soudan (Mali) and Ivory Coast claimed the support of the descendants of both Samori Toure and Al Hajj Umar as the contemporary resisters of the French.[9]

The military prowess demonstrated by the African during the occupation had to be borne in mind during colonial rule. Even where the French in the Western Sudan had smashed the armies that opposed them, during the 1914-18 War, when the French were at a disadvantage, large areas of the Western Sudan rose in revolt and slipped from French control for nearly two years.[10] The British and Germans in Central and East Africa learnt that occupation did not mean an end to resistance when many whites were slaughtered during the Shona and Ndebele risings of 1896-7 in Southern Rhodesia[11] and the Maji Maji rising in Tanganyika in 1905-6.[12] Lugard, despite the apparent ease with which he had conquered the Sokoto Caliphate, was well aware that a small miscalculation in his subsequent administration and diplomacy with the Emirs might lead to a revolt which he could not put down.

While a number of historians, both European and African, have in recent years undertaken studies of resistance to colonial occupation and rebellions against colonial rule once it had been established, they have been primarily concerned with the questions as to why Africans offered armed resistance. Little attention has, however, been paid to the actual mechanics of resistance; or to looking at colonial occupation from the point of view of the strategies adopted by the African armies. Although such strategies were unsuccessful, they were not those of 'barbarous hordes' but of generals, often with long years of experience, some so sophisticated that they taxed European forces, despite their possession of superior weapons, to the utmost; others so hidebound by traditional military thinking that, like the French at the opening of the Second World War, they were unable to appreciate that old methods were not suitable for dealing with armies equipped with revolutionary new arms, in this case the Maxim and Gatling guns. It is time to look at some of the major battles of the Scramble as two-sided affairs which all battles, of course, are. In so doing one may recall the change in character of the 'Western' film in recent years. Most old 'Westerns' showed a wild horde of all but naked Indians attacking the 'Cowboys' with seemingly no discipline or plan of attack. The 'Cowboys' were always triumphant since films had to have happy endings for an audience which was heir to the cowboy culture. In recent years more sophisticated films have shown the 'Cowboys' and 'Indians' pitting their wits against each other, with the latter sometimes triumphing, as indeed they did, and as indeed African armies sometimes did. Few films have been made of African battles, though there are great opportunities for them. When they are made it is to be hoped that, as with *Zulu*, that remarkable film of the near defeat of the British at Rourke's Drift, both sides will be given credit for their generalship and strategic abilities, though it must also be hoped that their account of actual events will not be so romanticised and distorted as in this film.

In considering African resistance it is not sufficient only to describe the organisation of the army in question, the weapons available to it, the nature of its generalship, the strategy employed against the Europeans. Consideration must also be given to the way diplomacy was used by leaders as a means of staving off military confrontation when they were convinced that the outcome would be unfavourable to them. Such was particularly the concern of Ahmadou of the Tukolor empire. And, although the European conquest was, as so many writers have rightly observed, ultimately a matter of time, demonstration of this fact relies not on an assumed superiority of European generalship but a careful analysis of the options open to the African leaders involved in the confrontation and why African strategies failed in the face of the technologically superior, but usually numerically far inferior, enemy.

In this essay we are concerned with the confrontation of African and European armies, and as such do not cover the resistance of segmentary societies or peoples divided into numerous petty chiefdoms which had no co-ordinated military organisation beyond the level of the village. Nevertheless, such societies — in particular the peoples of the Benue valley in Nigeria and the peoples of the southern Ivory Coast — provided some of the stiffest resistance the colonial forces of occupation experienced. Since each village offered its resistance, there was no identifiable army to defeat among the Ibo as there was, say, among the Tukolor, the Emirates of Nigeria, or Samori's

Mandingo empire. Each village or federation of hamlets had its own war-leader. These societies conducted what was in effect guerilla warfare against the invading armies, quite the best tactic that could have been adopted in the circumstances. Unfortunately no detailed study has yet been made of the nature and methods of the military resistance offered by these societies to colonial occupation.

In considering the opposition to European forces by the organised armies of centralised states, it must be remembered that the size and complexity of these states varied considerably. One of the smallest armies was that of Bai Bureh of Kasseh, a tiny Temne state in northern Sierra Leone, barely more than 400 square miles in area. As a war-leader of long-standing reputation, as well as chief of Kasseh, he was, however, able to unite the forces of most other Temne chiefdoms against the British and provide them with some of the toughest opposition they met in their occupation of West Africa. Nana Olomu, Governor of the Benin river, ruled over a state more conspicuous for its prosperity than its size. The military forces he used to maintain its monopoly of trade on the Benin river were used to defend it against the British who had to bring into play most of the forces at their disposal in West Africa. The Yoruba kingdom of Ijebu seems never to have been brought under the rule of Oyo, which controlled most of the west of Yorubaland as well as Dahomey during the eighteenth century. In the nineteenth century, with the opening of the Lagos lagoon to regular trade with Europe, Ijebu prospered on the middleman trade in goods and firearms with the interior, and became during the civil wars of the nineteenth century one of the most powerful of the Yoruba states. It was the only one to offer any effective military resistance to the British and, despite internal dissension, fielded an army of between 7,000 and 10,000, larger than that of Federal Nigeria at the beginning of the Civil War. It was defeated, however, in a short engagement, but acquitted itself with greater success than the British forces had ever anticipated.

Ashanti and Dahomey had both been founded in the seventeenth century and owed their expansion as states in great measure to their sophisticated military organisation. Though Dahomey was tributary to Oyo during the eighteenth century, and only secured independence between 1818 and 1822, its army, with its famed Amazons, was one of the most impressive in West Africa. Ashanti, a much larger state, based on resources of gold, kolanuts and slaves, had by the beginning of the nineteenth century made most of what is modern Ghana tributary to it. In 1823 it became the first major West African power to fight a war against the Europeans, in this case the British. In all, Ashanti fought eight major engagements with the British, and in two of these achieved significant victories, thus being the only West

African army decisively to defeat the Europeans in more than one major engagement.

Several states which fought with the Europeans were products of the Islamic revival that swept the Western Sudan in the nineteenth century: the Sokoto Caliphate, founded in 1804; the Tukolor empire, founded in 1852; the Mandingo empire of Samori, which almost immediately after its foundation in 1870 came up against French expansionist ambitions in the Western Sudan; and the short-lived Sarakole empire of Mahmadou Lamine, which threatened both French Senegal and the Tukolor empire, so that the Tukolor, whilst intent on resisting French encroachments on their own territory, saw Mahmadou Lamine as a more immediate threat and allied with the French against him.

Perhaps the most striking feature of the invading armies was their small size in comparison with the African armies which opposed them. For instance, Colonel Kemball took Sokoto with a force of only 1,200, half of which consisted of carriers, yet Sokoto had an army estimated at nearly 30,000. The British expedition against Ijebu-Ode in 1892 comprised just over 1,000, more than half of whom were again carriers, while the Ijebu fielded a force seven to ten times larger. Again, General Dodds led an expeditionary force of only 2,000 against the Dahomeyan army of nearly 12,000. There were, however, exceptions to this disproportion. While the British considered at the outset that only a small force was necessary to deal with Bai Bureh's army of 3,000 they ended up with almost the same number of troops and carriers in the field before they could bring him to bay. Again, while French armies in the early campaigns against Samori had been greatly outnumbered, by 1891-2 the French and Samorian armies opposing each other were of roughly the same size.

The composition of the European forces varied, but for the most part they were only European in leadership. French and British officers and N.C.O.s led African troops, trained in their drill and weapons, against their fellow Africans. The use of Europeans in other ranks was limited: Wolseley sent three British battalions to Kumasi in the Ashanti War of 1874. More regularly employed by the British were West Indian troops, who were better adapted to the climate and were permanently stationed in Freetown, Gold Coast and Lagos. They fought in the wars with Bai Bureh, the Ashanti and the Ijebu among others. The French armies were based on the *Tirailleurs Sénégalais* — founded by General Faidherbe in St. Louis in 1857. They were recruited from among local Africans, who were officered by Frenchmen. In the early years French troops were used in the rank and file: at the battle of Guemou against Al Hajj Umar, in 1859, 320 European soldiers as against 760 African soldiers fought in the

French army. Nearly half the Senegal garrison in 1874 was composed of French *disciplinaires* sent to Senegal as a punishment. By contrast with British practice some Africans did gain commissions in the French forces and it was an African lieutenant, Yaro Coumba, who successfully defended the French post at Senedoubou against Mahmadou Lamine. Medina was defended against Al Hajj Umar by Paul Holle, who was a *métis* from St. Louis, as was General Dodds who conquered Dahomey. The reluctance of the invading armies to use European troops was the result of the high death rate from the climate and tropical illnesses, in particular malaria and yellow fever, though by the time of the conquest the regular use of quinine as a prophylactic reduced deaths from the former. Cardwell, at the War Office, instructed Wolseley in 1873: 'If the employment of Europeans shall become a necessity, every preparation should be made in advance; and no European force should be landed on the Coast until the time for decisive action has arrived'. Wolseley was urged to use troops only during the 'period when the risk of loss from the climate is at a minimum ... [and to] spare to the utmost of your power the exposure of European soldiers or marines to the climate of the Gold Coast'.[13]

The fact that the invading armies were able to defeat African armies which sometimes outnumbered them 10-1 was due in part to the possession of superior weapons, and in part to the superior manipulation of those weapons which the African armies also possessed. The chief advantage of the European forces was that they had access to the most recent advances in military technology. While African forces were able to purchase small-arms, and some artillery, their own supplies were not only sparser than those of their European adversaries, but also less up to date. However, European forces did not have a decisive technological advantage over the Africans before the 1860s, since any superiority in small-arms, such as their possession of breech-loaders as against the muzzle-loaders employed by African armies, could be compensated for by the greater numbers their opponents could mass against them, and any superiority their cannon might possess was countered by the difficulty of transporting them into action. But the development of machine guns was to place the odds substantially in the Europeans' favour. In the 1860s the Gatling gun, consisting of a number of small barrels rotated by a crank, was invented, giving much more rapid fire than the single-round, breech-loaded gun: This was followed by the Mitrailleuse, which consisted of thirty-seven barrels of rifle calibre fixed together, also operated by a crank. These and further similar developments in artillery, such as the Gardener and the Nordenfeld, when use was made of their light weight and greatly improved manoeuvrability, increased the forward fire-power of the possessors enormously, and greatly compensated for imbalance in numbers. The major development in Western military technology as far as Europe and Africa were concerned was the single-barrel Maxim gun, the force of the recoil of which operated loading, firing, extraction and ejection at the rate of eleven shots a second. Much lighter than the Gatling gun and the Mitrailleuse, it could be used easily by the forward troops, and its devastating fire-power could hold down an army of much vaster numbers. The Gatling and its relatives were used by European forces in West Africa from the early 1870s onwards, and the Maxim from the early 1890s. No West African army appears ever to have obtained either of these machine-guns for use against their European opponents, though Johnson, the historian of the Yoruba, quotes a claim that the Ijesha had a Gatling gun in their war with Ibadan at Kiriji. The Amakiri faction in the state of New Calabar acquired a Gatling for use in the Civil War of 1879-82. This weapon stands in the Abbi compound in Buguma today. Also during the Satiru 'rebellion' against the British in Northern Nigeria in 1906 the 'rebels' captured a Maxim gun, but its water jacket was slashed and it could not be used.

Over and above their superiority in weapons the Europeans were also heirs to systems of drill and tactics devised to make maximum use of their weapons. African armies which did acquire relatively up-to-date European weapons rarely appreciated instruction in their mechanical and tactical advantages. Thus the Ijebu never took advantage of the fact that with a breech-loading rifle you can fire prostrate, thus presenting a smaller target to the enemy: they continued to fire them standing, as they had had to with muzzle-loaded guns. On the other hand Samori deliberately sent his soldiers to enlist clandestinely in the French Army to learn how to use the new arms to best effect. In addition he recruited African soldiers who had served the British and French armies. Over and above these, there was no means of learning the tactical advantages of the new weapons except through direct experience of battle with the Europeans.

Apart from Samori, few of the generals of the West African armies that opposed the Europeans appear to have realised that the new weapons they were acquiring needed special drills and gave specific tactical advantages. Herein lay the second major key to the success of the European armies: using African soldiers, they were much better drilled and disciplined than most of their opponents. The 'square' which the invading armies invariably used in any open engagement was, if it held fast, invincible. Disciplined troops, with rapid-fire rifles and fortified with Gatling and Maxim guns, could mow down opponents with vastly superior numbers, whether foot-soldiers or cavalry.

While the invading forces had clear advantages in weapons and discipline which compensated for differences in numbers, they suffered the severe disadvantage that they were fighting on foreign ground, with which their European officers were usually completely unfamiliar. They all too often had very extended lines of communication, having to rely on carrier pigeons, or runners, to keep in touch with headquarters. Their artillery was cumbersome, and they were much more heavily equipped on the march with both clothing and gear than their African opponents. Too often military dress in the tropics was conceived on a pattern more suitable for Europe, so that quick movement was impeded by the exhaustion heavy clothing would bring on. It is not surprising that the Colonel commanding the expedition against Bai Bureh died of 'Heat Apoplexy'.[14] Nevertheless Wolseley in his expedition to Kumasi did design a light-weight uniform more suitable for the tropics than the domestic uniform.

The greatest disadvantage of all faced by the invading armies was the fact that the only method of advance in the bush was in single file along narrow paths. The extended column, in particular with unarmed carriers trailing at the rear, was particularly vulnerable to attacks from behind or to ambushes from the side, as Bai Bureh and Samori showed. Bai Bureh in particular used bush-fires to cut off the advance or retreat of the British forces. The lack of knowledge of the countryside, however, was partially compensated for by the use of local scouts, the presence of African allies and the use of African troops themselves.

The armies which resisted the European invasion of West Africa varied considerably as to size, organisation and equipment. But they all faced the same dilemma. Their organisation, tactics and equipment had evolved to deal with local military situations, which continued to threaten them, at the same time as the presence of European forces demanded that they re-think their strategy to deal with the different tactics and superior weapons of their new opponents. Thus even if army commanders, one of whose common characteristics is their conservatism, had been inclined to devise new tactics to deal with the invading Europeans, there were powerful arguments in favour of sticking to the existing organisation, since for the most part they had still to deal with their African enemies, both external and internal. This was acutely the dilemma of the Sokoto Caliphate. And the European enemies were not, at least in the short-run, always considered the more dangerous foe. Thus Ahmadu of Segou allied with the French against Mahmadou Lamine; Tieba of Sikasso with the French against Samori; and Ibadan with the British against the Ijebu, who also had to cast nervous glances over their shoulders at a dissident Ijebu army led by their Seriki, Kuku.

To deal successfully with the European invading forces would have necessitated a complete reorganisation of the army in terms of strategy and equipment. Bai Bureh, Samori and to a certain extent Nana and the Ashanti managed to effect this. Bai Bureh adopted the strategy of guerilla warfare, avoiding direct confrontation with the enemy, which was so characteristic of the battles fought between African and European forces. Samori not only adopted guerilla warfare as a strategy but also managed to achieve some parity in arms with his adversaries. This he did not only through a remarkable network of commercial contacts, but also by manufacturing effective copies of some of the European originals. This enabled him to stave off the Europeans for longer than any other African military commander in tropical Africa, but ultimately he was doomed, as he himself knew, because he did not have all the weapons the Europeans possessed. He never obtained anything more than rapid-fire rifles and his fire-power could never equal that of the French. Nana's untrained riflemen, just by taking advantage of the natural defences of Ebrohimie, forced the British to withdraw on three occasions. The Ashanti used their superior knowledge of the forest to attack the British on the flanks where they were most vulnerable.

The major problem for all African armies was the difficulty of obtaining supplies of European arms. Before 1890, when the European powers formally forbade the export of arms to West Africa, obsolete European arms had been a staple of the export-import trade. Samori bought his from British traders in Freetown to fight the French, the Ijebu bought theirs from French traders to fight the British. Bai Bureh obtained supplies from merchants of the very country he was fighting. Indeed Joseph Chamberlain, the British Colonial Secretary, was considering a charge of treason against one such merchant.[15] But even where they did acquire arms from European merchants, these were very rarely the modern ones which the European armies, supplied by metropolitan military ordnance, had access to. The African armies became the dumping ground for discarded European models, which could give them immense advantage over African rivals who did not possess them, but left them, with the rapid development of gun technology at the end of the nineteenth century, often several jumps behind the European invading forces. This policy of dumping obsolete weapons on African armies continued in some cases into colonial days. When the British and French invaded Togo in 1914 they found the local forces equipped with rifles from the Franco-Prussian War of 1870-1.[16] Even where African armies did lay hands on modern arms, repair was difficult. Samori solved this by sending his armourers to St. Louis to gain experience from the French armoury.

African armies, apart from guns, relied on a variety of weapons — swords, spears, lances, bows and arrows — the complexity of which is indicated by the weaponry of the Hausa-Fulani forces.[17] But these were ineffective, except as irritants, against the European enemy. As late as 1916, in the Borgu rebellion against the French in Dahomey, the rebels met gun-fire with bows and arrows, albeit poisoned. The number of French forces killed in the two-month-long engagement, in which eleven battles were fought, was only ten, with thirty-three wounded. Of these only two were European: one N.C.O. killed, one N.C.O. wounded. The African rebels suffered losses which they admitted after the war to be very heavy. Two months after the war only 611 dane-guns (flintlocks) had been confiscated from the rebels.[18]

Too often the African armies fell back in defeat on their walled cities or stockaded towns. Designed to withstand long sieges against an enemy with no marked superiority of weapons, they were delightful targets for cannon and projected flares which could set alight the thatched roofs of the houses, a trick also used by the Fulani.[19]

Where most African states did not have standing armies as such, they had the mechanisms for the rapid recruitment and formation of an army of soldiers who had had military training. In most African societies youths were expected to learn the arts of warfare, so that in times of emergency they could be called up. Some states had a small standing army which formed the nucleus of the much larger army formed from the 'reserves' in times of war. The standing army might consist of just the recognised military commanders and the palace guard or be a regular force such as the Amazons in Dahomey, the war-boys of northern Sierra Leone or Samori's sofa.

Usually soldiers were expected to equip themselves: part of Samori's success lay in keeping his men supplied with rifles. The King of Dahomey equipped his standing army with flintlocks or carbines, though flintlocks were replaced for at least half the standing army with rapid-firing rifles immediately prior to the wars with the French. Soldiers usually brought their own supplies with them, and often, in traditional siege-type warfare, they were followed by their wives, who during the long static battles cultivated crops behind the lines.[20] In fast-moving battles soldiers lived of necessity off the land. The organisation of the armies again varied greatly from state to state. It is certainly impossible at this stage to generalise about them, except that in every African society, whatever its organisation, there was the obligation for young men to undertake military service in times of need, and train for it in advance. While the European forces had great advantages in weapons and discipline over their African opponents, they had all the disadvantages of the invading army coupled with paucity of numbers. Why in these circumstances did the African armies not mount more effective opposition to the Europeans? Though the great majority of West African peoples cherished their independence, they were invariably faced with a series of potential threats to that independence. Not only was their attention divided between African and European threats to their independence, but at times the European seemed less of an immediate threat to that independence and was, as we have seen, called in as an ally, or was joined in his conquest of a mutual enemy. In many cases the Europeans were assisted by African enemies of their immediate antagonist. In some cases there were enemies within the state. Thus the British allied with the Fanti against the Ashanti; the French with the Yoruba of Ketu against Dahomey; the British with the Ibadan against Ijebu; the French with the Bambara and other dissident groups against the Tukolor;[21] the French with the Tukolor against Mahmadou Lamine; the British with Dogho and other trade rivals of Nana Olomu in their expedition against Ebrohimie. The Europeans, though strangers, proved much more skilful in their diplomacy with regard to forging military alliances with African states than these states did among themselves. Indeed, as Flint points out, few West African states began the hostilities against the Europeans, and many tried, as was the case with Ahmadou of the Tukolor, to avert hostilities by diplomacy.[22] Rather, local European commanders on the spot invariably precipitated the wars of conquest. Flint speculates that, given the reluctance of most African leaders to engage in warfare and the desire of the metropolitan European to limit expenditure in West Africa and to gain control over African territories primarily to avoid them being taken over by rival colonial powers, West African leaders might have accepted a light form of European protectorate rather than go to war. The major weakness of African resistance was that it was undertaken state by state, where alliances of threatened states might not only have inflicted defeats on the Europeans but put the cost of conquest higher than the metropolitan powers were prepared to pay. As it was, the high costs of the Sudan campaign evoked violent criticism in the French Chamber of Deputies between 1891 and 1893.[23] The fiasco of the British expedition against the Ashanti in 1863 was in large part responsible for the decision of the 1865 British Parliamentary Select Committee's decision to limit British commitments on the West Coast. However, there was only one major attempt to combine forces against the Europeans and this was more significant as an exception in the pattern of resistance than as the threat it posed to the Europeans. Between 1889 and 1893, a number of states and groups allied to resist the French in the Western Sudan.[24] Unfortunately, while they all shared a common goal in seeking to preserve their independence from the French, within the alliance were groups who were equally anxious to preserve their independence from other members of the alliance. Thus Tieba of Sikasso joined a confederacy in which his long-standing enemy Samori was a leading member; the Bambara allied with the son of their erstwhile conqueror, Al Hajj Umar, against the French. But by the time the coalition had brought together all its members — Tieba did not join until 1890, the Bambara till 1891 — the French had already gained sufficient ground in the Western Sudan to make their conquest only a matter of time. Had, however, such an alliance been forged at the outset, the task of the French military would have been very much more difficult than it was. Attacked on all sides, without firm bases, they would have had to commit far more troops. Furthermore the African armies, freed from looking over their shoulders at potential and actual African enemies, could have devoted all their energies to the defeat of the Europeans. Just as the Europeans followed a policy of divide and conquer, so some African leaders followed a policy of divide and survive. Unfortunately the Europeans, though bitterly divided at home, managed to settle their differences amicably in Africa despite high tension in Borgu and the Gold Coast hinterland. The British in Sierra Leone turned down Samori's request for protection, a request which was designed to stave off the French. The Mogho Naba of the Mossi tried to play off the French and British and so preserve his independence. But in the circumstances the British, French and Germans in West Africa, though greedy for as much land as they could obtain, were not prepared to do so at the cost of a local African war that might provoke clashes in Europe.

Even though Africans were unable successfully to pool their resources, and even though they were unable to play off one European power against another, the African armies, despite their inferior weapons, their shortage of supply of arms and ammunition, and their less advanced discipline and drill, could have put up a better fight if they had been more tactically adaptable. If all African generals had appreciated, like Samori and Bai Bureh, that head-on clashes with the enemy's army, or the taking up of defensive positions in walled cities, gave the Europeans the fullest tactical advantage for their weapons, and had accordingly resorted to guerilla tactics, the story of the European conquest would have been very different. The forest regions were, of course, much better suited to guerilla warfare than the savannah areas, though we must remember that the savannah was then much more densely wooded than it is today, denuded as it is of trees by the cultivation of groundnuts. The European armies were particularly vulnerable at night, but for the most part they were only attacked by African armies by day, since many of the troops were too superstitious of the night to fight in the dark. The most difficult conquests for the Europeans were those where the African armies abandoned conventional warfare and resorted to guerilla tactics. Nana of Ebrohimie used to fullest advantage his superior knowledge of the creeks along which the British had to sail to reach Ebrohimie and made what the British thought would be a casual African conquest one of their most difficult. Bai Bureh appreciated that the African troops used by the British depended intimately on their white leaders, and instructed his men to pick off the Europeans. Similarly he saw that the most vulnerable part of the British columns was the line of carriers, and concentrated attacks on them. Samori took advantage of the extended lines of communication of his opponents, which forced them to live off the land, by pursuing a scorched-earth policy. The longest war fought by the Europeans in West Africa after that against Samori was against the peoples of the southern Ivory Coast, in particular the Baoule, who resisted occupation village by village, using to maximum advantage the dense forests of the area.

Even when African armies did adapt their tactics to meet the European threat there was a sense of inevitability about the European conquest. Even Samori, the most successful of the resisters, knew he was doomed but refused to surrender. So, too, did Ahmadu, but here he chose to stave off the inevitable by diplomacy. Threatened from within by rivals to the throne and by recently conquered subject groups, he knew he could not win against the French. Islam, whose hatred of subjection to the infidel could have provided, as it did for a short while between 1889 and 1893 in the Western Sudan, a unifying theme for resistance against the French and British, also held the seeds of a fatalist acceptance of the inevitable. It is clear that in the Sokoto Caliphate the leadership had given much thought to *hijra*, or the obligatory flight from the infidel, when there was no hope of resisting his rule. Sultan Attahiru Amadu thus after the conquest of Sokoto led a *hijra* to the east, where the British finally overtook him at Burmi and killed him. However, many of his followers continued to the Sudan where their descendants still live today under the chieftaincy of his grandson, Mohammadu Dan Mai Wurno. For many African leaders the confrontation between themselves and the technologically superior and vastly different European must have held something of the trauma of the encounter between Cortes and Montezuma or that between Pizarro and the Inca, so vividly portrayed in *The Royal Hunt of the Sun*. Furthermore, the myth of the white man's invincibility was enhanced by each conquest. Added to that was the ruthlessness of his methods of conquest. Much has been made of the bloodthirsty methods of the Africans in their wars with each other: too little of those of the Europeans in their wars with Africans when they often resorted to standards of warfare they would not have tolerated in Europe. In the British campaigns against Bai Bureh a policy of systematic burning of villages was followed. Crozier reported that the Hausa-Fulani wounded after the battle for Sokoto were shot 'to put them out of their misery' [25] The French in their conquest of the Western Sudan held out to their African troops the prospect of African slaves in reward for their services. The Voulet and Chanoine columns' ruthlessness in sacking towns, killing innocent women and children and enslaving adult males caused a major scandal in France. Above all, the Maxim gun, and the Gatling before it, evoked wonder and fear among the Africans. After the conquest of Ijebu, Carter trekked round Yorubaland displaying his Maxim gun. In the war with Ashanti the British forces in 1874 made a point of showing off their Gatling gun to the concealed but watching enemy.[26]

Guerilla warfare could only have staved off the inevitable. West Africa was an agricultural society with limited resources to finance a long-term war, whereas the Europeans came from an industrial society which had, by comparison, infinite resources, in particular the resources of fire-power.[27] Furthermore, at this stage the Europeans were not at war at home and could devote all their energies to the African conquest. Twenty years later, when the European powers fought each other and had limited resources to spare for Africa their African subjects were able seriously to embarass them in the Western Sudan and Dahomey, which rose up against the French taking advantage of their weakness. Lugard feared that in sending African troops to East Africa the British might become vulnerable in Nigeria. The Egba and Iseyin risings were treated very seriously. The tiny rebellion against the British-imposed Native Authority in Bussa caused concern because of the shortage of troops available.[28] It was Africa's misfortune that the Scramble for Africa occurred at a time of peace in Europe, when Europeans, instead of using their newly acquired weapons on each other, used them on Africa.

NOTES

1. 'Report of Captain A. T. Jones', appendix to J. F. Ade Ajayi and R. S. Smith, *Yoruba Warfare in the Nineteenth Century*, London, 1964, p. 139.
2. Roland Oliver and J. D. Fage. *A Short History of Africa*, London, 1962, pp. 194-5.
3. For a general account of the European conquest of West Africa see Michael Crowder, *West Africa Under Colonial Rule*, London, 1968, Part II.
4. See for instance, J. S. Gallieni, *Deux campagnes au Soudan français 1886-1888*, Paris, 1891; C. Braithwaite Wallis *The Advance of Our West African Empire*, London, 1903; one of the notable exceptions to this is Lugard, whose reports deliberately played down the importance of Hausa-Fulani resistance.

5. T. O. Ranger, 'Connexions between "Primary Resistance" Movements and Modern Mass Nationalism in East and Central Africa', Part I, *Journal of African History*, IX, 3, 1968, pp. 437-53, and Part II, IX, 4, 1968, pp. 631-41.
6. J. E. Flint; 'Review of West African Resistance' *African Historical Studies*, 3, 1972, p. 103.
7. In Sierra Leone when Colonel (later Brigadier) Juxon-Smith took over power he cited as the national heroes of Sierra Leone Bai Bureh, I. T. A. Wallace Johnson and Sir Milton Margai, *Daily Mail* (Freetown), 1 April 1967.
8. Ruth Schachter-Morgenthau, *Political Parties in French-Speaking West Africa*, Oxford, 1964, p. 234.
9. *ibid.*, p. 281 and p. 325.
10. National Archives of Senegal, 4D 45 Recrutement indigène: Execution — comptes rendus des colonies — 1915-16. See also Michael Crowder, 'West Africa and the 1914-18 War', *Bulletin de l'IFAN*, T.XXX, sér B., No. 1, 1968, pp. 227-45.
11. T. O. Ranger, *Revolt in Southern Rhodesia 1896-7*, London, 1967.
12. John Iliffe, *Tanganyika under German Rule 1905-1912*, Cambridge, 1969;
13. Quoted in Alan Lloyd, *The Drums of Kumasi*, London, 1964, p. 68.
14. P.R.O./C.O. 267/437, to Sec. of State, Conf., 31 March 1898.
15. P.R.O./C.O. 267/438, Draft reply dated 24 June 1898 to Governor of Sierra Leone's Secret (Conf.) of 28 May 1898.
16. Sir Charles Lucas, *The Gold Coast and the War*, London, 1920, p. 18.
17. See also Robert S. Smith, 'Yoruba Armament', *Journal of African History*, VIII, 1, 1967.
18. National Archives of Senegal, I.D. 178.
19. H. Clapperton, *Journal of a Second Expedition into the Interior of Africa from the Bight of Benin to Soccatto*, London, 1829, p. 62.
20. See S. A. Akintoye, 'The Ekitiparapo and the Kiriji War', Ph.D. thesis, Ibadan, 1966.
21. For a detailed study of dissident groups within the Tukolor Empire see B. Olatunji Oloruntimehin 'Resistance Movements in the Tukolor Empire', *Cahier d'Etudes Africaines*, 29, vol. VIII, No. 1, 1968, pp. 123-43.
22. Flint, *op. cit.*, p. 105.
23. See A. S. Kanya-Forstner, *The Conquest of the Western Sudan: A Study in French Military Imperialism*, Cambridge, 1969, pp. 202-9.
24. See B. Olatunji Oloruntimehin, 'The Anti-French Coalition of States and Groups in the Western Sudan 1889-1893', *Odu: A Journal of West African Studies*, New Series No. 3, April 1970.
25. Brigadier F. P. Crozier, *Five Years Hard*, London, 1932.
26. Lloyd, *Drums of Kumasi*, p. 97.
27. See J. B. Webster, and Adu Boahen, *The Growth of African Civilisation: The Revolutionary Years: West Africa since 1800*, London, 1967, pp. 243-4.
28. Nigerian Archives, Kaduna, SNP/331p Telegram Lt. Gov. Northern Provinces to Resident Kontagora of 17 June 1915 and Lt. Gov. Northern Provinces to Governor-General, Lagos, 17 June 1915.

IV

BAI BUREH AND THE SIERRA LÉONE HUT TAX WAR OF 1898 *
(1970)

In the early months of 1898 there was a general uprising against British rule in Sierra Leone. This was less than two years after the imposition of a British Protectorate over the hinterland of Freetown, the capital of the Sierra Leone colony. Sparked by the imposition of a hut tax in three of the five districts into which the Protectorate had been divided, the Hut Tax Wars, as they came to be known, were more than just a protest against a particularly obnoxious feature of colonial rule. They were rather a manifestation of African resentment against alien rule and of a 'desire of independence', as Governor Frederick Cardew himself admitted to Joseph Chamberlain, Secretary of State for the Colonies, on 10 May 1898.[1] A few days earlier, Chamberlain had told the House of Commons that he no longer believed that the wars were due to the hut tax but that they were 'a general rising against white rule'.[2]

The wars themselves consisted of two separate but related risings: that of the Temne in the north, which broke out toward the end of February 1898; and that of the Mende and neighbouring groups in the south, which broke out at the end of April. The Temne rising was under the leadership of an individual, Bai Bureh of Kasseh; that of the Mende was inspired and co-ordinated by a secret society, the Poro. Although the Temne restricted themselves to fighting the British forces and, with one notable exception, did not kill missionaries and traders, the Mende attacked every vestige of alien rule, murdering not only Europeans but also Africans dressed in European clothes. However, the underlying causes of the two risings were the same. And it seems fairly clear that Bai Bureh's highly successful stand against the British in the first two months of his war was an

*Reprinted by permission of the co-author. LaRay Denzer, and the Oxford University Press from *Protest and Power in Black Africa*, Robert Rotberg and Ali Mazrui (eds.), Oxford. 1970, pp. 169-212.

inspiration to the Mende.[3]

Bai Bureh's war against the British is the focus of this paper: why did he rise against them? Many of the reasons will apply equally to the Mende war. We shall then turn to Bai Bureh's career, starting with his early years as a war chief, when he acquired the military skills which he later used to such good effect against the British that it took them nearly ten months to defeat him. His career as chief of Kasseh follows: this brought him into direct involvement with the British administration of the Sierra Leone colony. Finally, we shall examine his war with the British, which, given the small size of his chiefdom and the limited forces at his disposal, was one of the most brilliant campaigns conducted by an African leader against European forces.

THE BUILDING UP OF RESENTMENT

Britain had been established in Freetown since 1787. In 1895 it had concluded a treaty with France delimiting respective spheres of influence in the area. In 1896 Britain proclaimed a protectorate over the city's hinterland. Although the appointment of two travelling commissioners in 1890 had extended Freetown's influence over its hinterland considerably, in 1896 Britain exerted a strong, effective influence only upon chiefdoms near the colony, but very little on those distant from it.[4]

Authority over those chiefs who had entered into treaty relationship with the British was buttressed by the establishment of a paramilitary force known as the Frontier Police, stationed in various hinterland chiefdoms. The main functions of these police were to patrol the roads and to ensure free passage on them, to prevent traders from being molested, and, where possible, to avert the outbreak of war in those districts to which they were posted. But they were given no authority to interfere in the governments of the chiefs in whose areas they were stationed.

When the Protectorate was declared in October 1896, some chiefs had already made treaties of cession to the British Crown, some had agreed to British arbitration of their disputes with their neighbours. However, some chiefs who had made no treaties whatsoever with the British were also brought under British rule at this time. And those who had made treaties had certainly not envisaged the alienation of their sovereignty to a foreign power. They had agreed only to certain limitations on it.

Nevertheless, the declaration of the Protectorate unequivocally vested sovereignty in the British authorities in Freetown. The District Commissioners were given extensive judicial powers which seriously curtailed the judicial authority traditionally held by the chiefs.[5] They could also direct arbitrary settlement of any question likely to cause a

BAI BUREH

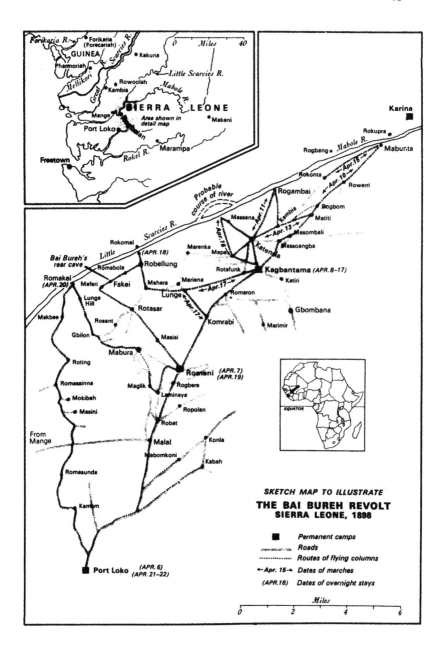

breach of the peace, even if it concerned local law and custom. The slave trade was abolished, and domestic slaves were free to leave their masters if they wished. For the chiefs, the Protectorate entailed not only the acceptance of the British District Commissioners, who were mainly young and inexperienced officers who interfered in every aspect of their administration, but it also contained provisions for the collection of taxes to support them. Governor Cardew having decided that the chiefs and people must help pay for their administration; this was done through a tax of 5/- a year for two-room houses and 10/- a year for larger houses. The tax became known as the 'hut tax' since most of the houses in the Protectorate were huts. Collection was to begin on 1 January 1898 in the three districts of Ronietta, Bandajuma, and Karene (in which Kasseh lay).

In March 1897, Cardew wrote to the Secretary of State:

> The Protectorate Ordinance as far as I can ascertain is working smoothly and the authority and jurisdiction of the District Commissioner is being felt and accepted. I gather this from unofficial as well as official sources, but of course the crucial time will be when the house-tax is levied but with an adequate police-force and a sufficient complement of white officers I have no apprehensions as to the results.[6]

This optimistic assessment of the situation in the Protectorate was confounded less than a year later when the peoples of the Protectorate rose up in protest against the introduction of the hut tax in particular and the British administration in general.

At the beginning of hostilities, both the local administrators and the Colonial Office believed that the primary cause of the war was the imposition of the hut tax. Direct taxation by the colonial administration in any form had already proved itself very unpopular in Sierra Leone. In 1872, Governor John Pope-Hennessy had made himself the best loved Governor in Sierra Leone's history by abolishing the house tax in the colony. 'Today', he wrote to Sir Hercules Robinson of the Colonial Office, 'I am the victim of popular ovations, bands, processions, religious services, public dinners and illuminations'.[7] In French Guinea, direct taxation in the Conakry region had met with resistance, which had only been overcome by 'incarcerating the chiefs until their people had collected sufficient produce to meet half the amount of the tax due'.[8] To explain his ordinance and the tax, Cardew undertook three series of tours up-country; these took place in 1894, 1895 and 1896. His tour in 1896 took him through the Karene district. At no meeting did the chiefs make any comment on the ordinance. To Cardew this meant acceptance, even if passive. However, Parkes, his shrewd Creole Secretary of Native Affairs, warned that from what he knew of the people, such passivity meant that 'they would not consent'.[9]

That Parkes was correct in his assessment became clear when, in mid-December 1896, a number of Temne chiefs, including Bai Bureh, wrote to Captain Wilfred Stanley Sharpe, who had just assumed duties as District Commissioner for Karene. They complained generally about the new administration. Then, protesting their friendship for the Queen, they begged the District Commissioner 'to tell the Governor that we are not able to observe the new laws and to pay house taxes'.[10]

Later, in June 1897, while Cardew was on leave, a group of influential Temne chiefs who had been invited to Freetown for the Jubilee celebrations took this occasion to draw up a petition to the acting Governor. In it they expressed fears concerning their own status, judicial powers, and lands. They also asked for relief from the hut tax.[11] Neither this petition nor the earlier letter had much impact on the administration. Only Parkes, long associated with the chiefs, perceived that their grievances were such that 'if it is decided to collect the hut tax during the coming dry season, considerable tact and patience will have to be exercised by the collectors in order not to alienate the loyalty and confidence of the natives concerned'.[12]

However, Cardew did not relent in his intention to collect the tax, even though the Temne petitioners waited in Freetown for two months until his return in September so that they could present their grievances to him personally. He did concede that 'it was desirable to grant considerable exemptions in view of the circumstances that next year would be the first year of its imposition, that natives were unaccustomed to be directly taxed by the government and that under the hope that their petitions against it might be entertained by [the Secretary of State] they had probably made no provision for its payment'.[13] Therefore, the tax was made a uniform one of 5/- for all houses irrespective of size. The other grievances of the chiefs, except those concerning their authority in land disputes in their own territories, Cardew dismissed as unfounded and the result of gross misrepresentation as to the nature of the Protectorate Ordinance. He seems to have been blithely unaware of the seriousness of the situation created by his determination to collect the hut tax and his reluctance to change any part of the Protectorate Ordinance despite the numerous complaints presented to him about it. Joseph Chamberlain was to note a year later that 'although I have supported Sir J. Cardew throughout I am a little afraid that he is inclined to be hard on the Natives and does not take sufficient pains to ascertain their views and to remove their suspicions'.[14]

How gravely Cardew had misassessed the situation was brought out by his dispatch to Chamberlain of 8 October 1897:

> I do not apprehend that the chiefs will combine to forcibly resist the collection of the tax, for they lack cohesion and powers of organisation, and there are too many jealousies between them for concerted action, but there may be isolated acts on the parts of some chiefs and their followers of forcible resistance to the tax which might spread to other tribes if not promptly suppressed by the Police....[15]

Within six months a large part of the Protectorate had risen against the British.

As the war progressed, it became increasingly clear that the hut tax was only one of many causes of the rebellion, even though its collection had undoubtedly set it off. It is not even clear whether the tax as such involved real financial hardship for the people. The Temne chiefs in their petition had complained that prevailing prices for the produce of the Protectorate were exceptionally low, and Parkes himself confirmed this assertion.[16] They had also complained of the difficulty of obtaining labour for their farms; if they worked their domestic slaves too hard, they could run away and obtain their freedom from the British. The acting chief of Port Loko had protested to the District Commissioner at Karene that it would be hard to pay the tax: 'They were not allowed to buy and sell slaves as they did nine years ago. There were no gold-mines, no quantity of palm-kernels or rice; they could only just get their livelihood'.[17] In the Colonial Office consideration was given to reducing the tax on the grounds that the people might be prepared to pay a lower one.[18]

Cardew, however, was able to marshal evidence from both official and unofficial sources in support of his contention that the level of the tax was not too high.[19] The Rev. J. A. L. Price, an American Negro missionary who was the Secretary of the American Soudan Mission, wrote Cardew that he did not think that the hut tax was 'exorbitant or oppressive'.[20] Methods of collection rather than the tax itself were put forward as the real cause of resentment. There were many allegations that brutality was generally used. The District Commissioner of Karene dismissed such accusations peremptorily.[21] In fact officials had received special instructions that nothing was to be done which might irritate or hurt the people's feelings.[22] However, the Chalmers Commission of Inquiry which investigated the war proved that the arrogant behaviour of the police and the misuse of their prerogatives had long been a source of grievance to the people and chiefs of the Protectorate.[23]

It does not seem that direct taxation was repugnant to custom, for chiefs throughout Sierra Leone were in the habit of imposing levies on their people. However, the notion that people should pay a 'rent' to the government for houses which they owned seemed to them preposterous, and 'an abnegation of their ownership rights in their own houses'.[24]

There was considerable resentment also over the fact that the people of Rokamp, as Freetown was called in the Protectorate, were exempt from the tax. The District Commissioner of Karene insisted that everyone would continue to resent paying the tax as long as their compatriots in Freetown were exempt.[25] That the chiefs of the Protectorate were quite aware of this point comes out clearly in the Chalmers Report. For example, Creole traders in Port Loko told the local people that in Freetown no such tax was paid and they should not have to pay it either. They introduced the chiefs to lawyers in Freetown who could advise them about the tax. Indeed a British trader gave evidence to the Chalmers Commission that if the hut tax had been imposed on Freetown a year before its introduction into the Protectorate, there would have been no trouble.

Nor were the Creole traders the only outside interest group to oppose the tax. British traders in Sierra Leone were against it from the start, considering it detrimental to trade. They made their opposition clear to the Governor. The Manchester and Liverpool Chambers of Commerce, which represented most British traders in Sierra Leone, sent petitions to the Colonial Office asking for its repeal. Chamberlain even asked the Manchester Chamber of Commerce to suggest an alternative means of taxation.[26] Cardew, however, dismissed the opposition of merchants who 'telegraph in the interest of trade'; he felt the administration of the colony was a matter of indifference to them as long as trade was good.[27] He even accused certain British traders of actively assisting the 'insurgents' by selling gunpowder to them, naming in particular G. B. Ollivant's, the Sierra Leone Coaling Company, and Pickering and Berthoods. 'The British Merchant out here has shown convincingly that he would not hesitate to sell arms and ammunition to the enemies of his country whenever he can get the chance...'.[28]

Chamberlain was so shocked by this news that he asked Cardew to find out whether there was sufficient proof of these allegations to prosecute the offenders for high treason.[29] Because of the difficulty of securing conviction, the disappearance of witnesses, and the fact that one of those to be tried had already been thanked by the Executive Council for his services to the Government (lending carrier pigeons for use in the war), Chamberlain reluctantly agreed that there should be *no prosecution*.[30]

In Britain, traders pursued their opposition to the hut tax in the press, gaining a notable ally in the popular *Daily Mail* which 'time and again . . . had called attention to the notorious hut tax'.[31] Other newspapers, despite their preoccupation with the Spanish-American War, and, in Africa, with the Sudan and Anglo-French tension on the Niger, also found space to publish the merchants' views.[32] Mary Kingsley, the celebrated traveller, came out in support of the merchants, describing the hut tax as 'a piece of rotten, bad law from a philosophic as well as fiscal standpoint'.[33] In the House of Commons, in 1898, Davitt, the member for Mayo South, described the tax as a blunder'. And, while Chamberlain defended its imposition publicly, within the Colonial Office walls he had as early as April described it as a tax 'which I strongly suspect ought never to have been imposed'.[34]

Despite the general opposition to his tax, Cardew never — before, during, or after the war — countenanced its abolition. For him there was 'a great principle involved in this struggle which is the right of the Government to compel the governed to contribute towards the support of the Government which ensures them the security of life and prosperity, just laws and all the other benefits of the most advanced civilisation'.[35]

But as Cardew soon came to realise, the people did not want the so-called 'benefits' of his government, and they were certainly not prepared to pay for what they did not want. They fought the government in order to regain their independence and be rid of what they considered an oppressive system of government. In a secret dispatch, Cardew himself attributed the war to 'the desire for independence and for a reversion to the old order of things. . . . They are sick of the supremacy of the white man as asserted by the District Commissioners and Frontier Police'.[36] T. Caldwell of the Church Missionary Society told Chalmers that he believed 'that the country was ready for any excuse to throw off British rule, because they complained of having to clean roads, build barracks, and obey the Government in what they called their own country'.[37] Rev. Price supported this view:

> The Temne people (the chiefs) do not want the English to rule in their country, or influence their customs in any way. . . . Their desire to throw off the English Power was not conceived last year nor the year before. They disdain the idea of being tributary. They want to dominate, hence the deep-rooted idea of slavery. For some years they have apparently been hesitating between two extremes, Rebellion or Submission, and the Hut Tax afforded them quite a pretext to decide one way. . . .[38]

If the hut tax was merely a pretext — a final straw — what were the underlying reasons why the Temne, and later the Mende, decided on rebellion? In addition to the desire for independence, the complex of resentments falls under three main headings: (1) loss of authority and prestige by the chiefs, in particular their loss of judicial authority; (2) resentment at the abolition of the slave trade and the liberty offered to domestic slaves by the British; and (3) hatred of the Frontier Police. These grievances, given focus by the hut tax, were encouraged by the Freetown press and by Creoles living up-country.

The overriding grievance of the chiefs was their loss of authority under the new regime. They were now subjected to young District Commissioners who knew little of the areas which they were administering. In an interview with Lord Selborne, Parliamentary Secretary at the Colonial Office, Dr. Edward Blyden, the West Indian nationalist, said that 'one main cause of the rebellion was the want of consideration shown by young District Commissioners in their dealings with the chiefs, many of them old men, who resented being dictated to by young men'.[39] In particular, the chiefs resented their loss of judicial authority to the District Commissioners' courts. They were now deprived of that great proportion of their revenue which had hitherto been derived from fines imposed in the cases which they tried.[40] What legal authority was left to them was further reduced by the new sanctions on certain types of judicial procedure such as the 'ordeal' – a form of physical torture used to determine guilt or innocence.

The chiefs also resented the tasks imposed upon them by the District Commissioners, such as building barracks for the Frontier Police, making roads, or collecting the hut tax. They were horrified by the provision in the Protectorate Ordinance that District Commissioners could punish them by flogging, a punishment which would disgrace them in front of their people. They felt that the Protectorate Ordinance had so reduced their authority in the eyes of their people that their wives, children, and domestic slaves would cease to obey them, and that they now lacked their former powers of punishment to enforce obedience.[41] Missionaries became the object of hatred in this connection. Not only did they expose 'malpractices' to the British authorities, but in educating children, they taught them to despise their illiterate and 'pagan' elders, thus arousing the jealousy of the uneducated.[42] (This grievance, however, was stronger in Mendeland where missionary efforts were concentrated, than in the Temne areas where Islam was making progress.)

Further, the prohibition on the internal slave trade deprived many chiefs of a major source of income from levying duties on slave caravans. This was particularly true in Kasseh, which lay astride the traditional trade route from Mendeland to Susuland. Although under the *Protectorate* Ordinance domestic slavery was not abolished as such, domestic slaves could obtain their freedom on application to the

British authorities. This deprived chiefs and other owners of domestic slaves of an important source of labour and obviously weakened their control over their slaves.

Probably the most directly irritating aspect of colonial rule was, however, the behaviour of the Frontier Police. Even before the imposition of the Protectorate they had far exceeded the powers delegated to them by either the colony's government or by the chiefs who had agreed to their being stationed in their chiefdoms. In spite of orders from Freetown, far from just keeping the peace, they set themselves up as 'little judges and governors';[43] they interfered in local disputes which were none of their business. Scattered over the hinterland, they were often unsupervised by senior officers who, when they made their tours of inspection, were inundated with complaints against these men. Parkes presented a volume of correspondence relating to complaints against the police to the Chalmers Commission.[44] One of the problems was that many of the Frontier Police were runaway slaves who had gained their freedom in Freetown, whence they were recruited. Chiefs thus resented the fact that they were open to arrest by men who had once been their slaves.[45] According to Parkes, the behaviour of the police improved with the appointment of Cardew as Governor, although he told Chalmers that they were still not what they ought to be.[46] Regimental Sergeant Major George of the Frontier Police, however, defended the force against criticism, asserting that it was largely manufactured by Creole traders.[47]

The grievances against the police were exacerbated by the Sierra Leone press and the Creole traders in the Protectorate. The Freetown press had a surprisingly wide circulation in the interior; Creole traders subscribed regularly and conveyed the news to the largely illiterate chiefs. In this manner, British reverses became known to the African opposition during the wars.[48] Important chiefs, such as Bai Bureh, employed educated clerks, who translated the newspapers for them. When Almami Senna Bunde, one of the leaders of the revolt in the south, was captured in April 1898, some thirty copies of the Sierra Leone *Weekly News* were found in his house.[49] Taiama's Foray Vons was also well acquainted with Sir Samuel Lewis's attacks on the Protectorate Ordinance.[50] When a prisoner of Bai Bureh, W. M. Pittendrigh, the chairman of Freetown's Chamber of Commerce, recorded that the chief would look for articles on the Port Loko disturbances of February 1898, and that he put great faith in them.[51] There was even a limited circulation of English papers in the interior.[52] Cardew went so far as to request the restriction of the freedom of the press in the Colony because of the role he considered that it was playing in stimulating trouble in the Protectorate. With these constant communications between Freetown and the Protectorate, he asserted, 'the disloyal sentiments contained in the Sierra Leone newspapers can be conveyed into and influences the minds of the natives'.[53]

In much the same category as the Freetown press were the Creole traders of the Protectorate, whom Cardew accused of deliberately fomenting trouble. In this regard the district commissioners of Karene and Ronietta backed him.[54] So did the superintendent of the Soudan Mission, the Rev. E. Kingman, who wrote a letter to Cardew in which he laid great emphasis on the role of the Creole traders in inciting resistance.[55] Cardew, who greatly despised Creoles, insisted that the Creole traders not only incited rebellion but that they were also one of its causes by alienating the chiefs and people 'with their loud and obtrusive ways, their contempt for the bushman and their property'.[56]

That the causes of the war were as complex for Bai Bureh as indicated above is brought out in the text of the letter he signed, with other Temne chiefs, in December 1898. It is reproduced here as the prelude to our study of his role in the war:

> We received one letter here from Governor sent to tell us that the Queen now takes the whole of the Timini country. The palavers are all left now to Queen's part, so we read the letter and we know the law that he the Governor puts on us now, viz., not to barter any slaves again, nor to buy again, nor to put pledge again, so who ever do that if Government find you guilty of that with the slaves they will catch you and put you for seven years Gaol.
> So that again who get his own country and if the place is empty and there is no one to work, the Governor will take the place and give to another people to work farms there. This we come to you Captain, to beg the Governor, to make him don't do that to us. Because we did not make war in our country.
> Again to say we must pay for our houses, we are not able to pay for our own houses. Because we have no power and no strength to do so, so that please tell the Governor we beg him to be sorry for us, and to consider the old agreement he made with our fathers.
> Suppose when your headman tells you to take up a heavy load, if you are not able to take it, you can only tell him by true words: 'Master, I am not able to carry all this at once, I am too weak.' Suppose you omit to tell him at the time itself that you are not able to carry the load, then when you tell him afterwards, he will ask you, 'why did you not tell me at the same time that you are not able to do this?' This is why we tell you, Master, we are not able to pay for our houses. Beg the Governor to leave us as we have been day before,

because the law tells us that we must not take our load to go up country again, unless we pay duty. Now the whole of the domestics we got before all stubborn and refuse to work for us. Now as we have no power to force them to work do, we beg you, Captain Sharpe, to tell Governor that we are not able to observe the new laws and to pay house taxes. Remember we all have been friends with the Queen for a long time. Also we beg the Governor must leave our woman palavers to ourselves because we are poor people, and because we do not get any power beyond our farm-work.

So, Captain, please beg the Governor to make him feel sorry for us, and beg him not to take any chiefs waste land and give to any man or stranger. This we beg him, all this, we do not get slaves to work for us, and we cannot trade as the road is closed say if any body kill person or snake bites person and die, and all the witch palaver so the Chief must not talk palaver alone, except the Captain present, the Chief and the Captain talk the palaver — concerning all this we send to beg the Captain to tell the Governor not to pull the power to judge these matters out of our hands but to leave all these matters to ourselves both all the big palavers and all the small ones we beg may be left to ourselves, any matter are not able to settle them we will go take it to the Captain, Do, we all pray God by the Governor to allow this for us and not be so hard on us.[57]

THE EARLY YEARS: BAI BUREH, THE WARRIOR

Little is known of Bai Bureh's life.[58] He spent his childhood in the small town of Rogbolan in the chiefdom of Kasseh, which covers a small area south of the junction formed by the Little Scarcies and Mabole rivers (see map). His father, a professional warrior, followed family tradition by sending his son to a well-known warrior training centre at Pendembu Gwahun, founded by the great warrior Gbamelleh. So successful was Bai Bureh in his profession that his peers soon nicknamed him Kebalai, or 'the man whose basket is never full', because of the number of men he killed in battle.[59] Since 'Bai Bureh' is the title of office of the chief of Kasseh, not a personal or family name, he did not become known as such until he became chief in about May 1887,[60] by which time his fame as a war leader extended throughout much of modern Sierra Leone. It was this fame which led the elders of Kasseh to invite him to assume the post of chief. In the absence of an hereditary claimant, such a step was not against traditional custom.[61] However, the British, with their theories of royal lineage and nobility, cast aspersions on Bai Bureh's right to rule because, to their way of thinking, he lacked the hereditary right.

Bai Bureh was a *kruba*, or war chief, whom other chiefs called upon to assist them in their wars. According to the traditional code regulating conduct in war, in return for his services he had certain rights of plunder. Among these was the right to enslave prisoners taken in battle – it is not certain whether he and his men had the right to all such prisoners or merely to a certain proportion. In English the name given to this transaction meant that one chief 'bought war' from the other: Governor Cardew and his predecessors interpreted this literally, describing the system as one of acquiring 'mercenaries'.[62] Much more research into the nineteenth-century social and political structure of the Temne must be done before the term 'mercenary', with all its derogatory implications, can be used with certainty to describe Bai Bureh and other war leaders like him. The authors believe that it cannot be so applied because, for one thing, the position of war chiefs and warriors, as professional men, was clearly institutionalised. There were very few war chiefs, and only they possessed the right to request permission from other chiefs to travel through their chiefdoms to collect armed followers.[63] Furthermore, the occupation of warrior was specialised and boys were specifically trained for it in centres scattered throughout the chiefdoms.[64] Often boys were sent out of their own chiefdom to another for such training, thus acquiring 'trans-chiefdom' loyalties. By the 1890s, political authority seems to have become concentrated in the hands of important military figures. Captain Sharpe, Karene's District Commissioner, observed that the war chiefs were the only ones who possessed any 'real authority' and that one of them was worth fifty ordinary chiefs.[65] It would seem that the warrior system was a factor unifying the many Temne chieftains into a broad alliance for achieving politico-military ends, and that Bai Bureh's leadership of the Temne against the British was thus a result of his status within this military system rather than the result of his strictly political position as chief of tiny Kasseh.

Although Bai Bureh led the Temne against the British, it is not clear whether he was a Temne or a Lokko. He himself told Cardew that he was a Temne during an interview shortly before his deportation.[66] All administrative reports prior to 1899 also refer to him as a Temne.[67] Elizabeth Hirst and Issa Kamara, however, maintain that he was really a Lokko who intended to restore Lokko prestige in the Scarcies-Port Loko area.[68] Christopher Fyfe compromises by maintaining he was partly Lokko by descent.[69] Linguistic evidence tends to support those who claim Lokko descent, for it is maintained that Temne in the Scarcies-Port Loko area still sing war songs about Bai Bureh's exploits in untranslated Lokko.[70]

Bai Bureh was an adherent of traditional religion but he must also have been influenced strongly by Islam, for the Susu, Fula and

Mandingo, most of whom were Muslim, had migrated into the Scarcies and northern areas of Sierra Leone during the nineteenth century. Many Muslims from these groups had married Temne, Lokko and Limba. Most important of all, as a war leader for the Muslim chief, Bokhari, in what Bokhari considered a *jihad* against Bokhari's own people, Bai Bureh must have been aware of Bokhari's desire to impose Islam on his followers. Nevertheless he seems not to have embraced the Islamic faith in terms implying anything other than the recognition of the abilities and influence of its adherents. Possibly he was a member of the Kefa or Kefung secret society, an elite group about which very little is known; membership supposedly endowed its members with the abilities[71] which Bai Bureh possessed according to myth — such as his wondrous abilities to change into an animal in order to escape from his enemies and to live either underground or underwater for long periods of time.

Nevertheless, Islam affected his rùle in a variety of ways, and he must have been profoundly affected by Islamic developments further to the north. Throughout his chieftaincy, he maintained an Arabic-writing clerk; the majority of his letters to the Aborigines Department — later known as the Native Affairs Department — were written in Arabic, as were the administration's replies. Hirst and Kamara suggest that there were close relations between Bai Bureh and a family of powerful Muslim traders who had immigrated into Temneland.[72] It was through influential Muslim leaders that he made various peace overtures to the British in 1898: once through the Alikali of Port Loko; at another time through the leader of the Muslims in Freetown.[73]

Before 1887, when he was installed as chief of Kasseh, Bai Bureh's contact with the British was indirect, always through the chiefs for whom he was fighting, and the result of his activities in 'French-influenced' territory as war chief of the Temne forces in Bokhari's service. The areas which were involved in the struggle were the hinterlands of Forikaria and the coastal region stretching from Freetown to Conakry. The scene of constant, gradual change for centuries, this area was at the time undergoing three major internal developments: (1) the establishment of Islam as a major socio-politico-religious force; (2) the attraction of trade from the interior to the coast by means of the main river ports; and (3) the migration of Susu from the Forikaria and Mellakori riverain regions to the Scarcies and upper Limba countries, and their subsequent assimilation in the political systems within which they had settled. Conflict was a natural result of such a situation. The evolution of events would probably have been very much different had it not been for the external forces set in motion by the exigencies of European expansion and control.

Much of the conflict focused on trade relations. The Susu and Temne, divided among themselves, were fighting to obtain footholds on the rivers which commanded European trade. There was an attempt to divert the direction of the interior caravan trade from the Mellakori River to the Scarcies rivers.[74] The internal trade was still active and important, a major route running from Mendeland along the road through Port Loko and thence to Mellakori.[75] Prisoners of war were an important source of slaves; they could either be sold or made a part of the domestic labour force. Either way they were a great source of wealth to war chiefs such as Bai Bureh.

The disturbed state of the region's trade had an immediate impact on the British and French, whose traders were active all along the coast. Not unnaturally they made frequent demands on their governments for intervention. The French, furthermore, were anxious to establish their protection over at least the northern part of the area. In Freetown, however, the British considered this area to be a part of the natural hinterland of the colony, but the Colonial Office restrained its administrators in Freetown from extending British responsibility there.

Kebalai first came to the attention of the British in Freetown in 1865 because of his role as Bokhari's war leader. Though Maligi Gbele received support from the French in return for signing a treaty putting his chiefdom under their protection, he was defeated and killed by Bokhari's force, which was under Kebalai's command. As a result of his success, Kebalai became Bokhari's principal war leader for many of the campaigns which he launched during the next twenty years. Bokhari's victory over his French-supported rival suited British interests in Freetown, for if they were unable to place Forikaria under their own protection, they preferred that it should remain independent of another power. Although the French made overtures to Bokhari, he did not co-operate with them in the way they would have liked and remained effectively independent until his subjects rebelled against him in 1876.

The cause of the rebellion was Bokhari's strict enforcement and observance of the laws of the Qur'an.[76] The anti-Islamic reaction was sufficiently violent that his people murdered his chief *imam*, and eventually drove Bokhari himself out of his chiefdom.[77] He sought refuge in the British sphere of influence at Kambia, where Kebalai was then living. Bokhari sent for him and they made arrangements for Kebalai to go into the Scarcies interior and to Yonni country to recruit 'warboys'.[78] Kebalai gathered a large army of four thousand 'warboys' and in January 1882, as had already been pointed out, led it in what from Bokhari's point of view was a *jihad* against his own subjects.[79]

In the meantime, Dowda, the Alikali of Forikaria, had usurped Bokhari's position as chief, and the French readily supported him. Although the early successes of Kebalai as Bokhari's commander suited British interests, they brought forth vehement protests from the French, who accused the British of actively assisting Bokhari. Mistakenly believing that Sattan Lahai and Bai Inga, the leaders of the Temne alliance supporting Bokhari, were under British protection, the French asked for their arrest as well as that of Kebalai, who had hitherto been a somewhat shadowy figure to them.[80] Governor Arthur Edward Havelock explained to the French that his treaties with the Scarcies chiefs merely specified terms of friendship but no formal protection; therefore he considered it completely beyond his political authority to arrest these persons.[81]

However, the geographical boundaries of the respective spheres of influence between the British and the French were becoming more strictly delimited, and international diplomatic lines were hardening. The British did not wish to provoke the French too much, and therefore the Governor warned the Scarcies chiefs to keep out of the war and to send Bokhari away from their country.[82] But at first the warnings had little effect. Sattan Lahai replied, explaining that he and his neighbouring chiefs had been insulted by Dowda in 1876 when they tried to arrange peace negotiations between him and Bokhari at the latter's request.[83] The French were dissatisfied with such explanations and indicated that if the British could not keep the chiefs in the area under control, the French would be forced to enter Kambia and arrest Bokhari themselves. Henceforth, British warnings took on sufficiently severe a tone to persuade Sattan Lahai and the chiefs of Kambia to expel Bokhari.[84]

Even after the departure of Bokhari from Kambia, the French (with some justification) continued to accuse the Scarcies chiefs of abetting Bokhari, especially as his war leader was still Kebalai.[85] This diplomatic wrangling between the French and the British was not brought to an end until mid-1885, when Bokhari was killed in battle, and Dowda became secure at last in his position as chief.

During the last three years in which Kebalai had led Bokhari's forces, his campaigns had been particularly bloody, especially by contrast with his restrained warfare against the British some fifteen years later. Pillaging and burning of villages was the order of the day. Adults taken prisoner were as often as not slaughtered. Toward the end of the war, in July 1885, there was an exceptionally violent campaign when Kebalai invaded the countries of Samo and Moria and took Gbarmooyah Island. His Susu opponents had hidden all their property and placed their wives and children on the island for safety. While Kebalai's warriors were on the island, the tide went down and it became impossible for them to cross by canoe until high tide. On the opposite bank, their opponents also waited for high tide to cross and defend their families and property. Before their eyes, the Temne killed everyone present on the island and burned all their property. When the tide finally came up, there was a violent battle in which the Temne were victorious. On their way back to their base, the Temne continued their destruction, burning every one of their opponents' towns in their path.[86]

In the course of the war, Kebalai had had his first contacts with Europeans. In 1882 he attacked Pharmoriah and captured a number of European traders whom Bokhari then held as hostages for three months in an attempt to secure French neutrality.[87] During his campaigns Kebalai had to contend with forces supplied with arms by the French; he clearly obtained his arms supplies through traders from Freetown and Port Loko. Above all, Bokhari's war gave Kebalai his best preparation for the brilliant campaigns which he was later to conduct against the British, and through his participation in it, he must have acquired from Bokhari some of the techniques of diplomacy necessary in dealing with Europeans. In 1887 he became chief of Kasseh, and although he was involved in wars over the next decade, none of them was on the same scale militarily as those he had fought for Bokhari.

BAI BUREH AS CHIEF OF KASSEH

When Kebalai was installed as chief of Kasseh in 1887, he assumed the name Bai Bureh and undertook the chiefdom's obligation of carrying out the terms of the 1871 treaty between Kasseh and the British. These included keeping the roads open to traders from the interior and the promise to refer any dispute with his fellow chiefs to the British Governor in Freetown. In return he received an annual stipend of £10 from the administration. Although on this occasion he did not question the terms of the treaty or the authority thus given to the British, as soon as the terms were invoked he showed how little they meant to him.

In the latter part of 1888, a land dispute broke out between Bai Bureh and his neighbour, Bai Inga. When it became apparent that war was about to break out, the acting administrator in Freetown reminded both chiefs of their treaty obligations to the British, and assured them that the newly appointed Governor, Sir James Shaw Hay, would settle the dispute on his arrival.[88] And soon after his arrival, Hay did summon the two chiefs to Freetown to discuss the dispute.[89] They agreed to submit the matter to three important Scarcies area chiefs for arbitration.[90] However, when Bai Bureh observed that the judgment of these chiefs was going against him, he made it clear that he would not accept their opinion. Deadlocked, they asked Hay to make the final decision, which he did, in favour of Bai Inga. So dissatisfied was Bai Bureh with the outcome that Hay had to warn him against preparing to fight with Bai Inga over the matter by sending a police officer to Bai Bureh with the message that whosoever broke the peace would be punished by the British authorities.[91] Bai Bureh finally yielded to this threat of British force.

Less than six months later, however, Bai Bureh came into more direct conflict with the British. Reports reached Freetown that he was organising a strong war party to attack Moriah.[92] The Scarcies-Kambia area seemed to be in such a general state of confusion — with 'warboys' patrolling the main roads leading from the interior to Kambia and Port Loko — that serious consideration was given by the British to the declaration of a protectorate over the area and the establishment of police posts at frequent intervals along the road.[93]

The situation deteriorated rapidly when a well-armed Susu war party led by Karimu, a Susu chief in upper Limba who was under treaty with the British, captured several towns in the country of the Limba.[94] The chiefs of upper Limba appealed to Bai Bureh to help them drive the invaders from their country. Bai Bureh assisted them, heading a coalition of Limba, Lokko, and Temne against the Susu. The Freetown administration was apprehensive lest the war extend into the French sphere and warned Bai Bureh against aggravating the extremely tense situation, reminding him that his chiefdom was in treaty relationship with the British. Their apprehension grew as Freetown came increasingly to suspect Karimu of collusion with the French.[95] Whatever the truth of this allegation, Karimu was able to retreat into the French sphere of influence with impunity and to receive support from Dowda of Forikaria.

Parkes feared that there would be a general uprising of Temne against Susu and tried to arrange peace talks. He summoned all the main chiefs in the area to the talks, but neither Bai Bureh nor Karimu came.[96] When the police constable arrived to summon him to the negotiations, Bai Bureh could not be found in this town. Parkes then told the chiefs who were friendly to Bai Bureh that if he did not return to his town in two days, he would be arrested.[97] Bai Bureh, however, remained out of reach of the short arm of Freetown. Parkes continued his attempts for negotiation even as he destroyed Karimu's stronghold at Kolunkureh, being 'strongly of the opinion that an exhibition of force would be of incalculable benefit in increasing the prestige of the Government and maintaining peace for the future'.[98] Finally, Parkes warned Bai Bureh that if he continued to make war he would suffer severe consequences.[99] Bai Bureh, however, continued to ignore the Government's demands.

In mid-September 1889, after the police had reported that they had been unable to find Bai Bureh at Roballan, his chief town, Governor Hay sent another party to look elsewhere. The officer in charge was ordered to tell Bai Bureh that all the reports coming to the Governor were so unsatisfactory that as a treaty chief, Bai Bureh must 'come to town without delay and explain otherwise [the Governor would] have to regard him as having broken his treaty'.[100] He made it clear that every measure short of actual arrest was to be taken 'to persuade' the chief to accompany the police to Freetown.[101] Although Parkes's letter, which the police were to deliver to Bai Bureh, acknowledged that Karinìu had destroyed some of the towns of the Limba, Parkes also warned the chief that instead of accepting the Susu's invitation to make war, he should have advised them to consult with the government: 'Take care Bey Boorey the Government have warned you once to be careful but it seems as if the time is fast coming when the things I told you would surely happen to you if you did not change will come to pass'.[102] However, Bai Bureh was not found, and six months later the government had made no further progress in its attempts to bring about peace. Hay next instructed the police to arrest Bai Bureh if they could manage to do so without undue risk.[103]

For his part, aware of the dangers implicit in the government's letters to him and the escalation of activities in the interior, Bai Bureh sent Parkes a letter explaining his actions. The Governor replied that he found his answer unsatisfactory as it was not at all in accord with a recent report of his conduct[104] and ordered him to come to Freetown, or a place where a British authority was represented, to explain himself personally. If, however, Bai Bureh persisted in his activities, the Governor continued, the government would have no alternative to treating him as an enemy and would take very active measure against him.

Again government threats had very little effect. Two weeks later, there were reports that Bai Bureh was collecting 'warboys' for an attack on Upper Sanda. By now the administration felt that even if Bai Bureh did come to them he would still continue his operations through the agency of his lieutenants.[105] The Sanda patrol was instructed to assume the offensive only if absolutely necessary. If it met Bai Bureh's 'warboys', it was to disperse them and call upon their leader to go to Freetown as directed.[106]

In May 1891, Hay brought the state of affairs in Sanda country before the colony's Executive Council. He explained that it was necessary to make a show of force in that area in order to disperse the 'warboys', and that he had therefore instructed the police patrol to go to Sanda. The patrol had reached its destination early in May. At Tambi, a stockaded town within the British sphere of influence, it met opposition and was forced to retreat. It appears from the nature of the reports of this battle that although the 'warboys' at Tambi were Karimu's, Bai Bureh's men also gave considerable trouble.[107] In any case, the unanimous opinion of the Executive Council was that Bai Bureh must not be allowed to defy the government with impunity and that force should be used to bring him to heel. Two days later the Council brought the matter up again, and considered the report of the Inspector General of Police, who maintained that the general warlike demonstration — the shouting, beating of drums, and war cries — obviously meant that the 'warboys' intended to make war. The Council members concurred in the opinion that a defeat of the police might encourage the 'warboys' to make more frequent raids, and they considered the possibility of stationing a strong police party in some adjacent town. It would remain there until 'such time as active measures could be taken if it is not possible to send an armed force at this time of the year to disperse the band'.[108] However they had to postpone their demonstration of force because of the approaching rains.[109]

In the event, Bai Bureh continued his war operations in upper Sanda, and destroyed towns in Bai Inga's country. The Governor asked the Alikali of Port Loko to intercede with him, to urge him to stop the war, and to come to Freetown as he had promised to do.[110] Captain Edward Augustus Lendy, then the acting Superintendent of Native Affairs; warned Bai Bureh that if he did not come to Freetown, the government would in future treat him as an enemy.[111] The government was particularly anxious to restore peace in Bai Inga's area, as the war had blocked the Port Loko-Futa Jallon trade route.[112]

Meanwhile Bai Farima reported that Karimu's 'warboys' had come as far as the outskirts of Kambia and were destroying various Limba towns nearby.[113] With the dry season, the situation deteriorated rapidly. Freetown therefore decided on a dramatic show of force to restore its authority in the area and recoup its prestige after the retreat from Tambi; the resultant expedition was primarily political in its objective. It was thought that Tambi had to be destroyed 'no matter what the cost' because it had successfully resisted an attack by the police.[114] To ensure the success of the expedition, Freetown made what at first seems a remarkable decision: to use Bai Bureh's 'warboys' as a 'native levy'. As Bai Bureh's objective was to defeat Karimu and drive him out of the country, in concert with the actions of the Limba-Lokko-Temne alliance, he agreed to collaborate with the British. The thought was that the British should ally themselves with peoples firmly based in the British sphere of influence, and against Karimu, who moved in and out of French territory. Captain Lendy, a European, was put in charge of Bai Bureh's 'warboys' to ensure that action would be co-ordinated and that there should be no doubt in the eyes of the Africans that this was the Queen s war not an African one.

At the last moment, London decided that the expedition should be conducted by the West India Regiment, commanded by Colonel Alfred Burden Ellis, instead of by the Frontier Police. At first, Ellis decided not to use Bai Bureh's 'warboys'. However, the administrator refused to dismiss them, fearing the political consequences of such a change.[115] In the actual expedition, Bai Bureh's 'warboys', numbering some fifteen hundred, acquitted themselves well, although Captain Lendy and Bai Bureh had some initial difficulties in restraining them once Tambi was in sight. The attack, however, was disciplined, the 'warboys' moving in concert with the police and regimental troops. They chased the Susu to the Scarcies rivers. Captain Lendy afterwards praised Bai Bureh's command and the conduct of his 'warboys', though his very laudatory account may have been partly designed to vindicate the original plan for a combined police and 'warboy' operation against Tambi.[116] Peace was restored temporarily, and all the Scarcies chiefs, including Bai Bureh, agreed not to cross the Scarcies rivers again.[117]

The importance of the Tambi expedition to Bai Bureh was that it gave him and his 'warboys' direct knowledge of the fighting techniques of both the Frontier Police and the West India Regiment, and not as opponents but as allies. He clearly did not consider that the experience placed him in the position of a permanent ally of the British nor as one who had recognised another's authority. Early in 1894, reports reached Freetown that Bai Bureh was about to attack Moriah, and the Governor, now Sir Frederick Cardew, had to issue a warning.[118] Although this attack never materialised, Temne 'warboys' crossed the Scarcies into Benna on March 23. It later became clear that Bai Bureh had participated in this attack as the ally of Surakata, a Susu chief who had been at war with the French and had taken refuge in the British sphere. British authorities had allowed Surakata to stay in Kambia on his promise not to use the British sphere as a basis for incursions into French territory.[119] As a result of this raid on Benna, Surakata was expelled and Cardew ordered the arrest of Bai Bureh.

At this point, under Captains Sharpe and Alexander Tarbet, a party of fifty police was sent to detain Bai Bureh on charges of aiding Surakata. When they reached Roballan, they discovered that he had departed, leaving behind a number of 'warboys' sufficiently large to resist the police force.[120] Not only did the 'warboys' resist the police, they also humiliated them by jeering at them. Cardew feared that the result of this failure to arrest Bai Bureh 'would have a bad effect in the Loko District and bring into contempt the authority of the Frontier

Police'.[121] He even proposed stationing a company of the West India Regiment in Port Loko to reinforce government authority, but Parkes reported from Port Loko that this step was not necessary, a view with which Cardew concurred after making a visit there himself early in June.[122]

After that Cardew wrote to Bai Bureh that he 'could not overlook his offence in gathering his warboys together and resisting and insulting the police and that in consequence he must surrender himself unconditionally and that if he did not do so, [Cardew] would hold no further communication with him and when convenient effect his arrest'.[123] From his place of refuge, Bai Bureh replied with an indignant letter in which he disclaimed any ill feeling against the British. He said that he had not refused to come to Port Loko, but that he feared to do so. He explained that when the police had come to his town, they had behaved in such a way that he feared what they might do to him. He claimed (in the language of his English-speaking clerk) that he did 'not know what offence [he had] committed against the Government on account of which the policemen entered into [his] town and spoiled [his] goods and carried away a good number of [his] wives'. He asked that Parkes and the Governor 'do not refuse communication from me nor deny a hearing. You must not be vexed at me nor condemn me before you have heard from me. If you send me a letter of invitation to answer any charge I shall willingly go down; but for the present I am afraid as I very much suspect some evil'.[124]

Subsequently, under a guarantee of safe conduct, a meeting was arranged at Port Loko between Bai Bureh and Cardew. There Cardew told Bai Bureh that he did not blame him for eluding arrest, for that was natural, but for gathering his 'warboys' to resist the authority of the police and for having permitted them to menace and insult the latter.[125] Cardew ordered him to pay a fine of fifty guns within a month or be arrested and deprived of his chieftaincy 'for a considerable period'.[126] Cardew informed the Secretary of State that if Bai Bureh did not pay the fine, he proposed to deport him to Bathurst, Gambia, until the Anglo-French boundary question was settled and the rest was restored to law and order. Optimistically, he said that this would take no longer than a year.[127] Bai Bureh, however, paid the fine and thus escaped the planned punishment. Cardew asked the messengers bringing the fine 'to exhort their chief to restrain in future his warboys from disturbing the peace of the country'.[128]

From this time on, until the proclamation of the protectorate over the Sierra Leone hinterland in August 1896, Bai Bureh had very little to do with the British. He continued to draw his stipend,[129] and on one occasion wrote Parkes a letter assuring him and the Governor that he did not forget their warnings and was doing his best at Kasseh.[130]

On another occasion he requested financial assistance in order to repair roads and bridges in his area.[131] There were, however, indications that he was not content with British jurisdiction. Judging from the frequency of administrative reminders to him concerning his obligations to clear and repair the roads, it would seem that he was adopting the tactic of passive resistance as a means of showing his displeasure.[132] However, British influence continued to grow in Bai Bureh's area, and in two years' time he was to find the British uncomfortably close to him. In 1896, with the establishment of the five districts into which the country was divided, he was to discover that the headquarters of the district in which Kasseh was included was Karene on the north bank of the Mabole River in the chiefdom of Sanda, on the very borders of Kasseh.

BAI BUREH'S WAR

Despite the obvious unpopularity of the hut tax, neither Cardew nor Captain Sharpe anticipated anything but a few isolated incidents of resistance to its collection. They certainly had no idea that, at least six months before its outbreak, the Temne chiefs of the Scarcies had already begun to plan their massive resistance.[133]

In late January 1898, shortly after he assumed office as District Commissioner, Captain Sharpe began collecting the tax at Karene. The first people asked to pay it were the Frontier Police. They protested on the grounds that they considered it unfair to have to pay taxes on houses they had been forced to rent as a result of the government's failure to provide them with barracks for their wives and children. But they gained no concession from Sharpe and had to pay, although with the greatest reluctance.[134] On the evening of the collection, rumours appeared that Bai Bureh was mustering his forces to oppose taxation and that he intended to attack the Karene garrison that same night. No attack materialised, but Sharpe's next preparations were made in an atmosphere of great uneasiness.

Sharpe then attempted to collect the tax in Port Loko, the largest and wealthiest town in his district. Here traders refused to pay the tax for fear of reprisals against them by the local people, all of whom opposed the tax. After much palaver, Sharpe detained the leading chief of Port Loko, Bokari Bamp, and warned him that there would be serious consequences if his people molested the traders in any way. Later he released Bokari Bamp for a while on the chief's promise not to hinder the traders' payments even though he would not agree to vouch for his people's conduct. Some traders still refused to pay, and Sharpe detained them also. It was clear that the traders were still not entirely free agents because of the continued hostility and threats of the local people concerning what would happen if they did pay. Sharpe therefore summoned Bokari Bamp, who took a day to respond. When he did finally arrive at the District Commissioner's residence, he came with all his subchiefs and a thousand followers. Sharpe demanded an immediate reply to two questions: (1) Would he permit the traders to pay their taxes without fear of reprisals? and (2) Would he assist in the collection of taxes in Port Loko? 'No', was the chief's categorical reply.

Almost immediately Sharpe had Bokari Bamp and four of his subchiefs arrested. He tried all of them summarily for inciting others to disobey, for refusing to collect the tax, and for attempting to overawe a public officer in the execution of his duty. Afraid of public response to their arrest, he sent them to Freetown as soon as opportunity arose, and then installed Sorie Bunki as chief in Bokari Bamp's stead.

All these events had taken place against a background of rumours that Bai Bureh was planning armed resistance. 'Warboys' had kept Sharpe under surveillance from the bush along the way from Karene to Port Loko. On the night of his appointment, Sorie Bunki reported to Sharpe that messengers had brought news that Bai Bureh intended to attack Port Loko that night because of his co-operation with the government. The traders, advised of this attack by the subchiefs and themselves personally afraid of the consequences of an invasion by Bai Bureh, fled.[135] Most of the townspeople also fled. From the deserted town Sharpe wrote to the Governor that he could not return to Karene because of the danger of imminent attack by Bai Bureh. He also sent a messenger to the latter ordering him to collect his chiefdom's tax and have it ready when his party came to collect it.

Bai Bureh's 'warboys' turned back the messenger, saying that if he wished to go to Karene the road was open, but if he wanted to go to their chief, there was no way.[136] Sharpe, convinced now that there could be no peace in his district unless Bai Bureh were removed from it, determined to arrest him. He requested an additional twenty veteran police from Freetown to assist in the arrest, because he felt that his own force was too raw and because only fifteen out of the force of sixty were presently available.[137]

Police reinforcements embarked on 16 February under the command of Major Tarbet, who in 1894 had already tried to arrest Bai Bureh. After great difficulty in obtaining a guide who would admit to knowledge of Kasseh, Tarbet set out with Sharpe and forty-six police. Their main problem was to discover Bai Bureh's location. What they did find was that the road to Karene was full of groups of armed men. To strengthen their force, they decided to ask the Frontier Officer at Karene to meet them at Kagbantama with as many men as he could spare. On their way, the officers tried to talk to some of the armed men they met on the road near Romeni. Only one would talk to the administrative party. While Sharpe was talking to this man, armed men began to surround him, and he decided he had better return to the column. He seized the man, thinking he could interrogate him later, but the 'warboys' became so threatening that Sharpe finally released him.

As it went along, the 'warboys' followed the column, jeering at it from all sides and throwing stones. The stoning became so intense that Tarbet ordered the police in the rear guard to open fire. Hearing these shots from the rear, soldiers at the head of the column rushed back to give assistance without orders to do so, leaving the carriers without any protection. The 'warboys' then seized some of the latter, several of whom were later found to have been sold in French territory. The 'warboys' themselves returned the fire, and only after several more volleys from the police did they retreat. This marked the opening exchange of Bai Bureh's war.[138]

At Kagbantama the force met the Karene party, whose officer reported that there were armed men all along the road to Karene. Tarbet therefore decided to proceed at once to Karene. While fording a river at Massoangball, the column was again attacked by Temne 'warboys'. Tarbet found Karene safe; however, this was of little comfort, since from Port Loko to Karene all the towns and all the villages except one were deserted. Everyone was in open revolt. The Karene-Port Loko road was now quite unsafe for messengers or small parties. The British had no indigenous allies: the people of Brima Sanda's chiefdom, which neighboured on Kasseh, had joined Bai Bureh, opposing their chief, who remained loyal to the British. It was clear to Sharpe and Tarbet that no British administration could function without the removal of Bai Bureh and a show of British force.

Meanwhile in Port Loko, rumours were circulating to the effect that Sharpe had been captured, taken to Bai Bureh, and killed. The threat of attack on the small garrison of police was ever present. In response they disarmed everybody in the town, not taking much trouble to distinguish between friendly and hostile Temne. There were one or two incidents.

All communication between Karene and Port Loko ended when the Temne captured most of the canoes at Rokupru on 19 February 1898 (see map). The only way to send messages to Freetown from Karene was by a circuitous route through Kambia or by carrier pigeon. On 22 February, Tarbet took a party of forty-eight police from Karene to Rokupru, where he had to cross his troops in four relays in the only remaining canoe. He staved off the fire of the Temne 'warboys' on the opposite bank by firing rockets at them. He then rushed the village, but the Temne retreated, waiting until the police recrossed the river to fire on them again. During this confrontation it became evident that the Temne were much better armed than the administration had thought, being equipped with better guns than the Dane guns normally sold by the traders.

On his return to Karene, Tarbet requested reinforcements from Freetown. Cardew did not inform his Executive Council of the seriousness of the situation until this time, when he recommended that 'a demonstration of force should be made to compel the natives to return to their allegiance'.[139] The Executive Council finally agreed that a company of the West India Regiment should be sent to Karene to strengthen the police force there. Cardew then cabled the Secretary of State that there was armed resistance to the collection of the hut tax, and requested the use of the West India Regiment, adding optimistically that he hoped that the 'service of troops will not be required for more than one month'.[140]

Two days later Tarbet informed him that the situation had deteriorated. The number of armed warriors in the area had continued to increase and more and more villages on the Karene side of the river had come out in support of Bai Bureh. Meanwhile, Sorie Bunki appeared to have fled from Port Loko, although much later it was learned that he had been captured by supporters of the Temne warriors and murdered. Panic prevailed in the town and surrounding areas. Cardew ordered Sharpe to consult with the officer in command of the troops he was sending from Freetown to determine how many troops he would need to occupy the whole district. The country to the east of Kasseh feared attack from the Temne, but the country to the north supported them.

Major Richard Joseph Norris, the commander of the company of West India Regiment troops leaving Freetown, had instructions to remain at Karene 'to support the Frontier Police who will thus be left free to operate in the Kassi District against the insurgents and to effect the arrest of Bai Bureh'. If the police could not accomplish this mission, he was to give the District Commissioner what assistance he required and assume full control of operations. However, the District Commissioner was to retain his civil jurisdiction and to bring to trial any prisoners taken in battle. Cardew hoped that once the troops arrived, resistance to the administration's authority would collapse, and that the District Commissioner could then make an example of Bai Bureh, whom he described as a 'great drunkard and a worthless character'.[141]

The role the regimental troops were to play in the operations soon became an extremely controversial point in the tactics and strategy of the war. Cardew preferred the lightly equipped Frontier Police and was of the opinion that their numbers would be sufficient to bring Karene under control. According to him, the West India Regiment was only to garrison Karene and Port Loko in order to allow the police to concentrate on Bai Bureh's arrest, aiding them when they needed assistance. Because of their light field equipment, Cardew believed that the police could move more easily through the bush and that they would be an excellent match for the similarly unencumbered Temne. (For example, when Norris's company had left Freetown accompanied by 540 carriers and 912 loads, Cardew had felt compelled to complain to the officer in charge that such equipment was far in excess of what the expedition demanded.) However, when the troops arrived on the scene of field operations and saw how serious the actual situation was, their commander decided that lightly equipped police could not re-establish administrative control in the area, and that the government's only alternative was to use fully equipped troops in full force to impose its authority.

Norris disembarked with his troops at Robat on the Great Scarcies and marched to Karene without being attacked, although he was closely observed all the way. When he reached the Karene garrison, he found the men tense, fearful, hemmed in, and expecting attack at any moment. Food was in very short supply. Norris quickly concluded that the country around the garrison was held by the Temne, and that the lack of food supplies would make it impossible for his company to stay more than three days in Karene. He suggested that Karene be evacuated since he felt that too much attention was being given to the question of maintaining communications with it. But Cardew objected violently that such an evacuation was politically impossible since it would 'reveal great weakness and cause the rising to extend not only throughout the district of Karene but probably all over the Protectorate'.[142] He was also very angry at Norris's decision to return to Port Loko, since his doing so prevented Tarbet and Norris from setting out on their planned expedition with the police.

In Karene, the situation became so serious that, on 2 March 1898, Sharpe asked Norris to declare martial law in his district and to assume full responsibility for Port Loko and Karene.[143] On the day following the declaration of martial law, Norris marched to Port Loko, twenty-five miles from Karene, in an attempt to restore communication between the two places. From hiding places in the bush along the road, Temne 'warboys' constantly sniped at his column, every so often coming out in full attack. Only after intensive fighting did the troops drive them off. For ten consecutive hours, all the way to Port Loko, the company fought hard: they stormed and captured seven villages and three strongly fortified towns. Upon their arrival in Port Loko, Norris felt that matters were so grave he immediately requisitioned two additional companies from Freetown. He informed

Cardew that he had decided to make Port Loko his headquarters and would wait there for further reinforcements before he determined his next moves.

As soon as Cardew received Norris's report, he conferred with Colonel Arthur Bosworth, the Commander of Troops in West Africa. They decided that only one company was needed as reinforcement. Cardew justified this decision on the grounds that he did not believe that Norris was as hard pressed as he made out, and that he could easily hold his own. Norris was furious at Cardew's intervention and his refusal to appreciate the seriousness of the situation in Karene.

The Temne attacked Port Loko three days after the declaration of martial law. Early that morning, the fire alarm sounded, and a house near the Church Missionary Society station was set on fire. This appeared to have been a signal for attack for, immediately afterward, 'warboys' fired on the town from the direction of Old Port Loko. The tempo of their attack increased throughout the morning, and only after four and a half hours of steady battle did the regimental troops force them to retreat. Once the attack subsided, the regiment set about enlarging and strengthening its position by clearing more of the surrounding bush and demolishing any huts within the area. Later that day, a company of reinforcements from Freetown arrived on the H.M.S. Fox. Norris took the opportunity to request assistance from the naval officer in charge for a combined attack on the Temne. Late in the afternoon all Temne 'warboys' were driven out of Old Port Loko by shellfire from the Fox, supported by fire from the seven-pound gun manned by Norris's troops.

Norris straightaway requested another company, and another seven pounder from Freetown, stressing that he could not return to Karene without more troops and more supplies. He proposed to distribute his troops in three directions: one company to garrison Port Loko; another to garrison Karene; and one to form a flying column under his command to patrol along the Port Loko-Karene road.

On the night of the sixth, Temne 'warboys' attacked Karene itself, but the police drove them back. Captain Stansfield arrived in Port Loko bringing the new company of reinforcements which had disembarked at Robat. He reported that the Temne had attempted to burn his column by setting fire to the dry bush along the line of march, but that they had never actually attacked it. After receiving this report, Cardew ordered the Frontier Police to intensify their efforts to arrest Bai Bureh, and Sharpe to resume his political and administrative duties as soon as practicable.

Cardew was still optimistic that the situation was not nearly so serious as Norris and Sharpe maintained, gaining confidence from the fact that no reports had come in from Norris since the last reinforcements had arrived. He drafted an ambitious, but quite unrealistic plan for putting down the resistance and arresting its leaders. But before he could send his instructions, reports arrived from Norris, doubting whether he had sufficient troops to arrest Bai Bureh and requesting yet another company. Cardew, however, considered that Norris was exaggerating the seriousness of the situation and asked him to wait until he had seen how the operations of the two companies already under his command fared before requesting more. But Norris was soon asking for not one but two further companies because Sharpe, on his way to Port Loko with twenty police and twenty soldiers, had been seriously opposed at Malal by Temne 'warboys' from newly constructed stockades. Sharpe now concurred with Norris that the police were 'absolutely powerless' to quell the rising.[144] Cardew informed the Secretary of State that he felt he could no longer shoulder the responsibility of withholding further reinforcements in the light of Norris's repeated requests even though he still contended that 'the troops he had should have been sufficient to quell the disturbance had he made more use of them on the offensive'.[145]

Actually, during the period from 23 February to 1 April, government forces had taken the offensive only once. Throughout this period it was Bai Bureh and his 'warboys', estimated at three thousand, who held the initiative. Their tactics were simple but effective against the heavily encumbered troops of the West India Regiment whose officers knew little of the terrain over which they were fighting. They concentrated primarily on attacks on the columns, paying particular attention to eliminating the white officers. The insistence of Cardew that Karene be maintained as a garrison, and the consequent necessity of keeping the road open to it for supply and communication purposes, made the troops patrolling the road an easy target for ambush. Bai Bureh's strategy was primarily defensive and obstructive. His 'warboys' avoided direct confrontation in battle; they preferred sudden raids, ambushes, and, in particular, attacks from behind stockades and war fences.

The stockades were built so that they supported each other and were generally positioned in places difficult to reach. They were never very large, usually from twelve to forty yards long, and were not visible from the opposite side of the road. Usually built out of blocks of trees, with a firing trench running the length of the stockade just inside the wall area, the stockades were placed on high ground so that the Temne were able to retreat swiftly down the slopes, if necessary At times British troops were able to outflank the stockades but, because of the dense bush, this occurred only rarely.

The Temne maintained communication among themselves concerning the movement of the British troops by a network of spies and a system of signals: often three guns were heard by the troops whenever a column halted. By concentrating on ambush instead of open attacks, the Temne had the advantage since, except for the Kagbantama road, the entire countryside was dense bush. The roads were little more than bush paths. Generally speaking, the Temne used guerilla hit-and-run tactics which were ideal for dealing with an extended column moving slowly along roads and paths it hardly knew.

Only once did the British go on the offensive before 1 April, and it was then that the Temne showed just how effective their tactics could be. A large British column consisting of 6 officers, 90 soldiers, and 640 carriers set out from Port Loko for Karene on 13 March. It had to operate in thickly wooded country interspersed with hills and intersected by rivers and swamps. On the first day's march, the column's commander, Major Buck, razed to the ground the villages and stockades of Ropolon-Rosannie, Robat, Malal, and Robant. He met with no opposition. He encamped at Mahera for the night and burned it to the ground as he left the next morning. On the second day, his column was greatly delayed going through the swamp, not reaching its destination of Butien until that afternoon, when it encountered heavy resistance. Temne, led personally by Bai Bureh (as it was later discovered), fired at them from stockades in the town as they approached. Only after long, intensive fighting did the troops succeed in taking the town. Later that evening, Temne again attacked the column and continued harassing it until dawn. As the column left Butien the next morning, it burned the village and proceeded unopposed to Kagbantama where it was ambushed. After a long battle, the soldiers dispersed the 'warboys' and moved on toward Rotigon, where they were again attacked from five stockades which had been placed at intervals of fifteen yards on both sides of the road. The column was barely able to withstand this attack.

Consequently, when the 'warboys' retreated the commander of the troops decided not to pursue them but instead followed paths through the bush on the windward side of the town. When the Temnes discovered that the troops were neither following them nor attacking the towns along the way, they suspected that they had inflicted severe damage. They set fire to the extremely dry grass and bush along the windward side of the road, and the country was in flames for a mile in every direction. To counter it, the troops were ordered *to set fire to* the bush on the leeward side of the path, which gave the company sufficient space to wait out the fire with little or no danger of attack. Nevertheless, the result was that it could not move until the next day.

Resuming the march at daybreak, the column encountered more

intense resistance at the stockaded towns of Romaron and Katentia (one of Bai Bureh's strongest towns). Only after heavy firing with the 'magazine' gun did the troops manage to disperse the 'warboys'. After this battle the column marched to Karene with no further resistance except for occasional Temne sniping. Although the column was able to destroy more stockades along the route, Bai Bureh's forces had by this time exacted a heavy toll.

Cardew was very alarmed by the systematic burning of villages and towns. If villages and towns were to be burned, he urged that they be carefully selected and limited to Bai Bureh's chief towns. Sharpe, however, supported Norris's decision and tactics, pointing out that before the column had started out Norris had advised the troop commander to use his discretion as to which towns to destroy. He assured Cardew that only those towns which were fortified or offered resistance would be destroyed, and that all the officers concerned appreciated that this policy would be hard on the women and children. Nevertheless, 'events necessitated the destruction of the principal towns of Bai Bureh's and of all villages where armed people met. The whole of his country had risen, and [Sharpe could] see no other way of punishing the offenders than by destroying their towns...'.[146] Criticising the hut tax, a local correspondent of the *Daily Telegraph* noted sourly: 'So far as we are informed, most of the huts on which he (the Governor) intends to collect the debts have been burnt down, if not by the people themselves, by the soldiers'.[147]

On 17 March a company commanded by Major Stansfield, which had set out for Kambia from Karene, was driven back to Magbolonta, only six miles from Karene. This reverse was of such gravity that Cardew agreed that Colonel Bosworth himself should assume command in the field. Bosworth left on the evening of the nineteenth for Port Loko with a company consisting of 8 officers, 92 troops, 300 carriers, and a seven-pound gun. He decided that Port Loko was a more suitable base for his operations than Karene. Before determining what further operations would consist of, he asked Captain Carr Smith to report on his column's operations which had begun on 22 March. When Cardew received Bosworth's report, he concluded that the situation was so serious that he should go to Port Loko himself.

Meanwhile on 25 March, Carr Smith began his return to Port Loko, but the Temne opposed the troops so stubbornly outside of Matiti that they forced the column back to Karene. Carr Smith and one other officer were wounded, leaving the column under the command of its only other able-bodied officer. Receiving news of Carr Smith's retreat, Bosworth decided to march immediately for Karene in order to clear the road of opposition. He selected 100 soldiers and 4 officers and took as little equipment as possible. He experienced strong opposition at Malal and Romeni but managed to push on to Kagbantama, where he met even greater opposition. By the time the troops had dispersed the 'warboys', they were so exhausted that they were barely able to reach Karene. Bosworth himself collapsed and died from what was described as 'heat apoplexy'.[148]

The Temne tried to close the road again, entrenching themselves in stone stockades which were at least two feet thick; these had firing holes formed by inserting bamboo in them. They were almost bullet-proof and the seven pounder had little effect on them. They were destroyed only after severe fighting and many British casualties.[149] It was obvious that continuous patrols would be needed in order to prevent the frequent reconstruction of the stockades.

Keeping the Karene-Port Loko road open had involved so many casualties and had so diverted the troops from their main aim of tracking down the leaders of the resistance that Major Burke, from the Port Loko garrison, once again urged the abandonment of Karene: 'It will never be possible to take active measures against Bai Bureh with any chance of success as long as this station is occupied'.[150] Despite Cardew's assurances that Burke was exaggerating the gravity of the situation, Bosworth's successor, Lieutenant-Colonel John Willoughby Astell Marshall, found on his arrival at Port Loko that the troops were working under every possible disadvantage.[151] Political reasons, however, dictated that Karene should not be abandoned although the Colonial Office sympathised with the soldiers' point of view.[152] Chamberlain considered that 'Sir J. Cardew is inclined to interfere too much in the details of the military action',[153] and he later cabled Cardew not to interfere in the conduct of the operations.

Given the necessity of keeping the road to Karene open, Marshall decided to establish an auxiliary garrison at Romeni, as the best intermediate point between Karene and Port Loko. Once it had been established, he set out to implement a scorched earth policy in Kasseh country. From 1 to 10 April, he concentrated his attention on the road between Port Loko and Karene. Taking out a flying column each day, he razed every village which offered resistance to his advance. The Temne opposed him all the way, but by 10 April, he had gained complete control of the road. He left garrisons at Romeni and Karene which were to maintain the government's position and prevent further construction of stockades. He then extended his operations to the entire area, moving through the country systematically, destroying every village as he came upon it. Temne resistance was steady, increasing in strength after the fifteenth. Sometimes the column destroyed as many as twenty stockades a day, and fought three or four hard battles. The Temne offered particularly strong resistance at Katentia and Matiti on 11 April, at Kagbantama on 13 April, and at Mafouri on 25 April.

Once Marshall gained control of the country of Kasseh, he began operations in that of the Sanda. Wherever he was opposed, he destroyed the villages as he had done in Kasseh; where he was not, he assembled the villagers and explained to them what the troops were doing and that they would surely catch Bai Bureh soon. Toward the end of April, Marshall turned his attention to the countries of Bai Bureh's allies. By 13 March, he felt that the government had re-established control over the country. He sent letters to the chiefs warning them to desist from their hostile activities and to withdraw all their support from Bai Bureh.

By that time, of course, the war had spread to other parts of the Protectorate, and Cardew had requested a European battalion to deal with the situation in a telegram which had 'a look of panic' about it.[154] By the end of May, however, Cardew was writing to the Secretary of State eulogising Colonel Marshall's 'energy, enterprise and endurance'.[155] But Marshall's victory had been achieved only by using military methods that ruined much of Temne country and exhibited the civilisation of the white man in its worst aspects. That Marshall had to resort to such methods is a tribute to the fighting skills of Bai Bureh who, as is appropriate for a guerilla leader, remained a shadowy figure in the reports of the British campaigns. Nevertheless, it was clearly recognised that the length and stiffness of Temne resistance was due to him. While Cardew wrote optimistically that he hoped that 'Bai Bureh's powers of resistance were completely broken', he acknowledged that 'he will be a disturbing element till he is caught'.[156] Still, the government could not contemplate the capture of Bai Bureh and other war leaders until after the rains, which in Sierra Leone fall with an intensity that made impossible British operations in Temne country. Thus there were only a few isolated incidents during the rains (May to October), the most serious of which was the attempt by a band of Temne 'warboys' stationed at Robarrong to burn the Karene barracks.[157] This attack proved unsuccessful, and Cardew was not unduly worried, feeling confident that the situation was mostly under control in both the Mende and Temne areas. So sure was he that he made a provisional request for leave in October.[158]

Cardew rejected all attempts at mediation between Bai Bureh and the government, insisting that Bai Bureh's 'submission must be precedent to any proclamation of a general amnesty',[159] and offered a reward of £100 for information leading to his capture. However, he did inform the chief through intermediaries that his life would be spared if he surrendered.[160]

Although Cardew insisted on the surrender of Bai Bureh, he proposed to treat the people of the Karene district leniently. A general amnesty would be proclaimed in the district where 'the insurgents have carried on their warfare on fairly humane principles. I do not say that they would have spared any of our troops had they fallen into their hands, but with the exception of the murder of the Rev. W. J. Humphrey (the Principal of Fourah Bay College), Chief Suri Bonkeh and a few other cases, they have refrained from killing non-combatants'.[161] (Such leniency was not the case in the Mende areas where many European and Creole civilians had been murdered indiscriminately.)

Cardew continued to reject offers for mediation even though his optimistic assessment in June that there was 'every hope that peace [would] soon be effected by the surrender of Bai Bureh'[162] had by early October proved unjustified. Freetown Muslims passed on letters from Bai Bureh, in which he expressed 'every earnest desire for peace',[163] to Sir Donald Chalmers, sole Commissioner conducting the inquiry into the causes of the Hut Tax War. Chalmers offered to mediate, much to the chagrin of Cardew, who detested him and was sensitive to any action on Chalmers's part that might demean the gubernatorial authority. Meanwhile demonstrating his opposition to Cardew's uncompromising stand, Chalmers, as the Queen's Commissioner, wrote to Bai Bureh through the Secretary of Native Affairs and conveyed peaceful greetings to him: 'He wishes peace for him and all this troubled country. He advises that for the good of all the people, Bai Bureh should listen with a good ear to the proposal which the Governor makes to him'.[164] Mediation, however, proved impossible due to Cardew's insistence on unconditional surrender.

On 11 November Bai Bureh was finally tracked down in swampy, thickly vegetated country by a British patrol.[165] Under constant sniping from Temne 'warboys', Captain Goodwyn and 40 troops caught up with him near Roballan. The Temne fired on the troops from a stockade. Two of the 'warboys' rushed to the bush at the soldiers' return of fire, and the resulting drama ended the war: 'Sergeant Thomas ran forward in pursuit of one who seemed to move rather slower than his companion. Getting close to him he shouted to him to stop or he would shoot, at the same time firing over his head. The man threw himself on the ground and was secured. He proved to be Bai Bureh'.[166] At 1.00.p.m. on 12 November, the elderly warrior, who had a striking face dominated by a very long aquiline nose and a remarkable protruding lower lip, was brought to Karene. He had lived in the bush for twenty-three weeks. Earlier in the month, Captain Goodwyn had destroyed his *fakai* (bush camp) and he had only narrowly escaped at that time.[167] In London, they were delighted: 'The success will no doubt greatly simplify matters . . . it will no doubt much diminish any resistance by the natives all over the

Protectorate', Mercer wrote to Antrobus on the fourteenth, 'and the need either for a white battalion or for reinforcements from the Niger should be disposed of'.[168]

It remained only to dispose of Bai Bureh. The government planned to bring him to trial in Karene since it felt that a trial in Freetown would cause too much popular excitement. Sharpe's original plan had been to try him for treason.[169] Cardew concurred and cabled the Secretary of State that he intended to try him for high treason or treasonable felony though he would not impose the death penalty.[170] The Colonial Office, however, doubted that Bai Bureh could be treated as a British subject, a necessary prerequisite for trying him for treason,[171] and instructed Cardew to delay proceedings. The local law officers opined that treason had not been committed by Bai Bureh since, in fact, he owed no allegiance to the Queen; therefore it was impossible to convict him of this charge. He was never brought to trial.[172]

Bai Bureh was detained while awaiting London's decision on Chalmers's recommendations. At first he was kept in Karene, but, after a Temne guard in the West African Regiment attempted to help him to escape, the District Commissioner decided to move him to the Freetown jail. There he received a special diet and was kept separate from the convicted prisoners. In April 1899, the administration removed him from the jail to a house on the outskirts of Freetown in Ascension Town, near the residence of the exiled Asantehene, PrempehI, and kept him under guard. The Governor gave two reasons for his removal: first, there was a smallpox epidemic in the jail; and secondly, 'the evil accommodation which that building affords at the best of times is an unnecessary addition to the punishment of political offenders of importance'.[173]

Crowds flocked to the house hoping to catch a glimpse of this great opponent to British rule. Sir Matthew Nathan, the acting Governor, decided against allowing Bai Bureh to return to his own country, fearing that to do so might be regarded as weakness on the part of the government.[174] Instead he ordered him deported to the Gold Coast along with Bai Sherbro of Yonni and Chief Nyagua of Panguma. Neither of these two latter chiefs had taken part in the war, but the government greatly feared their influence. Both died in exile, but in 1905 Bai Bureh was allowed to return to Sierra Leone and resume his position. Then very old, he remained there without further incident until his death in 1908.

CONCLUSIONS

Like Samori in Guinea, Bai Bureh's sustained resistance to the British has made him a national hero of independent Sierra Leone.[175]

In 1967, shortly after assuming power as Chairman of the National Reformation Council, Colonel Juxon Smith declared that his Council 'had decided to work on the principles of three eminent Sierra Leone citizens — the late Prime Minister, Sir Milton Margai, the late Bai Bureh, and the late Mr. Isaac Theophilus Wallace-Johnson — that is, honesty, integrity and nationalism'.[176]

Over the years, both before and after his capture, many myths have been woven about Bai Bureh. Many tales have been told of his magical powers, of his ability to disappear at will, or to live underwater. Cardew had reported that he was 'regarded by the natives throughout the Protectorate, and I may add, by many in this Colony as a great Fetish man. For the stories current about him are that he had the power to transform himself into animals and live under water...'.[177] However fantastic the accounts that have grown up about him, most agree that he was a superb soldier. Creoles spoke of him as the Big Black General.[178] Captain Braithwaite Wallis, Frontier Police Officer, although not in Karene district, wrote that Bai Bureh:

> besides being a man of acute intelligence, was a renowned and successful leader... His name is now a household word for miles around, and in many villages mothers stilled their crying babies by whispering the name of their redoubtable Ethiopian into their infants' ears. This was the man who successfully defied the power of Great Britain for many months together, and thereby made for himself a name that will never die so long as the brave and misguided people whom he led remain a nation.[179]

However, one English writer, Elizabeth Hirst, has tried to show, from oral tradition, that at heart Bai Bureh was a man of peace.[180] According to her and her co-author (and main informant), he had given up fighting for a long time, taking a vow of peace which he broke only when his sense of Lokko patriotism forced him into action when Samori's Sofa menaced the Lokko. While their thesis is apparently supported by some oral Lokko traditions, it conflicts with many Temne traditions which emphasise Bai Bureh's essentially warlike character. Moreover, the archival records reveal that he was almost continuously engaged in war from 1865 until 1898. Indeed, many of the events recorded by Hirst and Kamara, none of which are dated, do not correspond with what the archives show clearly did happen. Since their book is used in the schools, their portrait of Bai Bureh as a man of peace and a model for Christian schoolchildren has gained wide currency in Sierra Leone.

It is essential, however, to contradict their thesis that Bai Bureh gave up war for a long period of time both because it is not true, and because it is clear that the major explanation for his success against the British was his experience as a war leader — unparalleled in those parts not only for its length but also for its continuity. Bai Bureh never suffered from that bane of generals — a long period of peace. The significance of his war with the British was that while many other Africans had the will to resist European penetration, he was one of the few who also had the skill.

NOTES

1. PRO. CO/267/438: Telegram of 10 May 1898. Governor to the Secretary of State.
2. Hansard, 4th Series, LVII, 5 May 1898.
3. Cardew made this point in various dispatches, both confidential and ordinary. Many of the witnesses whom Sir Donald Chalmers called before his Commission of Inquiry agreed.
4. Parliamentary Papers 1899, LX, Report . . . on . . . the Insurrection in the Sierra Leone Protectorate (Chalmers Report), I, II.
5. The judicial powers delegated to the District Commissioners included: (1) trying all civil cases involving non-natives; (2) trying all land cases; (3) trying all criminal cases involving non-natives; (4) trying all cases of pretended witchcraft, faction or tribal fights, slave raiding or slave dealing; and (5) trying all cases of murder, rape, cannibalism, or offences connected with Human Leopard or Alligator societies. For further explanation, see J. D. Hargreaves, 'The Establishment of the Sierra Leone Protectorate and the Insurrection of 1898,' *Cambridge Historical Journal*, XII (1956), 63-64.
6. SLA/GCDSS, 18/97: Governor to Secretary of State, 23 March 1897.
7. Cited in James Pope-Hennessy, *Verandah* (London, 1964), 143.
8. SLA/GCDSS, 10/98: Governor to the Secretary of State, 25 February 1898. The French, however, were to contrast their collection of the hut tax favourably with that of the British. For instance, *Le Temps* of 13 May 1898, quoted in the *Daily Graphic* (London) of 14 May 1898, crowed: 'We levy in French Guinea, as well as in our other West African colonies, a tax which has analogies with the English hut tax which has provoked the rising in the British possessions in Sierra Leone. But with us the tax is not oppressive, and its collection is made easier under such conditions that it has never excited discontent among the natives of our territories.' (Translation in the *Daily Graphic*.)
9. Evidence of J. C. E. Parkes, Chalmers Report, II, par. 850.
10. Appendix XIV, Letter from Timini chiefs to Capt. Sharpe, 17 December 1896, Chalmers Report, I: the signers of this letter were the following: Alikalie Morribah of Port Loko, Bai Foki of Mafokki, Bai Farima of Saffrako, Bai Kanarie of Tinkotupa, Bai Shakka of Dibia District, and Bai Bureh of Kasseh District.
11. Hargreaves, 'Establishment of Sierra Leone Protectorate,' 66.
12. SLA/NALB, 211/97: Parkes to Col. Sec., 14 September 1897.
13. SLA/GCDSS, 49/97: Gov. to Sec. of State, 8 October 1897.
14. PRO. CO/267/440: minute by Chamberlain of 9 November 1898 on Sierra Leone Conf. Desp. 81, 13 October 1898.

15. SLA/GCDSS. 49/97: Gov. to Sec. of State. 8 October 1897.
16. SLA/NALB. 211/97: Parkes to Col. Sec.. 14 September 1897.
17. Evidence of Mala. the spokesman of the sons of the Port Loko chiefs who were detained by the government in 1898. Chalmers Report. II. par. 1653.
18. PRO. CO/267/437: minute of W. A. Mercer on Gov.'s telegram to the Sec. of State. 5 March 1898.
19. The District Commissioner of Karene wrote him that it was certainly not excessive: 'A person only has to bring in a hamper of rice. half a dozen pine-apples. yams. Kassada. firewood. etc., and a year's payment of tax is easily secured.' SLA/CMP. 102-Enc./98. District Commissioner (Karene) to Col. Sec.. 10 August 1898.
20. PRO. CO/267/439: Conf. Desp. 59-Enc./98. Letter from Rev. J. A. L. Price to Gov.. 28 July 1898.
21. SLA/CMP. 102-Enc./98: District Commissioner (Karene) to Col. Sec.. 10 August 1898.
22. SLA/CMP. 102-Enc./98: District Commissioner (Ronietta) to Col. Sec.. 4 August 1898.
23. Chalmers Report. I. 12-13.
24. Editorial entitled 'The Madness of the Hut Tax'. in *Daily Mail* (London). 6 May 1898.
25. SLA/CMP. 102-Enc./98: District Commissioner (Karene) to Col. Sec.. 10 August 1898.
26. Reuter's Liverpool representative in *Daily Graphic*. 13 May 1898.
27. PRO. CO/267/438: Telegram. Gov. to Sec. of State. 9 May 1898.
28. PRO. CO/267/438: Gov's Conf. Desp. of 28 May 1898. and Gov's Conf. Desp. 43. 31 May 1898.
29. PRO. CO/267/438: Draft of reply dated 24 June 1898 to Gov.'s Conf. Desp. of 28 May 1898.
30. PRO. CO/267/440: Gov.'s Conf. Desp. of 12 October 1898. and Chamberlain's minute on it of 3 December 1898.
31. *Daily Mail* (London). 6 May 1898.
32. For instance. see *Daily Telegraph* (London). 4 April 1898: *Daily Graphic* (London). 6 May 1898: *Outlook* (London). 30 April 1898.
33. Letter to the editor in *Outlook* (London). 7 May 1898.
34. PRO. CO/257/438: minute by Chamberlain on telegram from Gov.. 21 April 1898.
35. PRO. CO/267/438: Gov.'s Conf. Desp. of 28 May 1898. Gov.'s Secret despatch to the Sec. of State. 28 May 1898.
36. That the chiefs were anxious to regain their independence was confirmed by the District Commissioners of Karene and Ronietta in their reports to Cardew on the causes of the war. See their reports in SLA/CMP. 120-Enc./98. District Commissioner (Karene) to Col. Sec.. 10 August 1898: and District Commissioner (Ronietta) to Col. Sec.. 4 August 1898.
37. Appendix E.. Interview with Mr. T. Caldwell of the CMS Mission at Rogberi. 12 May 1898. Chalmers Report. I.
38. PRO. CO/267/439: Gov.'s Conf. Desp. 59 of 28 July 1898: also its enc.. letter from Rev. J. A. L. Price. 28 July 1898.
39. PRO. CO/267/439: Gov.'s Conf. Desp. 57 of 2 July 1898. minute by Lord Selborne of 5 August 1898.
40. PRO. CO/267/438: telegram. Gov. to Sec. of State. 9 May 1898. minute by R. L. Antrobus referring to chief's memorials in Gov.'s Desp. 27603/97. 9 May 1898.
41. Appendix J. letter from J. C. E. Parkes to Gov.. 31 May 1898. Chalmers Report. I.

42. SLA/CMP. 102-Enc./98: District Commissioner (Ronietta) to Col. Sec., 4 August 1898.
43. Chalmers Report. I. 13.
44. Evidence of J. C. E. Parkes. Chalmers Report. II. par. 974.
45. PRO. CO/267/438: telegram. Gov. to Sec. of State. 9 May 1898 with minute by R. L. Antrobus. 9 May 1898.
46. Evidence of J. C. E. Parkes. Chalmers Report. II. par. 974.
47. Appendix M. Letter from R. O. George. R.S.M. Frontier Police, to Adjutant. Frontier Police, n.d., Chalmers Report. I. These criticisms gained surprisingly wide currency before the publication of the Chalmers Report. In an editorial of the *Daily Graphic* (London) of 6 May 1898, the Frontier Police were criticised as the 'worst of all rules, black rule backed by white authority, but without the efficient supervision of the whites'.
48. SLA/CMP. 102- Enc./98: District Commissioner (Karene) to Col. Sec., 10 August 1898.
49. PRO. CO/267/440: Gov.'s Conf. Desp. 68. 23 August 1898.
50. SLA/CMP. 102-Enc./98: District Commissioner (Ronietta) to Col. Sec., 4 August 1898.
51. Evidence of W. M. Pittendrigh. Chalmers Report. II. par. 436.
52. Evidence of J. C. E. Parkes. Chalmers Report. II. par. 715.
53. PRO. CO/267/440: Gov.'s Conf. Desp. 68, 23 August 1898.
54. SLA/CMP. 102-Enc./98: District Commissioner (Karene and Ronietta) to Col. Sec., 10 August 1898 and 4 August 1898, respectively.
55. Appendix F. Letter from E. Kingman. Supt. of the Soudan Mission to Gov., 18 May 1898, Chalmers Report. I.
56. PRO. CO/267/438: Gov.'s Conf. Desp., 28 May 1898.
57. Appendix XIV. Letter from Timini chiefs to Capt. Sharpe, 17 December 1896. Chalmers Report. I.
58. The main source for information on Bai Bureh's life is Elizabeth Hirst and Issa Kamara. *Benga* (London, 1958), which is based on oral tradition.
59. Ibid. 35.
60. The date of Bai Bureh's assumption to office was previously fixed at about 1889 by Cardew in SLA/GDSS. 43/99: 'Report on the Antecedents of Bai Bureh', 10 February 1899. Christopher Fyfe. *History of Sierra Leone* (London, 1962), 501, accepts this date. However, the stipend records and letters of the Aborigines Department show that the office had been vacant since 1883, but that in May 1887, a messenger arrived in Freetown with Kasseh's treaty book in order to collect the stipend due for the intervening years on Bai Bureh's behalf. Also, by August 1888, Bai Bureh was involved in a land dispute with Bai Inga. This was mentioned in SLA/ADLB, 31/88: J. M. Baltby to Bai Bureh, 18 August 1888.
61. Hirst and Kamara. *Benga*. 42-45.
62. SLA/GCDSS. 43/99: 'Report on the Antecedents of Bai Bureh'. Cardew to Sec. of State, 10 February 1899. So too did the French. The Commandant de Cercle Mellacourie reported the difficulties experienced by his opponent Bokhari, for whom Bai Bureh fought, in recruiting soldiers 'car le vieux dicton "pas d'argent, pas de Suisses" s'applique dans toute la rigueur aux Tymenes'. NAS/7G22/1/6: Commandant de Cercle Mellacourie to Lt. Gov. Senegal, 25 May 1883.
63. Evidence of Capt. Sharpe. Chalmers Report. II, pars. 3349-50.
64. Hirst and Kamara, *Benga*. 9-12.
65. Evidence of Capt. Sharpe. Chalmers Report. II. pars. 3349-50.
66. Report on the Antecedents of Bai Bureh'. SLA/GCDSS. 43/99: Cardew to Sec. of State, 10 February 1899.

67. E.g., SLA/ADMP. 110/82: T. Lawson to Gov., 16 August 1882.
68. Hirst and Kamara, *Benga*. 38-45.
69. Fyfe, History, 432.
70. We are indebted to A. K. Turay, a doctoral research student of the University of London presently engaged in field work on the Temne language, for this information.
71. Merran McCulloch, *Peoples of Sierra Leone* (London, 1950), 70.
72. Hirst and Kamara, *Benga*. 13-18.
73. SLA/NAMP. 154/98: Alfa Yanusa, Alikali of Port Loko, to Supt. of Native Affairs, 18 April 1898; and SLA/GDSS, 219/98: Gov. to Sec. of State, 6 October 1898.
74. We are indebted to Allen Howard of the University of Wisconsin for this information.
75. PRO, CO/267/439: Gov.'s Conf. Desp. 59/98, 28 July 1898 with enc. letter of Rev. J. A. L. Price; and 'Report on the Antecedents of Bai Bureh. . .'. SLA/GCDSS, 43/99: Cardew to Sec. State, 10 February 1899.
76. SLA/ADMP. 64/83: T. Lawson to Col. Sec., 28 September 1883.
77. NAS/7G/21/7/135: letter of Bokhari to Gov. Havelock which was forwarded to the French Consul in Freetown, 26 January 1882.
78. SLA/ADMP. 32/82: W. B. Harding to Gov. Havelock, 28 January 1882; SLA/ADLB. 6/82: Gov. Havelock to Bai Inga, 24 January 1882; SLA/ADLB, 8/82: Gov. Havelock to Alimami Sattan Lahai, 24 January 1882.
79. See above, 185.
80. SLA/GLLB, 81/22: Gov. Havelock to Bareste, 8 March 1882; and NAS/7G/21/7.
81. SLA/GLLB, 81/82: Gov. Havelock to Bareste, 8 March 1882.
82. SLA/ADLB, 6/82: Gov. Havelock to Bai Inga, 24 January 1882; and 8/82: Gov. Havelock to Alimami Sattan Lahai, 24 January 1882.
83. SLA/ADMP, 26/82: with Encs. 3, 4 and 5, translations of letters from Alimami Colleh, Alimami Lunsenny and Alimami Sattan Lahai, respectively, to Gov. Havelock, 2 February 1882.
84. SLA/ADLB, 28/82: Circular from Gov. Havelock to the chiefs of the Great and Small Scarcies River Districts, 11 April 1882; and SLA/ADMP, 29/82, with enc. 9. Memo from T. Lawson to Gov. Havelock, 13 April 1882.
85. SLA/GLLB. 267/82: Gov. Havelock to Bareste, 17 August 1882.
86. SLA/ADMP. 66/85: Memo from T. Lawson to Gov., 15 July 1885.
87. SLA/GLLB, 267/82: Gov. Havelock to Bareste, 17 August 1882. W. M. Pittendrigh, a trader, gave evidence to the Chalmers Commission that he had been held captive for three months by Kebalai. See Evidence of Pittendrigh, Chalmers Report, II, 428.
88. SLA/ADLB, 38/88: Maltby to Bai Inga, 3 October 1888.
89. SLA/ADLB, 47/88: Gov. to Bai Bureh, 27 October 1888.
90. SLA/ADMP. 7/88: Memo from T. Lawson to Gov., 23 November 1888.
91. SLA/ADLB. 116/89: Gov. to Bai Bureh, 11 March 1889.
92. SLA/ADLB. 291/89: Parkes to H. C. Sawyer, 9 August 1889.
93. SLA/ADLI. 382/89: Parkes to Gov., 25 September 1889. Parkes was instrumental in the foundation of the formal protectorate. For further information, see J. D. Hargreaves, 'The Evolution of the Native Affairs Department,' SLS 3 (1954), 168-84.
94. SLA/ADLB. 397/89: Parkes to Alimami Bomboh Lahai, 14 October 1889.
95. SLA/ADLB. 5/89: Parkes to Garrett, 30 November 1889.
96. SLA/ADLB. 432/89: Parkes to Garrett, 6 November 1889; and SLA/ADLB. 446/89: Parkes to Sgt. Crowther, 16 November 1889.
97. SLA/ADLB. 446/89: Parkes to Sgt. Crowther, 16 November 1889.

98. SLA/ADLB. 450/89: Parkes to Garrett. 20 November 1889; and SLA/ADLB, 4/89: Parkes to Garrett. 24 November 1889.
99. SLA/ADLB, 450/89: 20 November 1889.
100. SLA/ADLB, 639/90: Gov. to Actg. Insp. Genl. of Police, 15 September 1890.
101. Ibid.
102. SLA/ADLB, 640/90: Parkes to Bai Bureh, 15 September 1890.
103. SLA/ADLB, 182/91: Parkes to Insp. Genl. of Police, 8 March 1891.
104. SLA/ADLB, 223/91: Parkes to Bai Bureh, 2 April 1891.
105. SLA/ADLB, 240/91: Parkes to Gov., 14 April 1891.
106. SLA/ADLB, 253/91: Gov. to Insp. Genl. of Police, 15 April 1891.
107. SLA/ECM, 14 May 1891.
108. SLA/ECM, 16 May 1891.
109. SLA/ECM, 23 June 1891.
110. SLA/ADLB, 419/91: Actg. Supt. of Native Affairs to Alikali of Port Loko, 15 July 1891.
111. SLA/ADLB, 450/91: Actg. Supt. of Native Affairs to Bai Bureh, 15 July 1891.
112. SLA/ADLB, 454/91: Actg. Administrator to Alikali of Port Loko, 31 July 1891.
113. SLA/EGDSS, enc. 3 to Desp. 414 (December 19) 91: Police Report from Kambia, 24 November 1891.
114. SLA/GLLB, 170/92: Administrator to Insp. Genl. of Police, 17 March 1892.
115. SLA/GLLB, 191/92: Administrator to Insp. Genl. of Police, 29 March 1892; and SLA/GLLB, 194/92: Administrator to Col. A. B. Ellis, 31 March 1892.
116. SLA/EGDSS, enc. 2 to Desp. 169/92: Report of Capt. Lendy, 20 April 1892.
117. SLA/ECM, 20 April 1892.
118. SLA/EGCDSS, enc. 1 to Conf. Desp. 37/94: Police report from Kambia, 24 April 1894.
119. SLA/ECM, 28 May 1894.
120. SLA/GDSS, no number: Gov. to Sec. of State, 13 June 1894.
121. Ibid.
122. Ibid.
123. SLA/GCDSS, no number: Gov. to Sec. of State, 13 June 1894.
124. SLA/NALB, 5 and enc./94: Bai Bureh to Parkes, 31 May 1894.
125. SLA/GCDSS, no number/94: Gov. to Sec. of State, 13 June 1894.
126. Ibid.
127. SLA/GDSS, no number/94: Gov. to Sec. of State, 30 August 1898.
128. Ibid.
129. SLA/NAMP, 26/94: Bai Bureh to Parkes, 9 January 1894; SLA/NALB, 53/94: Parkes to Bai Bureh, 22 January 1894; and SLA/AMP, 45/94: Administrative comments, 4 May 1894.
130. SLA/NAMP, 362/94: Tr. of letter from Bai Bureh to Parkes, 12 November 1894.
131. SLA/NAMP, 354/95: Tr. of letter from Bai Bureh to Parkes, n.d. 1895.
132. SLA/NALB, 579/94: Supt. of Nat. Affairs to Bai Bureh, 19 December 1894; SLA/NALB, 65/95: Actg. Supt. of Nat. Affairs to Bai Bureh, 16 February 1895; SLA/NALB, 218/95: Supt. of Nat. Affairs to Bai Bureh, 24 May 1895; SLA/NALB, 320/95: Supt. of Nat. Affairs to Bai Bureh, 22 July 1895; SLA/NALB, 448/95: Supt. of Nat. Affairs to Bai Bureh, 17 September 1895; SLA/NALB, 524/96: Supt. of Nat. Affairs to Bai Bureh, 15 September 1896.
133. Evidence of Capt. Sharpe, Chalmers Report, II, pars. 3942-47.
134. C. R. Morrison, 'The Temnes and the Hut Tax War,' Sierra Leone *Weekly News*, 13 January 1934.
135. Evidence of C. J. Warburton, Chalmers Report, II, par. 183-4.
136. Evidence of Lance Cpl. Stephen Williams, Chalmers Report, II, pars. 7576-77.

137. Letter from Capt. Sharpe to Col. Sec., 13 February 1898, Chalmers Report, II, pars. 598-601.
138. For full account of the day to day progress of the war, see La Ray Denzer, 'A Diary of Bai Bureh's War,' SLS, 23 (July 1968); 24 (January 1969). Full details of archival sources for the account of the campaigns that follow are given there.
139. SLA/ECM, 22 February 1898.
140. PRO, CO/267/437: tel. from Gov. to Sec. of State, 22 February 1898
141. SLA/GDSS, 10/98: Gov. to Sec. of State, 25 February 1898.
142. SLA/GCDSS, enc. to 14/98: Gov. to Maj. Norris, 1 March 1898.
143. SLA/GCDSS, enc. 4 to 15/98: Report from Capt. Sharpe to Col. Sec., 2 March 1898.
144. SLA/GCDSS, enc. 2 to 17/98: Report from Maj. Norris to Gov., 9 March 1898.
145. SLA/GCDSS, 17/98: Gov. to Sec. of State, 12 March 1898.
146. SLA/CMP 40/98: Sharpe to Col. Sec., 16 March 1898.
147. *Daily Telegraph* (London), 4 April 1898.
148. PRO, CO/267/437: Conf. Desp. 22, Gov. to Sec. of State, 31 March 1898.
149. Ibid.
150. SLA/GCDSS, enc. 1 to 23/98: Report from Maj. Burke to Gov., 29 March 1898.
151. SLA/GCDSS, enc. 7 to 23/98: Report from Lt. Col. Marshall to Gov., 3 April 1898.
152. PRO, CO/267/437: minute by W. H. Mercer on Gov. to Sec. of State re Conf. Desp. 23, 2 April 1898.
153. PRO, CO/267/437: tel. from Gov. to Sec. of State, 4 April 1898 with minute by Chamberlain, 4 April 1898.
154. PRO, CO/267/438: tel. from Gov. to Sec. of State, 5 May 1898 with minute by W. H. Mercer of 5 May 1898.
155. PRO, CO/267/438: Conf. Desp. 39, Gov. to Sec. of State, 27 May 1898.
156. Ibid.
157. PRO, CO/267/440: Conf. Desp. 73, Gov. to Sec. of State, 17 September 1898.
158. PRO, CO/267/440: Desp. 174, Gov. to Sec. of State, 28 August 1898.
159. PRO, CO/267/439: no number, Gov. to Sec. of State, 28 July 1898.
160. PRO, CO/267/439: Conf. Desp. 45, Gov. to Sec. of State, 7 June 1898.
161. PRO, CO/267/439: no number, Gov. to Sec. of State, 9 June 1898.
162. SLA/GDSS, 110/98: Gov. to Sec. of State, 2 June 1898.
163. SLA/GDSS, 219/98: Gov. to Sec. of State, 6 October 1898.
164. SLA/NALB, 447/98: M. G. Wingfield (Sec. to Chalmers) to Supt. of Nat. Affairs, 11 October 1898.
165. SLA/GDSS, tel. from Gov. to Sec. of State, 12 November 1898. Fyfe incorrectly gives the date as 16 November, see Fyfe, History, 590.
166. PRO, CO/267: enc. to Conf. Desp. 273, Report of Capture of Bai Bureh from Lt. Col. Cunningham, Commanding Karene Dist. to Col. Woodgate, C.B., 23 November 1898. Cf. the death of John Chilembwe, below, 342.
167. Ibid.; also enc. report of Capt. Goodwyn.
168. PRO, CO/267/441: tel. from Gov. to Sec. of State, 12 November 1898 with minute of 14 November 1898 by W. H. Mercer.
169. SLA/CMP, 149/98: District Commissioner (Karene) to Col. Sec., 14 November 1898.
170. PRO, CO/267/441: tel. from Gov. to Sec. of State, 16 November 1898.
171. Ibid.: with minute by E. Wingfield of 16 November 1898.
172. Fyfe, History, 590.
173. SLA/GDSS, 135/99: Gov. to Sec. of State, 24 April 1898.
174. SLA/GDSS, enc. to Desp. no number/98: Gov. to Sec. of State, 10 April 1898.
175. See above, Yves Person, 'Samori and Resistance to the French', 80-112.
176. *Daily Mail* (Freetown), 1 April 1967.

177. SLA/GCDSS. 277/98: Gov. to Sec. of State. 30 November 1898.
178. Appendix M. Letter from R. O. George. R.S.M. Frontier Police. to Adjutant. n.d.. Chalmers Report II.
179. C. Braithwaite Wallis *The Advance of Our West African Empire* (London. 1903). 50-51.
180. Hirst and Kamara. *Benga*.

Key to Archives and Journals

ADCMP	Aborigines Department Confidential Minute Papers
ADLB	Aborigines Department Letter Book
ADMP	Aborigines Department Minute Papers
CO	Colonial Office
ECM	Executive Council Minutes
GCDSS	Governor's Confidential Despatches to the Secretary of State for the Colonies
GDSS	Governor's Despatches to the Secretary of State for the Colonies
GLLB	Governor's Local Letter Book
NACMP	Native Affairs Confidential Minute Papers
NALB	Native Affairs Letter Book
NAS	National Archives of Senegal
PRO	Public Record Office
SLA	Sierra Leone Archives
JAH	Journal of African History
SLS	Sierra Leone Studies

V

BLAISE DIAGNE AND THE RECRUITMENT OF AFRICAN TROOPS FOR THE 1914-18 WAR*
(1967)

In the vocabulary of present day nationalist politics, Blaise Diagne, first African deputy for Senegal, often appears as a stooge. He is remembered as the 'Pan-Africanist' who told the Third Pan-African Congress held in Paris in 1921 'I am a Frenchman first and a Negro afterwards'[1] and forced on that Congress a weak resolution about Belgium's colonial policy because of his own high position in the French government. He was the deputy who, in 1914, was elected on a platform which attacked the stranglehold of big Bordeaux business houses on Senegalese commerce, yet who in 1923 signed the famous Bordeaux pact whereby he arranged a truce with them. He would cease his attacks in return for their political support. As his rival for the deputyship, the *métis* or Mulatto, François Carpot, complained acidly: 'The Deputy Blaise Diagne, worshipping what a little while back he would burn, has become the ally of the Bordeaux coffers, the collaborator of what his friends called not so long ago Sharks'.[2] He is recalled as the African who told the Second Pan-African Congress in 1919 that France had given French Africans every liberty yet who, in 1930, had defended France at the International Labour Conference at Geneva in 1930 against critics of her forced labour policies.[3] It was hard for politically conscious Africans who saw their brothers subjected to the *corvée* or to impressment into labour on European plantations to have much respect for a Deputy who could declare to the International Labour Conference:

> ... at this time when the International Labour Conference at Geneva is engrossed ... with the question of forced labour, the

---
*This paper was originally delivered as a Public Lecture under the auspices of the Institute of African Studies, University of Ibadan in November, 1967. Sections of it were incorporated in a different version in Michael Crowder, *West Africa under Colonial Rule*, London, 1968.

presence of the delegate of France in my person is already symbolic; it signifies that my country has intended to show through my presence here what her true feelings are. The French government is in favour of the total suppression of this contemporary form of slavery and enslavement, and you will perhaps be surprised that a man who belongs to one of those races on whom, for four centuries, slavery has weighed heavily, has come here to bring at the same time the adherence of both France and himself in solidarity with those very races.[4]

This lie was told only two years after André Gide had created a furore in France by revealing in his *Voyage au Congo* how women with children on their backs in French Congo worked on the *corvée* making up the roads with their bare hands since the administration did not provide them with tools.[5] Diagne's lie was told fifteen years before forced labour, that 'contemporary form of slavery' as Diagne put it, was abolished in French Tropical Africa. In 1931 when Diagne became Under-Secretary of State for the Colonies, far from using his unique position as an African Minister in the French Government — he was at one stage acting Minister of Colonies — to better the lot of his fellow men, the price of prestige was for him complete cooperation with the French and the suppression of any demands for the liberalisation of the colonial regime in West Africa. The most he achieved was the negotiation of subsidies for Senegalese groundnuts during the depression, but this was in return for a promise to persuade the peasants to increase their production, which had fallen drastically as a reaction to low depression prices. All this seemed bad enough: but what many Africans today find especially hard to forgive is the fact that Blaise Diagne was responsible for the recruitment of over sixty thousand of his fellow men for active service on the European front in the First World War.

But there is another side to this story: Blaise Diagne, in agreeing to recruit African troops for the French, did so on the understanding that there would be major reforms in the colonial regime.[6] By successfully recruiting over twenty thousand more troops than he was asked, he, as an African, achieved something that had been considered by the local administration in French West Africa to be quite impossible.[7]

Blaise Diagne became first African deputy for Senegal on the eve of the First World War. Hitherto all the deputies of the Four Communes of Senegal were French or *métis*, despite the existence of African voters. Before the 1914 election Senegal had been very much a rotten borough in which sacks of rice and five franc pieces flowed freely from the hands of the Bordeaux merchants and their increasingly prosperous *metis* rivals.⁽⁸⁾ The election of Diagne was thus of more than symbolic importance in that he was the first deputy of full African blood to be elected: it marked the first time that a majority of Senegalese voters realised that you could do more with a ballot paper than sell it to the highest bidder.⁽⁹⁾

Diagne started the campaign as an outsider. He had been away from Senegal twenty years, serving in the French Colonial Customs Service where he gained a reputation for being ready to defend persecuted comrades or egalitarian ideas. He was married to a Frenchwoman and was hypersensitive to any criticisms about his own race. He had been sent on leave in 1913 from Guinea because of his hostility to his superiors and to local French merchants, and in Paris he made speeches and wrote articles attacking French colonial policy. It was at this time that he decided to stand for election as deputy for Senegal. Despite the presence of an incumbent Deputy of great prestige and wealth in the form of Francois Carpot, and despite the presence of six other candidates, all of them French, Diagne gained the largest number of votes − 1,910 to his nearest rival Carpot's 671 Since it was not an absolute majority there was a second ballot in which he beat Heimburger, who had come third in the first ballot, by 175 votes. Carpot only gained 472. Of the many forces of discontent in the Quatre Communes that helped Diagne to secure election, one of the most important was the attempt by the French administration to deprive the Senegalese *originaires* of their rights. And this is important for an understanding of Diagne's political significance, since by promising to secure his voters their rights, he was to commit them to military service for France.

The French had since 1848 begun to question whether the inhabitants of the *Quatre Communes* could be considered citizens since the majority of them were Muslim, illiterate in French, and often polygamous. Some were fearful of the dangers of a 'native electorate'. Thus the 1885 *Le Réveil* of Saint Louis wrote that the greatest dangers to the colony were 'yellow fever, Clericalism, and the native electorate' and warned that if the Africans were allowed to vote 'from conquerors, we will become, we French, we masters of the country by right of conquest and civilisation . . . humble subjects and tomorrow's slaves'.⁽¹⁰⁾

In 1908 the Lieutenant Governor of Senegal had tried to have 1,563 voters struck off the electoral roll on the grounds that since they had not been naturalised as French citizens they could not vote and were not in fact citizens. The Court of Cassation in Paris upheld the view that those concerned were not French citizens but confirmed that they had the right to vote. This meant that the non-naturalised citizens, the *originaires*, of the *Quatre Communes* were, apart from their voting rights, not citizens. If they went to the Protectorate they would be subject to the hated *indigénat* or system of summary administrative justice whereby Africans could be imprisoned without trial, in some cases for up to two weeks. The Decree of 1912 said categorically that only *originaires* who complied with all its requirements were citizens; the others, and this included automatically all Muslims, had the right to vote, but were liable to the *indigénat* in the Protectorate. Lamine Gueye, the first Senegalese advocate, whose parents were *originaires* but who was born outside the *Quatre Communes* and was therefore not eligible for the vote, summed up the horror of the *originaires* at being subjected to the *indigénat:* 'Our fears were more than justified by the spectacle of what happened in the interior of the Colony, where administrators, reviving in certain respects feudal practices, imposed upon the persons of our compatriots of the Protectorate acts which are neither human nor French'.[11] Deputy Carpot did little to protect the rights of the *originaires* and was in fact blamed unfairly for the 1912 Decree, a fact which accounts in large part for his poor performance in the 1914 campaign for the Deputyship.[12] In 1911 a number of *originaires* doing their military service in metropolitan units of the army in West Africa and serving under the same conditions as Frenchmen, were discharged. Diagne therefore campaigned for a law for obligatory military service for those living in the *Quatre Communes* without distinction as to race or colour. In return he would ensure that the rights of the *originaires* as citizens would be confirmed. To a St. Louis rally he declared 'They say that you aren't French and that I'm not French! I tell you that we are, that we have the same rights'.[13]

Diagne, whose own right to sit in the French Chamber of Deputies was challenged on the grounds that he was not a French citizen, kept his promise to his electors and by the Law of 29 September 1916 gained from the French Government the confirmation that 'the natives of the *communes de pleine exercice* of Senegal are and remain French citizens subject to military service as provided for by the law of October 15th, 1915'. Using France's need for troops in the War, Diagne had been able to extract this at the price of obligatory military service for his voters.

He told the Minister of War in a debate in the Chamber of Deputies: 'That group which sent me to this Chamber has the right to consider that the mandate which has been given me will not be complete except on condition that you place this group in the same situation as that group of the population which sent you to Parliament. . . . The question is this: if we can be here to legislate, it is because we are French citizens; and, if we are such, we demand the right to serve in the same quality as all French citizens'.[14]

The law was popular with the *originaires* for it secured them the rights of citizens, that is the opening up for them of a full-scale assimilation policy which for the most part they desired. In 1911, even before Diagne was elected, the Conseil-Général had through one of its Commissions asked that voters, without distinction of colour, be called upon to perform obligatory military service. And the 1919 election, which he won by 7,444 votes against Carpot's 1,252, showed clearly the extent of his popularity as a result of his policy.

The *originaires*, despite the improvement in their status as a result of Diagne's laws, did not prove willing volunteers. Diagne had to cable his lieutenant, Galandou Diouf, to set an example by volunteering. The majority of the *originaires* who served in the army after the passage of the Diagne laws were conscripted in the same manner as Frenchmen, and served on the same terms. These were very much better than those for the *sujets*, who proved exceedingly reluctant to serve, even to the point of revolt. *Sujet* soldiers received half the pay of the *originaires*, were not given beds, had no prospect of promotion to the officer grades or to hold authority over French troops, and on discharge received under a third the pension given to the *originaires*.[15] The *sujets* provided the mass of soldiers who served France during the 1914-18 War.

France had first used West African troops outside their homeland in 1828 when two companies of Wollofs were sent to Madagascar. In 1838 a company was sent from Senegal to French Guinea. Senegalese soldiers fought in the 1871 German war and in the Mexican war. They helped the French in their conquests of Madagascar, French Equatorial Africa and Morocco. Up till 1910 recruitment of soldiers had been on a voluntary basis. At this time the French were becoming increasingly concerned at the possibility of a revolt by their Algerian troops in Algeria. General Mangin in his famous book *La Force Noire* suggested that by using West African troops in Algeria rather than Algerian troops, thirty-two thousand French troops could be released to serve on the France-German border and the dangers of an Algerian revolt be averted. 'The result', he wrote, 'would be the creation of an African Army, whose camp would be in Algeria, but whose reservoir would be in West Africa'. Furthermore if war broke out in Europe and 'the struggle were prolonged, our African Forces', he wrote, 'would constitute almost indefinite reserves, the source of which is beyond the reach of the adversary'.[16]

In 1910, Mangin toured West Africa at the head of a governmental Commission and reported that forty thousand soldiers a year could be recruited for service in the French Colonial Army. The Senate of France agreed to send Senegalese troops to Algeria. In 1912 by the Decree of 7 February the French took the first step towards the creation of a permanent Black Army by introducing obligatory military service for Africans. Under this decree, which was opposed by the Senegalese Deputy Carpot, recruitment by *voie d'appels* through local chiefs for four years was authorised for men between twenty and twenty-eight years old. Once war broke out, the French turned to French Black Africa as an inexhaustible reservoir of men for their army largely as a result of Mangin's recommendations. The problems raised by the subsequent attempts at large scale recruitment nearly plunged French West Africa into chaos during the First World War. First there just were not indefinite reserves of men of military age available in sparsely populated French Black Africa. Secondly, those called up were for the most part reluctant to go, and their families even more reluctant to let them. In some cases reluctance expressed itself in open revolt or flight across the border into neighbouring British West African territories. Thirdly, a policy of taking away from West Africa its able-bodied men conflicted with the other role France had assigned it — that of provisioning beleaguered France. Finally, as one Frenchman remarked after the conquest, 'French West Africa was a country without Negroes'.[17]

On the outbreak of war, the French West African army consisted of 14,785 African troops in West Africa alone. In addition there was one batallion of *Tirailleurs Sénégalais* abroad in Algeria. The first full year of recruitment, 1915-1916, was limited to fifty thousand. Of these twenty-three thousand were to be found from Haut-Sénégal-Niger (roughly Mali, Upper Volta and Niger). By the end of the year the Governor-General was writing to the Minister of War giving him a sorry tale of resistance to the operation.[18] The Lieutenant-Governor of Haut-Sénégal-Niger reported that he could not recruit in Mossi until the Koudougou revolt was put down. He also reported that many in the area were leaving the fields and arming themselves.[19] A month later he reported that recruiting had had to be suspended along the Niger from Timbuctu to Gao because of feared resistance.[20] The whole of Dedegou, Bobo and Ouagadougou were in revolt. Approval was given for the enlistment of men taken prisoner in the suppression of the Dedegou revolt, and the Governor-General laid it down as policy that in suppressing subsequent revolts, prisoners taken would be recruited.[21] Something of the desperation of the Governor of Haut-Sénégal-Niger over his task is given by his demand that the doctors be less rigid in their selection and be required to accept men with 'only slight symptoms of goitre or umbilical hernia of small size'.[22] In Guinea the main problem in recruiting was flight across the border into Sierra Leone or Liberia. In Sierra Leone reports of *disturbances in Kissi country* in French Guinea were sent back to the Secretary of State for Colonies.[23]

In Ivory Coast, too, common borders with the Gold Coast and Liberia presented the same problem. But while the Lt. Governor of Guinea reported that the recruiting campaign had generally good results, Lt. Governor Angoulvant of the Ivory Coast, who had only recently completed his bloody 'pacification' of the territory,[24] was fearful of the consequences of further recruitment, which he described in a fifty page report as 'a man hunt'.[25] 'I concluded by cautioning', he wrote, 'that a new effort could not be undertaken without provoking in the country a certain discontent, a political and economic upheaval, without risking spreading amongst the native masses, who already have before their eyes the spectacle of the British colonies where compulsory recruitment by *voie d'appel* is still unknown,[26] the dangerous idea for our future rule that we are not strong enough in Europe to defend ourselves'.[27] He went on to cite reports from individual administrators complaining that only by force could they gain recruits, and that the removal of these ablebodied men was going to be disastrous for the economy. Angoulvant protested bitterly against the despatch of troops from sparsely populated West Africa to the European front, reminding the Governor-General that 'if the inhabitants of French West Africa previously lived in a state of continual war, our mission has consisted precisely in establishing French peace and to develop these warlike instincts towards the peaceful work of agriculture and commerce'.[28]

In Dahomey the problems were the same: flight across the border to Nigeria, the need to use force to recruit, the medical unsuitability of many candidates, willing or unwilling, and the threat of revolt. Even self-mutilation to avoid enlistment was reported.[29]

In the event the Lieutenant-Governors were only able to recruit 39,798 of their required 50,000. Haut-Sénégal-Niger was 9,000 men down on its prescribed 23,000.[30] Of these a tiny proportion were real volunteers.

The French administration tried desperately to secure the cooperation of their British allies in returning deserters and carrying out token recruiting drives along their common borders at the same time as the French were recruiting in the area. British co-operation was half-hearted. In the Gold Coast an Ordinance was passed permitting the Commissioner to deport Africans liable to French military service.[31] Lugard repatriated Dahomeans who had crossed into Abeokuta province. In Gambia, where the Travelling Commissioner reported that 'not one of my people will cross the boundary for fear of being caught',[32] the Gambia Company in December 1916 undertook a trek to show force in areas where immigration of deserters had created unrest and apprehended a number of them.[33] The British, however, refused to undertake wide-scale recruiting, the only way in which they could effectively have discouraged the French Africans from crossing into their territory.

The situation had so deteriorated in French West Africa by the time Van Vollenhoven became Governor-General in early 1917 that he reported to the Minister of Colonies in July that further recruitment was impossible without risking revolt, especially in Haut-Sénégal-Niger, and Dahomey. 'To extract from this country yet another few thousand men will set it aflame, drench it in blood and we will ruin it completely'.[34] There had been serious revolts in Haut-Sénégal-Niger, Dahomey, Ivory Coast and Guinea. Among the Ouilliminden Tuareg near Timbuctu and the Tuareg of Air, these revolts had amounted to full-scale challenges against French authority. The Tuareg of Air, who besieged Zinder in the military territory of Niger, were only defeated with the help of troops despatched by Lugard from Nigeria.

It is not surprising that the recruiting campaign caused such violent reaction. Chiefs were told how many people were needed from a particular town or village. If they could, they supplied people of slave status, or without influence in the community. Strangers were seized. Above all the recruiting drive deprived West Africa of its finest farmers, for little recruiting was done in the urban centres, since the administration and commerce did not want to be without their workers especially as their European personnel were being sent to the front. The only urban group that did enlist voluntarily and, as we have seen, only on a small scale were the 'Citoyens' of the *Quatre Communes* of Senegal, and they served on a privileged basis as 'Frenchmen'.

Van Vollenhoven, like Clozel his predecessor, was as much concerned about the economy of the country as the problem of recruitment, for the two were inextricably linked, since increased recruitment meant decreased production. In his report on the recruitment of troops made in September 1917, he pleaded: 'This African Empire which is poor in men is rich in products — leave it its wretched population for *ravitaillement* during the war and after the war'.[35]

The initial economic impact of the war on French West Africa was very similar to that in British West Africa. Germany had been a major importer from and exporter to French West Africa where she had a number of trading firms. New markets had to be found for crops previously sold to Germany. Shipping was scarce, and freight rates increased. In French West Africa European company officials and clerks were subject to what Governor-General Clozel described in his speech to the Conseil du Gouvernement as a *'mobilisation un peu excessive'*.[36] By November 1915, when he made his speech, there had as a result been an 'enormous diminution of revenue' though even so the budget had balanced, and 5,860,000 francs had been given to France for the war effort. For the next year, however, he estimated that they would have to call on French support to the tune of 5,500,000 francs. The mobilisation of Europeans in the administration and commerce forced the government to review its policy towards the training of Africans for these posts. Angoulvant, when Acting Governor-General in 1916, wrote to his Lieutenant-Governors: 'The difficulties which become graver day by day of recruiting European personnel make it necessary to associate our natives more closely than ever with our work of colonisation, and of ridding the formation of our cadres of local origin of their character of improvisation which they have too long maintained'.[37] Plans were therefore made to train Africans in a large number of fields hitherto predominantly occupied by Europeans: agricultural supervisors (*moniteurs*), postal officials, customs officers, mechanics and surveyors of public works. A medical school and an agricultural school were established. The medical school would train African assistant-doctors. This Africanisation was entirely the result of wartime economic expediency. But it was also seen as of long-term benefit since war forced the government to count the cost of employing Europeans in 'subaltern' posts, which could easily be filled by Africans with sufficient training.[38]

By the time Van Vollenhoven became Governor-General the problem of staffing, production of foodstuffs and shipment had become acute. But France demanded West Africa's food as well as her men. Not just her cash crops, but also her subsistence crops: sorghum, millet, maize, paddy-rice, yams and beans.[39] He urged the governors and their administrators to encourage the farmer to maximum effort, and to ensure that he knew a good price would be paid for his crops. But Van Vollenhoven found himself in what seemed to him an impossible predicament. At the same time as the Minister of Production (*Ravitaillement*) demanded food, the Minister of War demanded more troops. On the Governor-General's doorstep the Lt. Governor of Senegal was telling him that further recruitment would be an irreparable disaster, removing the only remaining labour force from the farms.[40]

On top of this, up to three-quarters of the European staff of French companies had been mobilised, and foreign trading companies and Lebano-Syrians, not subject to recruitment, were profiting from the French predicament. By 1 January they had increased the number of their trading posts from seven hundred and forty-six before the war to eight hundred and fifty-seven. At the same time many French companies were forced to close down shops. Public works had come to a standstill. It was calculated that sixty-one and a half thousand able-bodied Africans had left French West Africa for the British territories. Columns had to be maintained to put down revolts brought about by recruitment: the number of companies stationed in French West Africa had been increased from twenty-six to fifty.[41]

Almost at his wits' end as how to find the men required, the food required, and maintain France's commercial interests against the foreigners and avoid revolt, Van Vollenhoven wrote to the Minister of Colonies at the end of September in the same terms as his letter of July 1917: 'I beg of you, Minister, not to give the order to recruit any more black troops'. Repeating his earlier fears in the same words, he warned: 'You will set this land afire, you will ruin it completely ... without any gain'.[42] At the same time he had written in his report on recruitment of African troops '... the brutal fact is there. Recruitment has achieved what the African conquerors never saw rise up before them: the unity of people of the most varied kinds, of religious sects the most opposed to each other; Muslims and pagans, for the first time since our arrival in Africa, expressly or tacitly came to terms in order to resist us'.[43]

France under its Premier Clemenceau, who also became its Minister of War in November 1917, however, was determined to find more troops to replace the massive casualties the French had suffered since the outbreak of the war. By January 1918, Van Vollenhoven had resigned himself to it, telling the Minister of Colonies that recruitment could only be effective if neighbouring British West African countries and Portuguese Guinea co-operated by carrying on a counter-recruitment.[44] But the Government had by 11 January decided that recruitment should be entrusted to one who appeared to it 'suitable to enlighten the natives about the future of their race under Mother France. He will know how to provoke the more intensive collaboration in our war of all the African people whose attachment and loyalty to our flag are well known'.[45] He was the African deputy for Senegal, Blaise Diagne, who by a Decree of 11 January was appointed Commissioner for the Republic for the Recruitment of Troops in French West and Equatorial Africa. He would have powers equal to those of the Governor-General (Article 3) and had the right to demand the communication to himself of any instructions and measures taken by any authority from the Governor-General downwards. (Article 5)[46] Diagne, himself, was not over eager about serving in the French Cabinet as a Commissioner, since he feared his Senegalese constituents, not all of whom had understood why they should have to join the French army to become French citizens, would question why he now came to ask for more men.[47] This decision was taken to appoint Diagne without consulting Van Vollenhoven, who arrived in Paris the day the decree was promulgated. On 17 January,

Van Vollenhoven handed in his resignation, not in protest against the further recruitment, which he had come to accept as inevitable, though he still drew to the attention of the Minister, as he had done his *Conseil de Gouvernement*, its dangers. He resigned because he would not share power and have his decisions subject to the scrutiny of another.[48] Van Vollenhoven's admirers present him as the champion of the African who tried to save him from service at the front and, when he could not, resigned his post. His critics say he resigned for racial reasons, since he could not share power with an African. Neither can be substantiated. It is clear Van Vollenhoven had reluctantly accepted the necessity of further recruitment even though he was fearful of the consequences. He protested against division of power at a time when the political situation in the colony was delicate and an intensive recruitment was about to be undertaken.[49] The arrogant young Governor-General, in whose circulars the first person singular appears more frequently than in those of any other man who held his post, was unlikely to share power with anyone, so one cannot attribute his decision directly to the fact that Diagne was an African, though Van Vollenhoven had earlier described Africans as 'children'.[50] Diagne, by contrast, has frequently been the subject of attack for sending his fellow Africans as cannon fodder to the front, for despite Van Vollenhoven's gloomy predictions, he recruited all the soldiers that were asked of him without any trouble. In fact, Diagne agreed to undertake recruitment, which was going to be pursued anyway, in return for special privileges for those who served, and for development programmes for French West Africa as a whole. He gave his reasons publicly for taking on the task in the Chamber of Deputies: 'The first reason was that in fact it was aid given in tribute of recognition of what France, hitherto, had brought to these peoples... The second was that thus they were gaining the ransom for their liberty in the future'.[51] For those who served there would be relaxation of the *indigénat*, increased facilities for naturalisation, improved medical facilities, and reservation of jobs for them; generally there would be efforts to ameliorate the standard of living of all Africans including the establishment of agricultural schools, a *lycée* and a medical school in Dakar. In the letter to the Governors-General of A.O.F. and A.E.F. which the Minister of Colonies wrote describing these proposed reforms, he said that Diagne would make the Africans understand that 'this victory which will save our race will also save theirs; he will assure them, so that they can never henceforth doubt it, that their generous assistance (*élan*), creates for a grateful France a debt which she will acquit fully one day'.[52] France never really did, and most wartime promises were forgotten in victory and subsequent economic depression.

To back up Diagne's forthcoming recruiting drive, Angoulvant sent telegrams to all the British governors in West Africa asking them to send back those French Africans who had escaped before, and to deter others by carrying on parallel recruiting drives. In sending these telegrams, he noted sourly to the Minister of Colonies, 'Up to this year we have obtained but courteous promises without any real or effective follow-up, giving the impression that the Franco-British alliance is not known about in British West Africa'.[53] However, this time he gained better response: Gambia, as we have seen, co-operated. So too did Lugard, in Nigeria, even going so far as to promise a recruiting drive along the Dahomey frontier. Even Monrovia was approached. Sierra Leone said it could not recruit further because of the heavy enlistment of men for the labour corps, but it would agree to expel any fugitives from Guinea.

Diagne arrived in Dakar on 14 February 1918 and was received when he disembarked from his ship by the Acting Governor-General of French West and French Equatorial Africa (Angoulvant), the Secretary General of the Government-General, the Lt -Governor of Senegal, the Commandant of French Forces in West Africa as well as European and African notabilities and the Diplomatic Corps. His status was exactly equal to that of the Governor-General and superior to that of the Lieutenant-Governors who would later receive him. It is difficult today to conceive the significance of this reversal of status except to imagine Herbert Macaulay suddenly taking precedence over Lord Lugard in Nigeria. Diagne was well aware of the problem. On arriving in Dakar he wrote to Angoulvant that he would not insist 'on observing strictly the protocol which would have it that I remain personally, in my capacity as Commissioner of the Republic, outside and above the administrative hierarchy, to receive the Governor-General'.[54] He added: 'I will accompany the Governor-General in charge of the two Governments-General to his residence by sitting on his left in his vehicle'. He thus courteously yielded the precedence to the Governor-General which should have been his. French officials had already been warned to forget past battles and ancient prejudices when welcoming Diagne.[55]

On tour he made it clear to the Africans that this status reversal heralded a new era. 'When you return', he told them, according to a bitter report in a newspaper, by a European who signed himself, 'Un Vieil Africain', 'you will replace the whites in the administrations. You will have decorations and you will gain the same salaries as the whites who are here'.[56] Another European, under the pseudonym 'Administrateur', wrote 'The natives are holding up their heads again: they show (on every occasion) with regard to the Europeans a detestable attitude'.[57] Diagne used his authority to the full. Two

French traders who did not turn out to greet him were reported for disrespect to the Governor-General. In Bamako his African cortège, which had been allowed special privileges on the train, were put into houses which Frenchmen had been forced to evacuate. The wife of one European administrator was alleged in the *Conseil-Général* to have wiped the dust off his shoes. Later, there were to be allegations of French administrators' wives sleeping with the Deputy to secure advancement for their husbands.

Apart from their resentment against the position of Diagne and his entourage, there were many administrators who felt piqued that he was being allowed to undertake a task which they had failed to accomplish. The pseudonymous 'Administrateur' complained that the government had not believed it its duty to show 'confidence in our colonial administration which would have served much better, at less cost and without any disorganisation, the interests of France'.[58] There were others who alleged that the French administrators had recruited all the necessary troops before ever Diagne and his commission arrived. The lie to this is given by Angoulvant, no political friend of Diagne's, who in his reports gave full credit to the Deputy for the successful recruitment of that year. In Senegal, where recruitment was not started until after Diagne's arrival, Angoulvant reported that Diagne with the administration had 'caused the mass of the population to understand that rights are not acquired without sacrifices'.[59] A great part of the successful results of recruiting in Senegal, where even the formerly dissident Casamance produced troops, was due to 'the personal action of M. Diagne, to the moral authority which he exercises over his compatriots. . . .'[60]

After touring Senegal, Diagne travelled extensively in Haut-Sénégal-Niger (roughly Soudan, Upper Volta and Niger), briefly in Guinea, Dahomey and Ivory Coast. In Dahomey, Angoulvant had feared that it would be impossible to recruit more troops. Yet three thousand of the three and a half thousand required were obtained, though Diagne's critics suggest that he can hardly be credited with their recruitment since he spent so little time in the colony. In Haut-Sénégal-Niger, especially, Diagne was able to recruit from hitherto dissident areas.

The success of Diagne's recruitment was based partly on showing the Africans that soldiers who left for the front had returned bemedalled and promoted and that some of them had even become officers, and partly by the accompanying promises of a brighter future for all. These, together with Diagne's undoubted personal charisma, seem to have been the chief factors accounting for his recruiting 63,378 men, that is 23,378 more than the 40,000 required of French West Africa in the year in which he was in charge of recruitment.[61] Above all the presence of an African with such power, whilst it put a number of European noses out of joint, was certainly a great boost to African morale. Angoulvant, successor to Van Vollenhoven, and a man politically opposed to Diagne, summed it up thus: 'An evident enthusiasm was raised up in a large number of native milieux by the presence of one of them who had achieved high position in the country. His course of action certainly had a great influence on the decision taken by many chiefs to enlist themselves or their near relatives in order to give example to the masses'.[62]

Diagne, himself, believed that the Van Vollenhoven administration had been misinforming the Government when they assured it that (1) it was impossible to recruit more men from Haut-Sénégal-Niger since there were no more who could be recruited; (2) that revolt in Haut-Sénégal-Niger would be certain and widespread if further recruitment were undertaken; (3) that it was impossible to recruit 20,000 men within six months from Haut-Sénégal-Niger even using every coercive method conceivable. His proof was the fact that he had recruited 20,000 men without coercion and without revolt and without desertion in less than two months.[63]

For French West Africa the impact of the war was tremendous. Counting those already enlisted on the outbreak of war, some 200,000 able-bodied men were removed from a population of only 11,000,000 spread over an area of three and half million square kilometre miles. The British colonies, with a much larger population and spread over a much smaller area, only recruited 30,000.[64] This meant that even by 1918 over two per cent of the French African population had left West Africa for Europe.

As far as Diagne himself was concerned, he had been unable to secure the reforms he had been promised. Angoulvant, while emphasising that Diagne had recruited more soldiers than they could have hoped for, later remarked: 'Not one of the social measures we announced would soon be undertaken in the "palavers" preceding the recruitment has been undertaken; worse still, the little we had already undertaken is in the course of disappearing. Is it wonder then that the natives are losing confidence and are disturbed by the promises we make them without having the power to keep them'.[65] But Diagne had nevertheless excited the imagination of people both within Senegal and in French West Africa as a whole.

The French in Senegal were clearly worried by Diagne's impact. A hard-line Governor-General, Martial Merlin, was appointed to succeed Angoulvant just before the 1919-20 elections to the Deputyship, the General-Council and the Municipal Councils. Merlin was determined 'to re-establish strong French rule in West Africa and bring Diagne's party into line'.[66] But Diagne returned to Senegal as a conquering hero, gaining re-election to the Deputyship by a six thousand majority over Carpot. His new party, the Republican Socialist Party, swept into the General and Municipal Councils, so that all representative institutions in Senegal were now under his control. After his election, Diagne confirmed the worst fears of Frenchmen, consolidating his position as radical spokesman for African rights, not only in the *Quatre Communes*, which he represented in the Chamber, but in the Protectorate. He still retained his official position as Commissioner of the Republic. Governor-General Merlin had a secret report made on Diagne's politics and in it he was accused of having used his position as Commissaire to spread ideas of political equality throughout West Africa and diminish the standing of Europeans in African eyes.[67]

Diagne supported the reform of the General Council in 1920 into a Colonial Council with jurisdiction over the whole Colony. He and his supporters saw the reform, which gave the Protectorate twenty seats, and the Communes twenty seats, as one way of establishing the unity of Senegal. The reform also broke the monopoly of the *métis* of Saint-Louis in that it redistributed the twenty elected seats for the Communes more fairly. But Diagne found himself in the odd position of having supported a reform that also had the whole-hearted backing of his antagonist Governor-General Merlin, who felt that the presence of twenty nominated chiefs from the Protectorate would enable him to control the Council.

This alignment between Diagne and his opponents was fortuitous. Diagne continued to fight the forces of reaction that confronted him, and was certainly considered a radical by the French right up until 1922, when in fact he was already clearly seeking compromise. In 1921 he had helped the privately owned Banque de l'Afrique Occidentale retain its privileges as the sole issuer of currency for West Africa by opposing the creation of a State Bank. But in 1923 when Diagne signed the notorious Bordeaux pact, he withdrew from opposition and became a close collaborator with commerce and administration. African radicals in Paris became increasingly disenchanted with Diagne. Some of his lieutenants deserted him and opposition to him increased. He only won the 1928 election to the Deputyship with the assistance of the French administration. When he died in 1934 he had been completely absorbed into the life of Metropolitan France, visiting Senegal rarely. One of the honours noted in the short biography of him in his personal file in the archives in Dakar was that he was President of the National Committee for Monuments for Borgnis-Desbordes and Archinard, two of the French conquistadors of West Africa. By the time of his death Diagne had succeeded in raising a journalistic onslaught against him in

Dakar which attacked not only him but his two pillars of support: the Administration and Bordeaux Commerce. The fact that he co-operated so closely with these two after 1923 has led many of his critics to see all his actions in an unfavourable light. But if we look objectively at what Diagne hoped he would obtain for Africans as a result of his recruiting drive, and situate him in the context of the options open to African politicians in the colonial situation of the time, however reprehensible the recruitment of Africans by an African for slaughter on the European front may appear, it was going to take place anyway. And, in the event, few of the troops he did recruit completed their training in time to reach the European front before the Armistice in November 1918. In undertaking the recruitment himself, Diagne sincerely believed he would reap benefits for his fellow men — and some of these he did gain. But that he was, by and large, disappointed was the result of a perfidy in the French that they have too often attributed to their neighbours across the Channel.

NOTES

1. Cited in Rayford W. Logan, 'The Historical Aspects of Pan-Africanism, 1900-1945' in *Pan-Africanism Reconsidered*, Berkeley and Los Angeles, 1962, p.44.
2. L'A.O.F., 1 May 1924 cited in J. Suret-Canale, *Histoire de l'Afrique Noire; l'ère coloniale*, p.550.
3. See Charles Cros, *La parole est à M. Blaise Diagne, premier homme d'Etat Africain*, Aubenas, France, 1961.
4. Cited in *ibid*, pp.119-20.
5. André Gide, *Voyage au Congo*, Paris, 1929, p.89.
6. See Michael Crowder, *West Africa under Colonial Rule*, London 1968, p.265.
7. *ibid*, p.264.
8. Pierre Mille, 'The Black Vote in Senegal', *Journal of the African Society*, I, 1901, pp.64-79.
9. G. Wesley Johnson, 'The Ascendancy of Blaise Diagne and the Beginning of African Politics in Senegal', *Africa*, XXXVI, 1966, pp.235-52.
10. Cited in Roger Pasquier, 'Les débuts de la presse au Sénégal', *Cahiers d'Etudes Africaines*, 7, 1962, p.482.
11. Cited in Raymond A. Buell, *The Native Problem in Africa*, I, p.950.
12. See G. Wesley Johnson, *The Emergence of Black Politics in Senegal: The Struggle for Power in the Four Communes 1900-1920*, Stanford, 1971, p.169, where he points out that in fact Carpot had the 1912 decree modified in favour of the *originaires* so that they would be tried by French courts for offences committed outside the *Quatre Communes*.
13. Cited by Johnson, 'The Ascendancy of Blaise Diagne', pp.247-8.
14. Cited in Cros, *Blaise Diagne*, p.77.
15. See Johnson, *The Emergence of Black Politics*, p.190.
16. General Mangin, *La Force Noire*, Paris, 1910.
17. Source mislaid.
18. N[ational] A[rchives] of S[enegal] 4D.45 Governor-General, French West Africa to Minister of Colonies 'Recrutement de tirailleurs en A.C.F.'

120 COLONIAL WEST AFRICA

19. *ibid* Lt.Governor Haut-Sénégal-Niger to Governor-General, FWA, 26 Nov. 1915.
20. *ibid*. Lt-Governor, HSN to Gov-Gen. FWA, 19 Dec. 1915.
21. *ibid*, Gov-Gen. FWA to Lt-Governor HSN, 14 Dec. 1915.
22. *ibid*, Lt-Gov. HSN to Gov-Gen. FWA, 17 Oct. 1915.
23. S[ierra] L[eone] N[ational] A[rchives] Governor's Confidential Despatches, 10 April 1915, encl. Intelligence Return for the Quarter ending 31 March 1915.
24. G. Angoulvant *La Pacification de la Côte d'Ivoire*, Paris, 1913.
25. NAS/4D.45 Lt-Governor, Ivory Coast to Governor-General, FWA, 18 Dec. 1915.
26. In fact recruitment in British West Africa though formally on a voluntary basis was in effect often compulsory since chiefs were asked to recruit volunteers but in fact frequently impressed men into service.
27. NAS/4D.45 Lt-Governor Ivory Coast to Governor-General, FWA, 18 Dec. 1915.
28. *ibid*.
29. *ibid*. Lt-Gov. Dahomey to Gov-Gen., FWA, 2 Sept. 1915.
30. *ibid*, Gov-Gen. FWA to Minister of Colonies 'Recrutement de 50,000 tirailleurs. Rapport no.117', 28 Jan. 1916.
31. *Ordinance for Ashanti no.9, 1915* 'An Ordinance to provide for the deportation for certain persons liable for French military service, 29 Dec. 1915'
32. G[ambia] A[rchives] Colonial Secretary's Office, Confidential Minute Paper No.175, 22 Dec. 1915. 'Immigration of Natives from French Territory to escape Military Service' Hopkinson to Colonial Secretary, 22 Dec. 1915.
33. *ibid*. pp.68, 73, 89.
34. NAS/4D.75 Gov-Gen. FWA to Maginot, July, 1917.
35. NAS/4D.72 'Rapport sur le recrutement des Troupes noires' 25 Sept. 1917.
36. Gouvernement-General de l'A.O.F. *Discours prononcé par M. Clozel, Gouverneur-Général de l'A.O.F.*, Séssion Ordinaire du Conseil du Gouvernement, Gorée, 1915, p.4.
37. Gouvernement-Générale de l'A.O.F., *Textes relatifs à la formation et la réorganisation des cadres indigènes en A.O.F.*, Gorée 1916: 'Circulaire relative à la formation du personnel des cadres indigènes.' Dakar, 1 Oct. 1916. pp.3-4.
38. *ibid*. 'Circulaire relative à la réorganisation des cadres des agents indigenes de l'A.O.F.', Dakar, 1 Oct. 1916. pp.27-8.
39. 'Circulaire au sujet du ravittaillement' of 7 June 1917 cited in *Une âme de chef: le Gouverneur-Général Joost-van Vollenhoven*, Paris, 1920, p.122.
40. NAS/4D.73. Lt-Gov. Senegal to Gov-Gen FWA, 25 Dec. 1917.
41. *ibid*. 'Projet de recrutement 1918'.
42. *ibid*. Gov-Gen. FWA to Minister of Colonies, 29 Sept. 1917.
43. NAS/4D.72 'Rapport sur le recrutement des Troupes Noires' 25 Sept. 1917.
44. NAS/4D.73 Minister of Colonies to President du Conseil, Paris, 12 Jan. 1918.
45. NAS/4D.73 Minister of Colonies in report to President of the French Republic.
46. *Decret portant organisation d'une mission chargee d'intensifier le recrutement*, Paris, 11 Jan. 1918.
47. Johnson *Emergence of Black Politics in Senegal*, p.193.
48. *Une âme de chef*, allocution prononcée par le Gouverneur-Général Van Vollenhoven à la clôture de la session du Conseil du Gouvernement de l'Afrique Occidentale Française (24th Dec. 1917), pp.264-5, and letter to Minister of Colonies, pp.265-6.
49. *ibid*, p.266.
50. *ibid*. 'Circulaire au sujet des chefs indigènes', Dakar, 15 August 1917, p.191.
51. Cited by Bakary Traoré in Bakary Traoré, Mamadou Lô and Jean-Louis Alibert, *Forces Politiques en Afrique Noire*, Paris, 1966, p.8.

52. NAS/4D.73 Minister of Colonies to Gov-Gens. A.O.F. and A.E.F. accompanied by the series of decrees dated 11 January instituting some of these reforms.
53. NAS/4D.75 'Correspondence with neighbouring colonies' 3rd File.
54. NAS/Personal File of Blaise Diagne. Diagne to Angoulvant. 14 Feb. 1918.
55. NAS/4D.74 Minister of Colonies to Governor-General (incomplete n.d.)
56. NAS/Personal File of Blaise Diagne: *Les Annales Coloniales* (un vieil Africain), 20 July 1918.
57. *ibid. Les Annales Coloniales*, 20 July 1918, 'Un Administrateur'.
58. *ibid.*
59. NAS/4D.77 Governor-General to Service de l'Afrique 'Recrutement au Sénégal: 12 Mars - 6 Mai', 18 July 1918.
60. *ibid.*
61. NAS/4D.74 'Recrutement' Governor-General to Inspector of Colonies, n.d.
62. *ibid.* For instance the heir of the Mogho Naba volunteered for service.
63. 4/D.74 Diagne to Minister of Colonies, 20 June 1918.
64. See Michael Crowder, 'West Africa and the 1914-18 War', *Bull. IFAN*
65. NAS/4D.74 Report on 1918 Recruitment by Angoulvant. Angoulvant.
66. Johnson, *The Emergence of Black Politics in Senegal*, p.198.
67. *ibid.* p.207

VI

THE WHITE CHIEFS OF TROPICAL AFRICA*
(1970)

For the kings and chiefs of tropical Africa, colonial rule meant the alienation of their sovereignty to a new group of chiefs, the European 'bush' administrators. However much power chiefs may have retained under colonial rule – and some retained a great deal – one fact was clear to them as well as to their subjects: ultimate authority now lay with the white man. This authority was represented immediately in the person of the bush administrator, who arrogated powers that had hitherto been the exclusive preserve of the African chief. To these powers he added those delegated to him by his central government as its local agent. However, the extent and manner to which the administrator usurped powers from the chiefs depended both on the colonial power he served and on the particular territory in which he was serving. So too did his functions as agent of the central government.

The aim of the present essay is to study the role of this new white chief under five different colonial systems during the years between World War I and World War II: France in West Africa; Britain in Nigeria, where there were no settlers; Britain in Kenya, where settlers exerted great influence on the administration; Portugal in Angola; and Belgium in the Congo. This period represented the hey-day of European colonial rule in tropical Africa. The work of occupation, or 'pacification', as it was euphemistically called by Europeans, had been for the most part completed; and the colonial powers were unmoved by criticism of their policies either from non-colonial powers or from Africans themselves. It is during this period that the true nature of the differences in the administrative systems of the colonial powers in tropical Africa can best be seen – in particular the contrasts in the role and function under these systems of the new white chiefs of tropical Africa.

*Reprinted by permission of Cambridge University Press from *The History of Colonialism in Tropical Africa*, Vol. 2., by L. H. Gann and Peter Duignan (eds.), Cambridge, 1970.

THE AFRICAN CONTEXT

For the vast mass of Africans the advent of colonial rule made very little difference in their lives. Few found that their economic position had changed for the better. Most of them lived too far from the colonial railway lines and roads to sell cash crops to the European traders. Few produced cash crops that brought high enough prices or sold in sufficient quantity to make any appreciable difference in the economic status of the growers after they had paid the taxes levied on them by the colonial governments. There were exceptions, as in the case of the cocoa-farmers of southern Ghana, who enjoyed great prosperity because of high prices obtained for this crop. Tonga farmers in Northern Rhodesia began to sell grain and cattle to the Copperbelt. Shona cultivators in Southern Rhodesia started to compete with white farmers on the local grain market to such an extent that the whites called for protected quotas for themselves. In Tanganyika the government fostered the cultivation of cotton and *arabica* coffee by Africans. But the total effect of these innovations remained limited. In many cases, the few crops that did bring high prices were produced by Europeans. In numerous other instances, only Europeans with adequate capital were in a position to grow low-price crops profitably on a large scale. Moreover, both white and black cultivators suffered from sharp price fluctuations for their produce on the world market, with the result that cash farming remained an economically hazardous undertaking.

During the inter-war period, educational facilities for Africans in sub-Saharan Africa as a whole remained minuscule. Admittedly, there was some expansion. Between 1924 and 1939, for example, the number of African children at school in Northern Rhodesia went up from something like 40,000 to 120,000. But educational standards were usually low. Only a small number of Africans were able to go to schools of any sort, fewer still to secondary schools. The position during the 1930s of four of the colonies under consideration is shown in Table 1.

Sub-Saharan Africa did not therefore produce a substantial black westernised elite, though the impact of westernisation was, of course, uneven, and there were marked differences between the various African territories. Not many Africans were drawn into the non-agricultural sectors of the economy. The demand for clerks on the part of commercial houses and government offices remained small. Few processing industries were established on the spot. Only the railways, the plantations and the mining enterprises offered large-scale opportunities for wage labour. During the period, the wage-earning class as a whole remained tiny in comparison with the mass of peasants. Thus in Nigeria in 1936, out of a population of some 20 million there were only 227,451 wage-earners; in Kenya in the same year only 182,858 out of a population of 3,084,351; in French West Africa in 1935, only 178,908 out of a population of 14½ million; and in the Belgian Congo in 1936, only 409,274 out of a population of 11 million.[1]

Table 1. *Children attending school during the 1930s*

Colony	Estimated population	Year	Attendance in primary school	Attendance in secondary school
Belgian Congo	11,000,000 (1935, part enumerated, part census)	1938	716,857	7,540[a] (1946)
Angola	2,600,000 (1930-1, estimated)	1930-1	6,537	[b]
Nigeria (northern provinces)	11,500,000 (1931 census)	1939	25,067	[c]
Nigeria (southern provinces)	8,630,359 (1931 census)	1938	267,788	[d]
French West Africa	14,575,973 (1931 census)	1935	c. 60,000	c.600[e]

[a] In this year there were no secondary schools as such, but some post-primary education was given at a few of the primary schools. Two-thirds of the pupils at primary schools attended mission schools, which received no subsidies from government. (Source: Lord Hailey, *An African survey: Revised 1956*, London, 1957, p. 1207. Source for 1946 figures for secondary school pupils: Georges Brausch, *Belgian administration in the Congo*, London, 1961.)
[b] There was, for instance, an advanced *lycée* at Luanda to which assimilated Africans and *métis* were admitted. (Source: Lord Hailey, *An African survey*, London, 1938, p. 1278.)
[c] Michael Crowder, *West Africa under colonial rule* (London, 1968), p. 376.
[d] The figure given does not differentiate between students in different types of schools.
[e] Source: W. Bryant Mumford and G. St. J. Orde-Brown, *Africans learn to be French: a review of educational activities in the seven federated colonies of French West Africa based on a tour of French West Africa and Algiers undertaken in 1935* (London, 1937)

Black peasants thus constituted the mass of Europe's subjects in Africa. For them, the main feature of colonial rule was the maintenance of 'law and order', which was only rarely disturbed during the inter-war years. The agent of law and order was the European administrative officer, the only white man with whom the average African ever came into contact. For the African, he alone represented the new European government, based in a far-off capital, and ultimately responsible to a European metropolis of which most Africans had little or no conception. It is true that during the 1930s, the number of technical services began to increase in the more highly developed colonies. The administration began to assume new functions, which might range all the way from the collection of meteorological data to the compilation of ecological surveys, or to a more systematic provision of agricultural services. Generalisations in this respect are of course hard to make because there were significant differences, not only as between one territory and another, but also as between different regions of the same colony. The gradual invasion of the expert created various new problems for the district administrator, who often lost some of his accustomed powers, and sometimes tended to become more 'chair-borne' than in the olden days. But up to the 1930s, this process had not in most cases made much headway. In so far as colonial rule was brought home to the ordinary African villager, it was usually through the agency of the district commissioner. For the average African, the district administrator was a new chief working alongside or through indigenous dignitaries. The district officer thus became a 'white chief' exercising his rule directly or indirectly according to the rules of the colonial power which he served.

THE WHITE CHIEFS

The vast majority of the administrators of the four colonial powers under consideration were drawn from the middle classes of their respective mother countries. The British at first did not insist on any specific educational qualifications for the colonial service, and recruitment was made by selection under the direction of one man, Sir Ralph Furse, not by competitive examination. After World War I many army officers, without university degrees and some very poorly suited to their task, entered the British colonial service. By the 1930s a university degree was becoming increasingly necessary for entry; but recruits were usually, though not exclusively, drawn from the older and more prestigious universities and from elite 'public schools'. Cadets in the 1930s received one year's training at Oxford and were required to pass examinations in law and African languages. The French and Belgians, by contrast with the British, recruited on a competitive basis; and entry into their colonial services was dependent, with certain exceptions, on passing through special colonial schools established to train colonial administrators. The French administrator had to pass through the Ecole Coloniale, established in 1889, reorganised in 1927 and renamed in 1934 Ecole Nationale de la France d'Outre-Mer (E.N.F.O.M.). The Belgian administrator trained at the Université Coloniale at Antwerp or at the Ecôle Coloniale. Belgium and France recruited staff without these qualifications who, after serving a certain time in a separate grade, could be considered for promotion into the administrative grade proper.

A few brilliant and distinguished people managed to reach high office in the early Portuguese Empire, but by and large the quality of the average Portuguese administrator remained low until the reforms introduced by Salazar in the 1930s under the regime of the 'New State'. Low pay and bad conditions of service all too often meant the recruitment of men who were prone to corruption and to neglect of duty. Though the Escola Colonial Superior had been founded in the first years of the twentieth century, it was not until 1926 that it was integrated with the colonial administration. And only with the improved conditions of service under the New State did a better class of administrator, who had graduated from the school, begin to dominate the service.

Except in the case of many Portuguese officials, the average colonial administrator was a man of solid character; he had a university degree or its equivalent in experience or training, though he was usually rather unimaginative. Perhaps the best service was that of the Belgian Congo, where the reaction to the Free State scandals led to insistence on high standards under Belgian parliamentary as distinct from royal control. In their approach to the problems of African administration, the French and Portuguese officials represented powers with distinctly assimilationist and centralising tendencies. The British and Belgians, on the other hand, believed in a more decentralised system. They were preoccupied also with the problem of implementing indirect rule by using streamlined forms of traditional society. The British, however, did not apply this policy in Kenya, where the local white settlers enjoyed great political influence, or in Southern Rhodesia, where white immigrants dominated the state. In Kenya and Southern Rhodesia Africans were governed on a pattern closer to that of French West Africa than to that of Nigeria, Uganda or neighbouring Tanganyika.

The colonial administrative services of both Belgium and Britain, whether in Nigeria or in Kenya, were exclusively white. Until 1959, juridically no African could enter the higher grades of the civil service of the Belgian Congo, though some were in fact admitted after 1953. There were a few exceptions. In the Gold Coast, for instance, an African Solicitor General held office during the 1930s. In Nigeria, which was somewhat more backward, the first African Assistant District Officers were not appointed until 1951, though, unlike Kenya, a few Nigerians were employed in senior service posts in technical branches of the civil service, such as the medical and legal departments. The French and Portuguese made no discrimination as to colour, and a substantial number of French West Indians, Goanese and Portuguese mulattoes worked in the local administration. Very few Africans were employed. Though provision was made for their assimilation as French or Portuguese citizens, the educational facilities available to them were such that few became assimilated, let alone qualified to enter the colonial service.

The systems of grading and promotion of officers within the four services were in all cases competitive. For the most part, the standards of the administration were thus kept reasonably high, though in the case of the Portuguese colonies this was not achieved until the 1930s because the officers recruited in the early days were usually of such poor quality. The administrative services of all five colonies under consideration rarely contained representatives of the cream of the metropolitan generation, since Africa was not a popular choice for a career. Nigeria and French West Africa both had difficulties in recruiting, and frequently had large numbers of vacancies.

One of the main problems of all administrations was that of stability. In colonies of widely diverse populations, where few of the African subjects initially spoke English, it was of course desirable for the administrators to learn the local language and to study the culture of 'their' peoples. Yet the central secretariats of Nigeria and Kenya rarely kept a man for long in one station. Indeed in Kenya a study made in the 1930s showed a marked instability of administration, with one official being posted to eleven different stations in six years.[2] The British, as a matter of policy, rarely transferred administrators from one territory to another. In Southern Rhodesia native commissioners formed part of a locally-based service; Southern Rhodesian officials were not seconded to other British possessions, and native commissioners tended to stay in the same district for long periods of time. The Belgians, since they had no possessions other than the Belgian Congo and the mandated territory of Ruanda-Urundi, could not shift their colonial civil servants to other parts of the world. The French in West Africa, Equatorial Africa and Madagascar, on the other hand, systematically posted officials from one part of the empire to another, as well as from one *circonscription* to another within the same colony. For some time the French in West Africa indeed did so as part of a deliberate policy known as *rouage*, which was aimed at preventing officials from becoming corrupt by involving themselves too closely with local affairs. The Portuguese kept their administrators in the colony to which they were first appointed, except where a man secured promotion to the most senior posts within the colonial hierarchy.

The higher the rate of transferability from post to post, the less the administrator was apt to know about local institutions. This did not matter so much where the government aimed at a uniform administrative system, as in Angola or in French West Africa. But frequent postings did prevent that proper understanding of African social structures which was vital to a sympathetic local administration. Frequent postings were particularly serious where a policy of indirect rule was pursued, for indirect rule required that administrators should acquire a high degree of comprehension of the complexities of African society.

Despite the fact that a high rate of transferability tended to impede a good understanding of African society, promotion in the British system depended to some extent on progress made in an African language. Many British officials thus became fluent in African tongues, especially in linguae francae such as Swahili or Hausa. They also learnt and wrote much about the culture of the people whose tongue they spoke. In Nigeria, in particular, the British government not only directly encouraged its officers to make studies of the language and anthropology of its peoples, but financed the publication of such studies. While French cadets at the E.N.F.O.M. studied African languages, the fact that they rarely stayed long in one colony meant that they had little chance to pursue them. Whereas the British officer was encouraged to converse with his chief in the latter's language, the French tried to make fluency in French a prerequisite of chieftaincy. The Portuguese, too, insisted on their own language as the medium of instruction and education. However, administrative officers of these colonies have made some outstanding, if amateur, contributions to the anthropology of their African subjects. The tiny colony of Portuguese Guinea, for instance, is served by a Research Centre which has published studies by administrators of nearly every one of the many ethnic groups within its borders.

The administrators in each of the five colonies under consideration all shared the common function of 'political officer', that is, responsibility for the supervision of the maintenance of law and order in their areas of jurisdiction, and responsibility for implementation of central government orders. But their functions differed widely in other respects. As a rule, in Nigeria the British administrator governed, as did the Belgian administrator, through traditional authorities, The aim in both cases was to encourage local self-government by Africans through their traditional institutions. On the other hand, the French and Portuguese and the British in Kenya, whilst administering through 'chiefs', did not look on these chiefs as traditional African authorities (which in very many cases they were not) but as agents of the administration, who had in theory no initiative of their own.

In administration, the British and Belgians regarded their role as executive and advisory, while the French and Portuguese conceived of theirs as exclusively executive. This distinction will become apparent in the next section. Another major difference between the British officials on the one hand, and the French, Belgians and Portuguese on the other concerned the administrator's general role. Both in Nigeria and Kenya, the British administrator exercised no control over the technical services operating in his area of jurisdiction. Agricultural officers, public works officials and medical officers all worked independently of him, being responsible directly to their departmental heads. Since the administrator was meant to encourage local self-government by Africans, in which technical services were supposed to play an increasing role, this policy considerably hampered smooth development. Further, each department often worked independently of the others, in cases where co-ordinated planning would not only have been desirable but was actually necessary.

By contrast, under the French administrator all services were centralised; he was responsible also for economic development. He had under him *agents*, many of them Africans, of the technical services, whose work he co-ordinated. Similarly in the Congo, administrators at the various levels had overall co-ordinating authority. The main function of the territorial administrator (the equivalent of the British Resident) was to make twice-yearly inspections and to report on various services operating in his *territoire*. The Portuguese administrator was not only responsible for all services operating in his area of jurisdiction, but very often had to undertake their operation himself. As Duffy has remarked:

> untrained in colonial affairs, sent to dwell in an unhealthy region in which they had no interest, [they were] burdened with assorted responsibilities — legal, financial, technical — which would have tested the capacities of the most dedicated civil servant.[3]

The third major distinction between the various systems was to be found in the interchangeability of local administrator and central secretariat. While French, British and Portuguese administrators were expected to spend some of their tours working in the central secretariats in order to examine the problems of local administration in the context of the administration of the colony as a whole, such interchange was very rare in the Congo.

The last major difference was in the amount of time spent by administrators away from their desks. Belgian administrators, who were expected to be on tour twenty days of the month, appear not to have been overburdened with paper-work. Ideally, British district officers were supposed to undertake regular tours, but paper-work increased so much that they became more and more desk-bound. The official's responsibility for accounts, and, in Nigeria, the lack of qualified assistants for accounting, played a major part in bringing about this situation. The French administrator, in co-ordinating and having responsibility for so many services, managed very often by relatively junior staff, was in the same predicament. The Portuguese administrator had multifarious duties; he was the sole legal authority in his *circonscrição,* and hence he remained very much tied down to headquarters.

All junior administrators in these colonies enjoyed one tremendous advantage: this was the fact that up to the end of the 1930s communications were generally so poor that officials in out-of-the-way bush stations generally experienced little interference from their superiors. They were very much their own masters. They could conveniently fail to obey an instruction by being away when it arrived, and no one would be any the wiser. No colony was ever closely administered. The British in Nigeria were the most thinly spread; the Portuguese employed a relatively much larger number of civil servants. The distribution of administrators in each colony in proportion to the population is shown in Table 2.

Table 2. *Distribution of administrators*

	Population	Number of administrators	Ratio of administrator to population
Nigeria and Cameroun	20,000,000	386 (Late 1930s[a] — Includes those in the secretariat)	1:54,000
Kenya	3,100,000	164 (Late 1930s[a] — include those in the secretariat and locally recruited staff)	1:18,900
French West Africa	14,500,000	526 (1921 — include those in the secretariat)	1:27,500
Belgian Congo	11,000,000	316 (1936)	1:34,800

[a] See Lord Hailey, *An African survey* (1938), Table III, p. 226, where figures but no dates are given.

WHITE CHIEFS AND NATIVE CHIEFS

The administrative officers of all four colonial powers used African chiefs in one form or another to rule their African subjects. The relationship between the white chief and the African chief in each case reveals much not only about the character of the various systems of local administration of the colonial powers, but also about the nature of the task set to the colonial administrator.

Of the four administrations in question, that of the Portuguese in Angola was the most direct, that of the British in Nigeria the most indirect. On a spectrum ranging from direct to indirect rule, one would therefore place the Portuguese at the 'direct' extreme, moving through the French in West Africa, the British in Kenya and the Belgians in the Congo to the 'indirect' extreme of the British in Nigeria. The structure is illustrated in Table 3.

THE PORTUGUESE IN ANGOLA

The long-term goal of the Portuguese in Angola was the 'civilisation' of the 'native' and his integration into the Portuguese community. Hence any use of, let alone systematic preservation of, tribal institutions as a means of local government was inimical to this ultimate goal. The Portuguese favoured direct administration of their African population. They also employed many Europeans in lowly positions. (No published statistics are available concerning the total number of all Portuguese civil servants employed in the 1930s. Comparisons between, say, the Portuguese and the British colonies are in any case hard to make because of structural differences in their respective bureaucracies.) But even the Portuguese, in order to rule effectively, had to use African auxiliaries. The Portuguese, like all other European powers, were thus forced to rely on chiefs. These chiefs, however, were used not to preserve or develop traditional powers, but rather to bring home to their people the new authority represented by the Portuguese administrators.

The chiefs were called *regulos* and wore para-military uniform. Many of them carried traditional authority in that they came from ruling families, or because they would in any case have become chiefs according to traditional rules of succession. But in the 1930s old soldiers, loyal clerks and policemen without any claim to traditional authority were increasingly appointed to the position of *regulo*. These *regulos* had no authority of their own: they had no judicial functions, no right to raise traditional dues or taxes, nor did they maintain treasuries. They were mere extensions of the arm of the *chefes do posto* with clearly defined functions: to transmit government orders, to maintain peace in their areas, to report crimes, to prevent illicit sales of liquor, to report any suspicious persons, to register births, deaths and marriages, to furnish recruits for the army and for labour, to help conduct censuses, to put down 'witchcraft' and to help spread the Portuguese language. Under them the *regulos* had village heads for each of the villages in their respective areas. These village heads were responsible for collecting taxes, and their salary was derived from a percentage of taxes collected. Significantly, in order to minimise possibilities of corruption at this level, the *regulo* was not himself allowed to collect taxes. Village chiefs were responsible also for maintenance of roads in their areas.

The real chief was, of course, the Portuguese administrator. He alone administered the law, maintained a police force, controlled the movement of Africans. No African could leave his area without the authority of the administrator, nor indeed could a village move its site. Tax collection was under his direct supervision. He was an agent for the recruitment of forced labour, a commodity desired in the past by many entrepreneurs (though not by the more highly skilled and sophisticated employers, who had no use for unwilling draftees). There were few aspects of native life in which the district officer's presence was not felt through *regulos*, through his subalterns and village chiefs. Though the Portuguese administrator bore a basic resemblance to his colleagues in the British, French and Belgian possessions, the Portuguese administration, however, did show a marked difference from that of other colonial powers in its excessive formalism, expressed in its ritualistic regard for *papel selado* (official documents with the proper seals), in its curious mixture of chauvinism and a highly selective paternalism, and in its marked *étatiste* tendencies that often forced even the most law-abiding foreign entrepreneurs to operate in a curious twilight of legality that forced even the best-intentioned to become wholly dependent on 'right' official contacts.

The African revolution that has struck parts of Angola, Guinea and northern Moçambique brought about further changes which lie beyond the scope of this essay. The 'psycho-social' counter-insurgency programme run by the army has brought the military forces back into government, though perhaps on a different level. Suffice it to say that Portuguese counter-guerillas in Angola have tried to stem the tide of war, and to gain the confidence of the discontented people by providing a whole range of administrative services, including medical, educational and other forms of assistance. Whether these experiments will be more successful than similar attempts made by the French in Algeria is highly doubtful. All we can say is that they may introduce major, and perhaps irreversible, changes in the colonial Portuguese ethos.

Table 3. *Structure of administration*

	Angola	French West Africa	Kenya	Belgian Congo	Nigeria
European-hierarchy					
Central (1)	Governor-General *District* Governor	Governor-General *Colony* Lt. Governor	Governor —	Governor-General *Province* Commissaire de Province	Governor *Group of provinces* Chief Commissioner
(2)	*Circonscrição* Administrator	*Cercle* Commandant de Cercle	*Province* Provincial Commissioner	*District* Commissaire de District	*Province* Resident
(3)	*Posto* Chefe do Posto	*Subdivision* Chef de Subdivision	*District* District Commissioner	*Territoire* Administrateur de Territoire	*Division* District Officer
African-hierarchy	*Regulo* Village Chief	Chef Supérieur de Province Chef de Canton Chef de Village	Headman	*Circonscription* (Chief of *Chefferie/Secteur* Chief)	(N. Nigeria Example) Paramount: Emir District Head Village Chief

THE FRENCH IN WEST AFRICA

The French were assimilationist in spirit, and believed deeply that French culture represented the ultimate goal towards which their African subjects should aspire. But the problems experienced in applying a policy of assimilation in Senegal in the nineteenth and early twentieth centuries led the French to abandon this goal as a general governing principle. Instead, Africans were to be selectively assimilated; the administration of the vast bulk of the African population was to ensure the development of West Africa for the mutual advantage of ruler and subject. While never dismissing the values of traditional African society as forthrightly as the Portuguese, the French nevertheless believed in a system of rule that would be as direct and as uniform as possible.

But the French had fewer administrators in proportion to the population than did the Portuguese. Because they had to rule huge areas, the French had not only to use chiefs as auxiliaries, but often to accept, if not recognise, chiefs with traditional authority. Like the Portuguese *regulos*, the chiefs under the French were primarily agents of the French administration. They exercised no judicial powers and they were not legally permitted to exact traditional revenues from their subjects. As far as the French were concerned, the chiefs' authority derived not from their traditional position, but from their role as agents of the French administration. The powers of cantonal and village chiefs were uniform throughout French West Africa and did not, in theory at least, vary according to the traditional structure of the society over which they ruled. Wherever possible, the French broke down the powers of the great chiefs, sharing them among their immediate subordinates, though paying honour to the traditional influence of the paramount by recognising him as a *Chef Supérieur de Province*. Like the Portuguese, they frequently appointed old soldiers and loyal functionaries to chieftaincies, and even imposed as chief over one particular ethnic group a man from another. One of the principal qualifications which the French set up for an African to be recognised as a chief was his ability to speak French.

The chiefs collected taxes, recruited men for the army or for forced labour, maintained the roads, and were held responsible for keeping the peace. The fact that there were fewer French supervisors than in Portuguese territories often allowed chiefs to wield considerable unofficial authority, in particular through illegal collection of taxes. The frequency with which the French appointed chiefs without traditional claims to the office was reflected in the emergence of 'straw chiefs' or unrecognised chiefs, who had traditional authority, covertly settled customary disputes and carried out traditional

THE WHITE CHIEFS OF TROPICAL AFRICA 135

religious functions for their peoples. The French-appointed chiefs were treated with scant respect by the French themselves. They were subject to the *indigénat* or summary system of administrative justice whereby the administrator could imprison without trial a *sujet* (i.e., a non-French citizen) for up to fourteen days or fine him. Chiefs, in particular village chiefs, were frequently fined, imprisoned or deposed for failing to carry out their duties properly.

The relationship between the French administrator and the chief was that of officer to N.C.O. Indeed the chiefs became the sergeants and corporals of the empire, while the French administrators, with their judicial powers, their right to impose immediate punishment without trial, their para-military force of *gardes de cercles*, and their functions as agent of economic development, became 'les vrais chefs de l'Empire'. If their power was less than that of their Portuguese equivalents, it was that they were spread more thinly on the ground. In many cases they also had to deal with chiefs who, in the era immediately preceding the imposition of colonial rule, had wielded greater powers than the majority of, say, Angolan chiefs.

THE BRITISH IN KENYA

For the British, Kenya presented a special problem because of the presence of a vocal and prosperous white settler minority which had gained some power in the local legislative process, in particular with regard to the passing of estimates. There were two administrative systems in operation. One, which applied to the White Highlands, will not be discussed here. The other functioned in the native reserves, which were much larger in extent — though much less prosperous — than the Highlands.

The British government laid down clearly that African interests should be paramount in Kenya. But the administration did not govern the African through his traditional institutions, even though this policy was pursued generally throughout British tropical Africa. Instead a much more direct system of administration was devised. As in French West Africa and Angola, chiefs, known as headmen, were used as agents of government. Some of them exercised traditional authority, but many were appointed because of their educational background or experience in administration. They in no sense carried out traditional functions, and there was no such institution as a Nigerian-type Native Authority in Kenya. It has been suggested by some scholars that the Native Authority system was rejected in Kenya because the presence of a vocal European minority forced the administration to look with a more critical eye at traditional institutions as the basis of native administration.[4] Be that as it may, there were few chiefs in Kenya with wide areas of jurisdiction. Hence the British faced problems similar to those in eastern Nigeria, where tribal society was generally decentralised and where traditional institutions could not easily be used as the basis of local self-government.

While the district commissioners ruled through the headmen directly, they did not wield as much power as their Portuguese and French counterparts. In the first place, they did not have the latter's wide responsibilities for the technical aspects of local administration. In the second place, the British shared judicial authority with native tribunals, appointed by government but presided over by an African. This African was not, however, the 'chief', though headmen officially designated or with traditional authority could be nominated as members of these tribunals. The tribunals were supposed to be constituted in accordance with customary law, but this was not always done. They tried only petty cases, but Africans did exercise some responsibility for their own judicial administration.

As I have already pointed out, the French and Portuguese conceived of their role as purely executive, while the British and Belgians regarded theirs as both executive and consultative in nature. This held true even in Kenya, where British rule was more direct than anywhere else in British Africa except for Southern Rhodesia. In the first place, the native tribunals may be seen as an instance of this; their decisions, including the right to imprison offenders for up to six months, were made by Africans, though subject to the 'advisory' confirmation of the district commissioner. In the second place, district councils with African representation were established from 1924 onward. Though the district commissioner was the president and executive of these councils, he accepted and sought advice from the African members recruited from the modern rather than traditional ranks of African society. African members of the councils in the more advanced areas of Kikuyuland and Kavirondo were often very vocal. Though limited in functions to matters concerning roads, local schools, dispensaries, markets and cattle-dips, they did exert legal authority in that they were empowered to make resolutions, which, if approved by the Governor in Council, had the sanction of law. Many of them commanded only limited resources, but they raised their own revenues and administered their own budgets. The Machakos District Council in 1926 employed two European officials full-time, one as a forestry officer, another as a road overseer. While local self-government was encouraged neither in Angola nor in French Africa outside the urban areas, the British did foster local self-government in Kenya, though it was based on an English rather than on an African pattern. As Ingham notes, these councils were so modern that:

> frequently indigenous councils existed side by side with the authorities established by the Central Government although their existence was unknown to the Government. These traditional authori-

ties regulated much of the day-to-day life of certain of the tribes whose members would refer their disputes to the jurisdiction of the recognised elders rather than to the councils or tribunals created by the Europeans.[5]

Here we have a parallel to the 'straw chiefs' of French West Africa. Though the district commissioner in Kenya was much more limited in his functions than his French and Portuguese counterparts, the district commissioner's powers surpassed by far any possessed by Africans either of a traditional or a modern nature. The district commissioner was effectively the African's new 'chief'. He was magistrate for all serious crimes. He controlled the movement of Africans in his area, since all had to carry certificates and seek permission to move from one area to another. He alone exercised executive powers on behalf of the Native Councils. In areas where there were no such councils, the headmen formed what was described in the twenties as 'a native administrative service'.[6] Only the gravest crimes were sent to High Court judges for a hearing.

THE BELGIANS IN THE CONGO

In their administration outside the urban areas or the concessions (these formed a special case and will not be considered in this essay), Belgians showed little interest in assimilating the Africans. Indeed, the Belgians tried as far as possible to follow a policy of indirect rule similar to that pursued by the British. Africans should be ruled by their own chiefs according to tradition, shorn of those aspects repugnant to 'civilised man'. At the same time these chiefs would be the principal agents for transmitting to their subjects the orders of the central government. Thus, as far as local self-government was concerned, the chief determined policy but was subject to advice from the Belgian administrator, who could, where necessary, exercise a veto. But in his role as agent of the central government, the chief was in very much the same position as his counterpart in Angola, French West Africa or Kenya. The Belgian chief was to become 'une autorité qui, d'une part, participe à l'administration européenne, et est intégrée dans son cadre, et d'une autre part, continue à appartenir à l'organisation indigène. Cette autorité constitue le chainon entre les deux organisations'.[7]

In their efforts to pursue their policy of building up 'an autonomous self-ruling system of local government', the Belgians had by 1919 recognised 6,095 *chefferies*, many of which administered very small areas. While there were some chiefs who ruled over large areas, the majority governed only minute populations. Furthermore, the Belgians recognised also subordinate chiefs of paramounts along with the paramounts themselves. The problems arising from the existence of a plethora of small chieftaincies led the Belgians to reduce their number. This they did by withdrawing recognition from chiefs subordinate to paramounts and by grouping series of small chieftaincies into *secteurs* under the presidency of one of the constituent chiefs who alone was recognised as chief. Such chiefs thus exercised traditional authority (which was not formally recognised by the Belgians) only in the constituent chiefdom from which they came. Their authority as sector chief was Belgian-derived, though as sector chiefs they were expected to organise their sector government as though they were traditional chiefs.

In exercising local self-government, the traditional and sector chiefs had a fair degree of autonomy. They governed according to custom and administered customary law. Native treasuries were established to administer funds derived from court fees and fines, as well as so-called voluntary contributions collected at the same time as the central government tax. After 1933 the central government subsidised these chieftaincy treasuries. The official salaries paid to the chiefs were based on the number of taxpayers in their respective chieftaincies or sectors.

While chiefs had a certain degree of autonomy at the local level, the demands made on them by the central government as represented by the local Belgian administrator meant that much of their time was spent in the role of agent of the administration: as collector of taxes, as recruiter of labour for public works and for the concessions and as agent for the compulsory cultivation of crops. Thus, while a chief in the Congo exercised an autonomy never enjoyed by his counterpart in Kenya, Angola and French West Africa, the requirements of the Belgian administration too often emphasised his position 'as the lowest grade in the civil service'[8] at the expense of his position as head of a unit of local self-government. Though in theory he was a chief with a certain degree of independent initiative working both alongside and under a European chief, in practice it was the subordinate role of the chief rather than the dual role that was emphasised.

THE BRITISH IN NIGERIA

Nigeria was so vast and contained so many different ethnic groups of such widely differing structure that no one system of native administration emerged. Indeed, parallels may be found in Nigeria for all the systems described above, other than for the Portuguese in Angola. However, the system of indirect rule as formulated by Lord Lugard and his immediate successors in the north did become the goal for the administration of Nigerians even if it was never fully realised even in the north itself. Because of the limitations of space we will here consider only the ideal of indirect rule in northern Nigeria, the Hausa-Fulani emirate, followed by reference to the difficulties experienced in the application of this policy to non-Hausa-Fulani peoples. These difficulties demonstrate parallels between British rule in Nigeria and systems of Native Administration in the other territories under consideration.

Ideally, as Lugard saw it, local administration should be exercised through the traditional political institutions of the African, shorn of such aspects as were repugnant to Western concepts of civilisation. The Native Authority, as the traditional political organisation was termed, should be as far as possible autonomous in the management of its affairs. Its main obligation to the central administration should be the collection of taxes, the amount of which was determined by the central administration. Of these taxes, a certain proportion would revert to the native treasury. The essential feature of indirect rule in Nigeria was the regularisation of expenditure by these Native Authorities through treasuries, revenues of which would be spent only in accordance with a budget subject to scrutiny by the central administration. Chiefs and, where appropriate, councillors would become salaried officials not of the central government but of the Native Authority, and their salaries would form part of this budget. Native Authorities had their own courts, where customary law was applied; and only at certain levels were sentences and fines subject to administrative confirmation. The great emirs had powers even to impose the death sentence. The Native Authorities maintained their own police forces and prisons, which were subject to administrative inspection. In function, though not structure, the Native Authorities were similar to units of local self-government in Britain, responsible for roads, hospitals, education, water supplies, sanitation, etc. Some, like Kano, had budgets larger than some British colonies and employed European technical officers. Most important of all, they were the legislative authorities for local government.

The British administrator had no formal executive function in these Native Authorities. His role was designated merely as that of an adviser. His primary function was that of watchdog for the central administration: to see that the Native Authorities were running smoothly, that there were no abuses of the system and to give advice either where it was sought or when he considered it necessary. Lugard conceived of the role of the 'political officer' as one in which he would frequently advise even if his counsel was not sought. In practice, in the 1920s and early 1930s the British administrators in the larger emirates left their chiefs very much alone, pursuing a policy of minimal interference.

Such a policy worked in the great emirates, where the emirs remained very much chiefs despite reduction in certain of their powers. The relationship of the emir to the white chief was very much that of a head boy of a British public school to his headmaster. Provided there were no patent abuses, the headmaster left the head boy and his prefects to their own devices. Even when it was necessary to give the emir direct orders, every effort was made to ensure that further transmission of such orders appeared to emanate from the emir himself and not from the British administrator. This policy ran into difficulty only in societies where regular direct taxation was unknown, as in Yorubaland, in small chieftaincies where the British confronted the same administrative problems as the Belgians did in the Congo, or in societies where authority was decentralised or was shared among several groups.

In southern Nigeria the introduction of the Native Authority system and direct taxation provoked riots among both Ibo and Yoruba groups, to whom the idea was alien. The centralisation of powers in a single chief worked in the emirates of northern Nigeria. But it had a rough passage in Yorubaland because, through the Oba appeared to be the chief executive of state, decisions were in fact arrived at only after negotiation between a large number of policy-making groups in the state. In parts of northern Nigeria there were many small chieftancies which the British federated into more manageable units, as the Belgians did in the Congo. In Eastern Nigeria, particularly among the Ibo, the British, for want of actual chiefs, appointed as Warrant Chiefs those with some apparent authority among their people. These chiefs, whose claim to some form of traditional authority was sometimes questionable, were much closer in character to the appointed chiefs of the Portuguese and French administrations, or to the headmen of Kenya, than to the chiefs of Native Authorities in northern Nigeria. Even so, they enjoyed much more autonomy than any of these; and their abuse of this power, coupled with their lack of traditional authority, led to the 1929 revolt against them and the British who had appointed them. Finally, the British abandoned the Warrant Chiefs and, after anthropological inquiries, substituted as the Native Authority wherever possible the traditional political authorities, however diffuse.

In ruling Africans through their own political institutions, the British not only modified but in certain cases radically altered them. Nevertheless, the relationship of the British political officer to the Native Authority remained substantially the same: he was above all an adviser to the Native Authority. His role in the affairs of Native Authorities took on an executive aspect only in so far as Native Authorities were not fully capable of administering themselves. Thus, among the economically backward Plateau tribes, the district officer played an executive role inconceivable in large emirates like Kano and Zaria.

While the political officer was adviser on local government affairs, he had to carry out certain functions for central government such as recruiting soldiers and labour, as well as supervising tax collection. These, as far as possible, he performed through the agency of the Native Authorities. His other main functions were to co-ordinate the administration of the various Native Authorities under his control and to act as magistrate in cases which could not be considered within the jurisdiction of Native Authority courts. The British district officer in the emirates of northern Nigeria was a distant chief, a high god, to be appealed to in the last resort rather than to be consulted and negotiated with daily.

THE WHITE CHIEF AS MAGISTRATE

From a judicial point of view, by far the most powerful of the administrators in the colonies under consideration were the Portuguese. Since in most African societies there was no separation between the judicial and the executive functions of the chief, his status vis-à-vis his African subjects was extremely important. In Angola, however, no African, whether chief or *notable*, exercised judicial authority. All cases, civil as well as criminal, came before the *chefe do posto* in the first instance. In criminal cases the non-assimilated African was subject to the Portuguese penal code, though the administrator was required to place the offence in the context of customary law wherever appropriate. In civil matters the administrator was advised by two Africans, either *regulos* or those who were conversant with customary law. In any matter concerning an African and a non-African, only Portuguese law applied.

The African was permitted no legal representation, even though he was judged by Portuguese law. Punishments were severe: whipping with the *chicote* (hide whip) or the *palmetaria* (hand-bat) were common forms of corporal punishment. Imprisonment usually took the form of 'correctional labour' on public works projects. Political offences, though they were rare in the 1930s, were dealt with summarily.

In French West Africa the judicial powers of the administrators were somewhat more limited than those of the Portuguese. In the first place, civil cases were judged by *tribunaux de premier degré* presided over by an African *notable*, but significantly not a chief. Indeed, a feature of *justice indigène* in French West Africa was the elimination of the judicial functions of the chiefs. In criminal case. the *chef de subdivision* presided over the *tribunal de premier degré*, assisted by two African *notables* as assessors. Appeal from these tribunals was heard by the *tribunal criminel* presided over by the *Commandant de Cercle* assisted by two European and two African assessors.

The most important judicial weapon possessed by the French administrator was his power of summary imprisonment of African *sujets* under the *indigénat*. This allowed him to imprison any *sujet* without trial for up to fourteen days (later reduced to five days). He could also impose fines without trial. Until 1924 all chiefs were subject to the *indigénat*, but in that year a decree excluded all but village chiefs from its application. Africans committing 'political offences' could by terms of the *indigénat* be imprisoned for up to ten years; but it was required that the Minister for the Colonies be informed of the sentence. The French administrator thus had immense authority over his subjects.

The Belgian system, while allowing for native courts in which chiefs exercised authority in all civil cases and in some criminal cases, nevertheless gave its administrators summary judicial powers similar to those of their French counterparts. An African could be imprisoned by an administrator for up to seven days for *infractions aux mesures d'ordre général*. The only difference between these powers and those possessed by the French administrator was that they were subject to judicial process. However, in such instances the administrator, as police magistrate, was judge in his own case. But since the *Parquet*, or central judicial supervisory body, scrutinised all cases appearing in police magistrates' courts, there was some small check to his summary powers.

While civil cases were tried by African *tribunaux de chefferies* and *tribunaux de secteurs*, there was appeal from these courts to the *tribunaux de territoire*, composed of African chiefs as judges, but presided over by the Belgian *administrateur de territoire*. As police magistrate the *administrateur de territoire* could try all cases for which the maximum penalty was not more than two months' imprisonment. All offences of a more serious nature committed by Africans came before the District Commissioner's court, which served also as the court of appeal for the territorial courts. From the District Courts there was appeal to the professionally staffed Tribunals of First Instance. While allowing chiefs some function in the administration of civil law and some related criminal offences, the administrator had much greater legal powers than did the chief.

In British Africa the legal powers of administrators varied widely from territory to territory. Kenya and northern Nigeria present two extremes. In both systems the administrator was a magistrate and had supervisory powers over the administration of 'native' justice. In Kenya, however, native courts, which as we have seen were not chiefs' courts, could try only cases not involving sentences of more than six months, with the right of appeal in all cases, whereas in northern Nigeria the emirs' courts were empowered to try some cases for which there was no right of appeal. The emirs' courts themselves acted as courts of appeal from the subordinate Alkali courts. In Kenya the district commissioner acted as magistrate for preliminary inquiry into serious charges such as murder, rape and arson, and as judge in all other cases not dealt with by native courts. As far as the native courts were concerned, he had to confirm sentences of six months and acted as a court of appeal for all judgements made in them. He inspected their records; and even where no appeal was made to him, could on his own initiative order a retrial in his own court.

In the larger Nigerian emirates, as already noted, grave offences, including those involving the death sentence, came before the emirs' courts and were tried in accordance with the *sharia*. Death sentences had to be confirmed by the Chief Commissioner. Indeed, such was the confidence placed by the British in the judicial processes of the large emirates that it was seriously mooted in the 1920s that Europeans and Lebanese be subject to the Alkali's, rather than to British courts.

Up until 1933 the residents of the northern provinces presided as judges of the provincial courts, which had powers in cases not scheduled as coming within the province of the customary courts. In the northern emirates nearly all cases concerning 'natives', whether indigenous to the emirate or immigrants, came under the purview of the Alkali courts. Control of these courts was indirect: the colonial administration confirmed appointments, inspected the courts and reviewed cases. Where they were dissatisfied, they could transfer a case to the provincial court, or suspend sentences. They had no right to reverse a decision, only to order a retrial, in the provincial courts, of the case concerned. After the abolition of the provincial courts in 1933, the administrators retained their right to review cases, but were divested of their judicial role, since magistrates' courts now replaced the provincial courts, which had come in for considerable criticism on the grounds that their judges combined executive with judicial functions. Under the new system there was usually appeal from the customary to the British courts. However, in certain instances the final court of appeal for the African was still the emir's court. Thus an African arraigned before the district court could appeal against conviction to the Chief Alkali's court. From there he could appeal to the emir's court, which in this instance was designated a final court of appeal.[9] Thus in the emirates of Northern Nigeria the emirs enjoyed judicial powers unparalleled in any other African colony. Correspondingly, the British administrators there, after the abolition of the provincial courts, enjoyed more limited judicial powers than any of their counterparts in other colonies.

SOCIO-ECONOMIC ROLES OF THE BUSH ADMINISTRATOR

By far the most important role played by the administrators of the four colonial powers was that of the tax-collector. In all five territories under consideration Africans were taxed directly by the colonial administration through the intermediary of the chiefs. However, in parts of Nigeria Africans were not taxed until the late 1920s; and in the neighbouring British colony of the Gold Coast direct tax was not generally introduced until after the Second World War.

Taxation was vital to the colonial economy not only in raising revenue to pay for the cost of the colonial administration, but also for raising funds for development projects such as roads, railways and ports which would contribute directly to the expansion of trade. In those days the mother country gave very little financial assistance to the colonies. Individual British territories did, in fact, sometimes receive small grants-in-aid of local revenue, loans-in-aid, or interest-free loans. The British also gave a little help under the provisions of the Colonial Development Act of 1929. In addition, the British Treasury accepted a contingent liability by guaranteeing colonial loans, thus enabling the colonies to borrow on conditions more favourable than they might otherwise have secured on the London money market. The British also subsidised some colonial research.

But the modern concept of aid by the mother country to its dependencies was not accepted. Development was largely financed in one of two ways: by revenues raised either from direct or from indirect taxation, or by loans subscribed to by investors overseas. Direct taxation was never as important a source of revenue as indirect taxation on exports and imports. Direct taxation nevertheless forced Africans to grow crops for sale so that they could earn cash with which to pay their taxes. This was also a means of forcing Africans to seek work on the farms of white settlers or in mining industries. Thus, as a supervisor of the collection of taxes from the Africans, the white administrator not only contributed significantly to the expansion of the economy, but also had considerable impact on the taxpayers themselves. In French West Africa, for example, taxation compelled peoples from densely populated, non cash-crop growing areas of French Sudan and Upper Volta to seek work on the groundnut fields of Senegal and on the cocoa farms of the Ivory Coast. Many Mossi from Upper Volta preferred to earn their tax-money in the mines and cocoa farms of the Gold Coast, where remuneration was higher than in the Ivory Coast. Because most colonial administrators believed that all men had a moral obligation to work, direct taxation was one way of forcing them to do so.

A second method of gaining the same end was compulsory labour. In all five territories maintenance of local roads was effected through obligatory work enforced by the chiefs and supervised by the administrative officers. In Nigeria, after 1933, with the passage of the Forced Labour Ordinance the use of compulsory labour outside the Native

Authorities was forbidden, except in special circumstances; such a case apparently arose only once — during the Second World War. However, before the passage of this act administrative officers had conscripted labour for use on railway construction and other public works projects. In Kenya, when voluntary labour was not available, administrative officers could, with the authorisation of the governor, conscript labour for public works projects or porterage, though a limit of sixty days per man per annum was imposed.

In the Belgian Congo, with its legacy of excessive use of forced labour in the Free State, the question of compulsory labour was a sensitive one. As in Nigeria, inasmuch as the bulk of forced labour for public works projects was conscripted by the Native Authorities, the administrator was relieved of the necessity to intervene directly in its recruitment or use. Native Authorities maintained roads, built schools and rest-houses with such labour. Belgian administrators limited their demands largely to compulsory recruitment of porters and canoe-paddlers. There was no law permitting the use of forced labour on public works projects.

In Angola, compulsory labour was required of any African who had no apparent occupation. The moral obligation to work was written into law. Administrators could conscript labour for public works projects, in particular roads, within the areas administered by their *regulos*. In addition, they could use such labour on public works projects outside the area from which it was drawn. The Portuguese administrator thus was responsible for the miserable situation of the African in Angola, which outside visitors called variously a 'modern slavery' or 'serfdom'. It happened often that, because of the demands of the Portuguese for compulsory labour, villagers were unable to cultivate adequate crops to feed themselves.

In French West Africa all non-assimilated Africans had to undertake twelve days' labour for the administration, which they could redeem at one to three francs per day. In addition, administrative officers could recruit workmen for public works projects in return for payment. The most common use of such labour was on the construction and maintenance of roads and on large projects in areas where hands were scarce, as on certain stages of the construction of railways. In addition, Africans were conscripted into the army. The most massive 'compulsory recruitment' took place during World War I when France hoped, but was quite unable, to raise a black army of a million men.

In addition to drafting labour for government undertakings, administrators in some of the colonies acted as recruiting agents for white farmers, for European commercial companies and for mining industries. This practice was most flagrant in Portuguese territories.

Until 1921 it was carried on openly and quite legally. But in that year a decree was issued abolishing forced labour by private firms or individuals. Actually, however, the practice continued, if not always with the assistance of the administrators, at least with a blind eye turned towards the activities of the recruiters. In French West Africa, as distinct from Equatorial Africa, where there were large concession companies, the French administration undertook little recruiting of labour for private enterprise. The main example of compulsory recruitment of this kind was in the Ivory Coast on the European cocoa and coffee farms. Significantly, however, a number of rich African cocoa-farmers had access to this labour supply. These African growers complained bitterly at the discriminatory practices of the Free French administration during the Second World War in cutting off their supply of such labour and not that of the European farmers.[10]

In the Belgian Congo one of the legacies of the Free State was the administration's policy of supplying labour for European commercial enterprises. However, in 1926 administrators were forbidden to assist in the recruitment of labour for European companies. They were directed also to ensure that chiefs did not force their subjects to serve these companies. They were, however, permitted to use every legal means to persuade Africans to work for them. In practice, they continued to assist in such recruitment, which continued in many instances to be forced, though the responsibility lay with the chief rather than with the administrator himself. In 1931 the Colonial Minister announced that 'members of the territorial service had been forbidden to accompany the recruiting agents of private employers on their rounds'.[11]

In Nigeria, with one notable exception, British administrators never recruited labour for private enterprise. However, in the Second World War, when Britain was cut off from her Far Eastern tin supplies by the Japanese occupation of Malaya, increased production of tin in the Jos plateau became an imperative. To achieve this, forced labour for the private tin-mining companies was recruited by the administration.[12]

In Kenya, by contrast, European officials did assist in recruitment of labour, and by the notorious Labour Circular No. 1 of 1919 were instructed to use 'every possible lawful influence' to assist European farmers in obtaining African manpower. This policy was reversed in the early 1920s, when the British laid down that the administration had no formal obligation to recruit for European farmers and that as private entrepreneurs the settlers should take their chance on the labour market without public assistance. This was, however, provided indirectly, in that taxation of Africans in unproductive parts of the reserves forced them to seek labour on the European farms. Through compulsory labour, whether for public works projects or in private enterprise, European administrators were responsible not only for redistributing large numbers of African workers, but for causing much hardship and suffering in many instances both to those conscripted and to their families. This was particularly true of Angola.

In French West Africa and the Belgian Congo the administrator had the duty of forcing the African, where necessary, to cultivate certain crops. In French West Africa administrators in certain regions had *champs administratifs* on which the African peasant had to work without pay. In the Belgian Congo the administrator could compel Africans to produce crops for internal consumption or for export where he considered this necessary. In Kenya, however, the administrator found himself for a time in the reverse role. He had to prevent Africans in the reserves from cultivating coffee in competition with the white farmers on the grounds that African plantations would spread disease.[13]

Such were the principal economic functions of the local administrator, and each of them affected the social pattern of the local population in its own way. These functions increased, of course, as technical services were co-ordinated by the administrator, as in French and Portuguese Africa, where there were no African 'native authorities' or local government councils responsible for local development.

CONCLUSION

The bush administrators formed one of the few groups of Europeans who really knew anything about Africans. Sir Charles Temple draws a vivid picture of the ignorance of African life that existed in Northern Nigeria among the departmental officers of 'the Secretariat, Treasury or any and all the technical departments':

> In the morning he is called and fed by native boys who are nearly always out of touch with their own people. He goes to work, which is done with pens, ink and paper, or possibly with various tools: in the course of work he may come into contact with a few native clerks in European clothes or with skilled native artisans, a special class entirely out of touch with the natives generally. He is fed at midday and returns to his work. In the evenings he takes his exercise for the sake of his health with other Europeans. He is fed again and goes to bed. This he does for 365 days and then gets on a steamer and goes home. He spends his leave recruiting his health, occupying his mind on matters as little connected with official duties as possible. This goes on for eighteen years. He retires.

Temple concluded:

> It is a point not to be lost sight of that few Europeans working in a native Protectorate are in a position to learn anything about the native population, even though they may spend a lifetime there.[14]

Temple's picture, drawn in 1918, was substantially true for all five colonies under consideration in the inter-war years. Even though the bush administrator could claim to know more about his subjects than any other European except the missionary, whose understanding was nevertheless usually distorted by the special optic with which he regarded Africans, he never had that intimate knowledge which gave African chiefs such great control over their subjects. Administrators relied for their information, especially where they did not understand the local language, or interpreters, on court messengers, on sepoys, on *gardes de cercles*. But these invariably exploited the administrator's ignorance, each to his own advantage, accepting bribes from Africans who wished them to intercede with the administrator on their behalf or threatening with exposure chiefs who had something to hide if they did not pay them what they requested. It was in the interest of this group of intermediaries to keep the truth from their employers. The stock-in-trade joke of the white administrator telling the people one thing, and the interpreter deliberately translating it to mean something different, was not far from everyday reality. Given these obstacles, it is surprising how much some of the white chiefs did manage to find out about their subjects, as evidenced by their notebooks, the records and 'anthropological' studies.

From the imperial point of view, the bush administrators were the key officials of the colonial régime. In many cases the European district officers and their wives also served as models or as a reference group in matters of dress, etiquette and behaviour to aspiring middle-class Africans, often with sad results. In French West Africa, the Belgian Congo, Kenya and Nigeria they were the last group of officials to be replaced by Africans. Yet with independence they were swept away. Their posts were either filled by Africans or neutralised or abolished altogether. While Europeans continued after independence as permanent secretaries of ministries or as senior officials in the central administration and technical services of government, African governments would not permit the survival of those Europeans — the bush administrators — who most clearly represented the colonial days. Yet in the final analysis these administrators, despite their intimate relationship with the Africans, left a far weaker imprint on the local population than that of the representatives of commercial companies and technical departments of government, whose demands and development schemes substantially changed African life.

Nor did the white administrator exert the personal impact on the individual African equal to that of even the missionary or the teacher. The primary concern of the European chief was with the traditional Africa of the bush; the Africans who were to take over control of the bush from him represented the forces of westernisation and modernisation generated in the schools, the churches and the new urban agglomerations. The administrators tried to defend themselves and their role by dismissing such Africans, as did Sir Charles Temple, as being divorced from the peasants and therefore unfit to govern them. What surprised these administrators was not that these Africans took over power from them, but that they did in fact summon mass support from the peasants from whom they were supposed to be divorced. The white chiefs were replaced by a new class of African chiefs who had the advantage over them that despite all their apparent alienation from traditional Africa, they generally, though not always, knew their subjects. The new rulers were able to exploit this knowledge to form the mass parties that characterised the period of decolonisation and the years immediately following independence.

NOTES

1. Lord Hailey, *An African survey: a study of problems arising in Africa south of the Sahara* (London, 1938), p. 607.
2. Hailey, *An African survey* (1938), p. 231.
3. James Duffy, *Portuguese Africa* (Cambridge, Harvard University Press, 1959), p. 252.
4. Hailey, *An African survey* (1938), p. 387.
5. Kenneth Ingham, *A history of East Africa* (London, 1962), p. 309.
6. Address of Acting Governor to the Kenya Legislative Council, 1925, p. 15, cited in Hailey, *An African survey* (1938), p. 388.
7. Belgian Congo, *Bulletin Officiel*, 1933, p. 951, cited in Hailey, *An African survey* (1938), pp. 492-3.
8. See Lucy P. Mair, *Native policies in Africa* (London, 1936), p. 244.
9. See B. O. Nwabueze, *The machinery of justice in Nigeria* (London, 1968); and Elliot A. Keay and S. S. Richardson, *The native and customary courts in Nigeria* (London and Lagos, 1966).
10. Michael Crowder, *West Africa under colonial rule* (London, 1968), p. 497; F. J. Amon d'Aby, *La Côte d'Ivoire dans la cité africaine* (Paris, 1951); and Edward Mortimer, *France and the Africans* (New York, 1969).
11. Cited in Mair, *Native policies in Africa*, p. 235.
12. *The Times* (London), 18 June 1942.
13. Hailey, *An African survey* (1938), p. 386.
14. C. L. Temple, *Native races and their rulers: sketches and studies of official life and administrative problems in Nigeria*, 2nd ed. (London, 1968), p. 189.

BIBLIOGRAPHY

Amon d'Aby, F. J. *La Côte d'Ivoire dans la cité africaine.* Paris, 1951.
Brausch, Georges. *Belgian administration in the Congo.* London, Oxford University Press, 1961.
Buell, Raymond L. *The native problem in Africa.* 2nd ed. 2 vols. London, 1965.
Crowder, Michael. *West Africa under colonial rule.* London, 1968.
Crowder, Michael, and Obaro Ikime, eds. *West African chiefs: their changing status under colonial rule and independence.* Ife and New York, 1970.
Duffy, James. *Portuguese Africa.* Cambridge, Harvard University Press, 1959.
Hailey, William Malcolm, 1st baron. *An African survey: a study of the problems arising in Africa south of the Sahara.* London, Oxford University Press, 1938.
An African Survey: revised 1956. London, 1957.
Ingham, Kenneth. *A history of East Africa.* London, 1962.
Keay, Elliot Alexander, and S. S. Richardson. *The native and customary courts in Nigeria.* London and Lagos, 1966.
Mair, Lucy P. *Native policies in Africa.* London, 1936.
Mortimer, Edward. *France and the Africans, 1944-1960: a political history.* London, 1969.
Mumford, William Bryant, and G. St. J. Orde-Brown. *Africans learn to be French: a review of educational activities in the seven federated colonies of French West Africa based on a tour of French West Africa and Algiers undertaken in 1935.* London, 1937.
Nwabueze, B. O. *The machinery of justice in Nigeria.* London, 1968.
Perham, Margery. *Native administration in Nigeria.* London, Oxford University Press, 1936.
Temple, C. L. *Native races and their rulers: sketches and studies of official life and administrative problems in Nigeria.* 2nd ed. London, 1968.

VII

THE IMPOSITION OF THE NATIVE AUTHORITY SYSTEM IN BUSSA: THE REBELLION OF 1915*
(1974)

... this supplies an example of one of the most inept pieces of mismanagement of native affairs that I remember to have encountered in Nigeria. The sacrifice of native institutions, desires, tribal sentiments, traditions and customs to the mere administrative convenience of the Government and its officers can hardly ever have been carried out with more cynical indifference and ineptitude.
His Excellency Sir Hugh Clifford, Governor of Nigeria, 1924[1]

In 1915 the British deposed Kitoro Gani, Sarkin Bussa, and completely reorganised native administration in the Borgu Division of Kontagora Province, Northern Nigeria, of which Bussa was part. That same year, in June 1915, Sabukki, younger brother of the deposed Kitoro Gani, led some six hundred armed men in an attack on Bussa in which several members of the newly British-imposed Native Administration were killed.[2] A patrol was sent out to suppress the rebels and succeeded in dispersing them although their leader, Sabukki, was never caught. For the next five months an uneasy calm reigned in Bussa, giving way to a second smaller rising in December 1915. Again a patrol was sent out, and though it established order in Bussa once and for all, it remained difficult to govern until the restoration of its rightful ruler, Kitoro Gani, in November 1924.

The basic cause of the rebellion of 1915 by a people who had accepted British colonial rule taciturnly enough was the imposition of the Northern Nigerian Native Authority system on Bussa and the deposition of its ruler, Kitoro Gani, as being, from the British point of

*This paper was presented at a meeting of the Seminar on the History of the Peoples of the Niger-Beuve Valleys sponsored by the two history departments of Ahmadu Bello University at Ilorin in March 1974.

view, incapable of ruling his people under such a system. The particular form in which the Native Authority system was introduced, apart from the fact that it was incompatible with the pre-colonial conception of Kingship in Bussa, only served to exacerbate hostility to these reforms. Bussa was not made a separate Native Authority but rather its status as an emirate was abolished and it was subjected to its pre-colonial enemy, Yauri, which in turn had its ruling dynasty replaced by an alien Fulani adventurer.

The Native Authority system originally devised for local government in the Fulani-Hausa emirates rested on a number of assumptions the most important of which, for our purposes, were: the presence of an effective executive chief, possessing a considerable degree of centralised power: the regular collection of taxes; the regularisation of the expenditure of these taxes through a Native Treasury; the residence of the District Heads in their districts, rather than in the capital. This system, imposed on Bussa between 1912 and 1915, coupled with the ineptness (and often lack) of the British administration in Borgu during the first decade of colonial rule in the area, sparked off the rebellion of 1915. Fully to understand the violence of the reaction of the people of Bussa to the administrative reforms of 1912-1915, however, account must be taken of the pre-colonial structure of Nigerian Borgu.

PRE-COLONIAL BORGU

Before its partition by the British and French at the end of the nineteenth century, Borgu comprised a series of related, but effectively independent states, linked by the common descent of their rulers from Kisra. Traditions of the arrival of Kisra, who is said to have migrated with his followers from the East through Borno, vary both within the individual states of Borgu and from state to state. What is clear from these traditions is that, although by the nineteenth century Nikki had, in terms of population and territory, become the most powerful of the Borgu states, Bussa, though the weakest among them, was acknowledged as senior among them because it was the first of the Borgu states founded as a result of the Kisra migration. While Nikki was independent of Bussa, the link of common ancestry could unite them in times of threat of external aggression.

The political system of pre-colonial Borgu was characterised by the fissiparous tendencies of all the units of which it was comprised, so that it is very difficult at any one time to say whether particular states came under the effective control of either Bussa or Nikki. Thus the rulers of the outlying provinces of Nikki were to all intents and purposes independent and only owed Nikki obligation in times of war with outsiders. This was exactly the obligation of Nikki to Bussa.[3] It is in this sense that Nikki can be said to have been in any way politically dependent on Bussa. And it is in this sense only that Bussa can claim to have had overlordship of Borgu in political terms. In spiritual terms, however, the overlordship was much stronger. Bussa was revered as the senior Kisra foundation. A new King of Nikki sent presents to Bussa, who sent a representative to install him together with two horses, which by tradition were the first horses he should ride in his reign. Other traditions emphasise the primacy of Bussa: the tradition that Bussa sent presents to the Mai of Borno and in return received camels, horses and suits of cloth which he then divided among the rulers of Nikki, Illo and Oyo;[4] the fact that Bussa kept the Gangan Kisra (the Kisra Big Drum) and the Kisra Kettle-drums[5] as well as having more state trumpets than other Borgu states — fourteen as distinct from Nikki's twelve.[6]

In political terms at the end of the nineteenth century Bussa could claim hegemony of a very loose sort only over Wawa, Illo, Kaoje and Rofia, Agwarra, and the eastern parts of Babanna, the western parts of which also looked towards Nikki — that is roughly those parts of Borgu which were placed administratively under its ruler at the beginning of British colonial rule. Nikki definitely had hegemony in pre-colonial days over the southwestern states of Nigerian Borgu: Yashikera, Okuta, Banara and Ilesha. The position of Kaiama is not very clear. It was a Nikki foundation dating from the late eighteenth century. By the end of the nineteenth century it was effectively independent of Nikki, which however still sent a representative to the installation of its kings. Tradition has it that in a succession dispute in Kaiama the matter was referred to Nikki and if he could not settle it, it was then referred to Bussa. Thus when Mura Bane De, 7th King of Kaiama, died in 1892, Mora Tasude, one of his brothers, realising he would not be chosen as King, because an elder brother had prior claim, went to the King of Bussa with a present of 100 calabashes of Kola nuts and the King of Bussa then sent a messenger to Kaiama to install Mora Tasude. Sarkin Nikki on hearing of Bussa's decision acquiesced in this action as did the people of Kaiama, even though the brother who would normally have succeeded had been passed over.[7] A possible explanation of Bussa's action is the fact that Mora Tasude had distinguished himself at the head of a contingent of Kaiama troops sent to assist Bussa in the Gebbe wars against rebellious Kamberri subjects of Bussa (see below). It is recorded by the present Emir of Borgu that the reigning Sarkin Bussa, Dantoro, rewarded Mora Tasude with a cap taken from his own head.[8]

Even where Bussa or Nikki hegemony was acknowledged by dependent states, their rulers often acted as if they were independent. This is explained largely by the system whereby the throne was filled on the death of a Sarkin Bussa or Nikki. In principle succession went from elder to younger brother and when the last of a line of brothers had reigned and died, not to his sons but to those of his immediate predecessor. In practice the throne was often contested by rival princes. In effect, then, the throne went to the strongest claimant among them. In Bussa, if the choice of the king-makers was disputed, rival claimants battled for possession of the sacred skin which the new king had to wear for a prescribed period. Unsuccessful princes would move to outlying districts or even live in exile awaiting another chance to take the throne. Sometimes a king would be attacked by a rival claimant after he had acceded to the throne as in the case of Dantoro's successor, Kisan Dogo, who was attacked by Kwara, a son of Dantoro's predecessor. The path to the throne was through both the hereditary principle and force. Where a succession in Nikki or Bussa was not disputed, this was because the kingmakers chose the candidate who was clearly the most powerful. The rulers of Bussa could not be deposed: only die or be killed in battle. There was no concept of permitting the exile of an incumbent monarch.[9]

In these circumstances the position of the monarchs of Bussa and Nikki was not a strong one. With little authority over their dependent rulers, and always subject to challenge by rival claimants. their control over their 'states' was in no way comparable to that of the Amir al-Mumunin over the Emirs of the Sokoto Caliphate. In the case of Bussa, both Wawa and Illo, which paid him tribute, in practice were autonomous. Even in those areas directly controlled by Bussa, the ruler was far from being an autocrat, having to govern through a state council.

The above description of the political structure of Borgu is designed to bring out those features that are necessary to an understanding of the events leading up to the rebellion. A further aspect of pre-colonial Borgu essential to the understanding of the revolt is the relationship of Bussa to its neighbour across the Niger, Yauri. Both Bussa and Yauri came under heavy pressure from the Fulani during the early years of the *jihad*. While Bussa retained its independence, Yauri had to accept protection from Gwandu, to which it paid *jizya*.

Until the accession of Abdullahi Abershi as Sarkin Yauri in 1888, Bussa and Yauri maintained good relations. The friendship of the two states culminated in the 1880s in the joint action of their *sarakuna*, Gallo of Yauri and Dantoro of Bussa, against the Kamberri of Gebbe Many Kamberri had migrated across the Niger from Yauri to Bussa because Gallo had been unable to afford them protection from slave-raiding by Ibrahim Nagwamatse, Sarkin Sudan of Kontagora.[10] Gallo was further hampered by civil war. The Kamberri settled on Bussa lands, in particular in the Kwanji, Agwarra and

Rofia areas. The Kamberri soon asserted their independence, raiding canoes of both Bussa and Yauri. Sarkin Bussa, Dantoro, led an expedition against them but had to call in Yauri forces to assist him. These combined forces were at first led by Dangaladima Abershi of Yauri who had to withdraw on succeeding Gallo as Sarkin Yauri. Dantoro, assisted by Mora Tasude of Kaiama, successfully completed the war and installed his administrator, Barje Bello, to govern the recently subdued districts. Abershi was, however, allowed to appoint the village heads of Kalkami and Kawara to serve under Barje Bello. Then, according to Bussa traditions, Abershi tried to drive out Barje Bello and re-assert Yauri control over its former Kamberri subjects, even though they were settled on Bussa land. But Yauri has it that Dantoro asked Abershi to rid him of Barje Bello who had overreached himself, but that the latter subsequently made his peace with Dantoro. As it was, Abershi was ultimately unsuccessful in his attempts to remove Barje Bello, who remained as Bussa's administrator up till his death in 1912. One version has it that the French buttressed up Barje Bello's position, another that the Emir of Gwandu called off Abershi, and his vassal Kontagora, who had joined forces with Abershi to remove Barje Bello. Whatever the facts of the matter, as far as Bussa and Yauri were concerned they were now bitter enemies with Yauri claiming that sovereignty resided in the origin of the people settled in the disputed area, while Bussa insisted that it consisted in ownership of the land. The British administration put an end to open hostility between the two: but if anything, as we shall see, it exacerbated their strained relations through consistent misunderstanding of the nature of the problem.

EARLY CIVILIAN ADMINISTRATION IN BORGU 1902-1912

In 1902, after a short period of West African Frontier Force administration, Borgu, which was a constituent province of Northern Nigeria, came under civilian rule. For administrative purposes the Province, some 12,000 miles square with a population of barely 40,000, was divided into two: Northern Borgu (Bussa) and Southern Borgu (Kaiama). The Sarki of Bussa was recognised as Paramount over Northern Borgu, and administered lands which, by and large, he could claim were his, were tributary to him or would accept his administration as the senior ruler of Borgu: Illo, Wawa, Babanna and Agwarra. Kaiama was recognised as paramount over Southern Borgu, even though Yashikera, Okuta, Banara and Ilesha had never been subordinate to him in pre-colonial times, but had been subordinate to Nikki.

In November 1903 Kisan Dogo, Sarkin Bussa, died, and on 19 December the Acting Resident, Lt. Stevens, summoned claimants to the throne together with their followers and king-makers to Kaiama and after hearing evidence from the last, installed Kitoro Gani as Sarkin Bussa. Officially his accession was not recognised until January 1904, since Lugard as High Commissioner, and not Stevens as Resident, alone had the right to approve the appointment of chiefs of this importance. Both Bussa and Kaiama were recognised as First Class Chiefs. In 1907 Borgu Province was amalgamated with the new Kontagora Province as Borgu District. At the same time Illo and other parts of north-western Borgu were excised from Bussa and handed over to Sokoto Province.[11] Despite Bussa's bitter resentment of this action, the history of the subsequent four years was an untroubled one.[12] In 1910 Assistant Resident de Putron was reporting 'The general attitude of the whole division remains, as before, eminently satisfactory'.[13] Yet in the first decade of civilian administration we can see sown and germinate the seeds of discontent which were to be fertilised by the disastrous administration of Mr. J. C. O. Clarke, who first took over Borgu Division in 1912 and introduced the Native Authority system into Bussa.

We shall not discuss the history of these years chronologically but seek to identify the origins of grievances that were ancillary to the revolt of 1915.

The appointment of Mora Tasude as Paramount over Southern Borgu gave deep offence not only to the Nikki dependencies of Yashikera, Okuta, Banara and Ilesha, but also to Bussa itself, which saw this relatively new kingdom, which traditionally had to acknowledge Bussa's seniority, raised to parity as a first class Emirate. Lt. Stevens had actually summoned the claimants to the vacant Bussa throne to Kaiama to settle the succession: even Lugard, who had elevated Mora Tasude to his present unprecedented position because of his services to him on the Nikki expedition, reprimanded Stevens for this: 'Quite wrong. You should have gone there not called in Bussa to Kaiama who is not his suzerain'.[14] In the case of the Nikki dependency of Yashikera, its ruler, Ojo, or Woru Yaru, refused to acknowledge Kaiama as his paramount and resigned his position and went to live in Nikki, to whose throne he was a claimant. He took with him half of the population of Yashikera.[15] Bussa's resentment of Kaiama's elevation had not abated by 1911 when Assistant Resident T. C. Newton wrote of the long-standing feud between the two Emirs and mentioned that if they met 'an open fight between their respective followers is always *sur le tapis*'.[16] The resentment of Bussa at what it considered the unnatural position of the Emir of Kaiama in the Borgu Division persisted through to 1955 when the Kaiama emirate was abolished and made a District of Bussa Emirate, which was restyled the Emirate of Borgu. It should be noted here that Kaiama did not accept this view of the relevant positions of the rulers of the ruler of Bussa and their own ruler.

The second major blow to the prestige of Sarkin Bussa was the decision of the British to hand Illo and the Fulani inhabited areas of northern Borgu to Sokoto province. The reason, 'curious enough I venture to think' wrote the Resident of Kontagora in 1910, 'was to compensate him (Sokoto) for the loss of lands he suffered from the last delimitation of the Anglo-French boundary'.[17] Bussa was thus deprived of its most populous land. While Illo had been under Fulani occupation for a short time in the nineteenth century, it retained its identity as a Borgu town and its ruler not only treated Bussa as a senior brother but was recorded as a tributary of Bussa at the beginning of the colonial period.[18] Macallister, Resident of Sokoto, recorded in 1909, after Illo had been integrated in his province, that Illo was never under Bussa but used to send presents, Bussa being head of the family.[19] We have already seen how difficult it is to ascertain the exact relationship between Bussa and Nikki on the one hand and their dependent states on the other. What is clear is that Illo owed allegiance at the beginning of colonial rule to Bussa and not to Sokoto. Certainly as far as Sarkin Bussa was concerned the loss of Illo was a 'very sore point indeed',[20] and was brought up frequently by him with British political officers.

From as early as 1902 the British political officers in Borgu reported disputes between Yauri and Bussa over land. These disputes centred over islands in the river, and land on Bussa's side of the river in which Yelwa subjects were settling. In 1902 Kitoro Gani's predecessor had complained that Yauri was collecting 1/- tax a head from villages in his District.[21] By 1910 a large number of Yelwa subjects had crossed over to Bussa land, in particular Kunji, to farm, attracted in part by the better land, in part by the fact that the incidence of taxation there was 1/- as compared with 2/2d in Yelwa.[22] The Emir of Yauri accused Bussa of enticing his subjects to settle in his land. At one stage the idea of transferring Kunji to direct administration by the District Officer at Yelwa was mooted but was rejected by Assistant Resident de Putron in 1910 both because of the trouble it would cause with Sarkin Bussa and because Sarkin Kunji would become unmanageable under the Emir of Yauri, who was unpopular.[23] The root of the dispute was both historical, as we have seen, and a result of the fact that under the British system of local administration in the Northern Provinces, regular taxation provided the main income for the Emir's administration, so that the more people you controlled the more revenue you had at your disposal. Up until the arrival of Mr. J. C. O. Clarke at Yelwa the dispute between Yauri and Bussa continued to fester despite an apparent reconciliation between them at Kontagora on the occasion of the Coronation Celebrations for King George V.[24] As far as the British were concerned the central problem of early administration in Bussa was Kitoro Gani. Northern Borgu covered a vast area and for most of the first decade there was only one political officer in the whole of Borgu. And then he was often either sick or desk-bound. Thus from the point of view of the administration of Bussa Emirate a great deal depended on the effectiveness of Kitoro Gani. While nearly all the reports on him confirm his pleasant and co-operative disposition and his willingness 'to do what he is told',[25] his actual capacity for carrying out the instructions or requests of the administration was from the British point of view limited. This was usually attributed by the administration to his lack of self-reliance, inefficiency, incompetence and, increasingly after 1905, to his addiction to *gia*, an addiction so pronounced that it is remembered in Bussa to this day. Fergus Dwyer, Acting Resident of Borgu wrote in 1907 that Bussa was 'quietly drinking himself to death'.[26] In 1912 Mr. Boyd, the Resident of Kontagora reported on Bussa's 'overwhelming weakness for *gia*'.[27] Indeed in 1907 Fergus Dwyer had actually mooted the deposition of Kitoro Gani for drunkenness.[28] Apparently Bussa had on several occasions been warned that he would be deposed if he did not stop drinking, and on one occasion his deposition was actually sanctioned on these grounds.[29]

The majority of political officers, however, held the view that bad as Kitoro Gani was, there was no-one much better to replace him. A more sophisticated understanding of the problem Sarkin Bussa had in administering his lands under the Northern Nigerian system of indirect rule was shown by Assistant Resident T. C. Newton when he wrote in 1911: 'The ties between the Emirs of Bussa and their people have always been weak compared to the strong Fulani methods in vogue everywhere. Laissez-faire seems to have been their ruling policy, and this naturally did not tend to strengthen the character of a naturally weak man like the present Emir, nor to produce a strong and capable set of Kofas and other men in the Emir's suite'.[30] Bussa himself was unfamiliar with most of his territory, residing most of the time in his capital, where he kept his *kofas* rather than have them reside in the lands they were supposed to govern. His control over subordinate rulers like Kunji and Wawa was slender and the difficulties he encountered in carrying out what the colonial authorities would consider effective administration is clear from his failure to obtain the requisite number of men for labour on the railways. Indeed the inhabitants of the Western part of his territory frankly told him that they would migrate to French territory if they were pressed, all of which showed how weak his hold was on the people of his western lands which still looked more to Nikki than Bussa.[31]

THE IMPOSITION OF THE NATIVE AUTHORITY SYSTEM IN BUSSA 159

In the circumstances many political officers, like Mr. Houlgate, were forced to fall back on direct rule: 'The administrative work has been wholly dependent upon myself and staff, indeed to such an extent that if the Emirate of Bussa was done away with, I should be better off, as at present issuing orders through the Emir is only to cause delay and I generally have to take the matter in hand myself'.[32]

The problem of ruling Bussa directly was that there was often only one officer administering the whole of Borgu, and, after 1912, frequently none at all. In 1911, when the Acting Governor of Northern Nigeria complained that all the tribute for Borgu was not in by 31st March, Assistant Resident Newton remarked sourly to his Resident: 'Did His Excellency know that I had no Police at Boussa from March 7th. I imagine in no other Province are there 2 totally distinct Emirates looked after by one official'.[33] In short the Borgu political system did not give Kitoro Gani the authority to rule on a neo-Fulani model, even if he had had the inclination. This is clear from the example of Mora Tasude, Emir of Kaiama, whose 'efficient' and strong-arm methods had led to emigration of many of his subjects to French Borgu.[34] Conversely the British had neither the political officers nor the police, nor even the knowledge of the people, to rule Borgu directly. Nevertheless, this was what Mr. J. C. O. Clarke attempted to do soon after he was appointed in charge of Bussa.

THE COMPOUNDING OF ERRORS

For most of the crucial period of three years leading up to the rebellion, Bussa and Kaiama were administered from Yelwa owing to shortage of political staff in Kontagora Province. During these three years Mr. J. C. O. Clarke was stationed at Yelwa except for short spells on leave. He had joined the colonial service in 1905 from the Navy. In 1908 his confidential report described him as possessing 'strength of character, great energy, and perhaps the over-zealousness of youth'.[35] After a quarrel in 1908 with a Mr. Corey, the High Commissioner expressed the hope that he would endeavour to show greater tact in his dealings with 'both Europeans and natives'. As a result he was posted from Niger Province though in 1912 he was recommended for promotion. By 1914, Hamilton-Browne, his Resident, wrote: 'Most tactful with Europeans and Clerks. Not popular with all the natives, but this is due to his thorough knowledge of their ways. Mr. Clarke is in my opinion an exceedingly clever political officer. He is untiring in his energy. He has done excellent work in Yauri Division'.[36] Hamilton-Browne, or 'Hammy' as he was known to his political officers,[37] also believed he himself 'knew the natives' and in particular those of Kontagora Province. The combination of these two men who believed they understood the peoples they were administering, was to prove disastrous. The actions which Clarke was to take in the next two years in Yauri, Bussa and Kaiama and his plans for their administrative reorganisation, had the full, largely uncritical support of Hamilton-Browne. The situation confronting Clarke on 31 December 1912 when he became political officer in charge of the three emirates was a difficult one. In Bussa, Kitoro Gani had already proved himself a weak agent of British rule. In Kaiama, Mora Tasude, the strong-arm Emir, had just died and had been succeeded by Jimi, who did not have his predecessor's strength of character. In Yashikera the Sarki had been deposed and replaced by Mashi, an old soldier who was not a native of Borgu but a Zabermawa. In Yauri itself, the Emir was not very popular and certainly not very effective as far as the British were concerned. Here, Clarke had already been an administrative officer and had identified what he considered able administrators, among them, Aliu of Yabo, a Fulani immigrant to Yauri, who was appointed Tukura by the Emir of Yauri and subsequently became Sarkin Yamma.[38] In his report for the first quarter of 1913, Clarke indicated the line of action he proposed pursuing in Borgu. Despairing of the incumbent chiefs of Bussa as 'incapable of ruling', he wrote 'probably when I know the District better, comparatively capable men will be found and employed as was done in the case of Yauri division'.[39] At this early stage he also indicated his attitude with regard to the land dispute between Bussa and Yauri. His solution to stranger farming was to keep the *talakawa* under their own *sarakuna*[40] and by June he was suggesting Kunji should be placed under Yauri and that Bussa land on the right bank of the Niger should be annexed to Yauri because Yauri farmers were using it.[41] These ideas had the sympathies of Hamilton-Browne who favoured the creation of an artificial boundary between Bussa and Yauri to include Yauri farmers across the river in Yauri emirate, rather than using the natural boundary of the river.[42]

In 1913 the British administration, with Clarke as its agent, took the major step of introducing the full-scale Native Authority system as developed in the Fulani-Hausa emirates into Bussa. The Emirate, as it was designated though Kitoro Gani was not a Muslim, was internally reorganised into a series of districts under district heads to replace the old Kofa system about which the British so frequently complained. Metropolitan Bussa and nearby towns were designated as Bussa District and were administered by Turaki, 'who also acts as chief adviser to the Emir'.[43] The other districts, each with their district head, who was either an hereditary chief, or an appointee of Bussa, were Wawa and Kunji which came in the first category, and Agwarra, West Bussa and Leaba, which came in the second category. The main objective of the administrative reforms, apart from bringing the 'emirate' of Bussa into line with those of the dismembered Sokot Caliphate, was to streamline administration, in particular tax collection.

Clarke was not altogether unsympathetic to the position of Kitoro Gani as head of the Bussa Native Authority, for he suggested in December 1913 that Bussa should share taxes with the Central Government on a 50%-50% basis rather than 37½%-62½% because £240 a year was quite inadequate for him to maintain his position and meet the numerous demands upon his purse without running into debt'.[44] Whatever sympathy he might have had had dissipated with the agitation in 1913 against payment of tax for which Clarke believed Kitoro Gani was partly responsible. Indeed his half-brother, Sabukki, was arrested for his part in the disturbances and jailed by the Emir though he managed to escape with, Clarke believed, the connivance of the Emir and the Alkali. Exasperated with affairs in Bussa, worried about the continued tax agitation in West Bussa, Clarke requested a Patrol.[45] To this the Acting Resident, Fergus Dwyer, who came to have little time for Clarke, replied 'not necessary', evoking the response from Clarke 'I have studied the question and I know when a firm attitude is necessary'.[46]

While the question of the patrol was being argued back and forth, Sarkin Bussa installed the new Sarkin Kunji, thus demonstrating Kunji's continued integration in Borgu despite Clarke and Hamilton-Browne's thesis that Kunji was really part of Yauri. During the first quarter of 1914, Clarke felt Bussa was being administered satisfactorily, despite the fact that Sabukki had escaped from Bussa jail. He reported also that he was suspicious that the Emir's brothers and relatives were acting against the District Heads.

Dwyer took over temporarily from Clarke when he went on leave and reported further that Sarkin Bussa was finding it difficult to get compliance with his instructions from the outlying districts. Dwyer lectured Bussa on the subject of his own conduct and 'explained to him that while he was giving in to his attacks of drunkenness that the Talakawa would only despise him and refuse to obey him'. He also discussed the question of Yaurawa farming Bussa land. The Emir replied by complaining to Dwyer that Illo, Kaoje and Lafagu had been taken from him. Now he was losing all the rest.[47]

Clarke on his return again emphasised the need for a patrol of Borgu to bring the peasants to heel. 'On my arrival in November', he reported, 'no progress had been made in the collection of tribute – the Sarakuna informed me that the people had intimated their intention of not paying until after the harvest. I visited some of the more difficult towns and assisted the native administration but in West Borgu little can be done until I get the escort . . .'[48]

In January 1915, despite the exigencies of the War, permission was at last given to send out a patrol as a result of reports that the *sarakuna* of Kaiama and West Bussa had been driven out of their districts and no collection of revenue had been made.[49]

On the patrol Clarke deposed the *sarakuna* of Ilesha, Banara and Okuta and replaced them with those he felt most capable.[50] Not one of these chiefs were brought to trial before or after they were deposed. The mass deposition of the district heads of Kaiama Emirate was followed by the request for the deposition of the Emir of Kaiama himself and his replacement by Mashi, Sarkin Yashikera, as Acting Emir, despite the fact that he had no claim to the *sarauta* of Kaiama.[51] Hamilton-Browne recommended Mashi because 'the Borgawa are an indolent drink-sodden people and need a strong man to rule over them'.[52]

These actions in Southern Borgu coincided with a larger scheme put up by Hamilton-Browne, very much on the advice of Clarke, for a reorganisation of Western Kontagora. The proposal was designed in their eyes to solve at one blow the inefficiency of the incumbent administrations of Yauri and Borgu *and* the land problem.

Briefly the proposal was that Borgu and Yauri should be amalgamated. The Emirs of Kaiama and Bussa should be deposed while the Emir of Yauri should be retired. The new administrative unit, to be known as Greater Yauri, would be placed under Aliu, Sarkin Yamma, who would now become Sarki of a Greater Yauri. Bussa's various districts would become districts of Yauri, thus solving the problem of disputed lands such as Kunji as well as the question as to whom its farmers would pay tribute. Now all would pay tribute to Aliu, even though he was not related to the ruling families of Yauri or Borgu. Hamilton-Browne, however, argued that 'as in the case of the present Emir of Katsina, Sar. Yamma is possessed of sufficient tact to overcome jealousy in the first two years of his reign'.[53] The time was ripe, Hamilton-Browne argued, to effect this change with the Patrol still in the area. As far as Bussa Emirate was concerned, he argued, Turaki, District Head of Bussa, Aliyara, District Head of West Bussa and Sarkin Kunji, all supported Aliu. Incredibly, Hamilton-Browne further asserted that the *talakawa* of both Bussa and Yauri would support Aliu. As far as Kaiama was concerned, Sarkin Yashikera, Mashi, could become Sarkin Kaiama and run the Emirate under the suzerainty of Yauri. In short Yauri would become a monster emirate with all its key rulers non-natives. The Paramount would be Aliu, from Sokoto; the District Head of Bussa would be Turaki, a slave; the District Head of West Bussa, would be Aliyara, a Lopawa; the District Head of South Bussa would become Ajia Umoru, a Nupe; and the District Head of Kaiama (a sub-paramount), Mashi, a Zaberma ex-soldier. Hamilton-Browne made no bones about this: 'The scheme put forward would bring the three Emirates under the control of picked men who owe their position to us and whose interests are identical with ours and who therefore would be loyal to us'.[54]

On 23 March the Acting Lieutenant Governor of the Northern Provinces followed Hamilton-Browne's suggestions, and recommended deposition of the Emirs of Kaiama and Bussa and the amalgamation of Yauri and Bussa. Kaiama was to be maintained for the time as a separate unit, although under Mashi, Sarkin Yashikera as Acting Emir. Sarkin Yauri was not to be retired, but since he was incapacitated, Aliu should act for him as Wakil.

Lugard on 30 March enquired whether 'Yauri-Bussa' would not be too large for one chief to administer. To this Hamilton-Browne replied that he felt confident that Sarkin Yamma could administer it effectively and that the amalgamation, by eliminating the friction which had existed for so long would point the way for more efficient administration.[55]

As a result of Clarke's and Hamilton-Browne's recommendations these sweeping administrative changes were sanctioned, and Yauri with Bussa Emirate was placed under Aliu. Bussa was deposed and Turaki, his slave adviser, ruled as District Head of Bussa taking his orders from Aliu, Sarkin Yamma, assisted by Abba, his political agent, about whom the records tell very little, but who is considered in Bussa to have been a prime instigator of the break-up of Bussa.

THE REVOLT

'This outbreak has come as a surprise to me', Goldsmith, the Acting Lieutenant Governor of the Northern Provinces wrote in a minute to his Secretary. 'Early in the year the Resident received approval for a military patrol which escorted the Political Officer and toured the District for a month. The Resident then reported the district as quiet and no mention as far as I can remember was made of Sabukki or his intriguing. No sooner have the troops left the Province than the Resident reports the return of Sabukki and serious fighting. From the Resident's telegram dated 1.7.15 he states that "this rising is not of recent growth but has been fomented for years". If this is so Res. Kontagora appears to have been kept in ignorance of what is going on in his Province? I do not remember any report being received in Headquarters which hinted at Sabukki's (illegible) or attached any importance to the influence he exercises in the Bussa district as likely to lead to serious trouble'.[56]

Despite Hamilton-Browne's subsequent wisdom of hindsight, the rebellion led by Sabukki took both himself and Clarke, with whom he was staying at Yelwa at the time, by surprise. Indeed the date of the rebellion is not absolutely certain, though it was probably 14 June.[57] The first they heard of it was on 16 June when survivors of the massacre reached Yelwa. We shall not be concerned here with the revolt in detail. In brief the fugitive Sabukki led an army of between 500-700 men armed with bows and poisoned arrows, and occupied Bussa. Prior to his attack, according to the present Emir, he was met by a mission from Turaki, to whom he gave the following conditions for peace:

(1) That Turaki should give up the District Headship of Bussa.
(2) That Turaki, Aliyara, District Head of West Bussa, and Ajia, District Head of South Bussa, should leave Bussa.
(3) That the exiled Emir should be reinstated, or else another member of the royal family should be appointed to the Sarauta.

These conditions were refused and at Bussa an ill-prepared Native Administration was assembled to face Sabukki's forces, having sworn on a *Tsafi* to support Turaki. Among them was the Kiwotede, or heir apparent, Kijibrim, a brother of the deposed Sarkin Bussa. The rebels, a party of whom led by Liangabba had already killed some members of the Native Administration at Shagunu including tax-collectors, took Bussa and killed more members of the Native Administration, though Turaki and two other District Heads of West Bussa (Aliyara) and South Bussa (Leaba) escaped. They were pursued by Sabukki's men and only Turaki survived, making his way to Zungeru.

Bussa and its immediately surrounding towns were under Sabukki's control. Wawa, which according to the British administration came out against Sabukki, in fact sympathised with the rebels because of the resentment of its chief and people at being placed under Ajia Umaru as District Head. In Kaiama it was 'half for and half against'.[58]

On hearing the news of the rebellion, Hamilton-Browne immediately cabled headquarters in Zungeru that he was sending Clarke to Bussa to find out what was happening and that he was calling up the detachment of the WAFF stationed at Zuru to join with him. He was reminded by the Secretary of the Northern Provinces that it was wartime and that 'troops cannot be spared to settle local disturbances'. To this Hamilton-Browne replied sharply that many towns had joined the rebels and that Sabukki was pursuing Turaki into Kaiama. 'I consider the ordering of troops to prevent the murder of those whom we have appointed justified under the circumstances'.

Clarke, accompanied by Aliu, Wakil Sarkin Yauri, joined forces with the WAFF detachment on 21 June and marched to Bussa via Garafini with a total force of seventeen Police and twenty-five WAFF together with a British N.C.O. He hoped that in a speedy action he could cut off the retreat of the rebels into Dahomey, whose administration had been informed of the situation and who were nervous about repercussions in their own Borgu Province.[59]

On 23rd the contingent engaged the rebels at Bussa and then Garafini. In both places they met considerable resistance, and Colour Sergeant Kerry, in charge of the WAFF, wrote in his report on the Patrol that 'if the troops had taken a defeat the whole of the Borgawa would have been up in arms, as they were all ready to take up arms'. In Garafini nine rebels were killed, and in Bussa ten, with no losses to the Patrol − the arrows of the rebels, according to Kerry, the British N.C.O., 'being extraordinarily devoid of aim'. From Bussa the patrol marched south to Kaiama, where many sympathetic to the rebels fled across the border into Southern Nigeria. After protracted negotiations with the authorities of Oyo Province six ringleaders were handed over to the Patrol. The Patrol marched through Borgu showing the flag and did not return to Yelwa until 9 July. Sabukki, however, eluded them.

By 1 July Hamilton-Browne was able to advise Zungeru that Clarke had reported that Bussa and District were quiet and that nothing remained except to effect arrest and punish those concerned after trial.

Over the next months there was considerable discussion as to the causes of the rebellion. Despite attempts to associate Kitoro Gani, under surveillance at Yelwa, with the rebellion, no evidence of his direct involvement could be found.[60] With the advantage of hindsight, and without the emotional involvement of a Clarke, a Hamilton-Browne, or a Dwyer, who was strongly critical of Clarke, the causes of the rebellion seem to have fallen into the following categories.

(a) *The Administrative Reorganisation of Bussa*

It is clear that even the abolition of the Kôfa system and the division of Bussa into districts, prior to its subjection to Yauri, had not been popular, especially as it was associated with more efficient tax collection and a higher incidence. The princes of Bussa clearly resented the power given to Turaki and Aliyara as district heads. This resentment was of course increased to boiling point when Kitoro Gani was deposed and as far as Bussa was concerned power was concentrated in the hands of Turaki in metropolitan Bussa, Aliyara in West Bussa and Ajia in South Bussa. None of these were Borgawa, and two of them, Turaki and Aliyara, were slaves, whose rule was acceptable if they were agents of Sarkin Bussa but not as district heads in their own right subject only to Yauri, a foreign ruler.

(b) *The Deposition of Kitoro Gani*
For the British, Kitoro Gani was an incompetent drunkard and even after the rebellion they dismissed the idea that his deposition was a cause.[61] Fergus Dwyer, Acting Resident of Kontagora, wrote categorically in 1916: 'The deposing of the Emir was not the cause of the disturbance'.[62] But given the difficulties the Kiwotede Jibrim had in ruling as Emir, even though he was heir apparent, after the dismissal of Turaki, and given the popularity of the decision to restore Kitoro Gani in 1924, it seems clear that the deposal of the Sarkin Bussa, with all his religious significance in Borgu, *and* the humiliation the Borgawa felt at being subjected to a slave, we can attribute this as a major cause. Furthermore, when Kitoro Gani went into exile in Ilorin in 1916 many Borgawa followed him. Interviews with the present Emir of Borgu and the Ciroma support this view.

(c) *Subjection to Yauri*
The subjection of Bussa to Yauri in view of the rancour existing between them at the end of the nineteenth century was tactless to say the least. And Aliu, Wakil Sarkin Yauri, exacerbated the problem by removing the Kisra relics from Bussa to Yauri. From the Bussa point of view, the administrative reorganisation that took place in 1915 was a plot with the connivance of Turaki and Aliyara to deprive them of their lands. In fearing such loss, they were perspicacious for, when Bussa was again made separate from Yauri, it was with much of its land excised.

(d) *Unsympathetic Administration*
At a more general level, the early docility of the Borgawa had been tried sorely by the British administration as we have tried to suggest. Periods of minimal interference by District Officers would be succeeded by short bursts of interventionist administration culminating in that of Mr. Clarke, whose wholesale deposals of *sarakuna* contributed greatly to the discontent in Borgu and helps to explain the sympathetic rising that took place in Kaiama, even though this had not been incorporated into Greater Yauri. Generally the Political Administration showed little understanding of the Borgawa and tried to make a Fulani-style administration work in a state of very different political traditions. Clarke himself relied heavily on the advice of men like Political Agent Abba and Turaki who had ambitions of their own. At one level Kitoro Gani was considered by the British as having the status of a first-class Emir equal to the Sultan of Sokoto and Shehu of Borno: at another he was a chief treated with contempt since he did not have the powers

to carry out what the British wanted. Furthermore he resented his constantly diminishing position with land being taken away, and with, in his eyes, a comparative upstart Kaiama being placed on an equal footing as himself.

(e) *Taxation*

It is clear that the increase in incidence of taxation and the stricter enforcement of it did much to exacerbate unrest in Borgu — in both Bussa and Kaiama. Significantly the District Mallamai (tax assessors) were a prime target of the rebels.

All these factors combined to give Sabukki, a prince who had the right to succeed to the throne, the support he needed for his rebellion. It seems clear that his rebellion was mainly focused on ridding Bussa of an unpopular native administration, albeit a British imposed one. There were, of course, no immediate representatives of the British, either in the guise of a political officer, or of Police or WAFF soldiers, for him to attack. I can as yet find no evidence that a motive of the rebels was a desire to return to independence, which was however a theme in the rebellion of the Dahomean Borgawa later that year.[63]

Over the succeeding decade the British administration were to admit tacitly or overtly that the above were the causes of the rebellion and took steps to rectify a situation which they were later to admit was largely of their own creation.

THE AFTERMATH OF THE REVOLT

Clarke's patrol did not bring peace to Borgu. In December the area was still unsettled and Sabukki was still at large, protected from capture by his popularity among the people, particularly in Aliyara District and Shagunu. Bussa was still subject to Yauri and the administration had difficulties in collecting taxes. The following year, despite the fact that the unpopular District Head, Turaki, had been replaced, for reasons which will be discussed later, the situation in Borgu was still tense. Towards November of 1916 it looked as though the rebellion of 1915 would be repeated. Across the border in French Dahomey the Borgawa had risen against the authorities and rumours were rife, particularly in Aliyara District, that the Dahomeyan Borgawa had killed five Frenchmen, 'they [the Nigerian Borgawa of Giddan Lalle, Kabe and Kano] express the intention of following their example if any Political Officer goes there'.[64] Reports of refusal to pay taxes, highway robbery, threats against native authority officials and movement of refugees across the border from Dahomey led the Resident of Kontagora to ask for another Patrol to be sent to Borgu. On 12 December, reports came in that Sabukki had entered Shagunu and was preparing to attack Bussa. Troops were authorised by Lugard on 13 December 'if Commandant can supply war shortage'.[65] The troops arrived on Christmas Day at Bussa and Lt. Whitworth and 30 rank and file set out for Shagunu on 27 December reaching it on the 29th. There they encountered armed men who offered little resistance, and collected all the overdue tax. At Giddan Lalle, the village was burnt down as an example. The reports available on the actions of the patrol are not as detailed as those for the 1915 patrol, but in Bussa memory, the patrol is credited with having been ruthless in dealing with the rebels.[66] Whatever the facts of the case, it is clear from the records that as a result of the patrol Shagunu was deserted for the next decade, the people taking to the bush.[67] Certainly this patrol added further to the sense of injustice the Borgawa felt at the hands of the colonial administration. A question yet to be explored, is how far the 'rebels' were inspired by the desire to rid themselves of the white man and return to a state of pre-colonial independence, as is clear was partly the intention of the Dahomean Borgawa. But the Resident Kontagora was probably right in his assessment: 'The fact that no resistance was met with was I think due to the crushing defeat of the natives at the hands of the French and the subsequent punishment that followed'.[68]

As a result of the continued disturbed situation in Borgu, the administration began to rethink its policy in the area and to try and make amends. Within a decade they had conceded effectively what the rebels demanded, so that, as the present Emir of Borgu has put it: 'it was not a hopeless revolt'.[69]

The grievances of the rebels were not met systematically, so it is difficult to treat the various moves of the British administration over the next decade chronologically. As far as the explicit grievances of the rebels are concerned these can be listed as:

(1) The demand that Turaki, the slave, be removed from the District Headship of Bussa.
(2) The demand that Bussa's integrity be restored.
(3) The demand that Kitoro Gani be brought back to the throne.
(4) The demand that Bussa's lost lands be restored.
(5) Implicit in the grievances of the Bussawa was resentment at the high-handed methods of the British administration.

We will now consider the way in which the British settled, or partially settled these five grievances.

(a) *The Removal of Turaki*

After the revolt Turaki was maintained in office in Bussa and was given government policemen in addition to his own *dogarai* to back up his authority. The Bussawa, however, were rid of him through his own agency. In December 1915 he was arrested and charged with the murder of Gani of Wawa in June 1915 and Gani of Kagogi in July 1915. Both men were suspected by Turaki of being among Sabukki's followers. Turaki was brought to trial on 20 January 1916 in the Provincial Court at Kontagora together with three co-defendants. He was found guilty of manslaughter on 29 January and sentenced to fifteen years' imprisonment.[70] A separate retrial of each case was, however, ordered because the four accused were tried in one trial on two different charges of murder of men bearing the same name which made the record exceedingly complicated.[71] At the separate retrials in March Turaki was sentenced to 10 years' imprisonment for the manslaughter of Gani of Kagogi who had been tortured to death with his knowledge, and to death for the murder of Gani of Wawa who had been shot on his instructions by the Government Police. However, on 20 May his sentence on this charge was reduced to twelve years' penal servitude on the grounds that the circumstances of the murdered man being held to have killed one of the N.A. officials in Sabukki's revolt were mitigating.[72] Turaki's conviction necessitated his replacement as District Head: it also raised the question as to why he had been elevated to such a position in the first place. When Clarke had recommended the reorganisation of Bussa as part of Yauri, he did not inform Hamilton-Browne that Turaki was a slave.[73] Of course while Turaki was merely the representative of Sarkin Bussa this did not matter. But once Bussa was deposed, his slave status became crucial.

(b) *The Restoration of Bussa's Integrity*

While the rebels, according to the present Emir of Bussa, had been prepared to accept another member of the royal family as replacement for Turaki, the choice of Kiwotede Kijibrim, though he was heir apparent, was not at all popular. Kiwotede Kijibrim would have nothing to do with the rebels and had actually supported Turaki. The alternatives to appointing Kijibrim were to make the popular candidate, Kissoin, district head or leave the choice to Sarkin Yauri. This latter alternative was briefly entertained by Hamilton-Browne despite all that had happened, although he did add in his memorandum to Zungeru: 'I would wish, if possible, to put a Borgawa over the Bussa people. I think it would be politic to, so far, concede to their wishes'.[74] Despite the clear hostility that existed towards Kijibrim in Bussa, his appointment was approved on 19 July 1916. At least the Bussawa were to be ruled in their own capital by a member of their own royal family, even if he was still reduced in status to a district head of Yauri and was generally considered a traitor, usurping his deposed brother's throne.[75]

The following February, Hamilton-Browne proposed that Bussa be separated from Yauri and that Kijibrim be appointed a Second

Class Emir.[76] This was duly approved but the question as to whether Bussa should be accorded the status of a Second Class Chieftaincy was subject to question. The possibility of his being graded Third Class Chief was seriously considered.[77] Kijibrim, as Emir, ruled over a reduced Bussa, since not all of Bussa's lands were handed back when it was separated from Yauri (see below). He had little authority over his people, who for the most part despised him for his role in the rebellion. The District Officers constantly complained about his inefficiency, and the fact that it was difficult to do anything in Bussa while he was on the throne. T. Hoskyns-Abrahall, A.D.O. Borgu, wrote in exasperation 'I have come regretfully to the conclusion that under the present regime Bussa Emirate will never be anything but backward, unsatisfactory, dissatisfied, and ridden with peculation, bribery and corruption'.[78] In 1922 Kijibrim had been deprived of his staff of office for general inefficiency. His position had been further prejudiced that year by an attempt on his life by his own brother and one of his two Councillors and half-brother, Kissoin. Having killed a peasant at Kagogi in a fit of temper, Kissoin went to Bussa on the 19th of March to kill Kijibrim. According to witnesses he had the day before shot an arrow at Sarkin Bussa, who was trying to track him down and bring him to justice, saying 'I won't die alone'.[79] Kissoin was eventually hanged for the murder, but the incident further lowered Kijibrim's prestige in the eyes of his people. By 1923 the administration was actively considering alternatives to him as Emir.

(c) *The Restoration of Kitoro Gani*

In 1923 Kontagora province was dismembered and Borgu was made part of Ilorin Province. For more than a decade Hamilton-Browne had overseen the affairs of Bussa as Resident Kontagora. Now, Bussa came under Hon. H. Hermon-Hodge, Resident Ilorin, and in this period under T. Hoskyns-Abrahall as its District Officer. The two were dynamic and prepared for reform. Very much at Hoskyns-Abrahall's insistence, Kijibrim was told that his services were no longer required and Kitoro Gani was restored to the throne. Kitoro Gani had not only been deposed but after the rebellion had, after protracted negotiations, been deported to Ilorin.[80] There a number of his supporters had joined him. Despite his long absence from Bussa he still enjoyed great popularity and his return in November 1924 was greeted with enthusiasm by the people. In 1925 Hoskyns-Abrahall reported: 'He is exceedingly popular and his return has caused universal rejoicing. He appears to have kept himself extremely well-informed of current events during his nine years of exile'.[81] Kitoro Gani thanked the Governor in a letter written in Arabic in December 1924: 'Thanks be to Allah who teaches man to write with pen and ink to establish the truth that cannot be altered'.[82] The Emir removed for purposes of 'administrative convenience' was restored in the words of the Governor, Sir Hugh Clifford, 'as a tardy act of justice'.[83] The drunkard of earlier years, was now viewed as the salvation for British administration in Bussa. However, by the early 1930s the administration was once more having doubts about him and on 25 June 1935 he was again deposed, this time for peculation from the Native Treasury.[84] This time his removal from office and replacement by his brother Babakki, who ruled until 1968, caused no stir.

Along with the restoration of Kitoro Gani in 1924, an amnesty was offered to Sabukki and all others who had taken part in the 1915 rebellion. Hoskyns-Abrahall had written in his Political Diary in 1923 that he did not think that the people of Shagunu, who still lived in the bush as a result of the 1916 patrol, would come out until 'the Sabukki business is cleared up',[85] For nearly ten years Sabukki had lived at large in the bush despite efforts in 1916, 1917 and 1918 to track him down. Actually it seems that he was all the time in the Shagunu area, protected by the loyalty of the Shagunu people. An earlier suggestion of amnesty had been made on the grounds that 'all efforts to capture him have proved fruitless; that his presence in the country as an outlaw is a latent cause of disaffection; that his pardon would be a most popular event; and that his crimes were the outcome of harsh and injudicious treatment by the Administration'.[86] But this was turned down preremptorily by the Lt-Governor in 1918 who urged further effort to secure his arrest. In 1919 Joyce Cary wrote to his wife: 'I'm trying here to get a noted rebel to surrender to me. I can't catch him in (illegible word) and he's been sitting in the bush for three years. One can't find a rebel in thousands of miles of bush with half a dozen police and all the people are his friends. My diplomacy is hardly in the highest style of Lagos and Kaduna. I don't know what the Governor or Chief Justice would say to it. In short, I'm letting it be known by private means that if he surrenders himself I'll give him a short sentence. This is information of the highest secrecy. A breath of it would ruin your worthy husband, so don't tell on me. I'm sorry for the man who has been unjustly treated. A year or two in jug is all that is required to save the face of the Government, and he'll be happier even in jug than he is now'.[87] In the event, once pardoned, Sabukki and his followers settled down quietly under Kitoro Gani.

(d) *The Restoration of Bussa's lost lands*

In 1917, when Bussa was made independent of Yauri, Agwarra, the Rofia hinterland and Kunji were left under Yauri largely on the grounds that the land, which Bussa claimed, was farmed by Yauris. In

1919, however, Agwarra, which had been administered as a sub-district of N'Gaski, was transferred back to Bussa. On the break up of Kontagora Province in 1923, while Bussa became part of Ilorin Province, Yauri was made part of Sokoto Province. Instead of land disputes between them being left to the same Resident to arbitrate, it was now a matter for negotiation between two separate Residents, each of them jealous of their frontiers. Hermon-Hodge, Resident of Ilorin, assisted by the able researches of Hoskyns-Abrahall, took up Bussa's case for the return of lands still lost to Yauri, namely Kunji and the Rofia hinterland. For impoverished Bussa, of course, these lands were vital as a source of revenue. After protracted, often acrimonious negotiations, the transfer of Rofia from Yauri to Bussa was approved. But Kunji was to remain in Yauri and the Governor minuted 'it is clearly understood that we cannot entertain any more claims of this nature'.[88] Captain P. E. Lewis, the District Officer, Borgu, wrote in his Annual Report for 1927: 'A long-cherished hope, partly fulfilled by the restoration of Rofia, has re-established the confidence in the justice of administration . . .'.[89] The loss of Kunji, Illo, Kaoje and other lands excised from Bussa over the first twenty-five years of colonial rule, however, still rankles in the minds of the Bussawa to this day.[90]

(e) *The Subjection of Kaiama to Bussa*

The position of Kaiama as equal to Bussa continued to be an issue in Bussa right up till 1955, when finally it was made a district of the new Emirate of Borgu, in which Nigerian Borgu was brought under the Sarkin Bussa, now restyled Emir of Borgu. In 1917, when Hamilton-Browne proposed that Bussa be separated from Yauri, he also suggested that Kaiama, Okuta, Ilesha and Yashikera be made districts of the Bussa Emirate, but this was not followed through.[91] It was however later suggested in the 1920s that on the death of the incumbent Emir of Kaiama, Haliru, the Emirate of Kaiama be abolished and Kaiama be united with Bussa.[92] However, Haliru was a young man and did not in the event retire until 1954, after which this suggestion was followed through. Between him, and Kitoro Gani, personal acrimony, particularly when they encountered each other at Chiefs' meetings, continued.

(f) *British Administration*

Clearly inept administration was in large measure responsible for Borgu getting into the lamentable state which led up to the rebellion. One of the reforms that followed the separation of Bussa from Yauri was the decision to station a District Officer permanently in Borgu. From the appointment of Joyce Cary as District Officer Borgu in 1917 till the end of Colonial Rule Borgu was never without a District Officer. Joyce Cary in his letters to his wife gives some fairly hair-raising impressions of the administration of Kontagora Province in general and of Borgu in particular: 'The state of this Province is rotten all through, police, native administration and all, and it won't wake up till we change the Resident who is simply marking time till he gets his pension. He is an awfully good fellow and as straight as you make 'em but damn slack and that's all about it'.[93] 'I am going off on Monday to the cheerful anarchy of my division. I find there is no administration at all. All the recent administration are either in prison or dead'.[94] 'Cowper (the D. O. Yelwa) says the Province hasn't advanced since 1902 and I believe him'.[95]

Perhaps the most important decision for Borgu was that of placing it in Ilorin Province which brought it under the more immediate attention of the Resident than had ever been the case in the Kontagora days. As the Resident of Ilorin, Hermon-Hodge, wrote in 1924: '... I do not think I should be far wrong in saying that the visits in *one year* twice by the Resident, three times by the Commissioner of Police, once by the Senior Sanitary Officer, and twice by the Superintendent of Education compared favourably with the attention this much neglected division received during the whole of its previous association with Kontagora Province'.[96] Nevertheless, this optimism bore few fruits for Borgu. As D. F. Heath, District Officer of Borgu wrote in 1935: 'To describe present day Borgu one could quite easily copy one of Lord Lugard's early reports and give an accurate picture'.[97]

Indeed for the next twenty-five years Borgu remained backward but peaceful. A sparse population of 40,000 spread over 11,000 square miles with few crops, and no natural resources, gave the British administration little room to manoeuvre. But at least they had learnt some lessons from the revolt in Borgu: that to administer a people successfully through indirect rule a legitimate chief, however bad, was essential; that they could not juggle land with impunity for mere administrative convenience; that the realities of pre-colonial history had to be taken into account, especially in applying indirect rule. Though the rebels of 1915 were defeated, the fact that the British conceded most of their grievances meant that it was not fruitless. Indeed the British admitted that they were in large part responsible for the sorry condition in which Bussa found itself. As the Resident of Ilorin, Hermon-Hodge, put it in 1926: 'I do indeed feel that some reparation should be made to Bussa for the sufferings and sacrifices which have reduced a proud and comparatively populous race to a soured and sporadic handful'.[98] But in one matter the British did not give way. They did not dismantle the structure of administration which they had imposed on Bussa between 1912 and 1915, and which had been a major cause of the rebellion. They merely adjusted their basic application of it, so that in 1924, when Kitoro Gani was restored, it was as an Emir in charge of a Native Authority patterned on those of the far north.

CONCLUSION

The imposition of the Native Authority system of local government on the non-Muslim chieftaincy of Bussa, and in particular the manner in which it was imposed, provoked a sharp reaction on the part of the traditional elite and the people. The fact that no revolt took place earlier can be attributed to two factors. First, resistance to colonial occupation had been very firmly put down by the French, who occupied much of what became British Borgu.[99] Second, the first ten years of British administration in Borgu, and in Bussa in particular, was very light in touch, and limited largely to keeping the peace, ensuring freedom of person and movement, and exacting tribute on a small-scale to indicate the new relationship of dependence in which the native 'authorities' found themselves. With such minimal goals, the British in Bussa, and in Northern Nigeria generally, used the pre-colonial authorities wherever they would co-operate rather than disturb the traditional status quo. In Bussa, Kitoro Gani proved more than willing to co-operate: the problem was that from the British point of view, even as far as achieving their limited goals in Bussa were concerned, he was ineffective. The options open to the British in such circumstances were to identify an alternative traditionally acceptable authority, as was done in Sokoto, or identify a man of ability without traditional claim to power but whom the people would at least passively accept, as was the case in Katsina. The key task of the local British administration in such situations was (a) to identify which course was the better to take in the circumstances and (b) having decided on the course to be adopted, identify the right man to appoint to the chieftaincy. In Bussa, both Clarke, the District Officer, and Hamilton-Browne were guilty of gross ineptitude because they signally failed to prescribe the correct remedy to the problem. Rather the remedy was, as we can see with the value of hindsight, almost calculated to provoke the armed protest which it was their duty at all costs to avoid because their reorganisation of 'native authority' in Bussa altered the relative position of politically and socially consequential persons in Bussa to an extent that was intolerable to those disinherited as a result of it.[100]

While, however, once the revolt had been put down, the British were prepared to undertake reforms in an attempt to settle the grievances — both expressed and unexpressed — of the traditional elite and people, in particular by restoring the position of the traditional elite as it existed prior to the rebellion, they did nothing to alter the fundamental structure of the Native Authority system which they had imposed on Bussa. The slave District Head may have been replaced by the Emir Kijibrim and he in turn by the restored Kitoro Gani and Yauri's suzerainty over Bussa dispensed with. But both Kijibrim and Kitoro Gani were required to rule as Native Authorities on the same lines as the Emirs of the Fulani-Hausa Emirates to the north. The slave Kofas who had gained so much power once they were required to reside in their districts may in the long run have been replaced as District Heads by members of the ruling family. But the fact remains that the Districts became realities, closely modelled on those of the Fulani-Hausa Emirates. Taxes were regularly collected by the District Heads and failure to do so involved the deposition of at least one District Head. The Emir was required to operate his Native Authority on a strictly controlled budget and failure to obey the rules laid down for the control of funds in the Native Treasury led to the deposition of Kitoro Gani for a second time. Significantly his second deposition did not provoke the reaction his first one did. By 1935 the Native Authority system had become well entrenched, the presence of the British administration was firmly established, and the character of chieftaincy in Bussa had been effectively changed. This became the more apparent with the accession of Mohamman Sani, brother of Kitoro Gani, who reigned until 1968. He became a devout Muslim and modelled his own conduct as chief as well as the style of his administration increasingly on that of the Fulani-Hausa Emirate. A visitor to Bussa today would find the traditional political set-up much more akin to that of a small emirate'like Hadeija or Gumel than that described for pre-colonial Borgu. While the Yoruba Chieftaincies retained much of their traditional Yoruba character despite the imposition of a Native Authority system derived from the Fulani-Hausa emirates, that of Borgu became assimilated to them.

NOTES

1. N[igerian] A[rchives] K[aduna] / S[ecretary]. N[orthern] P[rovinces] / 17/7/K.C. Series/K.2227 'Bussa Rebellion 1915' etc.
2. The 1915 Bussa rebellion is the subject of a monograph by the author entitled *Revolt in Bussa: A Study in British 'Native Administration' in Nigerian Borgu, 1902-1935*, London, 1973.
3. Jacques Lombard, 'Une système politique traditionelle de type féodal: les Baribas du Nord Dahomey. Aperçu sur l'organisation sociale et le pouvoir central', *Bulletin de l'IFAN*, T. XIX. ser B. nos. 3-4, 1957, p.481.
4. NAK/BORGDIV/6 Borgu Provincial Record Book, No.3.
5. D. F. Heath, 'Bussa Regalia' Man, May 1937, Nos. 90-91, pp.77-78.
6. R. Cornevin, *Histoire du Dahomey*, Paris 1963, p.162.

7. This tradition is related by W. Hamilton-Browne, Resident Kontagora, in a letter to the Lt. Gov. Northern Provinces, 20 February 1917, NAK/SNP/9/3405/1923.
8. Alhaji Musa Muhammed Kigera III, Emir of Borgu, *The History of Bussa*, typescript.
9. Interview with Alhaji Musa Muhammed Kigera III, Emir of Borgu.
10. See NAK/BORGDIV/DOB/BOU/17 Ag. D. O. Borgu W. Nash to Resident Ilorin, 6 August 1926 et. seq. Also Mahdi Adamu 'A Hausa Government in Decline: Yauri in the Nineteenth Century' unpublished M. A. Thesis, Ahmadu Bello University, Zaria, 1968; T. Hoskyns-Abrahall 'History of Bussa' NAK/SNP/13 × 14/K.C. Series/K.6.
11. The date often given for the loss of Illo is 1905 both in the records and publications. However, it is clear that it was not transferred until March 1907. See: NAK/SNP/420 p/1918 (attached file 5282/1907) in which Temple, Res. Sokoto, telegraphed High Commissioner 7.3.1907 asking that Sharpe, Res. Kontagora, be ordered to hand over at once towns restored to Sokoto. See also: SNP/7/1866/1908 Kontagora Annual Report for 1907.
12. Despite complaints by Residents and District Officers of Borgu that many of the records of the early period of Borgu had been destroyed or eaten by termites there is a surprisingly full documentation in the Kaduna Archives. See footnote 33.
13. NAK/BORGDIV/DOB/QHR/4 Reports on Bussa and Kaiama 2nd Quarter 1910.
14. NAK/SNP/15/ACC No.52 Borgu Province Reports 1903, Monthly Report for December 1903.
15. NAK/BORGDIV/6 Borgu Provincial Record Book. Also see NAK/BORGDIST/DOB/ARS/9 for Joyce Cary's record of Yashikera History. Woru Yaru eventually became, briefly, Sarkin Nikki in 1917.
16. NAK/BORGDIV/DOB/HIS/3 Report on Chiefs, 1911.
17. NAK/SNP/420 P/1918 (attached file 5282/1907) Sharpe Res. Kon. to Sec. to the Admins. of Northern Nigeria. 3 Jan. 1910.
18. NAK/BORGDIV/6 Borgu Provincial Record Book. Illo 1905.
19. NAK/SNP/7/10/1778/1909 History of Illo and District trans. by R. Macallister. Authority: Sarkin Illo and Council.
20. NAK/BORGDIV/DOB/QHR/4 Bussa and Kaiama Reports, 1910.
21. NAK/ILORPROF/3353 A Borgu Province. Monthly Report for July 1902 Harry Tremble Ag. Resident.
22. NAK/SNP/7/5011/1909 Kontagora Province Sept. Quarter Report for 1909. N. M. Gepp Ag. Resident.
23. NAK/BORGDIV/DOB/QHR/4 Bussa and Kaiama Reports for 1910 (1st Quarter & 3rd Quarter).
24. NAK/SNP/7/3648/1911 Kontagora Province June Quarter 1911, E. G. M. Dupigny Ag. Resident.
25. NAK/BORGDIV/DOB/QHR/3 Bussa and Kaiama Reports 1909. T. C. Newton Asst. Res.
26. NAK/SNP/7/1858/1907 Borgu Province Annual Report for 1906. Fergus Dwyer Ag. Res. Kontagora to High Commissioner N. N. 27 May 1907.
27. NAK/SNP/7/4037/1912 Report on Sarkin Bussa: A/R. C. E. Boyd to J. E. C. Blackeney, Res. Kontagora. Kontagora Quarterly Report, June, 1912.
28. NAK/SNP/7/784/1908 Kontagora Quarterly Report, December, 1907.
29. NAK/SNP/8/42/1915 Hamilton-Browne, Res. Kontagora to Ag. Lt. Gov. N.Ps. 18/3/1915. I can find no trace of either the warnings or the proposed earlier deposition in the files. However, this is not altogether surprising since in

THE IMPOSITION OF THE NATIVE AUTHORITY SYSTEM IN BUSSA 177

    1912 Mr. Boyd recorded 'At Bussa the whole office was one mass of white ants and I regret to say that a great pile of records, some of them reference files etc. were in such a state that the only thing possible was done and that to burn them'. NAK/SNP/4037/1912.
30. NAK/BORGDIV/DOB/QHR/5 Bussa and Kaiama Reports
31. NAK/BORGDIV/DOB/HIS/3 Confidential Report on Kitoro Gani by T. C. Newton Assistant Resident 19 April 1911.
32. NAK/BORGDIV/DOB/QHR/3/June Quarter for Borgu, 1907.
33. NAK/BORGDIV/DOB/QHR/5 Bussa and Kaiama. Reports for 1911.
34. NAK/BORGDIV/DOB/QHR/6 Kaiama Annual & Quarterly for 1912.
35. NAK/SNP/CR/108 Clarke J. C. O. Sub. Lt. R.N.R.
36. *Ibid.* And this despite criticisms in 1912 of Clarke's assessment report on Borgu, only 2½ pages of large manuscript, as 'most insufficient'. NAK/SNP/7/185/1912 Kontagora Province, Borgu Divison Assessment, 1912.
37. Bodleian Library, Oxford: Joyce Cary Papers Box 268. Letter to his wife 7 Oct. 1918.
38. P. G. Harris; *Sokoto Provincial Gazetteer.*
39. NAK/BORGDIV/DOB/QHR/7 1st Quarter March 1913.
40. *Ibid.*
41. NAK/BORGDIV/DOB/QHR/7 2nd Quarter.
42. NAK/SNP/354 P/1913 Kontagora Report March Quarter 1913.
43. NAK/SNP/10/7358/1912 Kontagora Quarter 1912.
44. NAK/SNP/27 P/1914 File 2 Kontagora Report December Quarter 1913.
45. NAK/BORGDIV/DOB/QHR/7.
46. NAK/BORGDIV/DOB/AR/5.
47. *Ibid.*
48. *Ibid.*
49. NAK/SNP/14P/1915 Borgu Patrol.
50. NAK/SNP/837 P/1917 Kaiama Chiefs 1915.
51. NAK/SNP/8/2/42/1915 Kaiama. Emir Deposition of.
52. *Ibid.*
53. NAK/SNP/8/42/1915 Amalgamation of Yauri, Bussa and Kaiama.
54. NAK/SNP/8/42/1915.
55. *Ibid.*
56. NAK/SNP/331 P/1915 Bussa Disturbance of 1915. Minute by Ag. Lt. Gov. to Sec. Zung. of 12 July 1915.
57. NAK/BORGDIST/DOB/HIST/2 Borgu Patrol 'Gani of Bussa being duly sworn in charges that on or about 11.6.15 I saw Bokko of Puissa leading a section of Sabukki's army at the attack on Bussa . . . .
58. *Ibid.* Except where otherwise stated, the account of the aftermath of the revolt is based on this file.
59. See Archives Nationales du Senegal, Dakar [ANSD] File 3F1 (105/106/108).
60. See NAK/SNP/8/25/1916.
61. *Ibid.*
62. *Ibid.* Dwyer to Sec. Zung. 15 Jan. 1916.
63. ANSD./8G7 Situation Politique au Dahomey. Lt.-Gov. Dahomey to Gov. Gen. Dakar 14 Dec. 1916 citing letter from M. Géay, Administrator of Borgu. Concerning resistance by Borgawa he wrote:
    Je crois que cela ne tient qu'à l'orgueil incommensurable et in-intélligent des Baribas — On leur a dit (à Nikki) que le moment était venu de reprendre leurs indépendances — Partout on s'est consulté; à Bagou la décision était pour la guerre *à tous* les étrangers et le premier acte a été le portage des troupeaux, non des peulhs qui sont la reserve, mais des nagots, haoussas etc.

puis la destruction des inventions des 'blancs' — Ceci a été la rupture définitive. See also National Archives of France. Section Outre-Mer. Mission 1919. Rapport fait par M. Ch. Phérivong, Inspecteur-Général 1er Classe des Colonies, concernant affaires des cercles de Djougou et du Borgou a l'époque 30 Janvier 1919 et explications fournies par le Lt-Gouverneur p.i. de la Colonie du Dahomey.
64. NAK/SNP/709P/1916 Res. Kon. to Sec. Zung. 2 Dec 1916.
65. *Ibid.*
66. *Ibid.* and interview with Emir of Borgu and Ciroma of Borgu. Also Emir of Borgu's *History of Bussa.*
67. *Revolt in Bussa,* p.191.
68. NAK/SNP/709p/1916 Res. Kon. to SNP Kaduna 15(?) Jan 1917.
69. Emir of Borgu, *History of Bussa.*
70. SNP/13/O/PC/40/1916.
71. *Ibid.*
72. SNP/13/O/PC/117/1916.
73. NAK/SNP/224p/1916.
74. NAK/SNP/481p/1916. Hamilton-Browne. Res. Kon. to Sec. Zung. 12 July 1916.
75. Interview with the Emir of Borgu.
76. NAK/SNP/9/10/3405/1923.
77. NAK/SNP/10/503p/1918.
78. NAK/BORGDIV/DOB/AR/17. Annual Report for 1923. See *Revolt in Bussa,* pp.176-177 for Hoskyns-Abrahall's view today of Kijibrim's position.
79. NAK/BORGDIV/5 Provincial Court Record Book.
80. NAK/SNP/8/3/25/1916.
81. NAK/SNP/18/CR.47. Annual Report on Chiefs Ilorin Province.
82. N[ational] A[rchives] I[badan] CSO/26/2/File 13556.
83. *Ibid.*
84. *Ibid.*
85. NAK/BORGDIV/5 D.O.'s Political Diary. 1923.
86. NAK/BORGDIV/HIS/3.
87. Cary Papers. Letter to his wife 27 Jan 1919.
88. NAI/CSO.26/12687/Vol. V.
89. NAK/BORGDIV/DOB/AR/22.
90. Interview with the Emir and Ciroma of Borgu.
91. NAK/SNP/9/10/3405/1923.
92. NAI/CSO.26/2/File No. 33625 Vol. II.
93. Cary Papers. Letter to his wife 26 June 1917.
94. *Ibid.* Letter to his wife 18 May 1917.
95. *Ibid.* Letter to his wife 13 May 1917.
96. NAI/CSO.26/12687/Vol.II.
97. NAK/SNP/17/3/24024.
98. NAK/SNP/17/7/K.C. Series/K.2227.'Bussa Rebellion 1915 etc.'
99. As Colonel Willcocks remarked, 'As far as the native races were concerned, the French had, of course, a far more difficult task than we had in Borgu. When we arrived it was only to find a submissive population who welcomed us, but it must be remembered they had received a sharp lesson from other white men; they had offered opposition, and had soon learnt that the game was not worth the candle'. Brigadier Sir James Willcocks, *From Kabul to Kumasi: Twenty-Four Years of Soldiering and Sport,* London, 1924, p.225.
100. I am grateful to Professor R. J. Gavin for his comments on my introduction and conclusion, and to His Highness the Emir of Borgu, Alhaji Musa Mohammad Kigera III, for valuable suggestions with regard to the final version of this paper.

VIII

THE FRENCH SUPPRESSION OF THE 1916-17 REVOLT IN DAHOMEYAN BORGU*
(1975)

INTRODUCTION

French demands for African recruits for their army fighting against the Germans in the European War of 1914-1918, led to large scale revolts throughout French West Africa. Indeed such had been the violence of the reactions of French West Africans against the compulsory drafting of their able-bodied youth that France lost effective control over large areas of her vast federation, and in 1917 the new Governor-General, Joost van Vollenhoven, reported that further recruitment was impossible in view of the revolts that had taken place in Haut-Sénégal-Niger (Modern Mali, Upper Volta) Dahomey, Ivory Coast, Guinea and the Military Territory of Niger.[1] While recruitment was the principal cause of these revolts which were on such a scale as to result in temporary loss of administrative control by the French over large areas of what are now Mali, Upper Volta and Dahomey, there were other contributory factors: the desire for a return to independence, resentment at taxes, head-counting, forced labour, appointment of chiefs without traditional rights to rule, breaking-up of traditional political units to form administrative units convenient to the French, and above all the knowledge that the French were in a serious situation in Europe, strikingly demonstrated by withdrawal of large numbers of Frenchmen from all walks of life from French West Africa to fight on the European front. Yet that recruitment was not such a basic cause of the revolts as has usually been considered is brought out by the fact that the Senegalese deputy for Senegal, Blaise Diagne, as Commissioner for the Recruitment of Troops, was able to raise peaceably a further 63,378 soldiers from West Africa, when Van Vollenhoven had said it would ruin the

*Published in a modified form in *The Journal of the Historical Society of Nigeria*, Vol VIII, 1, December 1975.

country.[2] Indeed, 3,340 out of the 3,500 required in 1918 were enlisted in Dahomey during Diagne's recruitment tour, though he spent only eight days there.[3]

This paper is an attempt to analyse both the causes of one of these revolts, that of the Bariba of French Borgu in 1916-17, and to show the way in which a recently conquered African people were able to hold the French administration to ransom by military resistance over a period of nearly six months.

DAHOMEYAN BORGU

Dahomeyan Borgu at the time of the outbreak of the revolt against the French on 21 September 1916 was for administrative purposes divided into two *cercles*, Borgou and Moyen-Niger, with headquarters at Parakou and Kandi respectively. Each *cercle* was divided into a number of units called *subdivisions*, administered by European political officers. These *subdivisions* were in turn divided into *cantons*, administered by an African *chef de canton* usually chosen from among the pre-colonial ruling classes. The *subdivision* of Nikki for instance was in 1907 divided into 25 *cantons*. Prior to the partition of Borgu between the British and French by the Anglo-French agreement of 1898, the country had no single overall political authority nor did it consist of a single ethnic group. However, the various kingdoms that comprised Borgu were ruled by the *Wasangari*, who shared a common culture. Although they ruled their various sections of Borgu independently in times of peace, they did come together in times of external threat. Bussa, the first of the Borgu kingdoms to be founded and the one from which all the other major kingdoms were founded, was acknowledged as the senior of the kingdoms, but this was in respect of its role as the origin of the other kingdoms. By the nineteenth century Nikki, founded by the second son of Kisra, the legendary first king of Bussa, was acknowledged as politically the most powerful of the kingdoms and the one which in times of external threat would assume leadership of the Borgawa. Thus in the c.1835 war between the Oyo Yoruba and the Fulani of Ilorin, the King of Nikki not only sided with the Oyo, but brought in all the Borgawa with him and indeed assumed leadership of the allied forces. In times of peace, however, these kingdoms or provinces were to all intents and purposes autonomous. By the end of the nineteenth century, Nikki, itself, had lost almost all semblance of suzerainty over its constituent provinces, in particular Parakou and Kandi. After the Franco-British occupation of Borgu, which was bitterly resented by the Borgawa, Nikki had part of its diminished territory cut off by the Dahomeyan-Nigerian boundary. Even so during the colonial period former Nikki dependencies in Southern British Borgu not only ack-

FRENCH SUPPRESSION OF BORGU REVOLT   181

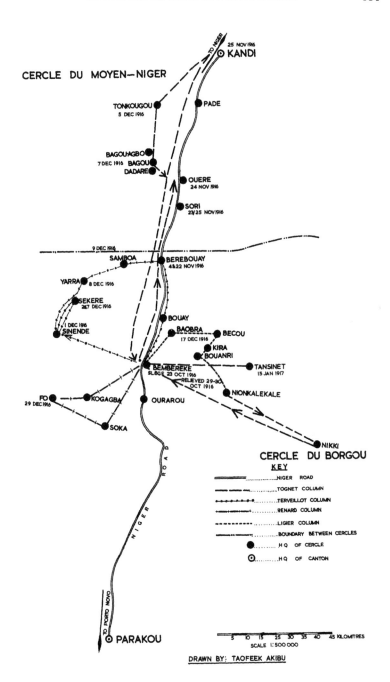

nowledged Nikki's suzerainty but in the case of Yashikera, its chief, who was a member of the Nikki royal family, actually aspired to the throne of Nikki when it became vacant. Whilst under French colonial rule the position of the King of Nikki was recognised in name, in fact he was reduced for administrative purposes to a simple *chef de canton*, with status equal to that of his former 'dependent' chiefs. Indeed in some ways he was worse off since the area over which he had acknowledged customary authority corresponded exactly to the sub-division administered by a French political officer. Furthermore, Parakou, which although a province of Nikki had exercised effective independence before the French conquest, was now made the headquarters of the Cercle of Borgou. The King of Nikki, Sero Toru Wonko, was thus summoned in 1911 to Parakou on the occasion of the visit of Governor-General William Ponty. This was contrary to Bariba tradition, by which it was taboo for the King of Nikki to enter Parakou and the death of Sero Toru Wonko shortly afterwards was attributed to this enforced violation of the taboo.[4]

Similarly the small Bariba chieftaincy of Kandi was raised in prestige by its creation as capital of the *cercle* of Moyen-Niger. But worse than the administrative reorganisation of the Bariba, which in many cases revised the pre-colonial hierarchy, was the way in which chiefs under French rule were stripped of their administrative, political, financial and judicial powers. Where under the British system of indirect rule chiefs were left with a real semblance of administrative and financial initiative and continued to exercise some of their pre-colonial judicial powers, under the French they were made simple subalterns in the administrative hierarchy.

Apart from their reduction in status, chiefs were liable to imprisonment like their subjects, and in 1902 the King of Nikki, himself, was imprisoned and committed suicide as a result.[5]

In addition to this, the presence of the French and the consequent abolition of slavery and establishment of freedom of movement, meant that many formerly dependent groups in Nikki and the other Borgu states were now free. Not only were the Fulani freed from the control of the *Wasangari* but they were also given their own chiefs parallel to those of the Bariba. Worse still, the *Gando*, or slaves of the *Wasangari*, were given their freedom. This was a blow to the prestige of the *Wasangari*, whose status in pre-colonial Borgu, and whose pretensions to the various thrones of Borgu, depended in part on the number of their slaves. The *Wasangari*, decisively defeated by the French during the conquest, now found the basis of their power removed. Furthermore, the relative status of the various rulers of what became Dahomeyan Borgu was reversed, particularly with regard to Nikki. This fact helps to explain the role played by Chabi Prouka, King of Nikki, in the 1916-17 rebellion.

Finally, the re-orientation of trade on a north-south axis as a result of the division of Borgu between France and Britain disrupted the old trade routes between Gonja and Hausaland which had been the principal source of Borgu's wealth, and further diminished the position of the traditional ruling groups.

THE ORIGINS OF THE REVOLT

Until September 1916, little overt resistance had been manifested by the Bariba either against the recruitment of able-bodied young men into the army, or against taxes and forced labour on the Niger road. There had been resistance against collection of taxes in Kandi in 1905, but otherwise everything appeared to be calm. The Bariba armies had been defeated in the occupation, while the Wasangari had been disinherited. The French administration, mistaking the reasons for this apparent calm, seem to have been blithely unaware of how deeply resentful the Bariba were, not only of their loss of independence but the character of the new regime imposed on them. When the rebellion in Nigerian Borgu broke out in June 1915, Noufflard, Lieutenant Governor of Dahomey, whilst he recommended taking precautions against it spreading to Dahomeyan Borgu, cabled the Governor-General in Dakar on 6 July 1915: 'Situation Cercle Borgou remains good and besides our policy continues to maintain it in such a state, if not to improve it. . .'.[6]

Indeed, the 1916-17 rising appears to have taken the local French administration by surprise. It began in the Nikki village of Becou, which lay thirty-five kilometres east of the French post of Bimbereke. The French had established a post at Bimbereke because it lay in an area distant from their principal administrative centres of Kandi, Parakou and Nikki itself, and because it was strategically situated on the new north-south Niger road, which was growing in importance because of the introduction of the automobile. By its establishment, it was hoped there would be better contact with the local people 'who are not hostile but are by nature independent and it is (therefore) necessary to be able to visit them frequently'.[7]

Bio Guera, chief of Becou until 1905, had continued in his hostility to the French ever since he first fought against them during their invasion. Because of his open disloyalty to the French he was relieved of his post in 1905 by a man faithful to them called Baguene. Bio Guera then took to the bush. The French were not particularly concerned by Bio Guera's disappearance because Becou was a village of little importance. In 1916, however, Bio Guera reappeared leading a violent campaign against Baguene, who collected taxes for the

French as *sous-chef de village*, claiming authority for this position from the King of Nikki. Chabi Pourka, to whom, in fact, Bio Guera was related. Baguene fled to Bimbereke, headquarters of the subdivision, where the *Chef de Subdivision*, Duthoit, responded by putting forward a plan to expel Bio Guera from Becou. He would seize him by surprise and bring him before the *Tribunal de Cercle*. The *Commandant de Cercle* of Borgou, Ferlus, felt his subordinate was too inexperienced to deal with the situation and proposed with his own 'profound knowledge of the Bariba' to settle it himself on one of his future tours. Meantime he let the matter lapse, while for several months Bimbereke was run, not by a political officer but by an official interpreter, Felix Vignon, whom Bio Guera asked to come to Becou to discuss his problems with Baguene.

Ferlus agreed to this, and Vignon went to Becou and informed Ferlus that all was well. He proposed that a new chief, a son of Bio Guera, considered to be loyal to the French, be installed in place of Baguene.

Meanwhile Ferlus advised Lt. Governor Noufflard that unless he had orders to the contrary he would leave Parakou for Nikki and Bimbereke. The next that was heard from him was a telegram of 21 September, saying that he had been attacked at Becou. At first it was not very clear to the Administration in Porto Novo exactly what had happened for Ferlus sent in a series of confusing and contradictory telegrams which were obviously designed to cover up his own humiliating role in what became known as the 'affaire Bécou'. Only after the Mission of Inspection of 1919, under Inspector-General of Colonies First Class, Ch. Phérivong, did the sequence of events which triggered off the Borgu revolt become clear.[8] Ferlus in his original long telegram of 21 September, reported that he and his party had fallen into an ambush. According to him he was attacked at dusk by 150 men with bows and arrows and he himself was only able to return to Bimbereke with difficulty. He reported that he had been lightly wounded by an arrow, and had been badly grazed on the legs whilst escaping through the bush.

In fact what happened at Becou was different from the version given by Ferlus. After detailed investigations by the Phérivong Mission, as a result of which Ferlus was reduced in rank, the actual sequence of events became clear.

Ferlus left Nikki with Baguene himself, Ali Bachabi, a *moniteur*, as interpreter, seven *gardes de cercle*, a convoy of porters and three cash-boxes with funds belonging to the administration. He by-passed Bimbereke, going direct to Becou where he arrived on 17 September. There he was installed in a hut belonging to Bio Guera, who in fact welcomed him. The *gardes de cercle* were lodged with Baguene in a compound some hundred metres from Ferlus' own hut. Ferlus did not forewarn Bio Guera of his intention to arrest him but ordered him to come and see him. Meanwhile Baguene had begun to threaten the villagers. So at night on 18 September, Bio Guera came to ask Ferlus to leave his house. The latter, however, was told by his cook that some people wanted to kill him. Ferlus in his report stated that he had then sent for his guards and while he was looking for his revolver in his baggage he was wounded in the neck by an arrow. Believing his life to be threatened, he took flight, half-dressed, leaving his personnel to look after themselves, and abandoning baggages and the money in the cash boxes. Like many villages in Borgu, Becou was 'fenced' by a hedge of thorns and he cut his legs scrabbling through them. It was established later that given the place where he had put his baggage in the hut, it would have been impossible for him to have been hit by an arrow while looking for his revolver.

After the cowardly flight of Ferlus, the *gardes de cercle* rushing out with their guns got into a fight with Bio Guera's men, who numbered some 15 and not the 150 reported by Ferlus. One porter and one *garde de cercle* were killed on the French side, while a brother of Bio Guera was killed and several of his men wounded.

Ali Bachabi was, however, able to bring calm to the situation promising that if order was restored he would see that nothing happened to the village or to Bio Guera. He retrieved all the baggages and funds, less 1,000 francs. He reformed the party and left the village conducted by Bio Guera himself.

The next morning, at Kira, the party was found by Ferlus who had spent the night in the bush. Ferlus took a horse and returned alone to Bimbereke that same day.[9] Soon afterwards, Chabi Prouka, King of Nikki, came to offer Ferlus his support. But, having been told to keep an eye on his people living along the Niger road, so the Administration later alleged, he went to Guessou where all his chiefs had gathered. The Administration had no means of telling what had taken place there but believed that he called on them to give support to Bio Guera.[10]

Meanwhile Ferlus had telegraphed Porto Novo for 50 soldiers or *gardes de cercle* and 2,000 cartridges so that he could deal with the situation; 30 *gardes de cercle* and 2,000 cartridges accordingly arrived at Bimbereke on 28 September. Later Inspector General Phérivong was to conclude that had the promises made by Ali Bachabi been kept, the whole matter might have ended there. Bio Guera himself remained at Becou, and did not make any trouble until either he got news of the telegram sent by Ferlus to the King of Nikki warning him and his people to keep away from Becou because of the impending punishment that was to be meted out to the village, or else because of news of arrival of the reinforcements demanded by Ferlus. Whatever the case, the promises made by Ali Bachabi were not kept and the revolt broke out. Communications were cut, bridges destroyed and four road-labourers were killed on the Niger road five kilometres from Bimbereke. European goods were boycotted and strangers were attacked and often killed.

The French took no action against the rebels until the 23 October, for they had much greater troubles elsewhere in Dahomey. The Somba of Atacora to the north-east of Borgu were in open revolt, as were the Pila Pila of Semere, and the Ohori along with other groups to the south, all primarily because of the recruitment of troops into the French army.

THE FRENCH 'POLICE OPERATION' AGAINST THE DAHOMEYAN REBELS

While the Becou incident was clearly serious, from the point of view of the Acting Governor-General in Dakar, Angoulvant, and the *Commandant Supérieur de Troupes* for French West Africa, who alone could decide whether a military operation should be undertaken in a constituent colony of the French West African federation, there were many other pressing demands on the small number of troops at their disposal in war-time. Apart from demands for troops for the European front, there were rebellions and troubled situations in other parts of the federation. As far as Dahomey was concerned they shared the opinion that Atacora should be dealt with before Borgu.[11] Preparations were made by them to send a detachment of troops under Commandant Renard to Dahomey.

Angoulvant, formerly Governor of Ivory Coast, for whose 'pacification' he had been responsible, laid down the principles by which the rebels should be dealt with. The expedition should be a police operation in character. 'There is no question that it should be a sort of expedition of conquest nor a *"colonne à grande envergure"'*,he wrote the Lt. Governor of Dahomey: 'Our aim is to strike hard in order not to have to strike over a long period of time nor on several occasions'. As soon as Atacora was dealt with, Semere and then Bimbereke should be tackled. Thereafter the Ohori should be suppressed. The population was to be disarmed for, in general, 'there are far too many guns in Dahomey'. Surprisingly for a man who, as 'pacificator of the Ivory Coast' had used the most ruthless methods in bringing the country firmly under French rule only a few years before, Angoulvant[12] also laid down strict rules for the 'Means of Repression and Intimidation to be employed'.

(1) Arms were to be used only if the troops were attacked or if it was clear the rebels could only be reduced by force.

(2) In the Acting Governor-General's own words 'I am entirely against the burning of villages and granaries and the systematic destruction of crops (*plantations*) since it only makes the population more disaffected'. Yet these were the very methods he had used in Ivory Coast.
(3) Everything that could serve as fortification was to be destroyed.
(4) Grain *really* belonging to a rebel or openly hostile people could be used to feed the troops but this must not take on the character of looting.
(5) There was to be no destruction of abandoned villages or fields, so long as there was no proof that the inhabitants of these villages had not attacked the French. Flight should not be necessarily taken as an indication of rebellion or of submission.

The conditions of submission were to be: (1) total disarmament and destruction of arms; (2) destruction of all fortifications; (3) capture and imprisonment of the leaders while other Africans who took up arms were to be incorporated on the spot into the Black Army 'in order that their warlike ardour find a useful outlet and this time is to our own profit'; (4) collective fines to be imposed on all villages or groups who had taken part in the hostilities; (5) all back taxes to be paid; (6) all bush camps to be evacuated and all destroyed and abandoned villages to be reconstructed, along with telegraph lines etc; (7) all young men who took part in the rebellion to be enlisted as *tirailleurs*; (8) hostages to be taken where this would serve a useful purpose.[13] The same day as he issued the instructions, Angoulvant wrote a personal and confidential letter to Noufflard telling him that he must put an end to his constant preoccupation with political questions which had bedevilled his own administration and that of his predecessors, and take the strong action he had outlined. No longer could he tolerate his 'methods of *petit paquets*, of delays, measures of benevolence or rather feebleness, which up until now have been favoured by the administration of Dahomey and which have finally resulted in a political situation of which you have not perceived the full gravity'.[14]

DETERIORATION OF THE SITUATION IN BORGU

Since Atacora had been assigned priority in the programme for the pacification of the country, there was little the administration could do in Borgu. An inquiry by *Administrateur en Chef* Sassias was ordered on 15 October into Ferlus' conduct. But Sassias did not get to Parakou until 23 October because of lack of transport.

Meanwhile the situation in the Bimbereke area deteriorated rapidly. On 17 October Lieutenant-Governor Noufflard telegraphed Commandant Renard to send up to Bimbereke a platoon of the 9th

Company then expected on the 18th at Djougou. But the telegram did not reach him till 22 October, both because the telegraph line was not functioning well and because of his own movements.

It was not until 24 October that Renard was able to despatch a platoon to Bimbereke.[15] Meanwhile news came through that a small hut had been burnt down by the rebels near the *poste* of Bimbereke. As a result Monsieur Lefilliâtre, *Administrateur-en-Chef* and head of the automobile service of Northern Dahomey, ordered the *Commandant de Cercle* of Moyen-Niger, Géay, to go to Bimbereke, in the *Cercle* of Borgou (hitherto commanded by Ferlus, now under investigation) to help capture Bio Guera. Noufflard, Lt. Governor of Dahomey, cabled Lefilliâtre that he had no right to assume the position of *Commandant de Cercle* of Borgou nor to call on the services of a neighbouring *Commandant de Cercle*. But Noufflard's cable arrived too late.

On 23 October, Bimbereke, where Géay was now stationed, was attacked by followers of Bio Guera, telegraph lines were torn down so that Bimbereke was cut off from Kandi to the North and Parakou to the south. Bimbereke, defended by three Frenchmen and forty-five *gardes de cercle*, was now in a virtual state of siege lacking water, food and with no means of obtaining them. More important, the Borgu rebellion had spread from the Cercle de Borgou into that of Moyen-Niger, also with a predominant population of Bariba, while the headquarters of the *Cercle*, Kandi, was itself menaced.

What subsequently became clear to the administration was that by this time Chabi Prouka, King of Nikki, had given orders to all those who in pre-colonial times owed allegiance to him to support the rebellion led by Bio Guera,[16] though not all responded.

On 24 October, Noufflard, informed of the crucial situation at Bimbereke and still without news of any action taken as a result of his telegram of 17 October to Renard, asked Captain Hegelbacher to form a detachment of sixty *tirailleurs* from the 12th Company and they set out the next day for Bimbereke.[17] Noufflard was later to be taken to task for giving orders to a military officer without consulting Renard, who alone was empowered to dispose of the troops sent to Dahomey. *General de Division* Goullet, *Commandant Supérieur des Troupes* in Dakar for French West Africa, was to write a month later to the Governor-General asking whether the Beroubouay situation was so serious that it needed action 'which had taken on the character of a veritable military operation'. He considered it necessary except in cases of extreme urgency that the local military commander be informed and consulted. The Governor-General then cabled Noufflard asking him to explain himself.

On the night of 29-30 October a detachment of thirty-two *gardes de cercle* arrived from Parakou under *Administrateur-Adjoint* Autié and got through to the besieged French forces and on the 30th drove back the rebels. On the same day a detachment of five Europeans and a hundred-and-twelve African *tirailleurs* from the 9th and 12th Companies of the Senegalese *tirailleurs* sent by Renard arrived at Bimbereke on 30 October, just after the relief of the post by Autié. Three days later, on 2 November, the detachment from Cotonou under Sub-Lieutenant Kiempinski arrived. Kiempinski put himself at the disposition of *Administrateur-en-Chef* Lefilliâtre, who asked him to escort Géay, the *Commandant de Cercle* of Moyen-Niger, back to Kandi.[18]

At Beroubouay the escort came up against rebels and in the engagement lost three African *tirailleurs* who were killed and seven wounded. Kiempinski attributed these relatively high losses (compared with those suffered in subsequent engagements) to the large number of rebels and the insufficiency of instruction and discipline among his soldiers. On these grounds he considered it advisable to return to Bimbereke and while awaiting reinforcements, conduct reconnaissances around the post.[19]

On 20 November Commandant Renard arrived at Bimbereke to prepare operations with the Lt. Governor of Dahomey, Noufflard. He had at his disposal four Companies of *tirailleurs* from the 3rd Senegalese Regiment and a section of Artillery. In whichever Cercle he was operating Noufflard of course automatically superseded the authority of the civil administrator. Significantly Chabi Prouka, King of Nikki, made no effort to go and greet the Governor at Bimbereke which was in his canton.[20]

Because of the deterioration of the situation among the Bariba in Borgu and Moyen-Niger and because the rebels blocked the road to the North and to the Niger, it was decided to change the earlier plan to deal with the Bariba after Atacora.[21]

The rebel-held country was, in general, flat with only a few isolated hills. Despite the flat nature of the countryside, vision was restricted at that time of the year by thick bush, often as high as a man on horse-back, since the bush fires had not yet cleared it. Trees themselves did not, on the other hand, present much of a problem, since they were rarely so heavily foliaged as to hide the view except near swampy land and certain villages. The villages themselves consisted of groups of huts separated from each other. The huts in each group were linked together by walls forming a compound. Many of the villages were surrounded by hedges of live thorn trees sometimes ten metres high. Entrances through these thick hedges were so narrow that at most only three men could get through at one time.

The Bariba themselves preferred to engage the French outside their villages in difficult terrain or to surprise them on the rear or flanks of the column as it tried to press through the high bush. They rarely used artificial defences like stone walls or stockades. Their bowmen placed themselves either in groups without any natural or artificial protection or behind large trees. Their arms were limited to a few trade guns, for which they lacked powder, and to bows and arrows which were usually poisoned — the Borgawa were notorious for the efficacy of their poisoned arrows.

THE CAMPAIGN AGAINST THE BARIBA

On 21 November Noufflard received a desperate telegram from Kandi saying that rebels were massed at Pade some 13 kilometres away, and had approached within 5 kilometres of the headquarters that day. There were only a few *gardes de cercle* and 500 cartridges with which to defend it. Noufflard and Renard agreed that priority must be given to the relief of Kandi and to the opening of the Niger road.[22] On 22 November Lieutenant Tognet set off with a column of two hundred and twenty five *tirailleurs* and the eleven *gardes de cercle* who had accompanied Géay on his ill-fated attempt to settle matters in Becou. Géay himself once again set out with the troops to see if he could get back to his headquarters. Once again the troops were met by the rebels at Beroubouay but this time, after a battle lasting only fifteen minutes, they were able to force their way through with only three *tirailleurs* wounded. The next day the detachment was again held up at Sori, this time much more seriously so, for the thick bush in which they were attacked prevented an easy solution to the battle which lasted two-and-a-half hours and resulted in three *tirailleurs* killed and thirteen wounded.[23] On 24 November the rebels were harassed for three hours by the inhabitants of Ouere who slid through the high grass to attack them on the flanks or from the rear. The French suffered no losses that day, and estimated they had killed fifteen Bariba. On the 25th the detachment got through to Kandi which in the event had not been attacked by the rebels as a result of the activities of pro-French chiefs in the area and the news of the impending arrival of the French column.

It now became clear that there were three major groups of rebels to deal with among the Bariba. The first were those in the Canton of Bagou, who disrupted communications between Kandi and the Niger. The second were in the Bimbereke-Beroubouay-Sinende area, disrupting communications with Atacora. The third group was centred in the Becou-Nikki area, but this last did not present any strategic threat. However, from a political point of view the Lieutenant-Governor considered it the most important group, because it was here that Chabi Prouka, King of Nikki, was most active.[24]

It was decided in Bimbereke to deal with the rebels in the Bimbereke-Sinende-Beroubouay area while waiting for Tognet to return from Kandi so that the combined forces could then deal with the Becou rebels. On 30 November the 7th Company under Captain Tirveillot left for Sinende arriving there the next day. On 2 December, the French forces lost their first French member killed. Five hundred metres west of Sekere they were attacked by rebels who had used the cover of the high grass to creep up on their flanks. At first the French were able to disengage themselves, but two hundred metres from the village they were again attacked, after which they finally took the village. The detachment then returned to Sinende in order to give the French sergeant a 'decent burial'.

Two days later the Terveillot column again joined battle with the rebels, this time on the road outside Sinende where they lost one *tirailleur* killed and one wounded.

Meanwhile Tognet had been effectively immobilised at Kandi for several days by lack of orders because the telegraph line to Bimbereke was down. On the 5th, however, he was able to leave Kandi with orders to crush the rebels in the *Cercle* of Moyen-Niger who were grouped in the Bagou-Sori-Ouere region. Thereafter he was to return to Bimbereke via the mountainous zone east of the Niger road. His own troops were reinforced by 90 *tirailleurs* from the 6th Company of the Senegalese Regiment under Lt. Croccichia brought down from Niger Military Territory. He left 40 *tirailleurs* in Kandi as a garrison. During his first day's march the rebels engaged him at Tonkagou for 20 minutes and wounded one of his *tirailleurs*.

Two days later at Bagou-Agbo, centre of the rebellion in these parts, the French forces met stiff resistance from the rebels, losing one *tirailleur* killed and one other wounded. Administrateur Géay was later to remark on the disproportion between the enormous number of cartridges fired by the French forces and the resulting damage to the rebels: 9,000 cartridges at Bagou-Agbo for seven or eight victims, a fact that did not escape the rebels' notice.[25]

From Bagou-Agbo the column marched to Ouere, which was destroyed along with other villages which had resisted — Tonkougou, Bagou, Bagou-Agbo, and Dadare. Géay was to cable the Lt. Governor a few days later on the uselessness of burning Borgu villages as retribution, since 'they have no fundamental attachment to them — their losses are relatively very small'.[26] At Ouere, Tognet set up a provisional French post. He reached Bimbereke on the 12th.

Terveillot stayed on at Sinende, where he had buried his European sergeant, until the 7th when he returned to Sekaere, taking it successfully. The next day at Yarra the rebels killed one *tirailleur* and one

European sergeant was wounded. Two days later on the 9th after taking Samboa, with only one African wounded, the Terveillot column returned to Bimbereke via Beroubouay where Tognet joined him on the 12th. The combined columns were now able to take on the rebel forces led by the Bio Guera himself, to whom, it was learnt, Chabi Prouka, King of Nikki, had sent reinforcements.

Renard himself took command of the two companies and the artillery section. His plan was first to attack Baobra, and there capture Chabi Prouka.

On 17 December, they reached Baobra where, eight hundred metres outside the village, they were attacked by the Bariba in the midst of heavily treed vegetation and thick high grass where their view was often limited to only a few metres. At the same time as impairing their vision, the dense bush and grass helped deflect the heavy rain of Bariba arrows that fell on them. The Bariba had either taken up position round the trees or in them and fought bitterly, several being killed at bayonet point. Outflanked by the French on both sides they nevertheless resisted right up to the village, which in turn they tried to hold against the enemy. The battle lasted one hour and twenty minutes. Because of the terrain the artillery was not used until the last minute. The French found forty-two dead bodies on the battle-field including that of Bio Guera. Their own losses in this bitter battle were only three wounded *tirailleurs*.

With Bio Guera dead the backbone of the resistance was broken. On the 18th Renard found Bio Guera's village, Becou, deserted and similarly Bouanri and Nionkalekale on the 19th. On the 20th Renard sent Tognet's company to Nikki to capture Chabi Prouka and take him to Bimbereke. On 24 December, Chabi Prouka, King of Nikki, whom the French had once thought a devoted chief, was brought before Governor Noufflard who after interrogating him 'established his culpability' and sent him for trial at Porto Novo. En route he tried to escape but was recaptured.

The final battle of the war of the Bariba against the French was fought against the 7th Company at Fo. Under Sub-Lieutenant Ligier the company had marched through villages south of the Bimbereke-Sinende road where rebels had been signalled. At Fo, within twenty minutes, the rebels were driven out and the French settled down to the problems of ensuring submission.

The Bariba rebellion had been put down none too soon: to the North West the situation in Atacora had deteriorated rapidly. Kouande itself was threatened by Samba, leader of the Atacora rebels. Furthermore Agades in Niger Military Territory was being attacked by Senussi rebels and the Governor-General ordered the return of the 6th Company of the 3rd Senegalese Regiment to Niamey reinforced by fifty *tirailleurs* from the Bimbereke region. Despite the seriousness of the situation in Atacora, the Governor-General decided that the peace imposed on the Bariba was so uneasy that they must be forced into complete submission before dealing with Atacora.

Columns were sent around the disaffected areas disarming the people throughout January. Only in the Bouanri-Nionkalekale-Ouararou area did the French experience further resistance when they came upon rebels who had taken refuge in bush camps on the banks of the river Tansinet some forty kilometres from Bimbereke. Lt. Tognet and seventy-eight *tirailleurs* took the rebels by surprise and killed eighty-nine of them, taking thirteen prisoners, ten rifles, sixty bows and some two-thousand arrows. After this the French had no more open trouble in Borgu, but the people were slow in making submission and handing in their arms. Certain rebel Borgu chiefs had taken refuge on the borders of Djougou and Borgou Cercles, and as late as August 1917, requests were being made by the Military Commandant of Dahomey to send troops to deal with rebel chiefs in the bush north of Nikki.[27]

By 30 June 1918, 3,027 bows and 60,306 arrows and 33 guns had been destroyed in the *Cercle* of Moyen-Niger while in Borgu 17,456 bows and 205,333 arrows and 725 rifles had been destroyed.[28] Collective fines were imposed and collected in the disaffected areas and an uneasy peace was restored among the Bariba.

CONSEQUENCES AND CAUSES OF THE REBELLION

From the Bariba point of view the overriding consequence of the rebellion was the demonstration that French power was superior to their own. Though they had succeeded in giving the French a stiff battle, the end result had been their submission and disarmament. They had lost some of their leaders, notably Bio Guera, and many of their men in battle. They were faced with paying a large fine to the French. Furthermore, the Sina Boco, ruler of all the Boco (Bariba), Chabi Prouka, King of Nikki, was arrested. Though he managed to effect a temporary escape, he was recaptured as a result of information supplied to the French by Ago-li-Agbo, the ex-King of Dahomey who had succeeded Behanzin, after his defeat by the French, but had no powers as King of Dahomey. He was taken to Cotonou and exiled for ten years to Guinea. Though the evidence against him was not direct, it was clear to the French Administration that he had taken a leading role in inciting the rebellion. Certainly, they believed, if he had opposed it, the rebels would never have been able to go as far as they did. It is not surprising that Chabi Prouka and other *Wasangari* should have taken what they saw as a golden opportunity to rid themselves of the white men who had so reduced them in status.

Undoubtedly, *Wasangari* resentment against the reduced circumstances in which they found themselves under French rule was a leading factor in the rebellion. It was not a cause readily recognised by the French. Indeed up until the Becou incident Noufflard, the Lt. Governor, and Ferlus, *Commandant de Cercle* of Borgou, had no idea that a rebellion was in the offing. Only Angoulvant, from the perspective of Dakar, was writing anxiously in August 1916 about the Bariba to the *Général Commandant* of Troops in West Africa: 'The Baribas of Bimbereke (*cercle* of Borgou) have a hostile attitude that the momentary abandonment of the post necessitated by penury of personnel could only render *plus entreprenante encore*'.[29] With hindsight senior Dahomeyan officials were able to enumerate, and quarrel as to the importance of, the causes of the rebellion, which the Becou incident sparked off. It became clear to them that taxation, forced labour and above all recruitment of young men for the armed forces had heightened Bariba resentment of French Colonial Administration, and that the Becou incident demonstrated to them clearly what they had come to believe: the French were not invincible. Inspector-General Phérivong wrote in his report: 'the Bariba peoples of Borgu and Kandi knew, and there is no doubt about this, of our difficulties in Europe, and the time seemed favourable to them to get rid of the whites and recover their independence'. Géay wrote afterwards that there was no immediate, well determined cause of the rebellion, but what became referred to as the 'disgraceful flight of Ferlus' showed the Bariba that 'one could defeat the whites'. Soldiers returning from the European front told the people 'that the whites were killing each other by the thousands; that the whites who remained in Dahomey were the last; everywhere their numbers were diminishing and they could not be replaced. In one word the whites were no longer strong and one could chase them out and regain one's ancient liberties'.[30] In evidence given to the inquiry as to the role played by Chabi Prouka, King of Nikki, in the uprising, Sorokou-Komani, a son of Bio Guera, alleged that Chabi Prouka had sent to his father a message that he was aware of what had happened at Becou and gave him the order to prepare for war against the whites for he (Chabi Prouka) was master of Bariba land.

It is clear from the widespread nature of the uprising and the analyses of the French themselves that the Bariba under Nikki did in fact see the chance for independence. In a study made by the author of a revolt a year before in British Borgu, it is clear that return to independence was not an aim of the rebels there. Taking this as a datum, we must then ask why the Borgawa under French rule were prepared to rise up against French administration as such and seek to drive the French out of the country, where the Borgawa under British rule merely sought to overthrow the unpopular Native administration imposed by the British. (See Chapter VII)

The simple answer is that the demands and imposition made on French Borgu were far heavier than in British Borgu. Where French Borgu was strategic to the French, linking as it did coastal Dahomey with their colony of Niger, British Borgu was of such little importance that for some periods of time no European official was stationed there, and it was the ignorance of the political structure of the area and the high-handedness of British officials in attempting to restructure native administration there which was the primary cause of the revolt.

In French Borgu a similar high-handedness in dealing with Borgu chiefs and their role in local administration was also a contributory factor. But on top of this, whereas British Borgu was administered in *absentia* by the British for much of the time, French Borgu was very closely administered by the French, so that discontent with local government was directly focused on the French whereas in British Borgu it was only indirectly focused on the British, the prime target of the rebels being the Native Administration of Bussa.

This discontent with French administration was exacerbated at this particular time by its imposition of taxes, forced labour and recruitment of young men for the army, in particular the last. In French Borgu taxation was much higher than in British Borgu; the demands for forced labour were systematic and much more onerous than the relatively casual demands in British Borgu. Finally in British Borgu there was no compulsory recruitment for the army.

As far as the French were concerned, Chabi Prouka had demonstrated that the kings of Nikki were still a power to be reckoned with. And though he was exiled, French policy towards chiefs was to be moderated into one which, while it did not give them powers in any way comparable to those of their British counterparts, at least tried to reinforce their positions and avoid humiliating them in the eyes of their subjects.[31] For the French the suppression of the rebellion was achieved just in time to open up the Niger road in order to shift supplies through to their forces beleaguered by the Senussist revolt in Agades and Zinder. But perhaps more fundamental, as far as the French were concerned, was the way the revolt demonstrated the precarious nature of their presence and their administration. Not only were Africans prepared to rise up against their white overlords, but these latter had not shown themselves very competent. Inspector-General of Colonies, Charles Phérivong, in his report on the rebellion, condemned not only the shameful flight of Ferlus, but his and the Governor's administration. Perhaps most significant of all was the *fact that the lines of* communication between the men on the spot and their superiors, at all levels, were so tenuous.

NOTES

1. N[ational] A[rchives] of S[enegal] 4 D.75, Recruitment indigène. Van Vollenhoven to Maginot, July 1917 and again in NAS Série D.4D 73 Van Vollenhoven to Minister of Colonies 29 September 1917.
2. See Michael Crowder, 'West Africa and the 1914-1918 War' *Bull. IFAN*, T XXX, ser. B, no. 1, 1968.
3. NAS/4/D/74.
4. Information supplied by the late Musa Baba Idris who before his death completed the first draft of a thesis on Pre-Colonial Borgu.
5. Information supplied by the late Musa Baba Idris.
6. NAS/3F/1 Lt. Governor Dahomey to Governor-General, Dakar, Kalale 5 July 1915.
7. NAS/8/G/15 Creation of Post of Bimbereke, Ag. Lt. Gov. Dahomey to Governor-General Dakar, received and noted by Governor-General 31 December 1912.
8. *National Archives of France*. Mission 1919. Rapport fait par M. Ch. Phérivong. Inspector-General ler classe des Colonies concernant affaires des Djougou et du Borgu à l'époque du 30 Janvier 1919, explications fournies par le lt-Gouverneur p.i. de la Colonie du Dahomey, referred to hereafter as Phérivong Report.
9. The above account is based on the Phérivong Report 'Affaire de Bembereke'
10. NAS/17G/56 Pièce 163: Extract of the Procés-Verbal of the 422nd Session of the Council of Administration of Dahomey of 1 May 1917.
11. NAS/1D178 Exchange of correspondence between Acting Governor-General and Commandant Supérieur de Troupes 5 October 1916 (folio 199), 9 October 1916 (folio 203).
12. G. Angoulvant, *La Pacification de la Côte d'Ivoire*, Paris, 1913.
13. NAS/1D178/4 (Acting Governor-General to Lt. Governor Dahomey) Instruction au sujet des opérations de police à entreprendre au Dahomey. Dakar, 24 October 1916.
14. NAS/8G8 Governor-General to Lt. Governor Dah. Personal and Confidential, 24 October 1916.
15. NAS/8G8/92 Governor-General to Commandant Superieur des Troupes Dakar, 6 December 1916.
16. NAS/1D178/37 Opérations Militaires du Haute Dahomey, Rapport d'Ensemble.
17. NAS/8G8/92 Governor-General to Commandant Supérieur des Troupes, 6 December 1916.
18. NAS/8G8 Governor-General to Commandant Supérieur des Troupes, 6 December 1916.
19. NAS/1D178/37 Opérations Militaires du Haut Dahomey, Rapport d'Ensemble.
20. NAS/17G56/piece 163.
21. NAS/1D178/28 Général de Division Goullet, Commandant of Troops for French West Africa to Governor-General, AOF; 26 November 1917 (folio 37).
22. Unless otherwise footnoted all the information in this section is derived from NAS/1/D/178 and NAS/8G8.
23. N.B. in this same file the date of the battle of Sori is also given as 25 November but it seems clear it did in fact take place on 23rd.
24. NAS/8G7/88 Noufflard to Renard, 27 November 1916.
25. NAS/8G7/ Letter from Géay to Noufflard dated, Ouere, 9 December 1916, cited by Noufflard to Governor-General Dakar, Bimbereke, 14 December 1916.
26. NAS/8G7/89 teleg. Géay to Noufflard, Kandi, 12 December 1916.

27. NAS/1/D/178 Lt. Col. Fourn, Commandant Militaire Dah. to Commandant Supérieur, Dakar, 2 August 1917.
28. NAS/8G9/
29. NAS/1/D/178/27 – 4 Letter from G.G. to Commandant Supérieur des lè Troupes, A.O.F., 29 August 1916.
30. NAS/1/D/178/22 Géay to Noufflard, 1 January 1917.
31. Luc Garcia, 'Les mouvements de résistance au Dahomey', *Cahiers d'Etudes Africaines*, X, 37, 1er Cahier, 1970.

IX

INDIRECT RULE – FRENCH AND BRITISH STYLE *
(1964)

In his witty and thought-provoking Lugard Memorial Lecture, 'Et maintenant, Lord Lugard?' (*Africa*, XXXIII. 4, 1963), Gouverneur Deschamps has provided us with an excellent general appraisal of the relative achievements and failures of French and British 'native' administration in Africa. But he does not do full justice to the fundamental differences between the two systems. Though he hints at these differences on several occasions in his lecture, he contends that, far from what is generally supposed, the two were in practice very similar, since they both reposed on indigenous chiefs.[1] He insists that 'la seule différence est que nous n'avons pas tenté, comme vous, Lord Lugard, de moderniser ces états anciens, ni de créer des embryons d'états là où il n'en existait point'; or '... (our administrative practice) ne différait de la vôtre (au moins en Afrique noire) que par une allure plus familière et des buts moins définis'. This seems seriously to underestimate the nature of the differences between the two systems, which were rather those of kind than of degree.[2] M. Deschamps rightly insists that there has been a tendency on both sides of the Channel to over-simplify the basic characteristics of systems of colonial administration in Africa. Nevertheless there were such fundamental differences between the French and British systems that, even if both did make use of 'chiefs', it is not possible to place the French system of native administration in the same category as British Indirect Rule. It is true that both powers had little alternative to the use of existing political authorities as a means of governing their vast African empires, and in most cases these authorities were headed by chiefs. What is important is the very different way in which these authorities were used. The nature of the position and power of the

---

*Reprinted by permission of the International African Institute from *Africa*, XXXIV, 3, July 1964, pp. 197-205.

chief in the two systems was totally different and, as a corollary, so were the relations between the chief and the political officer, who was inspired in each case by very different ideals.

The British in Northern Nigeria, which became the model for indirect rule, believed that it was their task to conserve what was good in indigenous institutions and assist them to develop on their own lines. The relation between the British political officer and the chief was in general that of an adviser who only in extreme circumstances interfered with the chief and the native authority under him. However, where chiefs governed small political units, and in particular where their traditional executive authority was questionable, the political officer found himself interfering in native authority affairs more frequently than ideally he should. This was true in many parts of East Africa and in parts of Yorubaland, where the borderline between 'advisory' and 'supervisory' in the activities of the political officer was not always clear. Though indirect rule reposed primarily on a chief as executive, its aim was not to preserve the institution of chieftaincy as such, but to encourage local self-government through indigenous political institutions, whether these were headed by a single executive authority, or by a council of elders.[3] In Northern Nigeria a policy of minimal interference with the chiefs and their traditional forms of government was pursued. But Lugard himself had insisted on a reform of the indigenous taxation system and of the administration of native justice when he was Governor of Northern Nigeria and believed that, while the colonial government should repose in the chiefs, their administration should be progressively modernised. And, though his successors left them largely to themselves, Sir Donald Cameron, Governor of Nigeria from 1931 to 1935, who had introduced indirect rule to Tanganyika and held similar beliefs to those of Lugard, was shocked by the situation in Northern Nigeria, where he felt the emirates were fast developing into Indian-style native states.

Indeed, in the earliest inter-war period many emirs and chiefs ruled as 'sole native authorities', a position which gave them for practical purposes more power than they had in pre-colonial days, where they were either subject to control by a council or liable to deposition if they became too unpopular.[4] They were permitted to administer traditional justice, which, in the case of certain emirs, included trying cases of murder for which the death sentence, subject to confirmation by the Governor, could be passed. They administered political units that corresponded to those they would have administered before the arrival of the colonial power. They were elected to office by traditional methods of selection, and only in the case of the election of a patently unsuitable candidate to office would the colonial power refuse recognition. There was thus a minimal undermining of the traditional sources of authority. The main change for the Fulani Emirs of Northern Nigeria, for instance, was that they now owed allegiance to the British Government rather than to the Sultan of Sokoto, and collected taxes on its behalf, though they retained, in most cases, seventy per cent of the amount collected for the administration of their native authority.

This system of indirect rule was, with modifications, practised wherever possible in Britain's colonies in West Africa and in most of her other African territories. There were notable exceptions, especially in Eastern Nigeria, where the absence of identifiable executive authority in most communities made indirect rule as practised in Northern Nigeria almost impossible to apply. In such societies, British assiduity in trying to discover chiefs, or invent them, might lend colour to M. Deschamps's argument; but, in practice, the goal of ruling through traditional political units in which local self-government could be developed was maintained, and after much trial and error a system of democratically elected councils was formulated as most closely corresponding to the traditional methods of delegating authority.

If, taking into account such variations, we use indirect rule in Northern Nigeria as a model we shall see just how greatly the French system of administration in Black Africa differed from that of the British.

The British system depended on the advisory relationship between the political officer and the native authority, usually a chief, leading a local government unit that corresponded to a pre-colonial political unit. The French system placed the chief in an entirely subordinate role to the political officer. M. Deschamps alludes only briefly to the role of the French political officer towards the end of his article, where he hints at the nature of his status as a *roi paternel* or *roi absolu*. But it is important to stress that the chief in relation to the French political officer was a mere agent of the central colonial government with clearly defined duties and powers. He did not head a local government unit, nor did the area which he administered on behalf of the government necessarily correspond to a pre-colonial political unit. In the interests of conformity the French divided the country up administratively into cantons which frequently cut across pre-colonial political boundaries. Chiefs did not remain chiefs of their old political units but of the new cantons, though sometimes the two coincided. In certain cases the French deliberately broke up the old political units, as in the case of the Futa Jallon where their policy was 'the progressive suppression of the chiefs and the parcelling out of their authority'.[5] Most important of all, chiefs were not necessarily those who would have been selected according to customary procedures; more often than not they were those who had shown loyalty to the French or had obtained some education. While the British were scrupulous in their respect for traditional methods of selection of chiefs, the French, conceiving of them as agents of the administration, were more concerned with their potential efficiency than their legitimacy. We need not wonder then that as a young French administrator, after serving in Senegal and Dahomey, M. Robert Delavignette should have been astonished, on his way to duty in Niger, to find that the British political officer in Kano actually called on the Emir when he had business with him and paid him the compliment of learning Hausa so that he could speak to him direct. 'Pour le jeune administrateur français, une telle manière d'administrer avait la charme d'un conte des Mille et Une Nuits'.[6] Contrast the position of the Emir of Kano with that of the Alaketu of Ketu in Dahomey. By tradition he was one of the seven most important rulers in Yorubaland, on an equal footing with the Oni of Ife and the Alafin of Oyo. A friend who visited him while Dahomey was still under French rule found him waiting outside the French *Chef de Subdivision's* office. He mentioned the fact that the King was waiting to the French administrator, who replied, 'Qu'est ce qu'il va se faire engueuler?', and kept him waiting a little longer.

It is clear then that the French explicitly changed the very nature of the powers of the chief and that 'his functions were reduced to that of a mouthpiece for orders emanating from outside'.[7] This is brought out clearly, for example, in the *Arrêté* of 28 December 1936 on the organisation and regulation of the local indigenous administration in French Equatorial Africa in the section dealing with *Chefs de Canton* (or *de Terre* or *de Tribu*).[8]

The *Chefs de Canton* (&c.) are recruited:
(i) for preference from among the descendants of old families traditionally or customarily destined to command,
(ii) from among notable natives, literate if possible, who have rendered services to the French cause and who are fitted to fill these functions by their authority or influence in the country,
(iii) from among the *Chefs de Canton* (&c.) who have satisfactorily carried out their functions for at least four years,
(iv) from among old soldiers who have completed more than the normal terms of service and who qualify for special treatment,
(v) from among local civil servants (clerks, interpreters, &c.) who have worked satisfactorily for at least four years in the public service.

The following are the disciplinary measures applicable to *Chefs de Canton* (&c.):
 (i) Reprimand by the *Chef de Departement*.
 (ii) Temporary withholding of salary.
 (iii) Temporary interdiction.
 (iv) Reduction of salary.
 (v) Dismissal.

Since the chiefs did not, except in rare cases, represent traditional authority and, since they were the agents of the colonial power for carrying out its more unpopular measures, such as collecting taxes and recruiting for labour, they were resented in most parts of French West Africa. While they retained no traditional judicial authority such as that of their counterparts in British West Africa in their Native Courts, they were agents of the law, in this case the unpopular system of summary administrative justice known as the *indigenat*.[9] In many areas in the post-war period they became identified with pro-French administrative parties, particularly in Soudan (Mali). Hence it was not surprising that when, in 1957, just before the independence of Guinea, Sekou Toure (then Vice-President of the *Conseil*) decided to do away with chiefs, the operation was effected with remarkably little protest from either the indigenous population or from the French administration that had made use of them. Of the twenty-two *Commandants de Cercle*, still mostly French, called to Conakry to discuss the proposed removal of the chiefs (from 25 to 27 July) only four felt that the *Chefs de Canton* had a useful role to fulfil in the territory, and nearly all confirmed that the chiefs no longer possessed political traditional authority and had become mere agents of the administration. As far as the *Commandant de Cercle* for Labe was concerned: 'Pour moi, qu'ils soient là ou pas, c'est la même chose'.[10] This is a far cry from Nigeria of the day, where in the North the opposition party (N.E.P.U.) were trying unsuccessfully to rouse the people against the chiefs and where the Government of Eastern Nigeria, an area in which traditionally most societies did not have chiefs, commissioned a former expatriate administrative officer to 'investigate the position, status and influence of chiefs and natural rulers in the Eastern Region, and make recommendations as to the necessity or otherwise of legislation regulating their appointment, recognition and deposition'.[11] In African countries where the British had imposed chiefs, as in Eastern Nigeria and parts of Uganda, their prestige had in fact gone up, but this has certainly not been true in the former French territories.

In formulating these general models it is once again essential to recognise exceptions to the general rule. For example, the kings of the Mossi in Upper Volta, the Fulani Emirs of the northern provinces of

Cameroun, and a number of chiefs in Niger retained some power. But in general the French system of administration deliberately sapped the traditional powers of the chiefs in the interest of uniformity of the administrative system, not only within individual territories but throughout the two great federations of West and Equatorial Africa. Thus it seems somewhat of an underestimate to describe the French attitude, as Gouverneur Deschamps does, as 'notre pratique nonchalante à l'egard des chefferies'. Robert Delavignette in *Freedom and Authority in West Africa* (London, 1950) bears this out in his chapter on the *Commandant*. 'The man who really personified the *Cercle* was the *Commandant*.... He was the chief of a clearly defined country called Damagaram (Zinder in Niger), and chief in everything that concerned that country'. Yet this was the Damagaram once ruled over by the powerful Sultans of Zinder, who are now reduced to little more than exotic showpieces of traditional Africa. So too does Geoffrey Gorer in *Africa Dances* (London, 1935), when he writes of the *Chefs de Canton*:

> In theory these local chiefs rule under the guidance of the local administrator: in practice they are the scapegoats who are made responsible for the collection of money and men. While they enjoy the administrator's favour they have certain privileges, usually good houses and land and in a few cases subsidies; but unless they are completely subservient they risk dismissal, prison and exile.

Gorer draws attention to a phenomenon that bears out just how much the French had changed the nature of chiefs in West Africa. In Ivory Coast, if a *Chef de Canton* with no traditional rights to 'rule' were imposed by the administration, the people often elected in secret a 'real' chief. Delavignette also notes this in *Freedom and Authority in French West Africa*.[12]

Why this great difference in approach by the two powers to the question of native administration, given that both for reasons of economy had to administer their vast African possessions with the aid of 'chiefs'? The difference has much to do with difference in national character and political traditions. While few would disagree that the British were inspired by the concept of separate development for their African territories, there is still much debate as to how far the French were inspired by the concept of assimilation even after its formal abandonment as official policy in favour of a *politique d'association*. Only by an examination of the extent of the survival of assimilationist goals in French colonial policy can we understand the reasons for the difference in the two approaches to native administration. This survival showed itself at two levels: as a dominant feature of the *politique d'association* and in the personal ethos of the French political officer.

One of the problems here is to define assimilation. M. D. Lewis has drawn attention to the many definitions of assimilation in use:[13] (1) Assimilation as the dominant colonial policy of France, i.e. its dominant and continuing characteristics; (2) Assimilation as the policy abandoned in favour of association; (3) Assimilation as opposed to autonomy, i.e. integration versus devolution; (4) Assimilation as a legalistic definition, i.e. representation in the mother of parliaments; (5) Assimilation as civilisation; (6) Assimilation as representing racial equality as against British tendency to the colour bar; (7) Assimilation as a highly centralised form of direct rule of colonies. It is of course difficult to choose any one definition as the satisfactory one. Assimilation as practised in the four communes of Senegal, the only instance of its full-scale application in French Tropical Africa, had the following distinctive features: political assimilation to the metropolitan country through the representation of Senegal in the *Chambre des Deputés*; administrative assimilation by creating a *Conseil-Général* for Senegal modelled on the *Conseils du Département* of France, and by the establishment of municipal councils on the French model; the personal assimilation of Senegalese in the communes by according them the status of French citizens, though they were allowed to retain their *statut personnel*; the extension of French educational facilities as part of the French *mission civilisatrice*.

This policy was abandoned not so much because men like Lyautey and Jules Harmand advocated Lugardian ideas about the relationship between the colonial power and African peoples, but because, to use Lewis's phrase, the French were 'not prepared to undertake the massive work of social transformation which alone could make it a reality'. But the *politique d'association* that succeeded it was certainly not that advocated by Jules Harmand, whereby the colonial power would respect the manners, customs, and religion of the natives and follow a policy of mutual assistance rather than exploitation. Rather it was one in which, while recognition was given to the impracticability of applying a full-scale policy of assimilation to African societies, a number of assimilationist characteristics were retained. First, the goal of creating French citizens out of Africans was not abandoned; it was just made more distant and much more difficult of achievement. Second, there was a high degree of administrative centralisation of the mother country, which was not compatible with a true *politique d'association*. We have already seen that the French made little concession to indigenous political units in dividing up their African territories for administrative purposes. Third, the French civilising mission was not abandoned, and though education might be sparse, it was modelled on the French system. Children spoke French from the day they entered school. No concession was made to teaching in the vernacular as in the British territories. Fourth, individual territories were not considered as having special characters, so that the same administrative organisation was imposed on them all. Political officers would be posted from one territory to the other sometimes every other year, which gave them little time to learn the local language or ethnography. On the other hand the British political officer remained in the same territory for a long period of time and, in the case of Nigeria, in the same region; and promotion depended in part on the ability of the political officers to learn indigenous languages. Thus under the French system the one constant for the political officer could only be French culture, while for the British officer every encouragement was given to him to understand the local culture.

As a corollary the French did give some encouragement to the formation of a native elite, which was absorbed into the territorial and federal administrative services, albeit not on a very large scale. The British, on the other hand, in the twenties and thirties actively discouraged the formation of a class of Europeanised Africans, particularly at the level of the central colonial administration. Miss Perham in the late thirties was advocating that no African should be appointed to the administrative service, which she regarded as an alien superstructure.[14] Rather they should be encouraged to work with the native administration. Nigeria was, in the words of Sir Hugh Clifford, Governor from 1919 to 1925, a 'collection of self-contained and mutually independent Native States' which the educated Nigerian had no more business co-ordinating than the British administration. Thus Nigerians were by and large excluded from the senior service of government, while a number of French colonials reached high posts in the administration. Professor Lucy Mair writing in 1936[15] about the status of the educated African in the French colonies remarked that:

> The assumption which governs the whole attitude of France towards native development is that French civilisation is necessarily the best and need only be presented to the intelligent African for him to adopt it. Once he has done so, no avenue is to be closed to him. If he proves himself capable of assimilating French education, he may enter any profession, may arise to the dignity of Under-Secretary for the Colonies, and will be received as an equal by French society. This attitude towards the educated native arouses the bitter envy of his counterpart in neighbouring British colonies.

Jean Daniel Meyer in *Desert Doctor* (London, 1960) writes of his experiences in French Soudan in the Army Colonial Medical Service before the Second World War: 'My colleague was a full-blooded

Senegalese. He had studied medicine in France, attending the Bordeaux Naval School, and had the rank of lieutenant'.

Fifth, the African colonies were considered economic extensions of the metropolitan country, and, as Albert Sarraut insisted in his *La mise en valeur de nos colonies* (Paris, 1923)[16], the colonies should provide assistance to France in the form of raw materials for her industry, and in addition to this troops in time of war, in return for which the African would benefit from French civilisation. Colonial policy in the inter-war period was to be 'a doctrine of colonisation starting from a conception of power or profit for the metropolis, but instinctively impregnated with altruism'.

Finally, it was at the level of the political officer himself that the tendency to assimilation so often manifested itself. Whatever official colonial policy may have been concerning the status of chiefs and the necessity to respect indigenous institutions, it is clear that the majority of French political officers believed sincerely in the French civilising mission and that it was their role to bring 'enlightenment' to the African. They certainly did not believe that indigenous culture or institutions had anything of value to offer except as a stopgap. L. Gray Cowan writing in 1958 observed: 'The young *Chef de Subdivision* in the bush is still a proponent of assimilation through the very fact of his education as a Frenchman although it is no longer a part of official policy'.[17] The administrator from republican France, particularly in the inter-war period, had little time for the notion of chiefs holding power other than that derived from the administration itself. This provides a marked contrast with the average British administrator, who believed sincerely that for Africans their own traditional methods of government were the most suitable, provided they were shorn of certain features that did not correspond to his sense of justice. Coming from a country which still maintained a monarchy that had done little to democratise itself on the lines of the Scandinavian monarchies, he had a basic respect for the institution of kingship and the panoply of ritual that surrounded it. The British officer respected his chief as separate but equal, though certainly not somebody with whom he could establish personal social relations. It was the educated African before whom he felt uneasy. Indeed many political officers openly expressed their contempt for the 'savvy boy' or 'trousered African'. In Nigeria, even as late as 1954, one could hear such epithets used by Northern political officers about Southern politicians. The African's place was in the Emir's court, not at Lincoln's Inn or Oxford.

The French political officer, on the other hand, was able to establish relationships with the educated African. M. Delavignette has published in *L'Afrique noire et son destin* (1962) a revealing letter which he received from Ouezzin-Coulibaly, late Prime Minister of

Upper Volta in 1939, concerning his application for French citizenship. Ouezzin-Coulibaly, then a young teacher in Upper Volta, had been friendly with Delavignette at that time for some ten years and expressed his devotion to France and her cause in the war in the warmest terms:

J'ai été à Sindou et c'est là que la nouvelle de la mobilisation m'est parvenue le 29 août 1939. J'ai pu admirer dans ce coin de brousse l'affection que les indigènes portent à la France. Le mouvement s'est opéré en silence et avec une rapidité qui suppose une certaine comprehension de devoir. J'en ai été émerveillé et cela c'est votre oeuvre, c'est l'oeuvre de tous ceux qui ont passé par là et qui ont inculqué au paysan indigène, qu'on frustre à tort, l'idée de la France et de la Patrie.

It would be difficult to find such an intimate relationship between a British political officer and a Nigerian teacher at that period. Even as late as 1954, such contact would have been rare. It would be interesting to make a comparison of the philosophy of the colonial service training courses of France, which were much longer established, with that of the British Devonshire courses.

In conclusion, the differences between the French and British systems of administration in Africa were not only differences in degree but in kind. Both may have used chiefs, but the position of the chief in each system was radically different. The basis for these differences may be sought in the fact that though assimilation as an official policy was abandoned after the early experiment in Senegal, it continued to be a most important inspiration both for the *politique d'association* and for the political officer charged with carrying it out. An understanding of the nature of these differences is not only essential to an understanding of colonial history in Africa, but also to an appreciation of the differences between the two main language blocks in independent Africa today.

NOTES

1. In the summary of the lecture in English it is put more explicitly: 'Indirect rule has been practised by local governors at least since the second empire; from the end of the nineteenth century the official policy was that of "Association" — very close to Lugard's ideas.'
2. See L. P. Mair, *Native Policies in Africa*, London, 1936.
3. See Sir Philip Mitchell's article on 'Indirect Rule', when Governor of Uganda, in *The Uganda Journal*, IV, no. 1, July 1936, where he says that indirect rule is founded on the assumption that 'every group of people must possess some form of ... natural authority, normally, of course symbolised in the person of some individual or individuals. The administrative system called "Indirect Rule"

endeavours in each place where it is to be applied to ascertain what are the persons or institutions which the people concerned look upon as the natural authority'.
4. See P. C. Lloyd's article 'Kings, Chief and Local Government', *West Africa*, 31 January 1953, where he remarks that the Yoruba kings became much more powerful under the British. 'They could only be deposed by the British administration which often tended to protect them against their own people'.
5. Overall report on the general situation of French Guinea in 1906, Conakry, 1906, cited by J. Suret-Canale in 'Guinea under the Colonial system', *Présence Africaine*, no. 29 (English ed.)
6. R. Delavignette in 'Lord Lugard et la politique africaine', *Africa* XXI, no. 3, 1951.
7. L. P. Mair, *op. cit.*, p. 210. R. L. Buell in his *The Native Problem in Africa* cites Joost Van Vollenhoven, Governor-General of French West Africa, 1917-18, as describing the chiefs as having 'no power of their own of any kind. There are not two authorities in the cercle, the French authority and the native authority; there is only one'.
8. Translated by T. G. Brierly.
9. Concessions were made to customary law prior to 1946, when native penal law was abolished and all inhabitants of French Tropical Africa became subject to the French code. Before that time only those Africans who were French citizens could claim justice under the Code. The vast majority of *sujets* were subject to the *indigénat* already referred to and to customary law. Customary law, however, was not administered by the chief but by the French administrator, who was assisted by two notables of the area who were versed in tradition. These courts could try both penal and civil cases. Now customary law survives in questions of inheritance, marriage, and land.
10. *Conférence des Commandants de Cercle*, Imprimerie du Gouvernement, Conakry, 1957.
11. G. I. Jones, *Report on the Position, Status and Influence of Chiefs and Natural Rulers in the Eastern Region of Nigeria*, Government Printer, Enugu, 1957-8.
12. A somewhat extreme point of view with regard to the French attitude to chiefs, which is the exact opposite of that of M. Deschamps, is held by J. Suret-Canale in 'Guinea under the Colonial System', *Présence Africaine*, no. 29, p. 53 (English ed.): 'Between 1890 and 1914 the system of "direct administration" was progressively established. The former sovereigns (including those who had rendered the best service to French penetration) were utterly eliminated and the former political leaders utterly overthrown; ethnic limits, the traditional limits of the former "diwe" in the Futa Jallon, all those were carved up and rearranged at the whim of administrative needs or fancies. The political reality was henceforward the Cercle, and where appropriate, the Subdivision, commanded by a European administrator, and below them, the Canton and the village commanded by African chiefs described as "traditional" or "customary". In reality, these chiefs in their role and in the powers devolved upon them had absolutely nothing traditional or customary; designed to ensure the cheapest execution (under their own responsibility) of the multiple tasks of administration, taxation, forced labour, recruitment etc., they were the exact counterpart of the *caids* of Algeria, subordinate administrators'.
13. M. D. Lewis, 'The Assimilation Theory in French Colonial Policy', *Comparative Studies in Society and History*, IV, no. 2, January, 1962.
14. P. C. Lloyd, 'Lugard and Indirect Rule', *Ibadan*, no. 10, 1960.
15. L. P. Mair, *op. cit.*, p. 189.
16. Quoted by L. P. Mair, *op. cit.*, pp. 186-9.
17. L. Gray Cowan, *Local Government in West Africa*, New York, 1958.

X

WEST AFRICAN CHIEFS*
(1970)

No subject has been more widely discussed by historians of the colonial period in Africa than Britain's policy of indirect rule. The apparent differences or similarities between indirect rule and French administration have excited considerable controversy. While there is a great body of literature on the subject of indirect rule, scholars are still not agreed as to how it should be defined, let alone what its essential characteristics were. Some see categorical differences between French and British local administration during the colonial period, others, while acknowledging that there were differences, see them as differences merely of degree rather than kind. In particular they insist that such differences were more apparent to the colonial rulers than to the Africans whose daily lives were affected by these administrative systems. Much of the argument really boils down to a question of semantics − what one scholar refers to as indirect rule is not what another one considers it to be.

The purpose of a seminar on West African Chiefs held by the Institute of African Studies at the University of Ife in December 1968 was, at the risk of going over familiar ground, to see if by studying the changing status under colonial rule of the chief, the keystone of both French and British local administration in West Africa, a better understanding could be reached not only of the differences between, and similarities to, each other of local administrative policy, which we would consider, constituted the most important element of colonial rule for the vast majority of Africans, but also what indirect rule really meant in the West African context.

The idea of approaching the question of the nature of indirect rule

*Reprinted by permission of the co-author, Obaro Ikime, and the University of Ife Press from the 'Introduction' to *West African Chiefs: Their Changing Status under Colonial Rule and Independence,* Michael Crowder and Obaro Ikime (eds), Ife, 1970, pp. vii-xxix.

and the differences between French and British administration in the colonial period through a study of the role of chiefs in that administration was mooted in a discussion between the authors after a seminar on indirect rule held by the Department of History of the University of Ibadan. We felt that far too many comparisons between French and British rule had been made without the benefit of detailed knowledge of its operation at the local level and that unless such detailed knowledge was brought together it was not much use pursuing the argument further.

The aim of the Ife seminar was not, of course, only to try and arrive at a better understanding of the relative nature of French and British administration during the colonial period, but to deepen our understanding of the institution of chieftaincy generally. Today there are few parts of Africa in which chieftaincy is not still an important social, religious and political institution. In Nigeria where the seminar was held, various state military governors had found it opportune, to the surprise of some of the educated elite, to summon meetings of chiefs to help advise on how best the affairs of the states were to be handled to produce the desired goals of peace and national unity. At the time the seminar was being held one state, the Midwest State, had set up a commission to study the status and functions of the chiefs and make recommendations as to their future. Mr. D. P. Partridge, who headed this commission, was with us at the seminar. We also had the one-time Sole Commissioner for Chieftaincy Affairs of the former Eastern Nigeria, Dr. G. I. Jones. In the northern states, a great deal of re-thinking was going on at the time as to the future role of chiefs, especially that of the great Emirs. Accordingly, at the seminar some twenty different chieftaincies were studied in depth hoping that this would deepen our understanding of the present and past role of chiefs and therefore aid planning for their future roles.

In presenting their papers, **contributors were asked to consider in particular the following points which we hoped would help us see differences and similarities not only between the various chieftaincies considered but also between French and British policy towards chiefs:

(1) Were the chiefs who ruled during the colonial period ones who traditionally would have had the right to assume the chieftaincy?
(2) How far did the colonial power interfere in the selection of candidates for appointment as chief?
(3) Did the chief rule over the same area as his pre-colonial

** Sixteen of these papers were subsequently published in Michael Crowder and Obaro Ikime eds, *West African Chiefs: Their Changing Status under Colonial Rule and Independence,* Ife and New York, 1970.

predecessor did?
(4) What was the relationship between the chief and the European political officer?
(5) How far did the chief retain his legal powers as a dispenser of justice and the one responsible for the maintenance of law and order, i.e. did he preside over criminal as well as civil cases? Did he maintain a police force? Did he run the prisons?
(6) How far did the chiefs lose or gain popularity under colonial rule?
(7) What changes in the economic position of the chief took place under colonial rule?

What follows is an attempt to re-examine the nature of British and French administration, the role of chiefs in those administrations, and their position in the West African society today under independent African governments.

WHO WERE THE CHIEFS UNDER COLONIAL RULE?

Perhaps the major obstacle confronted by the seminar was to determine what class of people we were discussing. The problem was particularly highlighted in Western Nigeria, the setting of the seminar, where there is a great array of people using the title of chief – the great paramount rulers such as the Alafin of Oyo and the Awujale of Ijebu-Ode, who all by tradition were entitled to wear a crown; 'obas', also entitled to wear a crown, who were either traditionally subordinate to the paramounts or made so for administrative convenience under colonial rule; the 'bales' or village heads of the obas; then a whole array of titled officials, heads of cults or lineages who are now referred to as chiefs. Since these title-holders did not have executive authority of their own independent of the oba, they might be easy to exclude. Yet the Western Region Government secured the entry of a 'commoner' into the Western House of Chiefs through a liberal interpretation of the meaning of the word chief. Wishing to appoint the distinguished lawyer, F. R. A. Williams, Q.C. as Attorney-General in their government, when there seemed no prospect of his being elected to a seat in the House of Assembly, once he had gained an Egba chieftaincy title, they made him a member of the House of Chiefs, thus extending the meaning of 'chief' from natural rulers to title holders.

It was quickly recognised by the seminar that it is very difficult to define a chief in the West African context: there is no apparent relationship between the role of the Emir of Kano and the Limba chiefs. It is only by accident that they have all been called 'chiefs', a distinctly colonial 'diminutive' term which effectively reduced the status of rulers like the Oba of Benin, who in pre-colonial times considered himself, and was considered by his subjects, a king. The Emir of Kano, one of the most powerful of the traditional rulers in the whole of Africa during the colonial period, would, however, not have considered himself a King, being himself subordinate to the Sultan of Sokoto, who in pre-colonial times would have considered himself Amir al mummin, Commander of the Faithful, rather than a King. By contrast, Limba Chiefs in pre-colonial times were leaders and rulers rather than officially recognised chiefs, though as Murray and Finnegan point out in 'more important centres, these leaders tended to be hereditary . . . the situation was fluid and the most important leaders in one generation were not necessarily directly succeeded by their descendants'. Again, as G. I. Jones points out, the sort of chiefs referred to by anthropologists as 'strong chiefs' did not, with a few exceptions, exist in Eastern Nigeria, and those who were usually referred to as chiefs in that area had more ritual than political authority, though it must be conceded that in practice ritual authority did tend to confer a measure of political authority. Again in French West Africa in colonial times a whole group of people were made chiefs who in pre-colonial times would have had no right whatsoever to such posts. This was a common administrative practice of the French, who selected chiefs as much on the basis of their administrative abilities, literacy in French and proven loyalty to their masters as on their traditional claims to office. While the British were much more intensely concerned with legitimacy, they did on occasions appoint chiefs who in pre-colonial times would have no claim to such office. Even where a ruling family had long been established in Bussa, they appointed a slave district head of the deposed 'king' of Bussa as his successor.

Whilst it is impossible to define 'chief' in pre-colonial terms, it is possible to define it in colonial terms. Chief, under both French and British colonial rule, was used administratively to designate African administrative authorities recognised by the colonial governments. These authorities fell into two distinct classes: those chiefs who were primary executive authorities, who dealt with the political officer directly, and not through intermediaries; and those chiefs who were subordinate to primary executive authorities, such as district heads and village chiefs, who in theory, if not always in practice, dealt with the political officer only through the intermediary of their superior chief. This was a distinction clearly recognised by 'subordinate' chiefs themselves, for one of the main issues in local chieftaincy politics was the attempt of subordinate rulers, district heads, and even village heads, to obtain their 'independence', i.e. achieve separate recognition by the colonial authorities. A major pre-occupation of Borgu during the colonial period was the equal status given to Kaiama and

Bussa, despite the latter's traditional senior position among the Borgu states, and the subordination to Kaiama of chiefdoms that considered themselves its equals. This was only resolved in the 1950s with the placing of Kaiama and its former dependants under Bussa, now re-styled the Emirate of Borgu. In Ekiti, one Annual Report recorded that there were years when 'claims for obas' crowns . . . threatened to vie with the number of applications to purchase Raleigh bicycles'. Similarly the Bale of Meko, a bale of the Alaketu of Ketu in precolonial times, profited from the fact that his territory was separated by the Anglo-French boundary between Dahomey and Nigeria from his former paramount to make himself into an 'independent' ruler, i.e. an oba dealing directly with the British authorities.

In this essay we are concerned with those 'chiefs' who under colonial rule were the primary executive agents of the British or French, whether or not they had traditional claims to such a position.

HOW FAR WERE THE 'CHIEFS' OF THE COLONIAL PERIOD LEGITIMATE

In a very real sense none of the chiefs who 'ruled' under the French and the British were legitimate. Before the colonial period chiefs derived their 'authority' or the right to rule from a wide variety of sources, whether right of conquest, membership of a particular ruling family, primogeniture, etc., but in every case their source of authority was an indigenous African one. Under colonial rule, whether they had fulfilled all the traditional prerequisites for assumption of office, which would have allowed them to rule in pre-colonial times, their right to rule depended on the colonial authorities. One could argue here that such a situation was not entirely foreign to African societies, particularly in the multi-ethnic empires of the Western Sudan where the ruling groups governed the many different ethnic groups in their empires through their traditional rulers, whose authority was limited by the existence of their overlords. But in these cases the overlords were African, whereas under colonial rule the overlords came from a totally alien culture and introduced very different norms of administration from those of their predecessors.

Within the limitations of an overall colonial authority how far were the chiefs of the colonial period those who would have ruled in pre-colonial times, and, subordinate to this, where they were the chiefs who would have ruled in pre-colonial times, how far did they rule over the areas they would have ruled on the eve of the colonial occupation?

In this connection one must note that where the colonial powers were concerned to use 'legitimacy' as a basis for the appointment of chiefs, they were faced with the major problem of how to determine what constituted legitimate succession in a chieftaincy.

One of the major distinctions between French and British attitudes towards chiefs, in particular 'strong chiefs' is that the French were far less concerned with 'legitimacy' than the British. The archives of the latter are full of 'Assessment Reports', records of oral tradition, special enquiries into dynastic history, largely aimed at establishing the rules of succession to chieftaincies. By and large the British were concerned to place on the throne the 'legitimate' heir. Fortunately for them, within this ambit, their choice was not limited. Benin was a rarity in that primogeniture had been established as the basis for succession since the eighteenth century, though even here disputes took place over the question as to who was the first-born son of the oba. In most chieftaincies several candidates presented themselves to the kingmakers, on whom the Resident or District Officer could put pressure in favour of the candidate in whom he most felt confidence as a potential executive agent of the government in local administration. District Officers, having established to their satisfaction, though not always correctly, the laws of succession, some of which were immensely complex, would keep detailed records on the candidates likely to present themselves on the death of the incumbent ruler. This did not mean that the British always appointed a 'legitimate' claimant, for whilst the kingmakers nominated, the confirmation of appointment came from the Governor. A notorious instance of this was the appointment of Gbelegbuwa II to the Awujaleship of Ijebuland. But by and large as far as the 'strong chiefs' were concerned, they were legitimate incumbents. The instances of chiefs being appointed to thrones to which they had no traditional claim, as in the case of Turaki, the 'slave' district head of Bussa referred to earlier, were rare.

The French took a much more pragmatic approach towards the appointment of chiefs. Whilst they recognised that for the most part a chief with traditional right to rule would be a more effective agent to their administration, they also balanced against this the ability to administer in the modern sense, particularly the ability to speak French. Where British administrators learnt the local language and spent a long time in their 'constituency', the French administrator, having learnt an African language in the Ecole Nationale de France Outremer (E.N.F.O.M.) in Paris, was almost certain to be posted to an area remote from any of its indigenous speakers. This, combined with the system of *rouage*, whereby an administrator was constantly on the move, meant that the ability of a chief to speak French was a considerable advantage to the French administrator who did not want to depend entirely on his interpreter. Over and above this was a French republican hostility to 'monarchs' so that where British officers, coming from a country in which the trappings and person of monarchy survive alongside a parliamentary democracy, found themselves sympathetic to African monarchs, their ritual, the complexity of their courts, genealogy, etc., the French saw the chiefs for the most part as a necessary evil. As such they rarely hesitated to replace an inefficient, illiterate, legitimate chief by an old soldier or retired clerk, who they felt would understand what was required of him. Yet the French from time to time had conscience about this, and in the famous circulars of Ponty and Eboué urged a return to a British type system of selection. It was clear that however efficient the old soldier, clerk or even governor's ex-cook may have been in the modern context, the legitimate chief had a call on his people that these parvenus never could. Hence the phenomenon of 'legitimate' chiefs ruling their people in secret, settling cases which the administration's 'straw chief' never could.

In the case of strong chiefs the British were concerned about their 'legitimacy', where the French were not only prepared to replace them by 'straw chiefs', but were indeed hostile to the presence of great traditional rulers. In cases where strong chiefs were not to be found, however, the British, as was the case in the former Eastern Region of Nigeria, were much more inclined to make administrative appointments. The British made similar appointments where strong chiefs ruled over small areas, in which case they federated chieftaincies under a single chief who traditionally would have no right to rule over other chiefs included in his area of jurisdiction. Examples here are in Ekiti, in Idoma, where the experiment seems to have been successful, whereas in Tiv they have been much less so. Even the British, ready as they were to tolerate great variety in the size and shape of their 'Native Authorities', had limits to this tolerance. So where in the strong chieftaincies they showed concern to establish the correct frontiers of the chieftaincy, in small chieftaincies they were prepared to federate them with others for administrative purposes. The French on the other hand made it deliberate policy to reduce great chieftaincies, and to organise their administrative system so that as far as possible *chefs de canton*, their primary executive agents, ruled over roughly the same area and/or population.

In conclusion we can generalise that the British were much more concerned than the French to retain as their executive agents chiefs who had traditional claims to office and also that they were more concerned to administer their territories through pre-colonial territorial units even at the expense of a bewildering variety of administrative units in shape, structure and size. The French on the other hand put a greater premium on modern administrative capability than on traditional claims to chieftaincy, and were also more concerned to rationalise the territorial organisation of their vast federation.

In all the above, there was less element of choice than has often been assumed. Whilst it is clear that both French and British had their distinct local administrative policies, West Africa was far from being a *tabula rasa* on which these could be imposed without reaction. Thus the French were never able to introduce 'administrative' chiefs into Mossi, and their policy of reducing the Emperor of Mossi's traditional powers, particularly with regard to his power over his former subordinates, whom they tried to make independent of him, was only partly successful because of the persisting regard of the Mossi for the Mogho Naba's person. As several papers suggest, policy and practice diverged in many cases. Policy could be changed in the field either by the strength of African tradition or by the personality of the chief himself. Within these variables, however, we can conclude that while the British were, generally speaking, inclined to allow the prevailing political, social and other circumstances of the territories acquired by them to influence their administrative organisation, the French were not similarly so disposed, though often these circumstances were so strong that they could not ignore them.

NATURE OF THE CHANGE OF AUTHORITY OF THE CHIEFS

We have already noted that in an absolute sense the authority of the chief was limited by the presence of the colonial powers in that he was now no longer independent. He was in the eyes of the colonial regime, if not of his people, a 'chief', not a 'king'. Where chiefs were those who would have had claims to rule in pre-colonial times, these same rulers had removed for them by the colonial regime many of the limitations to their authority from below. Thus we have the paradox, especially in British West Africa under the system of indirect rule, of kings losing their sovereignty but as 'chiefs' increasing their powers over their subjects because the traditional checks and balances to the exercise of their authority were neutralised by the same colonial authorities. Thus in British West Africa nearly all chiefs from the petty Limba chiefs to the Emir of Kano and the Alafin of Oyo increased their powers. Where traditional 'checks and balances' tried to assert themselves, a chief who was on good terms with the administrator could effectively neutralise them as malcontents and trouble-makers. The political officer, working in a strange land and with a vast amount of paper work to do, preferred to rely on the chief he had, than to deal with a complex series of negotiations between factions and groups such as characterised the decision-making process of most African chieftaincies in pre-colonial times. It took the educated elite to provide effective checks to the increasing authoritarianism of chiefs under indirect rule. Ijebu is an excellent example of how the Awujale increased his authority under indirect rule by neutralising traditional checks to it with the co-operation of the British administration but was eventually brought to his knees by the educated elite.

The case of the French chief was different, though not absolutely so. Where he was an administrative chief of course the issue of the change in the nature of his authority does not come into question. Where he was a traditional chief, like the great majority of British chiefs, he had removed from the political structure the traditional checks and balances, but had to contend with the 'interpreters' and *gardes de cercle* who became increasingly powerful as intermediaries between short-term appointment administrators and long-term incumbent chiefs. But more drastic as far as the change in the nature of their authority was concerned was the removal from their competence of functions that in pre-colonial times were the essence of their authority over their subjects.

The French chiefs had no criminal jurisdiction over their subjects, no police force, no prisons. Their jurisdiction in civil cases was severely limited. This did not of course prevent them from carrying out such functions *en cachette* but formally, and to a great extent in practice, their judicial role was reduced to a shadow of what it was in pre-colonial times. And it is clear that the mainstay of the continuing authority of chiefs was their judicial role. Certainly one of the root causes of the revolt led by Bai Bureh against the British administration in 1898 was the transfer of judicial powers of the chiefs to the British political officers. Furthermore, the French chiefs had no 'native authority' of their own with a budget and control of appointments as the British chief did. He collected taxes as his British counterpart did, but retained no percentage to run 'local government'. He thus had no patronage to offer.

The French chief had power insomuch as he had to recruit labourers, soldiers, collect taxes, report miscreants to the administration, but these were powers delegated to him by the administrator, and ones that made him very unpopular. He did not have the authority or initiative that the British chief had. We can say, then, that the British chief, while losing his sovereignty to the British, nevertheless increased his power over his subjects because he was no longer restrained by the traditional checks and balances from below. The great chiefs in particular, provided they did not flagrantly abuse their authority, were left to carry on local government with relatively little interference from the colonial political officer. When such interference was necessary, the political officer was careful to let it be seen that the resulting decision was made by the chief, however much the chief himself resented it. So in the eyes of the chief's subjects, though they knew he was no longer a free agent, there was no apparent diminution of his authority, in some cases there was a definite increase of his control of their lives. This increase in power, coupled with the elimination of checks and balances to restrain his abuse of it, was the principal cause of the unpopularity of many British chiefs during the colonial era.

Whilst the traditional chief under French rule no longer had to contend with traditional checks and balances, the French political officers made it clear that he had, at least formally, lost all initiative of his own. He was vested with many powers but lost much of his authority, since these powers belonged to him not as of traditional right but by dispensation of the latest circular or decree. Here, of course, it must be noted that whilst the British chief continued to exercise powers he had wielded in pre-colonial times, this was by specific dispensation of the colonial power, enshrined in statute – i.e. the Native Authority Ordinances or Proclamations. The essential difference thus lies in the nature of the powers vested in French and British chiefs during the colonial period. While the British chief retained a great many of his traditional powers, the French chief did not. By and large the latter was required to do the dirty work of the French administration: collect taxes, recruit and supervise forced labour, round up soldiers for the army. His traditional functions of justice, policing the state, and of administering the government of his people were removed from him.

FUNCTIONS OF THE CHIEF UNDER COLONIAL RULE

As far as the day to day local administration of France and Britain in West Africa was concerned, the British looked on their chief as a local government authority with legislative functions, albeit one who had often to be supervised by the representative of the colonial government. The French on the other hand looked on the chief as an agent of the colonial government who had to carry out the instructions of his colonial administrator. Where the British chief was acknowledged to have autonomy and initiative in certain spheres, just as a local authority does in Britain, no such authority or initiative was conceded to the French chief, though because of lack of supervision, or by a deliberate turning of a blind eye by the colonial rulers, he did in fact assume a considerable amount of initiative of his own.

The British deliberately tried to foster local self-government by the chiefs within a framework which they laid down. The chief on his own, or the Chief in Council, was known as the Native Authority which indicated that the colonial rulers were prepared to abdicate to him some of their governmental powers. As far as local administration was concerned the British political officer's role in regard to his chief ranged from that of adviser to the more sophisticated native authorities, particularly those they had constructed themselves. However, insofar as the political officer had to effect decisions made by the central government such as the building of a road, railway or telegraph line, etc., through one of his native authorities, he became an absolute ruler instructing the native authority concerned to carry out his orders.

No such dualism was apparent in the role of the French political officer in relation to his chief. The central government, at the level of the colony or the Governor-General of the Federation, laid down a policy which he had to put into effect. West Africa under the French thus inherited the tradition of French metropolitan administration which, as Alexandre points out, since the Middle Ages, showed a strong desire for uniformity and a refusal to accept diversity and originality in local structures. The chief had a set of duties explicitly laid down in circulars and it was the duty of the political officer to ensure he carried them out. The chief had no autonomy of his own as for instance chiefs in British West Africa did in the form of control of expenditure of a budget, the maintenance of a local police force, of a prison and most important of all control of justice up to certain levels depending on the sophistication of the chiefdom concerned. While he collected taxes for the administration, he did not as a matter of right retain a proportion for the local administration of his chiefdom. However, it was accepted that, since his salary was so small, he would illegally raise taxes from his own people over and above the rate set down by the administrator.

We can distinguish between the French and British chief under colonial rule: the French chief was an official or 'fonctionnaire' of the French bureaucratic hierarchy and like all subordinate bureaucrats had a set of tasks with little initiative of his own. On the other hand the British chief had a dual role: in local government he was an authority in his own right, though this authority was carefully circumscribed, even if it was considerable as in the great chieftaincies like Kano and Ashanti (after 1935). However, insofar as he was an agent of the central government required to executive decisions within his area of jurisdiction made by the central government, he was just as much a bureaucrat as the French chief. While at this level the political officer was not required to consult with his chief, at the level of local government, consultation, which was alien (at least formally) to the relationship between the French political officer and his chief, was the cornerstone of the British administrative system. Schematically the two systems may be seen thus:

220 COLONIAL WEST AFRICA

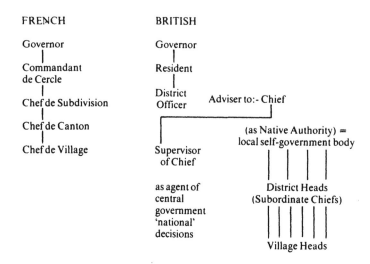

THE QUESTION OF INDIRECT RULE

Indirect rule has been variously defined, but the most general definition of it has been ruling through indigenous agencies. Yet French rule which used indigenous agencies has been defined as direct in contrast to British rule which has been characterised both by its administrators and outside observers as indirect. As pointed out much of the argument has been a matter of semantics, of how terms are defined.

It is argued by some that since the French 'chief' was so often not a traditional chief, nor even ruled over the land he would have done in pre-colonial times, he was a mere functionary. He had no authority of his own but a series of specific tasks which he, like any other member of the administrative hierarchy, white or black — and there were a few black political officers under the French colonial regime before 1940 — had to carry out according to the handbook. It is argued that effectively this was direct rule, and that if the French had been able to afford European substitutes, they would have had functions very little different from those of the chiefs, the 'sergeants and corporals of Empire' as Alexandre has described them. Yet the French reverted on frequent occasions to the thesis that only chiefs with traditional claims to chieftaincy could effectively act for them as the agents of local administration for while they had powers vested in them by the colonial rulers they also needed the authority that tradition vested in them if they were effectively to carry out their task. In the thirties there was a definite swing in French Black Africa towards using chiefs with traditional rights to office. Clearly such a system was not direct rule in the true sense, but nor was it indirect rule in the sense of ruling through an indigenous agency, since the concept of local self-government in which areas of initiative were left to the traditional authorities was foreign to the French.

Essentially indirect rule is about local self-government, and this was the essence of the British system. Within certain limits traditional authorities had initiative of their own, and the extent of these limits depended on the sophistication of the traditional administrative organisation which the British found. That the British tried to modify, streamline or develop these administrative organisations did not mean that they were abandoning indirect rule since their objective was so to develop such organisations that they could cede increasing local governmental functions to indigenous authorities, whether they were traditionally entitled to exercise them or not. However, even as regards the traditional authorities they were not very clear as to what or who they were. When confronted by chiefless societies or societies without strong chiefs they tried to identify an individual through whom they could indirectly rule, i.e. cede the province of local self-government. Later they were forced to realise that effectively to rule indirectly, one had to use an indigenous person or group of persons with real traditional claims to rule rather than a man who seemed capable of it, for in the eyes of the people the latter, even if he was meant to administer local self-government on behalf of 'his people', just because they were not his people, seemed to be very similar to the French *fonctionnaire* chief.

If we agree that indirect rule as an administrative system means local self-government by the traditional authorities, whether a chief as Sole Native Authority, or a Chief in Council, we can characterise most British local administration outside the towns as 'indirect', including even that of Eastern Nigeria during the time of the warrant chiefs. Yet we have the apparent paradox of areas like Gambia, Sierra Leone and Gold Coast (Ghana) where indirect rule was practised from the beginning (with certain notable exceptions) having 'Indirect Rule' introduced into them in the 1930s.

While in the loose sense indirect rule was generally practised in British West Africa from the start, we noted earlier that it was compatible with our definition of indirect rule that the political officers should try to streamline the indigenous administrations to make them more efficient self-governing bodies to which increased areas of authority could be delegated. In Northern Nigeria a pattern of native authority was developed which had certain characteristics which were later to become considered definitions of a system of government known as Indirect Rule. It could as easily have been called the Neo-Lugardian System of Local Self-Government, for it was a particular systematised form of indirect rule derived in large part from Lugard's ideas. Much of the confusion about indirect rule has been the use of the term to describe the special form of indirect rule practised in the north of Nigeria which was then exported to other colonies where indirect rule in the sense of administering the country at the local level through self-governing traditional authorities was already being practised. The next section attempts to define the characteristics of the special system of indirect rule that was introduced progressively throughout British West Africa before 1950 when local government was democratised.

'INDIRECT RULE' DEFINED

When British colonial governments in Gold Coast and Sierra Leone talked of introducing indirect rule into chieftaincies which in the case of Northern Ghana were, at the time, to all intents and purposes directly ruled by the British, or in the case of the Limba of Northern Sierra Leone, exercised a considerable degree of local self-government, what did they mean and, more important, what were they trying to do? What they meant, as we have already suggested, was that they were remodelling their chieftaincies or units of local self-government on the Northern Nigerian pattern.* Their objective was to streamline local administration with particular regard to the regularisation of raising of revenue. Indeed the cornerstone of Northern Nigerian Indirect Rule was the regularisation of the system of tax collection and the sharing of the tax between the central government and the local government unit raising it, i.e. the Native Authority. Apart from helping to support the colonial administration, the payment of taxes to the central government was a tribute acknowledging its authority, at least as Lugard saw it. Now in the Gold Coast no taxes were raised before Indirect Rule was introduced, chiefs running their governments on unsupervised levies and court fines. The second major feature of Indirect Rule was the establishment of a budget for expenditure of the portion of the taxes retained: this was seen both as a means to modernisation of local self-government as well as a check to peculation by the chiefs. These were the major features introduced in the guise of 'Indirect Rule' which otherwise combined features already common to the other local administrative systems of British West Africa.

We can say that once Indirect Rule had been successfully introduced into chieftaincies outside Northern Nigeria the following were its distinguishing features and we are indebted to John Paden's contribution to the discussion of the question at the seminar for

* To distinguish the Northern Nigerian system of indirect rule from indirect rule as a general pattern we designate it 'Indirect Rule'.

assistance in our formulation of the following identifying characteristics of Indirect Rule.
(1) Legitimacy: insofar as possible pre-colonial dynastic lineages were continued.
(2) Territorial Jurisdiction: the territorial jurisdiction of the traditional rulers was maintained, that is the land boundaries of pre-colonial times were respected except where the chiefs or people by their own consent agreed to federate for purposes of greater efficiency, larger revenues, etc.
(3) Native Authorities: chieftaincies were designated Native Authorities, in which the chief might be sole native authority or the Chief in Council constitute the native authority. A native authority had specific functions: (i) collection of taxes of which a fixed percentage was rendered up to the colonial administration; (ii) control of a budget established to spend the taxes retained by the Native Authority, which included initiating, local development programmes, building and maintaining native authority schools and dispensaries, building and operating permanent markets, and constructing local feeder roads to join up with central government roads.
(4) Legal System: the chiefs and their traditional legal officers controlled the administration of law, including local police functions and the prisons, according to customary legal principles shorn of abuses and repugnant aspects as determined by the colonial government.
(5) Appointment of Officials to Native Authorities: the Native Authority controlled appointment and dismissal of its officials; the colonial authorities, however, had to sanction the appointment of the chief himself.
(6) The Role of the Political Officer: essentially the role of the political officer in the Native Authority system was as an adviser, almost as a lobbyist vis-à-vis the Native Authority insofar as local government affairs were concerned. The less sophisticated the Native Authority, however, the more his role became that of supervisor rather than adviser. In matters of trans-Native Authority affairs, e.g. decisions made for the whole colony, the political officer could order rather than suggest action.
(7) N.A.'s as Legislative Bodies: The Native Authorities were legislative organs. With regard to legislation concerning traditional matters, the political officer would not interfere unless they were repugnant to 'human justice'. With regard to legislation concerning modern administration much of the legislation would originate from the political officer but be promulgated in the name of the Native Authority.

Up till 1945 Indirect Rule remained largely unchallenged as a system. So too did the local administrative system of the French. But from 1945 onwards increasing pressure was brought on both the colonial governments and the chiefs themselves for reform by the politically conscious educated elite. With the progressive concession of central authority by the colonial powers to this elite, the chiefs in both the French and British systems had to adjust, voluntarily or forcibly, their relationship with the central government and their subjects.

THE CHIEF DURING THE PERIOD OF DECOLONISATION

That the status of the chief and the nature of his authority changed noticeably as a result of the imposition of colonial rule is clear. We must now examine the further changes in his position that took place during the period of decolonisation when African politicians began to replace colonial officials in the central government.

Though at the time of the imposition of colonial rule some chiefs had resisted, and others collaborated with, the new masters, once colonial rule had been fully established and overtly hostile chiefs deposed, all chiefs became participants in the same political game. In this game the essential objective of the chiefs was survival: how to balance the demands of their new masters and yet retain a measure of authority of their own over their people. This they were determined to retain even when the nature of the political game changed radically and African politicians took the place of colonial officials. This is an important factor which has to be borne in mind in any study of the clash that developed between the chiefs and the educated elite in the period of decolonisation. The chiefs as a class had for the most part been the champions of independence at the time of the European occupation: they had fought, lost and learnt to co-operate, if not openly collaborate, with their new masters. The educated elite, itself in large part a by-product of the colonial situation, had not been involved as a class in the initial confrontation and defeat and were therefore much more optimistic about the future in terms of independence. The chiefs, while they too would have loved independence, provided they had a major political role to play in it, did not share the elite's optimism. Basically the chief's position was logical: they had learnt the hard way that by co-operation with the colonial powers they could retain some of their former powers, and indeed, as was the case in British West Africa, sometimes increase them. Their future under an independent regime dominated by the educated elite seemed very far from certain, especially as the radical politicians, who came increasingly to dominate the scene, saw the chiefs as lackeys of the colonial regime, paid little heed to the crushing defeat the chiefs had suffered at the latter's hands, and seemed to ignore that hard lessons had taught the chiefs that collaboration was the only way in which they could survive.

In French West Africa, while the chief lost a great deal of his power, up until 1945 he was the only African 'political' authority to be found outside the Quatre Communes of Senegal. Thus whether he was a 'legitimate' chief of greatly reduced powers, or an administrative appointee, he had a stake in the colonial regime. By and large, therefore, in the period of decolonisation, the chiefs allied themselves with French-backed conservative politicians to whom the French 'guaranteed' the support of the chiefs against the radical politicians. Because of the nature of the demands of the French administrative regime for forced labour, taxes, compulsory production and recruitment for the French army the chief in French West Africa became a more obvious target for the anti-colonial radical than the chief in British West Africa, who at least by the Second World War was no longer concerned with forced labour and had never been concerned, at least officially, with compulsory recruitment or with compulsory crop cultivation. Furthermore, divested of his judicial and police functions, the French chief had no formal power of his own and was in appearance and fact a mere administrative agent or 'lackey' of the French. Many chiefs, like the Mogho Naba, had cause to resent the French because of the break-up of their former territorial jurisdiction and the destitution of so many of their traditional powers; but when it was a matter of choice between French-supported 'conservatives' and the 'radicals', they knew where their best interests lay. As it was, in most of French West Africa, radicals (or parties, which while moderate, were anti-chief) came to power at independence. And while, with the exception of Guinea, which abolished the institution altogether, they still recognised chiefs as such, they had no political place in the constitution and at best were low-level local administrators. The one great chief who did survive the French colonial regime with much of his traditional authority intact, the Mogho Naba of the Mossi, when he did try to confront the politicians with a political showdown was defeated and disgraced by them. Chieftaincy in independent French-speaking West Africa today is an institution of little political importance as a result of the use made of chiefs by the French and the reaction of the people to them, for it was the people who put the radicals in power, even if some of these radicals, like Houphouët-Boigny, have in power become conservatives.

The same cannot be said of the chiefs in British West Africa though their experience can be seen in many ways as similar to that of their French-speaking counterparts. While chiefs in British West Africa also had learnt to accommodate themselves to the colonial situation if they were to retain any of their powers, the rules of the game, though the same in principle as the French, differed significantly. Whereas the French made their chiefs play according to very strict rules, the British evolved a fairly lax way of playing the game. Provided the chief under British rule demonstrated loyalty to the new regime, avoided overt corruption or acts repugnant to British humanitarian ideas, he was allowed to get on with the job of governing his people at the local level much as he wanted. The authority that was devolved on him by the British was backed up by the fact that in the vast majority of cases he had traditional claims to that authority, and in many cases administered the lands and people he would have governed in precolonial times. Such was not the case in French West Africa, as we have seen. Most important of all, at the local level, the chief retained responsibility for law and order. His authority over his people did not formally depend only on the colonial power as did that of the French chief: he still had traditional powers of his own which, provided he did not openly abuse them, he could wield very freely. In the eyes of his people, though it was clear he had lost his sovereignty, he still remained their chief, and not a mere administrative agent of the government.

By devolving local government on the chiefs, and making this real self-government, however localised, the British created two problems more complex and 'modern'. The chiefs chosen for their legitimacy rather than ability became less and less capable of running the bureaucratic structures of local government units which in the case of Kano were almost as complex as those of an English County Council. Either the District Officer had to take on much of the more specialised type of work, or members of the new educated African elite had to be employed. The second problem was that whereas chieftaincy was seen in French West Africa as primarily an extension of the French system of administration, so that once the French had been replaced, the chiefs would merely come under the administrative control of their replacements who were the African politicians, in British West Africa the chiefs, as head of local self-governing units, had power bases of their own which the politician sought to capture. Thus in British West Africa the politicians either sought to replace the chiefs as the government at the local level, or, recognising their very real power at this level, sought to identify them with their political goals. This dichotomy may seem to be the same as that between the French African conservatives allying with the chiefs and the radicals opposing them, but it is only superficial. The difference lies in the fact that in British West Africa the chief had real political power, which for the politician, whether radical or conservative, was worth gaining. This explains why the Action Group and the N.C.N.C., the radicals in Nigerian politics, spent as much effort in securing the support of chiefs as did the conservative N.P.C. in the North. Secondly, whereas in French West Africa independence was never pronounced as a political goal by the educated elite until 1958, and the French saw their colonies' future not as independent units but as part of a political community in which they would have autonomy while France wielded ultimate power, in British West Africa ultimate self-government and independence was conceded for the colonies, at least as a long-term goal, with the advent of the post-war Labour Government. The issues at stake were independence 'when' and for 'whom'. The chiefs knew this as well as anyone, and the more subtle of them played their political cards accordingly, promising their support to politicians for a secure future. Hence the fact that all the parties which came to power in British West Africa on independence had consented to constitutions in which chiefs had a political position, and in many cases, had chiefs as ministers in their governments. Even Nkrumah's C.P.P., the nearest thing in spirit in British West Africa to Sekou Toure's R.D.A., had to compromise with chieftaincy, making enemies of some, but careful friends of others. It is not without significance that Nkrumah himself chose to take on a chieftaincy title.

The fact that during the British colonial regime local government under the chiefs was such an important power base explains the frequency of complaints of the educated elite that they were deliberately excluded from it. This is not altogether true: the British, because of the increasing specialisation required of the various departments of the Native Authorities, did try to encourage recruitment of literates, though not the elite itself, into their service. Even before the democratisation of these Native Authorities during the period of decolonisation, the British had encouraged the chiefs to nominate educated men to serve as councillors, etc. The significance of the attacks on the Native Authorities by the educated elite is not that they were directed against the chiefs as such, but that they resented their exclusion from a potential power base.

When the British conceded democratisation of the Native Authorities, the political parties did their best to gain the elective seats. And while for the most part the councillors so elected were rarely of 'the educated elite' but men of local standing, they provided the elite, more concerned with national power, with a hold on the local power base. The French-speaking politician was concerned not with the chief's power base, for the latter had little except French support. He was concerned with the chief in so much as he was an obstacle provided by the French to his political ambitions. The chief, as agent of the French, could still be used to rig the elections as they did in

Guinea where later French administrators were themselves to admit that chiefs did not really matter, even in Fouta-Djalon. Such could never be said of the British chief. And whereas Sekou Toure was able to depose all chiefs in one fell swoop in 1957, over a decade later a Military Government, that of the Western State of Nigeria, has as one of its most delicate issues the difference between it and the people as to whom should be next Alafin of Oyo.

THE POSITION OF CHIEFS UNDER AFRICAN GOVERNMENTS

Once the African elite gained effective control over the government of their countries, which of course preceded formal independence, their attitude towards chiefs depended on how politically important they saw them to be. In Guinea, they clearly were seen as 'reactionaries' but not reactionaries of any political significance as the way in which they were abolished as an institution without any disturbance showed. The other French-speaking African states have used chiefs in much the same way as the French did, as agents of the central government for putting into effect its decisions, not those of the chiefs' own making. In many cases the traditional basis of the chief's appointment has been completely swept away and the office subjected to the ballot-box by universal suffrage. In French West Africa the chief has only been important in the period of effective African rule at times when there has been a struggle for power between two parties. Thus when Hamani Diori, leader of the opposition, sought successfully in 1958, with French support, to overthrow Djibo Bakary, the ruling Prime Minister, he brought out chiefs to help him in his campaign. But once his success was assured and he had created an effective one-party state the chiefs fell back for the most part into the oblivion to which the French had earlier assigned them. The reason for this is simple: while the chief could be given a temporary political role by identifying him with one party or another and thus adding to the weapons at the politicians' disposal, he was dispensable after he had been used successfully, for having no continuing power base of his own, he was no longer of any use to them. Even where the Mogho Naba, who by virtue of his extraordinary religious position vis-à-vis his people, was able to attempt to assume a political position as a result of the confused state of Voltaic politics after the death of Ouezzin-Coulibaly, Maurice Yameogo, his successor as prime minister, once he had won the struggle, was able publicly to humiliate him.

In British West Africa chiefs survived not only because they were the legitimate heirs to institutions that represented the traditions of their people, but also because they still had a power base. In any political struggle the two parties had to use chiefs, and while opposition still existed, the government of the day had to seek their continuing support, the opposition wean it away. Even in Nkrumah's retrospectively politically fragile one-party state, the chiefs could not be removed because their power base was such that while they could not challenge the regime, any attempt to abolish them would have caused a reaction which Nkrumah could not politically afford. The, obvious case in point is the Asantehene. Here one must add that the only chief in French-speaking West Africa today who could not be so removed would be the Mogho Naba.

As long as chiefs in English-speaking West Africa retain their power base, they will remain politically significant. But the fact that these African governments have tended to use the chiefs more like the French than the British, as agents of central government decisions, has reduced their power base and, most important of all, begun to alienate them from their people. African governments have treated loyal chiefs with the consideration the French did. Disloyal or uncooperative chiefs have suffered similar fates to those of their counterparts under French colonial rule. So, while chieftaincy is still a much more important institution in English-speaking West Africa in political terms, the fact that chiefs have been politicised, and are no longer fathers of all their people, has meant that they are being rapidly reduced to the position of French chiefs under colonial rule. Their use as tax-collectors under the military regime in default of anyone else able to do the job in Western Nigeria has meant that as a class they have become very unpopular, to the extent of assassination in Ogbomoso and the burning down of palaces in other towns. Indeed, military rulers, having banned politicians from their national scenes, have sought to use chiefs where they still exist, as administrative links between them and their people, thus further politicising the position of the chief. But insomuch as the chiefs are still legitimate heirs of their pre-colonial predecessors, as the Mogho Naba is, they can survive, if they can maintain a strictly neutral attitude, even though finally they are divested of all powers, in the exercise of their substantial residual influence. In French West Africa the damage has already been done, in British West Africa it is not complete. There is still a ceremonial future for the chief at the local level as a father of all the people without political functions.

One paper contributed to the Ife seminar even suggested chieftaincy might become a tourist attraction. But it remains to be seen whether chiefs can combine successfully both the ritual symbolism of monarchy and its popular pageantry without involving themselves in politics as the British and the other European monarchies which have survived have done.

BIBLIOGRAPHY

A. E. Afigbo, 'Herbert Richmond Palmer and Indirect Rule in Eastern Nigeria – 1915-1928' *Journal of the Historical Society of Nigeria*, III, December 1965, pp.295-312.

----------, 'Revolution and Reaction in Eastern Nigeria: 1900-1929' *Journal of the Historical Society of Nigeria*, III, 3, December 1966, pp.539-557.

David Apter, *Ghana in Transition* (Revised edition of *The Gold Coast in Transition)*, New York, 1963.

Raymond F. Betts, *Assimilation and Association in French Colonial Theory 1890-1914*, New York, 1961.

R. L. Buell, *The Native Problem in Africa*, 2 vols, New York, 1928.

Mary Bull, 'Indirect Rule in Northern Nigeria 1906-1911' in Kenneth Robinson and Frederick Madden (eds.) *Essays in Imperial Government*, Oxford, 1965, pp.47-87.

Sir Donald Cameron, *The Principles of Native Administration and their Application*, Lagos, 1934.

Henri Cosnier, *L'Quest Africain Français: ses resources agricoles -- son organisation economique*, Paris, 1921.

Michael Crowder, 'Indirect Rule French and British Style' *Africa* XXXIV, 3, July, 1964, pp.197-205.

----------, *West Africa under Colonial Rule*, London, 1968.

----------, 'The White Chiefs of Tropical Africa' in Lewis H. Gann and Peter Duigan (eds.) *A History of Colonialism in Africa*, Vol. II, London, 1970, pp.320-350.

----------, *Revolt in Bussa: A Study in British 'Native Administration' in Nigerian Borgu, 1902-1935*, London, 1973.

Robert Delavignette, *Les Vrais Chefs de l'Empire*, Paris, 1939.

----------, *Freedom and Authority in French West Africa*, London, 1950.

Hubert Deschamps, *Méthodes et doctrines coloniales de la France*, Paris, 1953.

----------, 'Et Maintenant, Lord Lugard' *Africa*, XXXIII, 4, Oct., 1963, pp.293-306.

Lord Hailey, *An African Survey*, 1938, London, 1939.

----------, *An African Survey* (Revised) 1956 London, 1957.

----------, *Native Administration in the British African Territories*, Pt. III, West Africa: Nigeria, The Gold Coast, Sierra Leone, Gambia, London, 1951.

Obaro Ikime: 'Chief Dogho: The Lugardian system in Warri 1917-1932', *Journal of the Historical Society of Nigeria*, Vol. III, No. 2, Dec. 1965, pp.313-333.

----------, 'Reconsidering Indirect Rule: The Nigerian Example', *Journal of the Historical Society of Nigeria*, IV, 3, Dec. 1968, pp.421-438.

G. I. Jones, 'From Direct to Indirect Rule in Eastern Nigeria', *Odu*, II, January 1966, pp.72-80.

Sir Frederick (Later Lord) Lugard, *Report by Sir F. D. Lugard on the Amalgamation of Northern and Southern Administration, 1912-1919* (1919) Cmd. 468.

----------, *The Dual Mandate in British Tropical Africa*, Edinburgh, 1918.

----------, *Political Memoranda*, Lagos, 1918.

L. P. Mair, *Native Policies in Africa*, London, 1936.

----------, 'African Chiefs Today' *Africa* XXVIII, 3, July, 1958, pp.195-206.

Margery Perham, *Native Administration in Nigeria*, 2nd Ed. London, 1957.

Jean Suret-Canale, 'La Fin de la chéfferie en Guinée, *Journal of African History*, VII, 3, 1966, pp.459-493.

C. L. Temple (later Sir Charles), *Native Races and their Rulers*, 2nd Ed. London, 1968.

Governor-General Joost Van Vollenhoven, 'Circulaire au sujet des chefs indigenes' Dakar, 15 August 1917 reprinted in *Une Ame de Chef: Le Gouverneur-Général J. van Vollenhoven*, Paris, 1920.

XI

WEST AFRICA 1919 – 1939: THE COLONIAL SITUATION* (1974)

By the end of the First World War, the British and the French, who had strengthened their dominant position in the area by sharing the former German territories of Togo and the Cameroons, could claim to be in effective control of their several territories in West Africa. The Portuguese, too, were firmly established in Guinea-Bissau and the Cape Verde Islands. Resistance continued in a few places, notably Mauritania and other desert, semi-desert and hilly areas where the writ of the conquerors still did not run especially in the hands of tax-collectors. The widespread rebellions during the war and the frequent anti-tax revolts showed that the colonial regimes could be shaken but armed resistance began to die down as the rebellions were usually suppressed with ferocity and the ultimate military superiority of the colonial rulers was hardly in doubt. The period of conquest was over; the few remaining military governors began to give way to civilian administrators, and the various regimes could settle down to the business of administration and economic exploitation.

By 1939 the colonial regimes were still congratulating themselves on the completeness of the conquest, or 'pacification' as they called it. Imperial law and order seemed to reign supreme. The pockets of rebellion had been conciliated or repressed. Colonial officials looked forward to many generations of quiet administration and evolutionary development, with the colonial decision-making process unfettered by any African initiatives or by international opinion, both of which were to become so important after the Second World War.

The two decades 1919-39 can, therefore, be looked upon as the years most characteristic of European rule in West Africa. The aim of this chapter is to examine the nature of the colonial relationship in

*Reprinted by permission of the co-author, J. F. Ade Ajayi, and Longman from J. F. Ade Ajayi and Michael Crowder (eds) *History of West Africa*, Vol II, London, 1974 and Columbia University Press, New York.

that period in terms of the administrative policies and structures, the economic systems and the general impact of colonialism on West Africans. The colonial regimes and their administrative policies and structures dominated the situation. The bulk of the existing literature on the period has been devoted to studies of these policies and the mechanics of administration based on the records of the administrators. To the obvious technological and military superiority, colonial propaganda has added legends of the moral and social superiority of European civilisation. In consequence, the colonial administrators and their impact on West African society have assumed a larger-than-life proportion. As they moved from the crisis-ridden period of conquest and initial establishment to a more settled period of administration they tried to rationalise their systems of administration. In doing this they tended to emphasise the differences in the attitudes and ideologies of the various regimes with the fervour of denominational evangelists. It is important to understand these differences as they had a significant effect on the roles, fortunes and opportunities open to both the traditional and the emergent Western-educated elites. The response of these elites to the Colonial Situation after the period of conquest had to be within systems created by the foreign rulers. But the dichotomy between the English- and French-speaking parts of West Africa must not be exaggerated.

In the first place, it must always be kept in mind that the rationalised systems never existed in reality. The settled conditions in which the foreign ruler could do whatever he wished with his African subjects never existed in practice. The maintenance of law and order remained even in this period the constant preoccupation of the administrator. The resources available to him in men, material and facilities for communication did not enable him to achieve an effective day-to-day dominance throughout vast areas of West Africa. The unexpected and unpredictable were daily features of the foreign administrator's life. Even under the most rationalised system pragmatism and laissez-faire, through policy or inertia, remained the predominant approach.

Secondly, it should be borne in mind that the colonial policies and administrative structures were only means to an end. When colonial propaganda about humanitarian intentions and burdens of empire is discounted, all colonial regimes will be found to have shared a common goal in the exploitation of economic resources of the areas they dominated, to the best of their abilities and with the least possible cost to the metropolitan countries. This overall ambition took precedence over differences in ideology and dictated a greater response, on the part of the foreign rulers and commercial interests, to the realities of the local situation. As we consider these realities and the impact of the social and economic systems of the colonial regimes, not just on the elites but on the mass of West Africans, it becomes more obvious that the long-term effects of the colonial period have been exaggerated. There was in the colonial period not only a common goal of the foreign rulers but also a common West African predicament, involving important African initiatives and continuities with pre-colonial African history.

THE ADMINISTRATIVE POLICIES OF THE COLONIAL POWERS *

Before 1919 the administrative policies of Europeans in West Africa had understandably been largely ad hoc. During the nineteenth century, when they controlled only small coastal enclaves, the usual approach in governing their African subjects was assimilationist; that is, the framework of reference was the metropolitan model. Thus the *Quatre Communes* of Senegal were governed through French-style municipal councils controlling their own budgets; the Communes elected representatives to a Conseil-Général similar to those of the Departements of France and during the Second and Third Republics in France they were allowed to elect a Deputy to the French National Assembly. In Sierra Leone, Freetown was constituted into a municipality with an elected Mayor and the Colony itself was governed by a Legislative Council and an Executive Council, presided over by a Governor, a device which was used in white settler colonies.

Furthermore, Africans or mulattoes could achieve the highest offices in the colonial administrative service. Indeed, a Creole, Honorio Pereira Barreto, was appointed Superintendent of the Portuguese fortress at Cacheu in 1834, and Governor of Cacheu and Bissau in 1837, and he became one of the real architects of Portuguese Guinea.[1] The Quatre Communes of Senegal elected a mulatto (*métis*), Durand-Valentin, as Deputy from 1848 to 1850. The French Expeditionary force that conquered Dahomey in 1894 was led by another Senegalese mulatto, Colonel, later General, Dodds. When Britain expanded into the hinterland of Sierra Leone its Secretary of Native Affairs, J. C. E. Parkes, was a Creole, while in Lagos in 1875 the heads of police, of posts and telegraphs, and of customs, and the Registrar of the Supreme Court, as well as the Anglican Bishop on the Niger, were all Africans. However, as the European powers expanded

---

*This section has been considerably shortened to avoid duplication of the discussions in Chapters IX and X of the administrative policies of France and Britain in West Africa. Where other sections have been edited to the same end this is indicated by. . . .

into the interior and extended their administration over millions rather than thousands of Africans they found the difficulties of governing their new subjects through metropolitan models overwhelming. It became clear that new administrative formulae had to be devised to govern peoples as disparate in political and cultural organisation as those to be found in a land mass larger than the United States of America. As they settled down to administer the various territories after the shortages and upheavals of the First World War, they tried to rationalise new systems of administration along the lines discussed in detail in Chapters IX and X.

Insofar as British administration during this period had a dominant model it was that of 'Indirect Rule' as developed in Northern Nigeria.

......

It was this system of administration that was gradually extended from Northern Nigeria to Southern Nigeria with the amalgamation of the two Protectorates under Lugard in 1914 and was later introduced into the Gold Coast, Sierra Leone and Gambia. Thus, on the Gold Coast, where the chiefs had always been used as the agents of local administration, the Colonial Administration could talk in the late 1920s of introducing Indirect Rule. What they meant by this was the Northern Nigerian model of administration, and in this case particularly taxation and control of expenditure by the chiefs through a budget.

......

The chief characteristic of French administration in West Africa was its heavy centralisation and consequent lack of scope for local initiative. Thus while the Native Authorities of British West Africa were legislative organs, albeit limited in scope, even the Governor-General of French West Africa had no legislative powers. The principal source of legislation was the French Chamber of Deputies, or, more usually, the Minister of Colonies in Paris who issued decrees. Concomitant with centralisation went a hierarchical and uniform administrative structure. Pierre Alexandre has emphasised the influence on the French administrative system in Africa of the military, who first established the administration of French West Africa.[2]

......

Perhaps the most important distinguishing feature of the French approach is that chiefs were not local government authorities. They disposed of no budget, the taxes they collected being rendered *in toto* to the French administration. Officially they did not exercise judicial functions, had no police force and did not maintain prisons. There was thus no local self-government in the British sense.

. . . . . .

ADMINISTRATIVE STRUCTURES

French West Africa

The administrative configuration of French West Africa was fixed for the next twelve years when in 1920 Upper Volta was excised from Niger, French Soudan and Ivory Coast and made a constituent colony of French West Africa. The French West African Federation, ruled by the Governor-General from Dakar, then comprised Mauritania, Senegal, French Soudan, French Guinea, Upper Volta, Ivory Coast, Dahomey and Niger. The greater part of German Togo was brought under French administrative control, under a League of Nations Mandate, but until 1934 it was governed as a separate entity with its own High Commissioner. From 1934 until 1936, because of the economic exigencies of the Depression, it was administratively integrated with Dahomey to save money. From 1936 until 1945, when it became a U.N. Trusteeship Territory, it was placed under the Governor-General in Dakar, who became its High Commissioner. Even when Togo was administered as part of French West Africa, however, the Mandate meant that certain restrictions were placed on its administration. Forced labour was restricted to four days a year on public works; this could be redeemed by payment of a tax and could not be used for private purposes. There could be no conscription into the army. Togo was kept open to Free Trade and protective tariffs were not allowed. There was comparatively more local participation in the administration than in the rest of French West Africa. Four unofficial members sat on the High Commissioner's Council of Administration, two of them Togolese, two of them French citizens. Though the High Commissioner was not bound by the advice of the Council he rarely acted against it. Between 1920 and 1931 the Council had 231 sessions.

French West Africa proper was ruled uniformly from Dakar, the only exception being Senegal, whose *Quatre Communes* continued to elect a Deputy to the French National Assembly and to elect municipal councils for Gorée, Rufisque, Saint Louis and Dakar. While the demand of the *Conseil Général* that its competence be extended over the whole of Senegal was granted, the French administration tried to curb its independence. The Governor-General Merlin, who had been appointed to counterbalance the influence of Diagne, the first black Deputy, and other elected representatives of Senegal, reconstituted the *Conseil Général* as the *Conseil Colonial*, in which there was to be parity of representation between twenty elected members from the Communes and twenty chiefs elected by fellow chiefs of the Protectorate. Since the chiefs were appointed by the Administration and subject to the *indigénat* — the summary jurisdiction of the French political officer — there was little fear of their opposing the Administration's policy. However, in order to persuade the elected members to pass the budget for the Colony in 1925, the Administration had to concede an increase in the number of elected representatives from twenty to twenty-four at the expense of the chiefs, who lost four seats.

For the rest of French West Africa, the pivotal administrative figure was the Governor-General. He was, as we have noted, not the source of authority, merely its instrument. Only the Minister of Colonies (or in rare cases, the Chamber of Deputies) could issue laws, in the form of decrees that were legally binding in the Federation. The Governor-General and the Governors often drafted these laws but did not make them, and they were limited to policy-making within the framework of the laws. This is the most obvious illustration of the highly centralised nature of the French administrative system.

While during the early years of the Federation there had been a natural struggle for power between the Governor-General in Dakar and the Lieutenant-Governors of the Colonies, by the inter-war years the Federation had become stronger than its constituent governments. It has been suggested that the Federation remained a rather weak administrative contrivance and that the *Loi Cadre* which broke it up in 1956 merely recognised the individual personalities of the constituent colonies. This may be an indication of the limited extent to which administrative policies affected the realities of the local situation, but there can be no doubt that the government of the Federation had overshadowed the government of each individual territory. No Lieutenant-Governor had direct access to the Minister, the sole source of authority, except through the Governor-General in Dakar. Circulars and *Arrêtés* of the Governor-General applied uniformly to all colonies.

Moreover, it was the Governor-General who controlled the economy of French West Africa. All revenues from customs were collected by the Federation and redistributed in the Federal Budget on the basis partly of derivation and partly of need. Roads, railways, telecommunications, ports, health and higher education were all federal concerns. The colonies did not have internal budgetary autonomy. As far as development was concerned only the Governor-General had the right to raise loans. In such circumstances Dakar dominated the colonial capitals. It did so to such an extent that Governor-General Jules Brevié in 1932 advocated a policy of decentralisation,[3] but as Lord Hailey pointed out some five years later, there was little evidence of such decentralisation having taken place.[4]

In a further attempt to decentralise in 1937, Governor-General de Coppet raised the status of the colonial governors from Lieutenant-Governor to Governor and attempted to give them greater initiative.[5] But by 1939 there had been no significant change, and both the Vichy and Free French regimes which ruled French West Africa during the war accentuated the earlier centralising tendencies of the Federal Government.

At the level of the colonies, the Lieutenant-Governors' principal pre-occupation was with political affairs. The administrative system devised for the eight colonies may have been more or less uniform, but the people administered differed radically. With his *Commandants de Cercle* the Lieutenant-Governor had to marry the diversity of the people with the uniformity of the administrative system.

From the point of view of the African peasant, who formed the overwhelming majority of those subject to French administration, the system was one directed to ensuring his production of cash crops for export to France. This may be to look at the system in crude economic terms, but insofar as the French *Commandants de Cercles* and their subalterns, the *Chefs de Subdivisions,* impinged on the lives of the Africans, it was mainly in the economic sphere. All Africans, men and women, who were not citizens were taxed directly, though the rates varied from colony to colony, and within colonies from district to district. The minimum age at which Africans could be taxed was often as low as eight or ten, though it was later fixed at fourteen years. The object of the tax was not only to raise money to pay for the administration but also to force people into production of crops which could earn cash. Such crops were, for the great part, export crops like groundnuts, cotton, palm-oil and cocoa. Where no such crops could be grown in a district, the young men had to migrate to areas where crops could be grown and work as tenant-farmers or labourers on other people's land in order to earn enough money to pay not only their own tax but also that of the rest of the family. In the inter-war years rates of taxation were raised considerably compared with those that had existed in the early days of colonial rule. The principal result of this was a vast increase in the seasonal migration of labourers, particularly from the poorer colonies like Niger, Upper Volta and

Soudan to the more fertile coastal colonies. The head tax was supplemented by the prestation, a tax in labour, which could, however, be redeemed by cash. All able-bodied males from eighteen to fifty years were subject to this tax of up to ten days' labour in a year, principally for maintaining roads. While large numbers of Africans did redeem their tax in cash, for the vast majority prestation was nothing but the *corvée* of the Ancien Regime and was hated as such.

Some idea of the importance of direct taxation to the French West African budget may be gauged from the fact that in 1933 it formed 28.7 per cent of revenue as compared with 18.5 per cent in Nigeria where all were also subject to direct taxation. On the Gold Coast only 0.7 per cent of the budget was of that date made up of direct taxation; for Gambia it was 6.3 per cent and for Sierra Leone 19.4 per cent. In observing that French West Africa's taxation rate was higher than that of British West Africa, we must also note that French West Africa was substantially poorer, sparser in population and that, in addition to his direct tax, the peasant had to work off his prestation.[6] The economic burdens placed on him by the regime did not end here. The compulsory recruitment of African soldiers into the army, begun just before the First World War, was put on a regular basis whereby all adult males were liable to three years' compulsory military service. Though they were paid for the duration of their service, this obligation removed some of the fittest men from the land and further increased the economic burden on those left to cultivate crops for tax payments. Some of the military conscripts did not serve as soldiers but were engaged on public work projects. The Sansanding Dam Project on the Niger in Soudan was built with the help of this class of labour.[7] As if these obligations to the new colonial masters were not enough, peasants were liable for work on the *champs administratifs* — that is, on crops which were deemed essential to the economy. In 1939 Delavignette estimated that obligatory cultivation of cotton in the Upper Volta was responsible for the migration of one hundred thousand peasants to the Gold Coast in search of work.[8]

While the *Commandant de Cercle* and *Chef de Subdivision* were responsible for seeing that these various taxes in labour, kind and specie were paid, the agent for their collection or enforcement was the chief. As in British West Africa the chief was the crux of the administrative system. But by the inter-war years in French West Africa the chief had taken on a very different character from that of the chief in pre-colonial times. By the 1930s the French had succeeded in their aim of breaking down large chieftaincies into smaller units, and had established the principle that appointment to chieftaincy depended not so much on traditional claim to the position but on ability. If no one with traditional claims was judged to have the right kinds of ability, an old soldier, *garde cercle* or clerk was appointed. Furthermore, as noted above, the chiefs had lost all legal powers.

. . . . . .

As a result of his unrepresentative role and his unpopular duties the chief lost respect in the eyes of the people to such a degree that in the independent French West African states, chieftaincy has become far less significant as an element than in British West Africa and in certain cases has been abolished altogether. Even in the 1930s, in the regulation of traditional matters, from customary law to religion, a large number of peasants often dealt not with the chief appointed by the French but with the man who would, according to tradition, have been chief.

While the chief was the agent of the French administration with whom the peasants most often came into direct contact, it was the French administrator who maintained discipline over them. The administration of the law, other than personal law, was at all stages governed by the French administrator. Supplementing the courts, he had powers of summary justice over all African subjects. This system of law, known as the *indigénat,* empowered the administrator to jail any African without trial for up to fourteen days. This applied equally to chiefs who failed in their duties and many were frequently jailed.

However, because of the comparative durability of his post, the chief had an advantage over the French administrators who, because of the system of *rouage,* rarely stayed in a particular post for more than a year and were thus unable to familiarise themselves with the workings of the chieftaincies under their command.[9] For this reason, the realities of the local situation with its variety of traditional African cultures often proved more operative than the uniformity which the French administration was trying to impose.

British West Africa
The four colonies of British West Africa were separately administered in the inter-war years, practically the only things they had in common being their currency and the West African Frontier Force. Nevertheless by 1936 the 'advantages of a closer relationship between the four British West African colonies and the appointment of a Governor-General for the whole' was, according to *The Times* of London, being repeatedly advocated.[10] The four colonies were each divided into 'Colony' and 'Protectorate', the Colony representing the original coastal enclave in which the inhabitants were technically

British citizens, the Protectorate being the vast hinterland in which the inhabitants had the status of British Protected Persons. The Protectorate of Nigeria was divided into two distinct sets of Provinces representing the former colonies of Northern and Southern Nigeria which Lugard had amalgamated in 1914. Nigeria as a whole was administered by a Governor in the inter-war years, with Lieutenant-Governors, later Chief Commissioners, for the Northern and Southern Provinces. The Lieutenant-Governors had a great deal more independence and initiative than their French West African counterparts, particularly in administrative as distinct from economic policy.[11] Indeed, administratively Northern and Southern Nigeria were treated almost like two separate countries, with the North-South boundary being often referred to as 'the frontier' in the correspondence between District Officers and their Residents, and political officers spending their lives in the exclusive service of either the North or the South, almost never serving in both.

The principal source of legislative authority was the Colonial Governor, not the Colonial Office. In the case of Nigeria in 1923 the constitution introduced by Governor Clifford made the Governor-in-Council the principal source of legislation for Southern Nigeria while the Northern Provinces were ruled by him through Proclamation. On the Gold Coast the Governor-in-Council legislated for the Colony while Ashanti and the Northern Territories were ruled by Proclamation. The Gambia and Sierra Leone made no distinction for legislative purposes between colony and protectorate, and their legislative councils had competence over the whole territory. However, while a Governor-in-Council could initiate legislation, the Colonial Office could, even after the Governor had given it his assent, disallow it in the name of the British monarch. Similarly, while what may be termed purely domestic legislation was in practice left to the local legislative councils or the Governors, certain classes of legislation involving constitutional changes or overall imperial policy required Acts of the British Parliament or the assent of the British Crown.

The Legislative Councils themselves were composed mainly of the principal and more senior colonial officials. Along with a few non-official Europeans nominated to represent commercial interests there were some African members, most of them nominated, with a few elected in the Gold Coast and Nigerian Legislative Councils. The Africans were always in such a minority that they were limited to criticising bills which they had not the power to reject. Indeed, composed as they were, the Legislative Councils provided little check on the authority of the Governors. Similarly, the Governors' Executive Councils, which were composed of a majority of officials with one or two nominated non-official members, were in practice largely instruments obeying the will of the Governors. Not until the Second World War were Africans nominated to them. Governor Graeme Thomson had in 1930 considered proposing two Africans for membership in his Executive Council in Nigeria but members of his existing Council persuaded him to drop the idea.[12]

That the Colonial Governors were so powerful at this time was also due to the size of the British Empire, the difficulties of communication, and the ignorance of the colonies that prevailed in the Colonial Office. Few Colonial Office officials had ever been to a colony, still less the particular colony on which they could be called upon at any time to advise the Secretary of State. Consequently, as one Colonial Office official told Ormsby-Gore in 1930, the Office's chief duty was 'to select the best man available for any particular job, and send him out to do it, and back him up'.[13] Thus in practice Governors of individual colonies in British West Africa, with their power to initiate legislation, and subject to few checks from London or within the colony itself, were much more powerful than even the Governor-General of French West Africa.

The British Governors were concerned not only with administration but with the coordination of the various technical services and in particular with the economic development of their colonies. Except in matters of major policy, it was their Lieutenant-Governors, Chief Commissioners, or Commissioners who supervised the administration of the African masses. Again, they too, because they had to coordinate the operation of the technical services at the regional or provincial level, had to rely to a great extent on their Residents and District Officers for the conduct of day-to-day administration. It is clear from a close scrutiny of the administration files for one particular division of Northern Nigeria, in this case Borgu,[14] that in a vast area such as Northern Nigeria real administrative power lay with the provincial Resident and his District Officers. The Lieutenant-Governor interfered only on major issues, principal control being through the annual budget exercise. Thus as far as the African was concerned, the main representation of the British administration was the District Officer or District Commissioner. The role of these officials in local administration has already been discussed above.

Portuguese Africa

Portuguese colonial policy in this period leaned towards the French approach of centralised control from the metropolitan capital. Indeed, the Portuguese system as rationalised in the 1930s provided for a greater degree of centralisation than obtained in French West Africa. However, in spite of the relatively greater importance of the colonies as a major national preoccupation of Portugal and a more plentiful supply of low-paid European personnel to draw on, the internal political and economic problems of Portugal ensured that more persistent bureaucratic interference in the colonies did not result in more effective administrative control.

Under the Republican Regime (1910-26)[15] the colonies were treated largely with indifference. Portuguese settlers and officials, led by the Governors and the colonial legislative councils, were left relatively free to attempt to consolidate Portuguese rule over the African populations, to raise loans for development and exploit the natural and human resources of the Africans. On the grounds of separating Church and State, the subsidy for Portuguese Christian missions was removed in 1911 but restored in 1919 as part of the effort to improve the cruel condition of the African subjects, whose sufferings under oppressive labour codes that were applied even more harshly reached the proportions of the Congo Scandals but were less publicised. There were also frequent reports of mismanagement of funds by colonial officials and of efforts to divert colonial riches away from Portugal, as well as the fear that the degree of local autonomy granted the settlers, and officials was likely to produce a disintegration of the Portuguese Empire.

The *Estado Novo,* the nationalist and authoritarian regime that came to power in 1926, was determined to reverse this trend. However, it was not till 1930 that new guiding principles were stated in the Colonial Act, and not till 1933 that these were elaborated in constitutional laws by the Organic Charter and regulations in the Overseas Administrative Reforms. Through these laws and regulations the new regime restored the State's control over the colonies at the expense of the settlers and officials. The Overseas Ministry with the Minister in charge became the main authority over the colonies. Though certain matters like the appointment of colonial governors, concessions to foreign companies and proposed loans had to be approved by the Council of Ministers, and the National Assembly also legislated on major issues, it was the Overseas Minister who directed the administrative, political and financial life of the colonies. The laws or decrees of the Council of Ministers originated from him. No colonial legislation was valid till his Ministry had released it for publication in the Official Gazette. The Governor-General of each province and the Governors who were directly responsible to him visited locations and supervised administration; they prepared budgets and advised on legislation; but, as in the French system, they had administrative but not legislative powers. What is more, financial control was so stringent that the Portuguese Governor-General was liable to prosecution if he exceeded or altered the budget passed by the Minister. It was one of the achievements claimed by the new regime that after 1931 colonial budgets were regularly balanced.

As far as the African population was concerned the effective unit of administration was the 'circumscription' under an administrador, though in the remote areas, to facilitate communication with the governor, some circumscriptions were grouped together as *intendencia*. Each circumscription was divided into a number of administrative posts, each under a Portuguese official called a *chefe de posto*. The administrador and his officials were directly charged with the political and judicial control of Africans under the *Regimen do Indigenato*. They had the powers of summary trial and imprisonment; they collected taxes and tried to encourage economic development in whatever way they could; above all, they coordinated labour recruitment and supply and dealt with the insatiable demands of private companies and concessionaires requiring labour. The colonial army was also an important feature of the administration, military service being almost as important an obligation on the Portuguese African as on the French African, but with a higher proportion of Portuguese non-commissioned officers.

Even more than in French West Africa, African political leadership had been undermined. While among the Fulahs, Malinke and Mandyako, Muslim religious leaders who were willing to cooperate with the regime were encouraged, it was the administrador and the *chefes de posto*, the white chiefs, who dominated the day-to-day life of the Portuguese Africans. The African chiefs, called the *regulos*, were uniformed Portuguese officials. Some of them claimed succession through the traditional system but this became increasingly irrelevant. They were appointed by the administrador and were usually former soldiers, policemen or interpreters rewarded for their loyalty and efficiency. They received token salaries and did the dirty work of the administration, especially in the collection of taxes and recruitment of labour. In this, they were assisted by the armed police, who were recruited largely from ex-servicemen and were infamous for their brutal methods.

Portuguese Guinea was different from areas like Angola, Mozambique, the Cape Verde Islands, or even São Tomé, with sizeable Portuguese and mestico populations. Guinea-Bissau, as it is now called, remained predominantly an African country with only 2,250 Europeans and 4,500 mesticos in 1950 out of a population of half a million. This meant a greater degree of neglect, fewer public works, fewer schools, particularly secondary schools. But the overall colonial policy remained the same. The Estado Novo emphasised the old doctrine of Luso-African solidarity and boasted of Portuguese miscegenation and absence of racial prejudice. It tried to reduce abuses in labour laws, in particular trying to stop private recruitment by channelling all requests through the administrador. But the obligation to work remained the cardinal Portuguese African policy. Beyond that, the ultimate goal that Africans through the regime of enforced labour would acquire Portuguese culture and one day qualify to be regarded as 'civilised' and fit to enjoy the privileges of Portuguese citizenship, remained a distant hope. Rather, it was increasingly stressed that the African had a culture of his own deserving of respect to the extent that his progress to the promised land of Portuguese civilisation should not be hurried with too much education or other interference, except by way of teaching him habits of industry through enforced labour. Meanwhile a few individual Africans, less than fifteen hundred by 1950, about a quarter of one per cent of the population, who were able to prove that they spoke Portuguese fluently, held lucrative jobs and had adopted Portuguese culture, were rewarded with certificates of assimilation, which enabled them to escape from the *regimen do indigenato* and join the *não-indigenas* in electing one member of the National Assembly.

ECONOMIC AND SOCIAL POLICY

The cardinal principles of the colonial economic relationship were to stimulate the production and export of cash crops — palm produce, groundnuts, cotton, rubber, cocoa, coffee and timber; to encourage the consumption and expand the importation of European manufactured goods; and, above all, to ensure that as much as possible the trade of the colony, both imports and exports, was conducted with the metropolitan country concerned. To facilitate the achievement of these objectives, new currencies, tied to the currencies of the metropolitan countries, displaced local currencies and barter trade. The state of the colonial economy was measured not by the welfare of African peasant producers, manufacturers, consumers, business-men or taxpayers, but solely by the increase of exports and imports and the proportion of this trade that was conducted with the ruling country.

In theory, the various governments adopted a laissez-faire policy of the state encouraging but not directly interfering with trade. In practice, colonial currencies, banking facilities, navigation, judicial processes, customs regulations and other measures ensured the domination of the economy by a relatively small number of large expatriate firms. These firms took action to ensure — through collusion concerning the prices both of imports and of exports, through agreements not to compete in one another's major spheres of interest and other monopolistic and discriminatory practices — that African businessmen were effectively eliminated from the import/export trade and that the African producer and consumer did not enjoy the benefit of a competitive market in relation to either the price of his exports or the price of the imported goods he bought. Similarly, when his labour was required, the firms, instead of paying a competitive price, agreed among themselves to fix a low wage. Sometimes the political officer enforced this through recruitment of contract and obligatory labour. Such price-fixing extended all the way to freight charges whereby the West African Shipping Conference, representing the major expatriate firms and having a virtual monopoly of the import/export shipping, imposed higher rates on non-members. Thus it was the European firms who reaped the benefit of the expansion of the colonial economy in the decade 1919-29. The few African merchants who had survived from the pre-colonial period found themselves in increasing difficulties. They tended to hold too much of their capital in goods, without reserves of cash to tide them over the difficult years, and the European banks would not go to their aid. The slump in the economy in 1920 ruined most of them and the Depression after 1929 virtually wiped them out of the export/import business. Their resentment was a major factor in the rise of nationalist politics in the inter-war years.

Similarly, the collection and transport to the coast of export crops and the retail marketing of imported goods, both of which in the nineteenth century had been almost exclusively in African hands, gradually passed to expatriates, not only to the large firms but to Levantines and a few Greeks and Indians as well. The European firms and banks showed greater confidence in these non-European expatriates by extending to them credit and banking facilities which they denied to African competitors. In the areas which produced cocoa, coffee and to a lesser extent palm produce in the Ivory Coast, Ghana, Dahomey and Southern Nigeria, the world price usually brought returns in relation to the labour invested that were sufficiently high to improve substantially the material living conditions of the African farmers. Indeed, faced by regimes little interested in their welfare, these farmers often had enough revenue to finance their own schools, roads, bridges and dispensaries.[16] It was in such areas that there emerged a number of relatively successful African businessmen. In the areas which produced lower-priced export crops like groundnuts, the role of Lebanese middlemen became prominent. Attempts at African cooperatives in this period were unsuccessful in gaining higher standards of living for farmers of such export crops. The only significant exception was in the Senegal where the marabouts of the Mouride brotherhood preached the heavenly reward of industry on earth and the regular payment of tithes to maintain the marabouts, who were thus enabled to expand the cultivation of groundnuts, accumulate capital and become powerful economic as well as religious and political leaders.[17]

In the inter-war years, therefore, it was in these cash crop-producing areas that West Africans were directly involved in the colonial economy. Even then, their material life was little affected since, apart from the exceptions noted above, the majority of export crops earned low prices and the return to the farmer was so small that after paying his taxes and usurious rates of interest on advances made to tide him over the cultivation season and other dues, he usually had little left with which to buy imported goods. Moreover, these imported goods were usually only substitutes for goods which had hitherto been manufactured locally — textiles, household utensils, etc. — rather than additions to the range of goods traditionally available to him. The major items imported during the colonial era do not differ greatly from the list of goods Heinrich Barth recorded as being the staples of the Kano market in the 1850s.[18]

The economic life of those West Africans living outside the cash crop areas would have been scarcely affected by the colonial presence but for the obligation to pay taxes — which was not enforced in some places such as the Gold Coast till towards the end of the period — and but for the obligatory labour and compulsory crop cultivation in Portuguese Guinea and French West Africa. Money to cover taxes had to be found either from internal trade in selling food crops in cash crop areas, or from the earnings of the younger members of the family who had to migrate voluntarily or through contract labour organisations to areas where cash could be earned. Large-scale migration for this purpose took place for instance between on the one hand Niger and Upper Volta and on the other Ivory Coast and Ghana where work was sought on the cocoa and coffee plantations or in the gold mines. Similarly, seasonal labour from French Soudan worked on the groundnut fields of Senegal and the Gambia. Again, such migrant labour did little more than provide taxes for the workers' families. In many areas throughout this period, barter remained an important form of exchange. In 1935 one British District Officer wrote despairingly on the slow pace of change: 'To describe present day Borgu one could quite easily copy one of Lord Lugard's early reports and give an accurate picture'.[19]

In principle only those areas that had potential for growing cash crops or had mineral resources were opened up by roads and railways financed by the colonial governments. Thus a map of the railways and major roads in the 1930s represents a grid draining the exportable resources of the interior towards the coastal ports. Roads and railways were not built for the specific purpose of developing internal trade. Thus in the 1930s goods from Ibadan to Enugu had to be railed via Jos.

Most economic studies of this period have been concerned only with the export of cash crops and the import of European manufactured goods. Comparatively little is known about the internal trade in subsistence crops and locally manufactured goods such as household utensils, woven and dyed cloth, metalwork, etc. Anthropologists have paid some attention to the economic importance of local trade and manufactures in particular areas. But relatively little, if anything, exists on the overall volume of internal trade in West Africa in such commodities as yams, cassava, cloth, kola-nuts, cattle, poultry, dried fish, etc., or locally manufactured goods such as cloth, hoes, knives, calabashes, jewellery, etc., or the fortunes of trade in these goods. What is clear is that internal trade meant as much to the well-being of the peasant as did the import/export trade, if not more. The depression which hit those involved in the colonial economy so hard in the 1930s probably brought some prosperity to others. French West Africa increasingly in that period and even more during the blockade of 1940-2, which cut it off effectively from European markets, had to rely on local industries and internal trade for textiles and matchets.

In the name of a laissez-faire policy, the various colonial governments did very little to encourage the production of food crops. Yet they did not hesitate to use the resources of the colonial regimes to encourage the production of cash crops. In Portuguese and French West Africa, labour was frequently recruited for European planters. The British in Nigeria did draw the line at the alienation of land to the Lever Brothers for plantations, but the agricultural research stations that were financed with the African taxpayer's money concerned themselves almost exclusively with the cash crops. If anything, as a result of the incessant demand for labour for public works, European farms, cash crop production, military service, etc., food production seems to have declined. Groundnut-producing areas of the Gambia and Senegal began to import rice and to endure annually what came to be known as 'the hungry season' just before and during the cultivation of groundnuts.[20]

Similarly, while France and Portugal, and even Britain to some extent, were willing to use tariffs and other measures to reserve colonial markets as much as possible for the trade of metropolitan companies, whether or not there were other more economically beneficial customers, there was no encouragement, to say nothing of protection, for local manufactures. No new industries were created to process the cash crops locally. For a long time not even the shells of the groundnuts were removed locally. Rather, cheaper imported textiles and household utensils were allowed to compete with traditional crafts and industries. The full effects of this on the economy deserve further study. While many household utensils began to be imported, farming methods and implements remained unchanged. Cheaper woven cloths were driven off the market faster than the more expensive ones for which there was always some demand. There is no doubt that the cheaper imports improved the standard of living especially in the cash crop areas where there was some money to buy them. But since most of the profit of the import trade was exported, the overall economic advantage to West Africa was limited.

In short the colonial regimes pursued only a one-sided laissez-faire policy. Where the interest of European firms was concerned, the administrations placed their resources at the firms' disposal at the expense of Africans. Where the interest of Africans was concerned, the administrations were indifferent and left the field free for the privileged Europeans to compete unfairly with the Africans. That was the essence of colonial exploitation. An important case in point is public works — roads, railways, harbours, schools, hospitals, agricultural stations, and later the occasional electric plant, pipe-borne water supply, aerodrome, etc. — which were a great source of pride to colonial regimes. It was a cardinal point of the philosophy of laissez-faire that colonial regimes should provide only what could be paid for from taxes, customs and excise duties, and loans serviced exclusively from local revenues. There was little conception that metropolitan funds could be invested in colonial infrastructure to stimulate development. The depression of the 1930s provoked one or two very tentative steps in this direction such as the Great Empire Loan in French West Africa for public works to relieve unemployment and the British Colonial Development Fund which made £420,000 available for the four British West African colonies, from which Sierra Leone alone received £250,000. Thus, while the public works represented long-term fixed capital assets, it was essentially the African taxpayers who paid for them but the European rulers who reaped the most benefits from them in the colonial era. Apart from the John Holt and the United Africa Companies which built private ports at Warri and Burutu, it was the African taxpayers who financed the harbours dominated by the monopolistic European shipping lines. They paid for the railways, which were designed for the import/export trade rather than for the expansion of internal trade and industries. They paid for the lighting and the water supply and paved streets of the exclusive European municipalities in West Africa.[21]

In spite of the laissez-faire philosophy, the colonial regimes could be as *étatiste* as they cared to be. In the absence of private companies willing to invest money in them, the colonial administrations operated railways, water works, electricity supplies, etc., thus fortuitously introducing ideas of public ownership of essential utilities. In addition, they not only directed what export crops should be planted, they often used taxation as a direct policy of encouraging migrant labour to assist cash crop production. In Portuguese Guinea, an administrador had the power under the Labour Code to recruit for obligatory work anyone who could not show evidence that he had a job to enable him to pay his taxes, as well as feed, house and clothe his family. Both the French and the British frequently fixed taxes at a rate designed not merely to pay for needed services, but to force as many Africans as possible to increase their production of cash crops or seek paid employment.

However, in matters that concerned the welfare of the Africans, the colonial administrations stuck rigidly to the philosophy of laissez-faire, balanced budgets, apathy and unplanned development. While the French had some notable success in combating major diseases, the Portuguese and British concentrated a disproportionate amount of available resources on safeguarding the health of European officials and paid only limited attention to the health of the African farmers. Similarly, the colonial regimes left the vital subject of education to a laissez-faire policy. Government involvement was limited to a few schools like the William Ponty of Dakar or the Bo School in Sierra Leone for sons of chiefs intended to produce clerks, interpreters, chiefs and other agents of colonial administration. The colonial administrations supervised and eventually began to subsidise Christian missions to produce more clerks and interpreters needed by the commercial firms or for the grades of staff in the administrative and technical services that were too expensive to import from Europe. Whenever Africans acquired higher education, it was usually through their own efforts or the encouragement of the Christian missions, and the denial of employment in the colonial administrations was calculated to discourage it. By administrative measures, the colonial regimes were willing to restrict the movement of Christian missions, for example in the Muslim parts of Northern Nigeria, or to limit the participation of missionaries from other than the metropolitan country. But they were unwilling to use administrative measures to prevent the consequent unevenness in the rate of economic, educational and social development.

For all the rationalisations of the colonial officials and all the impressive statements of the Annual Reports, Official Gazettes and other colonial publications, there is very little evidence of any conscious purpose or plan of the colonial regimes to create a new and improved social and economic order for the Africans. The policy of making Africans bear the cost of colonial administration, public works and services while large European combines enjoyed these services and drained the wealth, meant that colonial development in this period consisted of little more than increasing the exploitation of the resources of the forest areas in palm produce, rubber and timber. The forest areas, therefore, rather fortuitously felt more of the colonial impact. Apart from the expansion of groundnuts in Senegal and groundnuts and cotton in Northern Nigeria, the colonial regimes neglected the Sudan belt which at the end of the nineteenth century had appeared the more prosperous part of West Africa. With the seaward orientation of the colonial economy and the consequent total eclipse of the trans-Sahara trade, the Sudan lost its traditional role as the entrepôt of West Africa to the coastal harbours and new capital cities. In the long run, this uneven development was perhaps the most important legacy of the colonial period.

AFRICAN RESPONSE AND INITIATIVES

The West Africans were themselves the first to accept the reality of the colonial situation. It is clearer now in retrospect that, even in the heyday of colonialism in the inter-war years when the threat of revolts and rebellions had largely receded, the basis of the power of the colonial regimes remained shaky and they continued to fear uprisings. They were usually careful to avoid pressing unpopular measures unless they had first taken the precaution of assembling enough force to deal with protests and violent demonstrations. Yet, at the time, not even the most optimistic nationalists could guess that European political control would be so short-lived. No one questioned the reality of the conquest. The experience of some West Africans during the First World War had shown that the Europeans were human after all and not a race of gods but no one questioned their technological superiority and their ability to repress rebellion sooner or later. And no one, before the Second World War, seriously considered that force might successfully be used to overrun their regimes.

Yet, no African people were willing to entrust their fate permanently to the European ruler. He seemed to represent some powerful, unthinking irrational force that argued little and interfered much in matters he did not understand or try to understand. Faced with subjection to such a force, different West African peoples adopted different strategies to ensure their own survival as peoples and in relation to their neighbours. Many peoples, especially if they were outside the cash crop areas, and not close to mines or railway lines, found that they could get away with the minimum of contact. They paid their taxes, tolerated the officially recognised chiefs and courts, but very much went their own way. Others who could not avoid the colonial impact had to seek more positive approaches. Some tried to come to terms with the colonial power and outdo their neighbours in exploiting the regime's ignorance of the region's history in order to improve their own relative status and position. Others sought Christianity and Western education or organising cash crop production, while at the same time taking care to preserve their own identities. These responses and initiatives of the African peoples as ethnic, linguistic and historical units have so far received little scholarly attention other than from some social anthropologists. Most historians have tended to concentrate only on the policies of the colonial regimes and the direct reactions of the traditional chiefs and the rising educated elite. And yet no clear picture of the colonial situation, or the impact of colonialism on West Africa, can emerge without some understanding of these African attitudes.

Perhaps the most immediate problem posed to an African people by colonial conquest and the loss of sovereignty was the question of the most effective unit of organisation in the colonial situation. Given the variety of levels of political organisation in pre-colonial times — villages, village groups, city states, kingdoms, confederations, empires — and the different stages of consolidation of these groups at the time of conquest, the question of the most effective level of organisation became complicated through the apparent vagaries of colonial policy, breaking up existing larger units and forcing smaller units willy-nilly to consolidate. Indeed, the colonial policies seemed in a sense an attempt to create a chaotic situation in which previous historical development mattered less than the changing whims of the political officer in determining the units of local government and the political relationship between different peoples. That chaos did not result was due largely to the constant pressure of the African peoples to assert their wishes and establish some continuity with historical developments. The story is yet to be fully told, but behind the many little struggles against arbitrary amalgamation or the breaking up of historical states — through petitions, litigation, arguments before Tribunals and Commissions of Inquiries and sometimes uprisings — was the effort of African peoples to retain some control over their own destinies even under colonialism. It is remarkable how people who in most cases accepted the permanence of colonial boundaries so frequently forced the boundaries of the units of local government to change.[22] However much pre-colonial history was invoked, these struggles were not intended merely to re-create the pre-colonial situation. It was rather that different peoples were seeking to find new units of organisation that would best serve their own interest in the colonial situation by exploiting tendencies shown by the colonial powers, or sometimes by moving against those tendencies. Indeed, levels of organisation unknown in pre-colonial times sometimes came to be preferred, as when the Ewe, Igbo and several peoples in the Cameroons discovered new national consciousness.

At issue in the contest between the consciousness of African peoples and the will of the different colonial regimes was not merely the question of the best unit of organisation, but also the nature of the organisation itself. This, too, was a matter in which the colonial administration had a large stake. Just as they interfered with the units, so they tried to dictate who were to be the new political leaders and what powers they were to wield. Often, as we have seen, colonial powers found it convenient to recognise traditional leaders of the people as their agents of administration. Where, through policy or plain ignorance, the colonial powers insisted on persons without traditional status, African peoples often continued to recognise their traditional leaders and support them through customary dues paid clandestinely in defiance of colonial rulers.[23] They often went behind colonial courts to take their complaints and civil suits to the traditional courts, whose sense of justice they understood better. Sometimes, because colonial police institutions were remote, they continued to operate secret societies which detected and punished crime as understood in pre-colonial society. It was only gradually as colonial power became more effective, or colonial institutions became more responsive to people's needs, that these traditional law enforcement agencies fell into disuse.

Next to the question of the unit and the system of organisation was that of land tenure. Nothing threatened the African sense of identity and hope of well-being so much as a threat to his land. Colonial policies seeking to invest all land in the control of the metropolitan government, or to set apart uncultivated land as forest reserves or turn them over as concessions to European planters or concessionaires were resisted as fiercely as possible. With such pressures from the colonial regimes, along with increasing urbanisation, expansion of cash crop production, voluntary and enforced migration, the struggle to hold on to one's land and to seek to lay claim to more became for the majority of African peoples a most important feature of the colonial situation.

While most West Africans sought their survival within their own communities by holding on to their land and seeking a preferred unit and system of organisation, others were willing to try their fortunes further afield. The colonial era speeded up pre-colonial patterns of migration and encouraged new ones. This came about not only through the peace the conquerors established by proscribing war among their subjects or through their taxation policies and labour codes. To an extent not always appreciated, many people escaped unpopular measures by fleeing from the rule of one European power to another. The colonial regimes tried to be neighbourly with each other and discourage this but they could never prevent it. Indeed, it may be said that the Africans tolerated the colonial boundaries so well because they were not operated as lines of human divide. This was particularly so for the masses of unknown farmers who moved to and fro, to maintain traditional ties or search for new opportunities by simply walking across the boundaries carrying their belongings on their heads. The boundaries meant more to the elite, who spoke European languages, travelled in lorries or cars and were more conscious of opportunities in the metropolitan capitals than of the nearest markets or the natural outlets for one's goods across the colonial boundary.[24]

Even among those who migrated, the communal bond remained strong, either in the sense that they migrated in groups and invoked the communal ties to ease the problems of adjustment in their new homes, or in the sense that migration was only seasonal and the intention to return to their original homes and cultural background was always taken for granted. Thus the problems raised for the West Africans by the colonial situation were not only political and economic. Ultimately involved was a cultural confrontation.

The European ruler was more nervous than most Africans realised at the time, and he did not rely on the superiority of his guns alone. As Lugard preached, if a single white man were to assert rule over thousands of Africans he needed confidence and a sense of racial superiority more than technical competence.[25] Faced with this attitude, the West African came to rely more and more on his cultural traditions as the most effective armour against the arrogance and nihilism of the European. Some European rulers may have held the mistaken belief that the African was without history or culture and was waiting to be moulded at will by any European innovator. Yet it was precisely his sense of history and the consciousness of his cultural heritage that the West African had to rely upon in his struggle for survival and identity. The best commentary on West African attitudes to colonialism is to be found in the cultural and particularly the religious field.

The colonial regimes maintained an ambivalent attitude towards Christianity in West Africa. Even if some colonial officials were personally non-believers, the cultures of Britain, France and Portugal were officially Christian and the Christian churches were regarded as propagators of European culture. There was little disagreement on that. The ambivalence was to be detected in the extent to which they were anxious to see their African subjects acquire this Christian element of the European culture. Cultural assimilation was said to be the ultimate goal that the Portuguese held out for the Africans, for without it the African was not worthy of the Lusitanian community of which he was declared an involuntary member. To further the cause of assimilation, state subsidy, as we have noted, was restored to Portuguese Catholic missions. Yet, while many officials declared themselves pleased that a few Africans became converts to Catholicism, there was no great hurry to expand missionary activities. Up to 1950, African Christians in Portuguese Guinea numbered fewer than two per cent of the population.[26] It appears that illiterate Christians were welcome because they were thought to be generally loyal to the regimes. But the loyalty of Christians who sought Western education for themselves or their children as the only access not only to the privileges of citizenship but also to the better jobs ipso facto became suspect. Missionaries were therefore urged to show some respect for African culture and not hurry the pace of cultural assimilation unduly. The French adopted a similar attitude in restricting the work of missionaries, except that they did not share the added contradiction of offering state subsidy at the same time. The British were not as restrictive, except in predominantly Muslim areas. But they were equally critical of the supposedly adverse effects of missionary work not only on traditional African culture but also on the loyalty of Africans to the colonial regime. It was a firm British attitude that cultural assimilation was to be derided if not condemned, and certainly not applauded.

Yet the fact that Christianity was the religion of the rulers, and even more that it provided access to Western education, aided its rapid expansion during the colonial era. Many peoples who in the precolonial era had refused to accept Christianity began to show new interest. Indeed, the significant fact about the expansion of Christianity in this period was the extent to which it was due to the initiative of African evangelists and the patronage of communities demanding teachers and schools, rather than to any plans of the missions or colonial governments. This in turn meant that West African Christianity was never what the Christian missions or colonial governments wished. The independence movement among churches demanding that control be vested in African lay or clerical leaders remained strong. Such churches were trying to incorporate aspects of African ideas of worship into their liturgies and to show more tolerance for African social institutions like polygamy and the extended family. Other sects arose under African prophets who were anxious to relate Christianity to current West African beliefs in the existence of witches and other spirits which the Christian missions tended to ignore. They offered Christian prayers for the whole range of problems that plagued people in the villages and for which traditional diviners had offered assistance in the form of sacrifices to various gods. In addition, the new churches also showed concern and offered prayers to enable people to cope with the myriad problems of life in the cities — employment and promotion opportunities, good business for the traders, avoidance of accidents for the travellers, etc. In short, the new sects recognised the continued relevance to their followers of traditional beliefs and social practices and were helping them to make adjustments to the new urban situations. Even among those Christians who remained within the churches controlled by the missions, these traditional beliefs and practices died hard. Ethical and aesthetic values continued to be shaped to a large extent more by the traditional values of the old religions than by Christianity.[27]

For all the rapid spread of Christianity, the nagging fact that embarrassed all Christian missions was that Islam was spreading even more rapidly. Many of them sought to explain this by arguing that Islam was an easy religion, making few demands on the convert and being more willing than Christianity to become syncretic and make compromises with traditional African beliefs. They were loath to accept the unpalatable truth that many Africans in the colonial period embraced Islam almost as a form of protest against colonialism, because it offered the wider world-view that Christianity offered but without the indignity of assimilation to the colonial master's culture. Of course, Islam had other advantages. It had been in Africa since the seventh century. The preachers of Islam were Africans who understood the spiritual needs and social problems of their converts, and no doubt this made it easier for the converts to make the transition from traditional African religions to Islam. Islam had made significant advances in West Africa in the nineteenth century; it had consolidated its position in the Western Sudan, and had begun to advance into the forest areas of Yorubaland, Ashanti and the Senegambia. The colonial regimes quickly recognised that Islam could not be dislodged from this powerful position. They were therefore willing to encourage the spread of Islam provided they could wean Muslim leaders from their initial hostilities into supporting the colonial regimes. They succeeded in this to a large extent, by cutting West African Muslims away from the Islamic centres of the Middle East, by suppressing such universalistic movements as Mahdism, by breaking up the larger Caliphates into smaller, more localised emirates, and by encouraging the Sufi orders provided they limited their organisations effectively to the local level. Many officials who had no doubts regarding the superiority of Christianity over Islam as a way of life were more willing to see the African embrace Islam under those conditions than to see him claim to become heir to European Christianity and culture. For many West African peoples, particularly those in the Sudan belt, for whom Islam had become a way of life and their cultural heritage, the pressures of the colonial period provided added incentive to hold fast to their religion, even at the risk of shutting out many useful aspects of the invading cultures from Europe. In spite of colonial restrictions imposed on large universalistic and interterritorial organisations considerable movement of ideas went on through simple traders and other channels the colonial regimes could never effectively control. Nor could contacts with the Middle East be controlled as long as even a few Muslims continued to make the pilgrimage to Mecca. Moreover, these centres of Islam in the Sudan exploited the tendencies of the colonial regimes in order to spread their religion among peoples who had hitherto remained impervious to their preachings. It was in these areas where Islam was in direct competition with Christianity that Islam seems to have been preferred. Both religions offered literacy, though literacy in European languages seemed to offer the more immediate relevance. However, many coastal Muslims, partly through the effort of colonial administrations and partly through their own initiative, were able to combine literacy in European languages with Arabic. Both religions appealed to the urban trading communities, Islam more to those interested in the internal chain of markets, Christianity more to those focusing attention on the import-export trade. However, the subordination of Africans within the European orbit increased the attraction of Islam for people who were concerned about their self-respect and self-esteem. Sometimes there were elements of local politics involved: one community would go Christian and their rivals would go Muslim; the Creoles of Freetown held on to Christianity as their lifeline, while the Protectorate people who began to invade the town preferred Islam;[28] the foreigners in Lagos were Christian and the indigenous community chose to embrace Islam instead. Yet it is remarkable how the majority of the population of Dakar, Freetown, Lagos – those great centres of Christian and colonial activities – entered the colonial period as Christian and emerged as Muslim.[29]

With the rapid expansion of both Christianity and Islam it appeared that the traditional African religions were in danger of imminent extinction. The very act of conquest and loss of sovereignty seemed to have shaken many people's confidence in the old gods and the efficacy of their role in human affairs. The families charged with the rituals of the gods continued to hold their beliefs and warn of the consequences of neglecting the various festivals. But even among those who embraced no other religions, fewer and fewer people in the larger towns were willing to identify themselves as 'pagans'. But this was only a temporary loss of nerve. The vitality of the old religions was scarcely impaired in the villages. The whole cycle of religious festivals, daily prayers and sacrifices went on. Soon, some of the festivals began to move into the cities and the Christian-educated elite who had been taught to be ashamed of them began to rationalise that they were cultural, not religious, ceremonies which every patriot should preserve. The dances and the ceremonies were being increasingly divorced from the religions that produced them. The art that the religions had once patronised also survived and was being revived. The same was true for the oral literature and now it began to be written down. With varying degrees of religious conviction, the oracles and other methods of divination continued to be patronised. Times of stress, such as prolonged illness or unemployment, were apt to reveal that the hearts of many who had formally adopted Christianity or Islam continued to harbour many of the traditional beliefs. Indeed, on the eve of the Second World War, when so much had changed and was changing in West Africa, the remarkable thing was that so much more had been barely touched by European influence. It is easier now in retrospect to see that the impact of colonialism on West Africa had been exaggerated.[30]

NOTES

1. R. J. Hammond, *Portugal and Africa 1815-1910: A Study in Uneconomic Imperialism*, Stanford, 1966, pp.49-50.
2. See Pierre Alexandre, 'The Problem of Chieftaincies in French-Speaking Africa', *West African Chiefs*, M. Crowder and O. Ikime (eds), Ife, 1970, pp.24-78.
3. J. Brevié, *La Politique et l'administration indigènes*, Dakar, 1932, pp.13-27.
4. Lord Hailey, *An African Survey*, London, 1938, p.240.
5. Discours prononcé à l'ouverture de la session du Conseil du Gouvernment de l'A.O.F., Dakar, November 1937, p.9.
6. Hailey, p.547.
7. Hailey, p.626.
8. Robert Delavignette, *Les Vrais Chefs de l'Empire Français*, Paris, 1939.
9. Pierre Alexandre, 'Chiefs, Commandants and Clerks: Their Relationship from Conquest to Decolonisation in French West Africa', *West African Chiefs*, pp.2-13.
10. *The Times*, 28 December 1936; 'The Colonial Empire in 1937-1938', Statement to Accompany the Colonial and Middle Eastern Services, Cmd 5760, London, 1936, p.64.
11. This is borne out by a comparison of the detailed information which the Lieutenant-Governor of Dahomey had to provide for the Governor-General in Dakar about the revolt in French Borgu in 1916 and the brief reports the Lieutenant-Governor of Northern Nigeria sent to the Governor-General in Lagos when one year earlier rebellion broke out in Bussa, in British Borgu.

12. Tekena N. Tamuno, 'Unofficial Representation on Nigeria's Executive Council', *Odu*, new series, 4 October 1970, pp.54-8.
13. W. Ormsby-Gore, *Comparative Methods of Colonial Administration*, London, 1930, pp.10-11.
14. See Michael Crowder, *Revolt in Bussa: A Study in British Native Administration in Nigerian Borgu, 1902-1935*, London, 1973.
15. R. J. Hammond, *Portugal and Africa 1815-1910*; also his 'Uneconomic Imperialism: Portugal in Africa before 1910', *Colonialism in Africa, 1870-1960*, i, Gann and Duignan (eds.); James Duffy, *Portuguese Africa*, Cambridge, Mass., 1959; 'Portuguese Africa 1930-1960', *Colonialism in Africa, 1870-1960*, ii; Lord Hailey, *An African Survey*, revised London, 1957, p.228 ff.
16. Polly Hill, *The Gold Coast Cocoa Farmer*, London, 1956; David Brokensha, *Social Change at Larteh, Ghana*, Oxford, 1966.
17. Donal Cruise O'Brien, *The Mourides of Senegal: The Political and Economic Organisation of an Islamic Brotherhood*, Oxford, 1970; Lucy Behrmann, *Muslim Brotherhoods and Politics in Senegal*, Cambridge, Mass., 1970.
18. Henry Barth, *Travels and Discoveries in North and Central Africa*, London, 1857, II, pp.118-33.
19. National Archives, Kaduna/SNP/17/3/24024 Borgu Division, Development of. Resident Ilorin to Secretary, Northern Provinces, 114.1935.
20. The hungry season in the Gambia continued to be a major problem right up till the late 1950s. See Michael Crowder, 'Better outlook in the Gambia', *New Commonwealth*, 9.12.1957.
21. For the economy of this period see Alan McPhee, *The Economic Revolution in British West Africa*, London 1926; *Survey of British Commonwealth Affairs*, Volume II 'Problems of Economic Policy, 1918-1939, Part II' by W. K. Hancock, London, 1942; Margery Perham (ed.), *Mining and Commerce in Nigeria*, London, 1948; The Leverhulme Trust, *The West African Commission 1938-39*; Technical Reports, London, 1943; Report of the Commission on the Marketing of West African Cocoa, London, 1938, Cmd. 5845; Constance Southwark, *The French Colonial Venture*, London 1931; Henri Cosnier, *L'Ouest Africain Français*; Department of Overseas Trade, *Economic Conditions in French West Africa (1928-1930)*, Report by H.M. Consul-General in Dakar, London, 1930; Jean Suret-Canale, *L'Afrique Noire: L'ère Coloniale, 1900-1940*, Paris, 1964.
22. A good example are the Bussawa of Borgu. See Crowder, *Revolt in Bussa*: op. cit.
23. Delavignette, *Les Vrais Chefs de l'Empire*; A. I. Asiwaju, 'The Impact of French and British Administrations on Western Yorubaland, 1889-1945', Ph.D. Thesis, Ibadan University, 1971.
24. *Ibid.*, Chapter IX: 'Western Education and the Rise of the Educated Elite'.
25. F. D. Lugard, *The Dual Mandate in British Tropical Africa*, London, 1922 (1965 ed., pp.58-59).
26. Lord Hailey, *An African Survey*, op. cit., p.238.
27. See J. F. A. Ajayi, *Christian Missions in Nigeria, 1841-1891: The Making of an Educated Elite*, London 1965; James Bertin Webster, *The African Churches among the Yoruba 1888-1922*, Oxford 1964.
28. Edward Fashole Luke, 'Christianity and Islam' in *Freetown: A Symposium*, Christopher Fyfe and Eldred Jones (eds.), Freetown, 1968.
29. *Ibid.*
30. See J. F. A. Ajayi, 'Colonialism: An Episode' in *Colonialism in Africa, 1870-1960*, Vol. I. L. H. Gann and Peter Duignan (eds.), Cambridge, 1969.

XII

COLONIAL BACKWATER*
(1956/1957)

(a) PROBLEMS OF THE GAMBIA[1]

Richard Jobson, in his famous book *The Golden Trade*, wrote of the Mandinkas, the Gambia's largest ethnic group: 'the men for their parts do live a most idle kind of life, employing themselves (I mean the greater part) to no kind of trade nor exercise, except it be only two months of the year, which is in tilling, and bringing home their country-corn, and grain, wherein the preservation of their lives consists, and in that time their labour is sore'.

That was in 1623. Miss Elspeth Huxley, quoting this same passage in her own book, *Four Guineas*, commented: 'Life among the Mandingos does not seem to have changed during the past three centuries'. She further cited a young Irishman who had lived among the Mandinkas as saying: 'these sessions on the Bantaba (Mandinka palaver house) falsify the conclusions of the economists. Experts calculate that if you bring in mechanisation, say tractors, you save ten man-hours, and these hours can be spent on cultivating a larger acreage, and producing more food. But they won't be. They'll be spent on the Bantaba'. It is common practice in the Gambia to attribute the country's ills to the traditional idleness of the population, with the facile phrase, 'The problem of the Gambia is the Bantaba'.

Recent investigations in the Gambia have proved the Mandinka to be a much maligned character. Mr. D. P. Gamble, the Government sociologist, has shown in his economic survey of two Mandinka villages that the men work for a much longer period than two months, and the Genieri tests demonstrated that in the field work season all farmers, including women, work to the limit of their powers. In the 1948-49 season, in spite of poor soil, the Gambia's average export per

*Reprinted by permission of Times Newspapers Ltd., from *The Times British Colonies Review*, 3rd Quarter 1956 and 4th Quarter 1957 respectively.

capita was £16.90, and Nigeria's £6.20. Lately the number of immigrant or stranger farmers from Senegal has declined, but there has been no proportionate decrease in the Gambia's groundnut crop. The recent extension of rice cultivation, in which Mandinka men, contrary to all precedent, often assist the women, constituted a social as well as an economic revolution. To understand the problems of the Gambia one must look farther than the people's capacity to work. 'The problem of the Gambia is the Bantaba' is an inaccurate generalisation which does not admit the true complexity of the country's problems.

The Portuguese discovered the Gambia River in 1455, and in the following year settled an island, which later became known as James Island. For three centuries the history of that island was the history of the Gambia. The British first traded there in 1587, but it was only after 300 years, during which English, French, Dutch and Portuguese companies struggled for control of trade, that they finally occupied the Gambia. This was done by a boundary treaty with the French in 1889. This treaty, which determined the geography of the Gambia, has proved one of the major curses of the territory – for the Gambia is a geographical anomaly. It is merely a river stretching finger-like for 300 miles into French Senegal, and claiming for Britain a strip of territory some seven miles wide on either bank. It is a river without a hinterland; Britain possesses what would have been Senegal's most valuable natural waterway. The territory, 4,132 square miles in area, is flat and, by the river, marshy. The soil is sandy, deficient of certain components, overworked by the population, and ravaged by heavy tropical rains and an eight-month dry-season. The main system of communications is the river. The two lateral roads are extremely bad, and this, together with the lack of feeder roads, leaves parts of the territory economically unexploited.

The bulk of the population are Mandinka, Wollof and Fula. Of these the majority are Muslim. Ethnographically the Gambia is as much part of Senegal as it is geographically. Many villages alternate between the two territories regularly, and every ethnic group in the Gambia is represented in Senegal in greater numbers. Nevertheless, over the years a 'British' African has evolved, so that the African from Bathurst is as different from his cousin in Zuiginchor or Kaolack as a Londoner is from a Parisian. However, ethnic affiliations still present a considerable barrier to the creation of a true Gambian.

By British colonial standards the Gambia is over-administered. It supports a full-scale government for an area that in most other colonies would be administered by one or at most two district officers. Some 150 Grade I officials handle a budget of about £2,800,000. Admittedly the colony must have a government, but with so many officials and so small a budget, the country suffers from an overdose of bureaucracy. For administrative purposes the territory follows the normal British West African pattern of colony and protectorate. The colony, administered by a commissioner, is virtually Bathurst. Four commissioners, with two assistants, co-ordinated by a senior commissioner, administer the protectorate; to some extent this otherwise superfluous number of administrators is necessitated by the geography of the territory, but it means that much that would be done by the stroke of a pen in another district of similar size is delayed or hampered by conferences, committees, boards, and legislative and executive council meetings. This is one of the great drawbacks to the dispatch of reform in the Gambia.

By way of compensation native administration is the finest on this part of the coast. A comparison between the Gambian and his counterpart in French Senegal or Portuguese Guinea is enough to demonstrate this. The Gambian is more advanced and has a greater independence and enterprise than his neighbours across the border. For this the local government practised by the 35 district authorities, each with their own treasury and budget, is largely responsible. If the history of English political development in the nineteenth century is anything to go by, the Gambian will be far better suited to full political responsibility than his neighbours in Senegal and Portuguese Guinea.[2]

The Government services of the Gambia are among the most Africanised in the continent. Thirty-one per cent of the Grade I officials are Gambians, and many are heads of departments. On the whole these services are efficiently run – for example, the medical services, whose director is an African – but not all of them are good. In some cases this is due to inefficiency, but more often it is a result of the disproportionate expenditure between colony and protectorate. The main source of the Gambia's revenue is the heavily taxed protectorate, yet most of the expenditure is devoted to Bathurst, or the colony. Historically this is a natural phenomenon, but in the Gambia it has exceeded all reasonable limits. Thus, the Colonial Office adviser on Education, Mr. Baldwin, wrote: 'Justice must be done in the protectorate. At present nine times as much is spent on education in the colony as in the protectorate'. The same is the case with P.W.D. expenditure. Practically all development is undertaken in Bathurst, and that is largely wasted. For example, the recent road and drainage scheme for Bathurst was a lamentable failure. One member of the Legislative Assembly declared: 'We build roads and streets, only to repair them within a week of their completion. Wellington Street, more specifically, is lower than the drains intended to serve it; its surface is like a plush carpet in a West End cinema'. No wonder the Protectorate chiefs at a recent divisional conference complained about their roads. Yet while the demand for feeder roads becomes more urgent, the P.W.D. announces a new £180,000 scheme for resurfacing roads in Bathurst.

The Gambia has a single cash-crop economy. The recent fall in world market prices demonstrated how precarious such an economy can be. The Government has been compelled to lower the price paid to the farmer, and bring it in line with world prices. This action harms trading firms, to whose advantage it is to have as much money in circulation as possible. The Government was reluctant to take this step, not primarily for this reason, but because of the possible exodus both of stranger farmers and groundnuts across the border into Senegal, where prices are much higher than those of the world market. Whatever happens, the Government statement on the new policy concluded, the Gambia's economy might well receive a 'shock'. One magazine entitled its article on this statement 'The Gambia Gives Up'.

But the outlook is not so grim as at first it may seem. The steady decline in the number of stranger farmers in the past years has not, as already noted, met with a similar decline in production. The prices paid in Senegal fall steeply the farther away from the buying centre the producer is, whereas in the Gambia they are uniform. Indeed, a considerable quantity of nuts comes into the Gambia from Senegal. There is much to recommend bringing the Gambia's economy into touch with world prices, especially now that the rice-growing schemes have defeated the age-old problem of the hungry season.

Much can be done to solve the economic difficulties of the Gambia. At present the agricultural service is considering alternative cash crops such as cashew, tomatoes, mangoes and oil palms. But capital and transport costs present great difficulties. Private enterprise is helping. The new Atlantic Hotel will attract tourist trade,[3] and has already brought in two air lines to Yundum airport. Gambia Minerals Ltd. are exploiting the deposits of ilmenite on the beaches near Bathurst. These will bring in an added government revenue of some £100,000 or more, but can only be considered as a temporary asset, as supplies of ilmenite will be exhausted within about 10 years.

The most pressing problem, that of the improvement of groundnut production, is one of the few that can easily be solved. Bambey, the Groundnut Research Station in Senegal, with over 30 years' experience, has offered its help: advantage of this should be taken, and the Agricultural Service should be made directly responsible for the distribution of selected seed to the farmers. An extended agricultural sorvice, in liaison with Bambey, and based on the valuable soil research already done by Dr. Webb, could do much to help the Gambia.

Surprisingly enough these problems, and the succession of Colonial Development failures, such as the egg farm and the rice farm, have not produced political discontent in the Gambia. But the Gambia is too small for politics on the national scale. The new constitution provides for ministerial appointments. But politics are more a matter of personal followings than the beliefs of political parties. It is significant that Mr. Garba-Jahumpa, leader of the Gambia Muslim Congress, has the weakest party in a predominantly Mohammedan community. The other two party leaders, both Christians, depend for their backing on the Muslim elders. Politics in the Legislative Assembly are more those of a city council meeting than of the House of Commons. This is as it should be, for national politics could seriously damage a country as small as the Gambia.

What of the future? It is obvious that geographically the Gambia could be a valuable economic part of French Senegal. Rationally one would recommend giving it to the French. The main opposition to such a move would come from the population, as it did last time it was suggested. If we maintain the Gambia as our own protectorate, it must be accepted that possibilities for economic development per se are few. As Lord Hailey commented in 1951: 'It is the misfortune of the Gambia that the size of its population and the extent of its resources, which have been determined by accidents of history and geography, are such as must always make it difficult for it to achieve the reality of economic and political independence'. It was once suggested that it be made a part of a Federated British West Africa. But most remember the days when the Gambia was administered from Sierra Leone, and oppose it. Anyway, the Gambia would stand little chance in representation with its paltry 250,000 against Nigeria's 30 millions. The alternative, which meets with much approval, is representation in the British Parliament such as Malta has requested. The Gambia would be more suited to this than any other British African territory, and it might well be a worthwhile experiment. But whatever comes of the future, many of the present problems of the Gambia can be solved by a certain amount of reorganisation. Ultimately it must be accepted that if the Gambia remains British, *as it intends to*, it will have to be assisted by a considerable subsidisation – which it does not at present receive in any great measure.

(b) RICE REVOLUTION IN THE GAMBIA

In the past five years a socio-economic revolution of great significance has taken place in the Gambia, but it has passed almost unheralded. Basically this revolution has involved a large increase in the rice production of the territory, an increase whose significance can only be fully appreciated against the background of the notorious hungry season, which until recently had been the scourge of this small territory.

The hungry season prevailed in the Gambia from June until October. During that time there was a general shortage of food caused by the depletion of the previous year's rice harvest, and the exhaustion of the money earned from the cash crop of groundnuts.

The problem of the hungry season was threefold. In the first place it was undesirable since a large proportion of the population lived for a quarter of the year at near starvation level. Mr. D. P. Gamble, the anthropologist, who has made extensive surveys of the Central Division of the Gambia, where most of the new rice is now being grown, reported that from 24 July 1951, at Keneba 'only a quarter of the people were eating two main meals a day' and in August 'one found people who were not even getting one meal a day'. By the end of that month the number of people who were not having an adequate meal had risen as high as 30 per cent. Infant death rates rose sharply during this period.

The second aspect was that the hungry season coincided with the period when men were working on their groundnuts and women were planting the early rice. Their efficiency was impaired considerably by their poor nutrition, and Mr. Gamble reported that he 'found women collapsing by the roadside on their way back from the swamps and having to be helped home, the cause apparently being too much work and too little food'.

In a sense the third aspect of the problem was its most serious and demoralising. African villagers, desperate for food, involved themselves in heavy debts with local traders and Jula-men (combination of trader and money-lender). Imported rice was sold on credit to farmers, which brought the trader a double advantage of making over 50 per cent gross profit and being repaid with groundnuts. Thus he secured his share in the groundnut crop, a share he could not secure by price competition since the price was fixed annually by the Government and the Oilseeds Marketing Board. Traders and commercial firms, who significantly have mostly been against the rice extension, thus took advantage of the Gambian farmers' plight.

Extension of Cultivation

The solution to the problem was clearly an extension of rice cultivation, and a change-over from unproductive early rice to the highly productive late rice of the mangrove swamps. This would release women to help the men with groundnuts, and the men to help the women with the rice, ensuring a higher production of both groundnuts and rice. As early as 1946 Ilyasa, under its energetic chief Tamba Janneh, had shown the way, but it was not until 1950 that Government, under Sir Percy Wyn-Harris, took this problem seriously. For several years the gubernatorial progresses through the Gambia became more like those of a Bishop preaching rice to the unconverted. By 1953 the first effects of the changeover began to be felt.

To-day there has been a large extension of rice farming in the mangrove swamps, yielding 1,000-1,400 lb an acre compared with an upland rice yield of 400-800 lb. The main factor that militated against the extension of farming to the swamps was the difficulty of access, and the labour needed in a land that has always been short of it. Government, cooperating with the villagers, has in the past five years built well over 100 miles of access causeways in the Central and Macarthy Island Divisions. Last year over 1,800 acres of land were ploughed up by tractors, and in the Western Division extensive bunds have been built against flooding by sea-water. The measure of the resulting increase can be seen in Central Baddibu, which has three to four times more rice under cultivation to-day, and in Genieri, a flourishing rice village which hitherto had almost none.

The significant factor is the changeover from early to late rice. This involves a radical change in the argicultural traditions of the farmers, but with Government help little persuasion was needed. Of course, critics of this rice extension say that there has in fact been no real increase in the area cultivated, since it has involved only a changeover from one type of land to another. But even if this had any foundation it would be poor criticism, since production would automatically have doubled because of the higher productivity of swamp rice. And, as Mr. Ramaswami, the Indian rice expert at present on contract to the Gambia and the genius behind the rapid increase in rice production, has shown, the use of fertiliser could increase this further. The French have found that with submerged rice fertilised with ammonium sulphate they get yields of 2,000 lb. an acre.

The shortage of labour, chronic in the Gambia which for years has imported stranger farmers, who have recently been increasingly difficult to find because of the high price paid for groundnuts in neighbouring Senegal, has been partially solved by this changeover. Women now help the men with groundnuts, which is borne out by the fact that last year's was an exceptional groundnut crop with few stranger farmers working on it. On the rice fields the women are getting a far greater output for the same amount of labour. Mr. Ramaswami is now trying to introduce small rice threshing and rice hulling machines at low cost, which would save an immense amount of labour. The rice hulling machine he has in mind does in half an hour what the women take four days to complete by hand pounding.

To what extent have the rice areas increased? This cannot be ascertained accurately until the publication of a series of maps made from a recent aerial survey, but the evidence of officials, chiefs, the farmers themselves and of independent sociologists like Mr. Gamble and Mr. C. O. Van der Plas, from the United Nations, suggest it is considerable. One should not be confused by annual increases in rice imports figures, which many use to pooh-pooh the claims of the Government. Much of this rice is immediately re-exported, and the rest is mainly used for consumption in Bathurst, the Kombos and the poor Western Division, which is now increasing its purchasing power by its mounting palm oil production. It is indicative of the rice increase that one trader has already installed a rice mill at Ballinghoe, and is intending to build more.

The Director of Agriculture, who has seen most of the aerial survey photos, said: 'I am certain, after studying these photos of the Central River rice areas, that a very considerable increase has taken place. Naturally, the extent cannot be accurately assessed until the maps are completed, but at Katchang on the north bank a block of 500 acres has been cleared and put under rice in five years. What impresses me most is the enormous potential of mangrove and riverain grass swamps that have not yet been exploited'.

The hungry season is largely a thing of the past, though, as Sir Percy Wyn-Harris has admitted, earlier optimism has not been altogether justified. The increase in rice production has been sufficient to eliminate it in the rice growing areas, and reduce it considerably in other parts. It still appears in localised forms after floods or plagues of caterpillars, but only in such forms that the Government is able to deal with. There is room for further extension, as Seyfu Omar M'Baki, of Macarthy Island Division, declared recently in the Legislative Council. But with these qualifications the rice revolution of the Gambia has achieved its end, and reflects credit on both the people and the Government of a territory that has never had much money at its disposal.

NOTES

1. I have included in this collection of essays two pieces from my early days as a journalist, largely because they seem to me still to capture something of the flavour of colonial rule in microcosm. The first essay is a watered down version of a rather angrier essay written for *New Commonwealth* in the same year entitled 'What is wrong with the Gambia?' It was written when I was an undergraduate at Oxford, and I remember soon after its publication being telephoned at College by the Editor with the bad news that the Colonial Secretary of the Gambia having read it was threatening a libel action. The action was averted, but I sought what for me seemed appropriate revenge: setting the same article in different, more moderate language. I had it published in *The Times British Colonies Review*. It is interesting that this august journal actually submitted my article to the Colonial Office for vetting and I was

successfully able to parry their criticisms, so that what appears below was in fact 'passed' by the Colonial Office.

The companion piece, 'Rice-Revolution in the Gambia' also published by *The Times British Colonies Review* is included because it shows how much change one man was able to make in the colonial situation. The work of Ramaswami has always seemed to me the real proof that the colonial economy, and indeed the régime as a whole, need not have been as stagnant and unimaginative as it was.

Neither of these articles was footnoted, being essentially works of journalism and some of the sources used have since been mislaid. It therefore seemed to me invidious only to footnote partially where sources could be traced.

2. The subsequent history of independent Gambia, the only West African territory that has managed to maintain two-party democracy and does not have to back up its rule with the Military — indeed it does not have an army — suggests that this prognostication was a fair one.
3. The tourist trade has become a major industry in the Gambia. So too has smuggling of cheap goods into expensive Senegal.

XIII

VICHY AND FREE FRANCE IN WEST AFRICA DURING THE SECOND WORLD WAR*
(1970)

The Second World War is often seen as marking the prelude to decolonisation in British West Africa. During that war Britain introduced radical changes in the social, economic and political policies in her West African colonies. These colonies assumed a vital role in the war both from the point of view of strategy and from the point of view of men and materials. As a result, Britain felt increasingly obliged to make economic, social and political concessions to her African subjects. More important still, by bringing her African colonies into a world war in which resolutely anti-colonial powers like the United States and Russia were her allies, she was under strong pressure from them to undertake reforms. These reforms are well-known. In the socio-economic sphere the Colonial Development and Welfare Acts presaged a policy whereby the metropolitan government accepted that 'aid' for development was an obligation. In the political sphere, where prior to the Second World War self-government for the African colonies had been a vague goal which no administrator believed would be achieved in his life-time, limited measures of self-government and participation in the political process were initiated in the new constitutions promulgated at the end of the war.

In French West Africa, the war was to have equally important though somewhat different and less well publicised results in the liberalisation of the social, economic and political regime in the African colonies

Prior to the Second World War, French West Africa had been

---

*Originally published in Portuguese as 'Vichy e a Franca Livre na Africa Occidental durante a Segunda Grande Guerra' in *Afro-Asia*, 1970, No. 10-11. pp. 67-77 and subsequently partly incorporated in my chapter on 'West Africa and the Second World War' in J. F. Ade Ajayi and Michael Crowder (eds), *History of West Africa*, Harlow, 1974, and reprinted by permission of Longman Group Ltd.

economically and politically dominated by the metropolis. In the political sphere, apart from the *Quatre Communes* of Senegal, no Africans had rights other than a small group of *citoyens*, numbering not more than 2,136 in 1936.⁽¹⁾ The overwhelming majority of the population was classified as *sujets*, or subjects, who came under the harsh codes of the *indigénat* or code of administrative justice whereby they could be imprisoned without trial by the administration. It also subjected them to compulsory military service, obligatory forced labour, compulsory cultivation of crops and above all made any form of political activity all but impossible. Economically the West African colonies were treated as appendages of the metropolis and aid for the improvement of the economic lot of the African was almost unknown. The only major exception to this was the Sansanding Dam on the Niger which was designed to open up new lands for colonisation by land-hungry peasants in French Soudan and Upper Volta. In the social sphere, funds for the improvement of the lot of the African were sparse. Of a probable population of over 12 million in 1934 only 60,000 children were at schools of all kinds. The one shining light of France's social policy was in the field of health services, which by comparison with those of British West Africa were much more systematic and designed to reach the widest number of people possible. All in all, however, the political, social and economic lot of the African in French territory was much worse than that of the British, and perhaps the most concrete demonstration of this was the large-scale migration of French Africans into the British colonies, particularly the Gold Coast and Sierra Leone. There had, it is true, been attempts at liberalising the French administrative regime in West Africa under the Popular Front government, but these were cut short by the outbreak of war.

It is against this background that must be seen the struggle between adherents of the Vichy regime of Marshal Petain, who concluded an armistice with the Germans whereby France and her Empire would be neutral and the adherents of General de Gaulle, who proclaimed a Free France that would continue to fight against the Germans. This Free France, as we shall see, was based not on the metropolis, but on French Equatorial Africa, one of the most backward parts of the French Empire.

It is a myth of French colonial history that on the one hand the Vichy regime in French West Africa was much harsher than that of its predecessors and that of its successor in 1942, the Free French regime. It is also a myth that Africans were ready to regard themselves as Frenchmen and fight for France's liberty. As the Camerounian novelist, Mbella Sonne Dipoko, wrote in a recent review of the Free French regime in Cameroun:

I remember, as a child, seeing Camerounian men being conscripted by non-Camerounian Bambara soldiers [from French Soudan]. Some hid in the bush. Many others who were taken away clearly went against their will, not because they didn't want to fight against Nazi Germany and on the side of France, but simply because they couldn't be bothered one way or the other: ...

It wasn't Africans who vacillated between the Free French Movement and the Vichy regime. The *right* even to vacillate was denied them because, although French forces had been defeated in France, French-speaking Africans were still a colonised people, and there were French officials on the spot to carry on with the job of autocratic rule. It was these officials who were, with the handpicked African *notables* who were associated with them, for or against de Gaulle. And once they had decided one way or the other, all they did was to issue orders for the rank and file to follow suit.[2] The burden of this essay is that the dispute between Free France and Vichy did not concern Africans as active agents, but only as passive agents. Nevertheless the outcome of passive participation was the introduction of important political, social and economic reforms.

The French West African administration had hardly had time to adjust to the fact of the Second World War before France was defeated by the Germans and an armistice was signed on 21 June whereby Southern France was left in French hands under the so-called Vichy Government of Marshal Pétain and his Premier, Pierre Laval.

In French West Africa the main feature of the short months before the capitulation of France was the recruitment and training of African soldiers for the French army. In the First World War, some 180,000 Black African soldiers had seen service on the European front. From 1919 onwards military service had been obligatory for all adult males between the ages of 19 and 28. Before the capitulation some 80,000 African troops had already been sent to France,[3] while in French West Africa itself there were some 118,000 troops at the disposal of the French, the majority of them reservists, or recruits enlisted as a result of the 1939 and 1940 recruitments. Of these only some 20,000 were considered sufficiently trained to go into battle.[4]

Under the terms of the armistice France's colonies were to be neutralised which meant the disbandment of the majority of France's Black Army, whose level was reduced to 25,000 men. French West Africa ceased formally, like Vichy France, to have a military role in the war. Her reduced forces were merely for self-defence: economically she was limited to providing food for the truncated metropolis, that was if she could send food across the economic blockade imposed along the West Atlantic Coast by the British for whom the establishment of the Vichy regime in Dakar was a potential threat. Shortly before the establishment of the Vichy regime in Dakar the bulk of the Royal West African Frontier Force had embarked for East Africa for the campaign against the Italians in Abyssinia (Ethiopia) and Somalia. This left the four British territories practically defenceless.[5] They had no aircraft except some antiquated ones in Freetown belonging to the Navy. Freetown, vital as a convoy centre, and Takoradi, where planes were off-loaded in crates and assembled to be flown to the Middle East via Nigeria and Sudan, were both within bombing range of French West African airfields. The British, fearful that the neutrality of the Vichy regime would not survive German pressures to use Dakar as a base for attacks on Freetown, hurriedly increased their forces in West Africa. Three British battalions were shipped to Freetown and part of the Gold Coast Regiment was sent to the Gambia.

Right up to 21 November 1942, when the French West African administration decided to join the Allies, the British in West Africa looked nervously across their borders at their French neighbours, especially at Dakar with its large port, harbouring part of the French navy, and its air-base with a comparatively large number of planes. One of the reasons for the return of the West African troops before the end of the East African campaign was anxiety about the security of Freetown.[6]

The fall of France and the Vichy accords produced consternation among the overseas French administrators. On the one hand was their loyalty to a legitimate government of the Third Republic presided over by Marshal Pétain, the great hero of the First World War, who had successfully defended France against the Germans. On the other hand was the call of the comparatively unknown General de Gaulle to rally to his government in exile. If de Gaulle could secure the adherence of the colonies his French government would be more than a paper government. It would have land and, more important, men to recruit as soldiers. It could also supply the Allies with much needed foodstuffs. The administrators themselves, even before de Gaulle's call was made, had considered whether a bloc comprising France's African colonies might not be formed to continue the struggle against Germany. Governor-General Léon Cayla even sent a mission to North Africa to find out what General Nogues, General Officer Commanding in French North Africa, planned in this direction but finally decided he had not the forces to resist a German invasion.[7] What seems clear is that if, say, French West Africa had rallied against the Germans, the latter would almost certainly have invaded French North Africa. This certainly was the possibility that was uppermost in the minds of French administrators and is used as a justification by pro-Vichy writers for the policy pursued in French West Africa: by maintaining its neutrality, the Germans were kept out.[8]

As far as the European combatants were concerned, French Black Africa was strategic for two reasons over and above its resources in men and materials. First, Dakar was the third largest port in the French Empire after Marseilles and Le Havre. Secondly Niger and Chad had common frontiers with the Italian colony of Tripolitania (Libya) while Chad gave access to the Anglo-Egyptian Sudan and the British East African Colonies, all of which were under pressure from the Axis.

An important factor in the decisions made by the various French colonial governors as to which side to support was the destruction of the French fleet at Mers-el-Kébir in Algeria. Under the terms of the armistice the large French fleet was to be neutralised. One thing the Allies did possess in their favour at the time was British superiority over the seas. The British were very frightened that the French fleet, though neutral, would be taken over by the Germans whose fleet was a good deal smaller. The British, therefore, issued an ultimatum to the French Fleet that it should join the British fleet, or have its ships disarmed by the British who would guard them in their own ports until the end of the war. Alternatively the French could scuttle their ships themselves. The French refused all three alternatives so the British destroyed the bulk of the French navy in the docks at Mers-el-Kébir, killing over 1,400 French soldiers.[9] This action, justified by the British on the grounds that they could not afford the remotest chance of the French fleet falling into the hands of the Germans or Italians, indicated their lack of confidence in the Vichy regime and was reflected by its administrators in West Africa. It embittered many Frenchmen to such a point that they could not accept working with the British under de Gaulle. Furthermore in Dakar the reality of Mers-el-Kébir and the loss of French lives was brought home when the British crippled the French battleship *Richelieu*, then in port there.

In French West Africa, while de Gaulle had supporters, the majority of the administration preferred the easier option of neutrality under the terms of the armistice and acceptance of Cayla's Vichy-appointed successor, Pierre Boisson.[10] Many who had been wavering were shocked by the apparently unprovoked destruction of the French fleet. Finally, it must be remembered that de Gaulle was a relatively obscure and not very senior French general. The drama of conscience is nicely brought out in the following conversation when the Free French tried to persuade the Dakar government to throw in their lot with them.

Commandant Orfèvre, supporting the Vichy government of Dakar, having arrested D'Argenlieu, one of de Gaulle's delegates, told him: 'D'Argenlieu, you belong to a religious order and I myself am a believer. We therefore know how to examine our consciences. I have made my own examination and I am absolutely convinced of having done my duty.'
Argenlieu replied: 'Our duty is to fulfil our obligations to England.'
'I obey my legitimate leaders', replied Orfèvre. 'Our chiefs have betrayed us' objected D'Argenlieu.[11]

This conflict between obligation to legitimate leaders and their rejection on the grounds of betrayal was a very real one for most Frenchmen.

A former High-Commissioner for Cameroun, Pierre Boisson, himself a veteran of Verdun under Marshal Pétain, where he had lost a leg, was appointed Vichy High Commissioner for Black Africa, that is both French West and Equatorial Africa. His headquarters was Dakar, and he secured the support of all the constituent territories of French West Africa. Not so Equatorial Africa. There, Felix Eboué, the Guyanese Governor of Chad, the first Negro to be appointed a governor in French Black Africa, rallied to de Gaulle, in defiance of Boisson, his High Commissioner, who sent him a telegram: 'By your decision you have betrayed the duties with which you were charged. By taking the initiative in handing over to England the territory confided to you, you have by a deliberate and plotted act, broken the cohesion of the Empire'.[12] This was a major triumph for the Allies, since it gave them a staging post at Fort Lamy through Nigeria to East and North Africa. Shortly afterwards, Cameroun, whose High-Commissioner, Brunot, was hesitating over supporting de Gaulle, was taken over by Colonel Le Clerc in a rapid coup d'état staged from Nigeria. This secured the Chadien hinterland, for Chad had no territorial frontier with Nigeria, only the Lake. Soon afterwards Congo-Brazzaville rallied to de Gaulle and the pro-Vichy administration of Gabon was ejected by force. This gave de Gaulle the much-needed land-base for his Free France. Eboué, then, became Governor-General of the Equatorial federation based on Brazzaville.

Boisson was thus effectively only Governor-General of French West Africa. Only one administrator of major importance there tried to go over to the Free French: Ernest Louveau, head of Upper Volta, then dependent on the Ivory Coast. In an abortive mission to Dakar to persuade Boisson to support de Gaulle he merely succeeded in getting himself imprisoned.[13] Boisson's policy was clear: to preserve the neutrality of French West Africa to the extent of refusing access to it of any German. This policy he succeeded in pursuing and it is quite clear that despite propaganda to the contrary, no German submarine ever used the port of Dakar, and only one German official ever visited Dakar and that on sufferance and under close surveillance of Boisson himself.[14]

If Boisson ever doubted that he had the support of the majority of the French for his policy, such doubts were removed by the futile attempt by the Free French and British to invade Dakar. De Gaulle had persuaded Churchill that he had enough supporters in Dakar to take it without difficulty and an invasion force was assembled in Freetown. Thus on 23 September de Gaulle sent emissaries to Boisson, backed up by part of the British fleet and a Free French force to persuade him to rally to his cause. But they were received as invaders: one group was arrested, the other managed to escape. In the face of Boisson's refusal to negotiate, the combined Free French and British forces attacked Dakar, trying to land troops. Boisson successfully defended Dakar against the assault. The deaths of both French and Africans at the hands of the Allies hardened attitudes against de Gaulle and gave Boisson clear support for his policy. This was confirmed by an American visitor to Dakar at the time, Paul M. Atkins, who wrote: 'Practically all the citizens of the city, regardless of their basic sympathies, were proud that the British were successfully repulsed'.[15]

Thereafter Boisson continued his policy of strict neutrality though he restructured the Black African army in such a way that he did not arouse the suspicions of the Germans to the point of intervention. By the time he rallied to the Allies in 1942 he had, according to du Gard, a well-trained African army of 100,000, with a half-brigade of the Foreign Legion and a European battalion together with supporting arms as well as naval vessels and aeroplanes.[16] According to Boisson's supporters these forces accepted the decision to rally to the Allied cause in 1942 as 'the normal result of a policy whose inspiration, obligations and objectives they had understood. And it was from a well-controlled country that they left for battle'.[17]

When the Allies landed in French North Africa in 1942, Boisson decided to rally to them; he thus put over a hundred thousand soldiers at their disposal as well as providing them with the important port of Dakar and vital staging posts for their aircraft. It was the French Government in Algiers under General Gouraud to which he adhered in November 1942 and his decision to do so was not motivated by any concern with de Gaulle. In Dakar, de Gaulle's name was not even mentioned until April 1943, by which time he had become co-president of the government of which he was soon to become exclusive head.[18]

De Gaulle never forgave Boisson for his refusal to turn French

West Africa over to Free France in 1940 and he revenged himself by having Boisson imprisoned and nationally disgraced. Boisson had vehement supporters, even after his death, who felt that his policy had been the right one and that de Gaulle had shown gross ingratitude in not recognising that, by preserving French West Africa intact, Boisson had, when the time came, presented Free France with a most important supply of men and provisions as well as a strategically vital part of the Empire.[19]

For the British administration in West Africa the changeover of regime came as a great relief and meant that troops required for defence against a possible attack from French West Africa could be released for the Burma campaign. Furthermore the British blockade of the French ports was lifted and West Africa became a fairly safe staging-post for the Allies en route to the Middle and Far East.

For the French African the changeover of regime meant a return to systematic recruitment and service in the Allied armies: over 100,000 left for the front between 1943 and 1945.

Much play was made by the Gaullists of the 'loyalty' of the African to a Free France; Jacques Stern, Free French Minister of Colonies, in a eulogistic account of the French Colonies in which, he declared, no discrimination existed, speculated that the unknown soldier who rests under the Arc de Triomphe might be a coloured Frenchman.[20] But in reality as far as the majority of Africans were concerned the quarrel between Frenchmen — pro-Vichy and pro-de Gaulle — was of marginal interest.

Before the fall of France, French West Africa assumed its role of the First World War as a source of supply of foodstuffs for the metropolis. Léon Cayla, appointed in August 1939 as Governor-General, established committees at every administrative level to requisition foodstuffs while the possibility of economic cooperation between the French and British colonial administrations was explored by Malcolm Macdonald and Georges Mandel, respectively British and French Colonial Secretaries. For a brief period the rigid political and economic barriers established during the Colonial era between the two sets of colonial administrations were broken down. At the opening of his Council of Government, Cayla announced that priority would be given to construction of roads and railways and improvement of ports and airfields. Eight thousand five hundred kilometres of tracks were to be marked out and work was to go ahead on the second stage of the Mossi railway linking Ougadougou to Abidjan.[21] This was interrupted in June 1940 by the Armistice. Though French West Africa was still supposed to supply the metropolis with foodstuffs, the British naval blockade brought imports and exports to a virtual standstill. Groundnut production fell from

419,000 tons in 1940 to 114,000 in 1942, the lowest it had been since 1906,[22] while cocoa production fell from 55,185 tons in 1939 to 542 tons in 1943.[23] Though this meant that the peasant was no longer compelled to produce export crops and thus had more time to produce subsistence crops, it deprived him of cash income. In certain areas like Senegal, where there was great dependence on imported rice as a staple, the peasant was very hard hit. On the other hand, lack of imported cloth and other manufactured goods gave a new lease of life to the indigenous weavers and blacksmiths.

In April 1943 Boisson presaged the economic significance of the changeover of regime from Vichy to Free French in his declaration of French West Africa's new role: 'We must produce. The next groundnut crop in Senegal must in particular be a great success.... I conclude with an equation: Work = Victory = Liberation of the Motherland'.[24] In Senegal under the Free French a 'Battle of Groundnuts' was undertaken to increase production to pre-war levels.

The call for greater economic output was hampered by lack of transport and equipment as well as the imports which served as a means of exchange for the peasant farmer's export crops. Cut off from metropolitan sources, the Free French had to depend on the Allies for help.[25] To achieve increased production the administration requisitioned fixed amounts of produce and ensured the despatch of seasonal labour from Guinea and Soudan to work on the groundnut fields of Senegal. Forty-five thousand *navétanes* were despatched in 1943 'with the cooperation of the governments of these two territories'.[26] The battle for groundnuts was not so successful as had been anticipated; Senegal's Governor Deschamps' target had been four hundred thousand tons; actually only 275,000 tons were produced, partly because of sales over the border in the Gambia where a higher price for them was paid.[27]

Such were the administrative pressures that chiefs were ordered to produce so much of a particular crop on pain of house arrest. *Cercles* were required to produce crops they did not grow. There is the famous story of the cable received by one French administrator instructing him to produce honey in his district. He replied. 'Agreed honey. Send Bees'.[28]

Richard-Molard wrote of the Free French exactions thus:
... one cercle is required to produce so many tons of liana rubber, even though no liana grows in the territory. The native is therefore forced to travel on foot, sometimes over long distances, to buy rubber elsewhere, regardless of cost. He must sell this to the Commandant at the official price which is several times lower than the purchasing price to escape the hands of justice.[29]

While the peasant once again had access to cash income, the strict rationing of the war and the activities of German submarines meant that few imports reached West Africa. Furthermore the peasant had to devote time he would normally have spent on subsistence crops to export crops. Ivory Coast in particular suffered under the Free French regime. According to Amon d'Aby, farmers there were forced to change from one crop to another and since they were *sujets* they could not refuse. Plantations were destroyed on the grounds of disease, though often this was motivated by the fact that they were in competition with European plantations, which any way benefited from the premiums paid on all plantations of twenty-five or more contiguous hectares – there being few African plantations of this size. Europeans were also given priority in requisitioning forced labour.[30]

While the peasant suffered under the Free French regime with its determination to produce what the Allies needed regardless of the wants of the peasants, major developments took place in the cities where port and aviation facilities were improved. Furthermore, with half France occupied by the Germans and the Vichy portion opposed to de Gaulle, groundnuts could only be processed on the spot, which led to an expansion of industrial activity. There was also a revival of small industries which supplied other goods impossible to obtain from abroad. Perhaps the most significant development under the Free French was the intervention of the government in the economy on a scale it had never undertaken before. This was even more characteristic of the development of the economy in British West Africa during the war.

For those Africans who were at all conversant with the language of their colonial masters, the war brought into question the whole fabric of the latter's authority. Not only did they hear denunciations of the methods of their colonial rulers from German propaganda and attacks on the British by the Vichy French and vice versa, but through American and to a lesser extent Soviet sources they became increasingly familiar with arguments about the basic 'immorality' of imperialism. In Dakar, for instance, the French, through the major newspaper *Paris-Dakar*, delighted in pointing out that everything was not well in the neighbouring British colonies[31] while at the same time they forbade their subjects publicly to listen to British radio broadcasts in general and to any stations broadcasting 'anti-national' propaganda.[32]

For the prestige of the white man, on which colonial rule was so intimately based, the spectacle of Frenchmen attacking fellow Frenchmen, and of France under occupation by another European nation was particularly damaging. White supremacy, coupled with the hitherto monolithic structure of colonial rule, was for ever shattered as far as educated French-speaking Africans were concerned. In Dakar they witnessed the Free French savagely denounce officials of the Vichy regime, sentencing them to imprisonment and national degradation.[33] They learnt that Pierre Boisson, former High Commissioner for French Black Africa, had been disgraced and jailed. The benign Marshal Pétain, the hero of Verdun, whom countless Vichy posters had proclaimed the protector and saviour of France, was now discredited.

In British West Africa, though the administration was secure, Africans were well aware of the plight of the mother country. For the first time the administration appealed for the loyalty of their subjects rather than assumed it as of right. Even the Vichy administration in French West Africa, which abolished all consultative assemblies and reduced African *citoyens* to the effective status of *sujets*, appealed to the loyalty of the Africans. Pierre Boisson wrote in *Dakar Jeunes* that 'Africa is the white and black·associated. Let these two African groups of young people learn to know each other, learn to appreciate each other, learn to love each other'.[34] African intellectuals like Ouezzin-Coulibaly and Mamadou Dia were encouraged to, and did, contribute to this pro-Vichy journal. The pro-Vichy *Légion Française de Combattants*, formed in August 1940, grouped together both French and African veterans. The Legion's brochure reported a march past of six thousand members — 'Whites and Blacks united in the same desire ... to serve the flag, and not to betray the memory of heroes'.[35]

In Senegal, where elements of German-instilled racism had manifested themselves under the Vichy regime with the destitution of Jewish officials, in particular Governor Geismar,[36] who subsequently became Secretary-General of the Government under the Free French, a number of Africans were sufficiently motivated against the Vichy regime to cross into the Gambia to join the Free French Forces. Some, too, joined the Resistance and paid for this with their lives.[37]

Another important source of new ideas about the morality of colonial rule came from the huge numbers of white troops who passed through West Africa. African civilians and soldiers met, in the vast majority of cases for the first time ever, white men who were not of the ruling class. Some of them had radical views and communicated their ideas to the Africans, others demonstrated that there was little essential difference between the subject classes of Europe and those of Africa. In French West Africa French Communists encouraged the organisation of Groupes d'Etudes Communistes (G.E.C.s) after the establishment of the Free French regime. These anti-imperialist G.E.C.s were to become the basis of French West Africa's mass party, the Rassemblement Democratique Africain, after the war.

The brief, heady years of the Popular Front Administration in French West Africa, during which there was considerable liberalisation of the regime under which the *sujets* lived, were succeeded by a tightening up of the *indigénat* under the Vichy regime.[38] Not until the Free French took over the administration was there hope of renewed liberalisation. And this did not come about until after the war. In the short run the exigencies of war in the form of need for increased crop production and large numbers of recruits for the army entailed a continuation of the hated *indigénat*. If reforms did not accompany the progress of the war as they did in British West Africa, they were at least promised as a result of African assistance to the Free French by the famous 1944 Conference at Brazzaville where the whole imperial future of France was discussed by the Free French Government.

While the Free French regime made heavier demands on its West African *sujets* than the Vichy regime had, it promised reform in return for sacrifice. Whereas the promise of reforms at the end of the First World War was never kept, de Gaulle, at his famous Brazzaville Conference of 1944, was to initiate reforms which, with the advantage of hindsight, we can now see, had as their logical outcome the independence of French-speaking Africa.

Though for the most part Africans had been passively conscripted into support of the Free French regime in French Black Africa, de Gaulle in recognition of the contribution Africa had made to the liberation of France offered them political, social and economic reforms. Without Equatorial Africa as an initial base for his Free France, without Black African troops and the food supplied by African peasants, it is doubtful whether de Gaulle could ever have achieved his goal of the rehabilitation of a defeated France. As de Gaulle put it himself at the Brazzaville Conference: France found in Africa 'her refuge and the starting point for her liberation'.[39]

For Africans, the conference, which consisted of the three Governors-General of West Africa, Equatorial Africa and Madagascar, together with the sixteen governors of the constituent colonies, and nine delegates from the Provisional Consultative Assemblies and a Bishop, all of them non-Africans, proposed timid reforms or concessions in the political spheres. While there was to be no question of 'self-government', Africans were to play a greater part in the political process. The colonies should be represented in the constituent assembly of the Fourth Republic; each colony should, like Senegal, have a representative assembly; and a federal assembly should be established for each of the Federations. The franchise for Africans, though not universal, should be as wide as possible. However, while Africans were to be represented in the Constituent Assembly, the conference was against their continued representation in the National Assembly of France when it was established. The conference thus was essentially anti-assimilationist and advocated decentralisation with a co-ordinating Colonial Parliament.

In the social sphere the hated *indigénat* was to be abolished and forced labour was to be phased out over a period of five years. Labour conditions for African workers were to be improved. Education was to be increased down to the village level, though it was to be exclusively in French. Health services were to be improved, and a School of Medicine was to be established. More openings in the administration should be made available to Africans, though the higher posts would still be reserved for Frenchmen.

Finally in the economic sphere F.I.D.E.S. (*Fonds pour l'Investissement et Developpement Economiques et Sociales*) was established. Between 1945 and 1960 over £400 million was spent from this fund on roads, bridges, ports, argicultural and urban improvement. In the preceding years of colonial rule almost no aid had been given by France to her colonies, the notable exception being the dam across the Niger at Sansanding.

While French West Africans were largely passive participants in the events of the Second World War, and with the exception of two memoranda submitted by Fily Dabo Sissoko, a Cantonal Chief from French Soudan and a former school-teacher, had no voice in the Brazzaville Conference, the developments resulting from the replacement of the Vichy Administration by the Free French were of vital importance. Most commentators agree that the Brazzaville recommendations, many of them enshrined in the constitution of the Fourth Republic, paved the way for self-government and eventual independence for French Black Africa. Here it is interesting to note that the Brazzaville Conference was not even mentioned in the British Press at the time.[40] And so, though we have argued that French-speaking Africans had been largely indifferent to which of the regimes ruled them during the war, and that indeed the Free French demanded more of them, the success of the Free French regime opened a new chapter in the social, economic and political history of French West Africa. For what Brazzaville so clearly laid down was that Africans, whilst they had no right to self-government, had the right to representative government on the model of the old Senegalese Conseil-Général; and that France had an obligation to invest in the economic development and social welfare of her African subjects.

For both British and French West Africa the Second World War marked a major turning point. In retrospect we can see that colonial rule as it had been practised since the occupation of West Africa had come to an end. France and Britain were now embarking, whether they were conscious of it or not, on a period of decolonisation which was to prove much shorter in duration than either power, particularly France, could envisage at the time.

NOTES

1. Lord Hailey, *An African Survey*, London, 1938, p. 201.
2. Mbella Sonne Dipoko, review in *Journal of Modern African Studies* (J.M.A.S.), VII, 4, pp. 752-3.
3. Jacques Richard-Molard, *Afrique Occidentale Française*, Paris, 1952, p. 165.
4. Maurice Martin du Gard, *La Carte Impériale: Histoire de la France Outre-Mer 1940-1945*, Paris, 1949, pp. 137-8. N.B. This is an explicitly pro-Vichy account of the war years in the French Empire but has some very useful material despite its bias.
5. For an account of the British West African territories during the Second World War see my chapter in J. F. Ade Ajayi and Michael Crowder (eds), *History of West Africa*, Vol. II, London, 1974, pp. 596-621.
6. The above is based on A. Haywood and F. A. S. Clarke, *The History of the Royal West African Frontier Force*, Aldershot, 1964.
7. Daniel Chenex, *Qui a sauvé l'Afrique?*, Paris n.d.
8. *Ibid.*, also du Gard, *La Carte Impériale*.
9. According to du Gard, p. 39.
10. When he was appointed High Commissioner for Black Africa Pierre Boisson had to work carefully at first, on his own admission, because of elements favourable to the Free French cause. Jean Suret-Canale, *Afrique Noire: L'ère coloniale 1900-1940*, 1964, p. 571.
11. du Gard, *La Carte Impériale*.
12. *Paris-Dakar*, 30 August 1940.
13. See his pro-de Gaulle version of the situation in French West Africa at this time: E. Louveau, '*Au Bagne': Entre les griffes de Vichy et de la milice*, Bamako, 1947.
14. This official was a German Foreign Ministry official, Mülhausen, kept under close surveillance by Boisson. The other German to visit Dakar was Dr. Klaube, a former representative of Lufthansa in Gambia, who came to supervise the repatriation of Germans interned in Dakar on the outbreak of the war. Mulhausen passed only nineteen days in Dakar in September 1942. Verification of this lack of German activity was given by the American Consul-General in Dakar, Thomas C. Wasson, in an article, 'The Mystery of Dakar', *American Foreign Service Journal*, XX, 42, April 1943. Wasson was Consul during the Vichy period even after the Americans had joined the Allies.
15. Paul M. Atkins, 'Dakar and the Strategy of West Africa', *Foreign Affairs*, XX, 2, 1942, p. 362. A few pro-de Gaulle French were, however, interned at the time and deported, including the Mayor of Dakar, Alfred Goux, and Silvandre, a West Indian, who later became a Deputy and President of the Chamber of Commerce.
16. du Gard, pp. 137-40.
17. *Ibid.*, p. 140.
18. See, for instance, the principal Dakar newspaper of the day: *Paris-Dakar*.
19. See du Gard, *La Carte Impériale*; Chenex, *Qui a Sauvé l'Afrique?*; and Atkins,

'Dakar and the Strategy of West Africa', who quoted Boisson as saying, 'I defended Dakar against the British; I will defend it a hundred times more so against the Germans' (p. 365). *The Times*, 29 January 1943, wrote that Boisson could not 'be regarded as pro-German in sympathy' and was 'in a narrow and rigid way patriotic'.

20. Jacques Stern, *The French Colonies*, New York, 1944 (trans. Norbert Guterman), p. 12.
21. *West Africa*, 27 January 1940.
22. 'Discours prononcé par M. Hubert Deschamps, Gouverneur du Sénégal, à l'ouverture de la séssion ordinaire du Conseil Colonial', 23 August 1943.
23. F. Amon d'Aby, *La Côte d'Ivoire dans la cité africaine*, Paris, 1951, p. 77.
24. *Paris-Dakar*, 21 April 1943.
25. 'Discours prononcé par le Gouverneur-Général de l'A.O.F., Monsieur Pierre Cournarie, à l'ouverture de la session du Conseil du Gouvernement', December 1943.
26. Deschamps. 'Discours du 23 août'.
27. 'Discours du M. Charles Dagain, Gouverneur du Sénégal. à l'ouverture de la session ordinaire du Conseil Colonial', 3 October 1944.
28. Jacques Richard-Molard, *Afrique Occidentale Française*, Paris, 1956, p. 167.
29. *Ibid*, p. 167.
30. Amon d'Aby, p. 74.
31. See in particular *Paris-Dakar*, 1 July 1942.
32. *Journal Officiel de l'A.O.F.*, 21 December 1940.
33. See for instance the Gaullist paper, *Clarté*, which started publication in Dakar in January 1944.
34. *Dakar-Jeunes*, no. 1, 1941.
35. *Légion Française des combattants de l'Afrique noire* (Brochure), Dakar, 1941.
36. See Arreté published in *Journal Officiel de l'A.O.F.*, 19 April 1941.
37. See Abdel Kader Diagne, *La résistance française au Sénégal et en A.O.F. pendant la Guerre 1939-1945* (Mimeographed), Dakar, n.d., but preface dated 16 August 1949.
38. *Journal Officiel de l'A.O.F.*
39. *La Conférence Africaine Française*, Commissariat aux Colonies, Algiers, 1944. On the Brazzaville Conference see: Hubert Deschamps, *Méthodes et Doctrines Coloniales Françaises*, Paris, 1953 and René Viard, *La Fin de l'Empire Colonial Français*, Paris, 1963.
40. Edward Mortimer, *France and the Africans 1944-1960*, London, 1969, p. 27.

XIV

INDEPENDENCE AS A GOAL IN FRENCH WEST AFRICAN POLITICS: 1944-60*
(1965)

By the end of 1960 all the states that comprised the administrative federation of French West Africa had become independent. Yet the word 'independence' was for long excluded from the public vocabulary of French-speaking African politicians, and the demand for independence was not formally made by any major political party until well over a year after Ghana had become a sovereign state. On 25 July 1958, at its inaugural meeting at Cotonou, the *Parti du Regroupement Africain* (P.R.A.) was pressured into demands for immediate independence by its more radical members, to the embarrassment of some of its older leaders, particularly Léopold Sédar Senghor of Senegal, who were still committed to the creation of a Franco-African community in which the French-speaking African states would share with France the control of such matters as defence, foreign policy, currency, and higher education. Only the night before the meeting, Senghor had prepared a policy statement in which he had written: 'We will be careful not to abuse the word independence, which is a word only too useful for hiding our lack of imagination and our cowardice,' and 'Independence has no positive content, it is not a solution'.

Although the question of independence had been raised within the party, particularly by the Niger and Senegalese radicals, it had seemed that in fact the prevailing view would be Senghor's. It was still the view held by the other major party, the *Rassemblement Démocratique Africain* (R.D.A.), whose president, Félix Houphouet-Boigny of the Ivory Coast, had sent a telegram to the Congress in which he urged the participants: 'Apportent éléments réalistes construction communauté franco-africaine' ('Bring realism into the creation of the Franco-African community').[1] Two months later, however, Hou-

*Printed by permission of Walker and Company from *French-speaking Africa: The Search for Identity*, William H. Lewis (ed), New York, 1965, pp. 15-41.

phouet's own lieutenant, Sékou Touré of Guinea, led a successful campaign in Guinea against the proposed Franco-African community and declared independence. De Gaulle had put the terms for voting in the referendum bluntly: Anyone could take independence, with all its consequences, by registering a 'No' vote to the Constitution of the Fifth Republic. These consequences, it was openly hinted, would involve the withdrawal of all French aid and technical assistance.

Guinea became officially independent on 2 October 1958. By the end of 1960 all the other French African territories had followed suit.

This chapter attempts to trace the rise of the demand for full self-government and independence in French West African politics, to explain the tardiness in its growth, and to assess the strength of the appeal for politicians of the rival goal of membership in the French Union and its successor, the Franco-African Community, during the period 1944-60.

Although the Brazzaville Conference (30 January to 8 February 1944) was essentially one of administrators, it marks the end of the era when political activity in French West Africa was restricted to the four communes of Senegal. The participants were called upon to make recommendations as to the future relationship of France to her colonies. They proposed an assimilationist framework within which the political development of France's African colonies could take place after the war. René Pleven, Commissioner for the Colonies in the Free French Government, made it clear in his opening speech that France had no intention of prescribing independence as a goal for her colonies, not even in the distant future:

> In the Greater France there are neither people to set free, nor racial discrimination to abolish. There are peoples who feel themselves to be French and to whom France wishes to give an increasingly larger part in the life and democratic institutions of the French Community. There are populations which we intend leading stage by stage to a more complete personality and to political freedom, but who will know no other independence than the independence of France.

The Brazzaville Conference was summoned partly as a response to the growing anti-colonialist sentiment in the world, which demanded the early granting of self-government to colonial dependencies by the metropolitan powers, and partly in recognition of the debt Free France owed to the colonies in her struggle against the Germans. The Free French Government was based in Algeria and owed much of its success to the loyalty of French Equatorial Africa under Guianese Governor General Félix Eboué. Indeed, at one stage in the war, more than half of the Free French troops were of African origin.[2] However, although Britain was quite prepared to envisage eventual independence for her colonies, the whole colonial tradition of France excluded such a future for her own. Before the Brazzaville Conference, France had never really worked out what political future she intended for her African colonies. The early experiment in assimilation in Senegal had not been followed up elsewhere in Africa, and the dominant policy had become that of *Association*, which in theory was similar to Lugardian indirect rule, but in practice was paternalist, albeit with strong assimilationist traits.

A policy of assimilation carried to its logical conclusion would have involved the cultural, political, and economic integration of the empire with France. This was rejected not only on the grounds of expense but because many French officials were becoming increasingly doubtful as to whether Africans and Indo-Chinese could be successfully absorbed into French culture. In the last analysis, a full-scale policy of assimilation had been rejected, and was never to be put in force, because France, with a population of 40 million would be dominated by her 60 million colonial subjects, or become a 'colony of her colonies,' as President Herriot put it so neatly to the Second Constituent Assembly on 27 August 1946. Assimilation was abandoned in favour of a policy that in theory recognised the separateness of African culture and the need for a separate framework of development from France's, but that in practice had strong assimilationist elements, particularly in the field of education and administration.

For our present purposes, the most important features of French administration in the interwar years were its centralisation in Paris and its uniformity of application irrespective of territory. The policy followed involved the denial of political rights to all Africans who did not take up French citizenship (which demanded a certain level of education and the acceptance of French civil law) and the classification of those who were not citizens as *sujets*, liable to the *indigénat*, or summary administrative justice, and to the *corvée*.

The Brazzaville Conference stated in clear terms the renewed faith of France in a policy of assimilation, and, in making its recommendations as to the political future of the colonies, it declared that 'The ends of France's civilising achievements in the colonies eliminate any idea of autonomy; all possibility of evolution outside the framework of the French Empire, [and] the eventual establishment, even in the distant future, of *self-governments*[3] in the colonies, is to be dismissed.' In pursuance of its assimilationist aims, the Conference advocated the abolition of both the *corvée* and the *indigénat*, and with them the humiliating status of *sujet*. Further, it advocated greatly increased economic development in the colonies, as well as the extension of education, which, true to assimilation, was to be in the French language.⁽⁴⁾ However, while the Conference recommended that the colonies be represented in the Constituent Assembly, it was against their representation in the National Assembly. Rather, it proposed a Federal Assembly, in which the colonies would be represented not in proportion to their population, but only on a very restricted franchise. At the Conference, the Sudanese Fily Dabo Sissoko backed up this decision to limit the number of overseas deputies, citing the example of Rome 'foundering under the domination of all the barbarians she had wanted to assimilate'.⁽⁵⁾ All colonials were to be granted citizenship and, at the same time, to retain their *statut personnel,* meaning that they were not required to accept French civil law as a prerequisite of citizenship. What in effect was being proposed was a new type of French citizenship, that of a Greater France, a citizenship different from that obtaining in Metropolitan France, which was automatically accompanied by voting rights. Further departing from the ideals of assimilation, the Conference proposed two electoral colleges for the Constituent Assembly, one for citizens under the old dispensation and one for the proposed new class of French citizens. This would ensure the election of one European delegate for each colony with the exception of Senegal, where French citizens of African origin were in the majority.

From the associationist point of view, the Conference's most important recommendation was the one for administrative and political decentralisation. A high degree of centralisation in Paris had, as we have already emphasised, characterised the interwar period and was compatible with an assimilationist rather than an associationist policy. Since the Conference was one of administrators, many of whom had had cause to resent directives from Paris that showed ignorance of local conditions, it advocated decentralisation, stating:

> We also want the colonies to enjoy a large measure of economic and administrative freedom. Further we want the colonial peoples themselves to experience this freedom and to have their responsibilities gradually defined and increased so that they are associated with the conduct of their political affairs in their own country.

Here we find an indication of the dilemma that was to dog French African policy throughout the postwar period. In part, it is the conflict between the traditional universalist approach and the realisation that there were differences between cultures; but mainly, it was that France, unwilling to accept a full-scale assimilation policy, was forced to satisfy the Africans' demands for fuller participation in their own affairs by devolving administrative and political control to the territories. But, at the same time, France was not prepared to take this to its logical conclusion of self-government and independence, because of the firm belief in the 'republic one and indivisible'.[6] French policy then was a constant search for a compromise between these two extremes, for a formula that would conserve the unity of Greater France by retaining ultimate political control in Paris and yet allow a degree of local autonomy both compatible with this thesis of unity and yet sufficient to turn the African politicians' attention away from ideas of independence.

The first Constituent Assembly of 1945 did not meet with the intention of writing a constitution that would envisage independence or even a limited form of self-government for the colonies. Both of the left-wing parties, the Communists and the Socialists, on whose benches the West African deputies sat,[7] were essentially assimilationist in outlook. Yet the Assembly met against the background of revolt in Indo-China, the foundation of Istiqlal, the Moroccan Independence Party, and the demands by Ferhat Abbas for self-government in Algeria — demands that were also being taken up in Madagascar. Independence was becoming popular in the colonial empires. Britain was preparing to give independence to India. France herself had signed the Charter of the United Nations with its liberal sentiments as to the future of the colonies of the Great Powers.

The chief concern of the West African deputies in the Assembly was not independence, or even self-government, a goal openly sought by Ferhat Abbas, but, rather, how to obtain the fruits of France's assimilationist promises, held out at Brazzaville. Thus, they concentrated their energies on securing the abolition of the *corvée* and *indigénat* and on gaining public liberties such as the right to associate, the right to hold public meetings, and the freedom of the press. Their main goal was to obtain French citizenship, which was achieved with the passage of the first *Loi Lamine Guèye* on 9 May 1946. This gave French citizenship to all *sujets*, while allowing them to retain their *statut personnel*. The importance of these series of reforms is emphasised by the joy with which they were received in the colonies.[8]

Right up until 1956 most of the activities of the African deputies in the National Assembly were concerned not with the achievement of local self-government but with squeezing as much juice as possible out of the assimilationist lemon, whether it was in the form of increased aid, or in securing the passage of the Second *Loi Lamine Guèye*, which established the right of African senior civil servants to equal pay and work conditions with their French counterparts, and the passage of the Labour Code in 1952, which accorded African workers many of the benefits enjoyed by their French counterparts.[9]

Their second preoccupation was to ensure that that part of the constitution that concerned the colonies be acceptable to them. Here again we must remember that they were operating in an assembly where no party, not even the parties with which they were allied, saw self-government or independence as a possible goal for the colonies.[10] Furthermore, the deputies were, for the time being, intent on making the most of the assimilationist revolution. Nevertheless, there was considerable enthusiasm for the Brazzaville proposals that there be devolution of administrative and political affairs to the colonies and that a Federal Assembly be established for discussion of the affairs of the overseas territories. The Brazzaville solution, apart from being supported by the African deputies, gained greatest support in the Assembly from the left.

As it was, the first constitution proposed for the Fourth French Republic proved an almost ideal compromise between the general desire of French parties to follow an assimilationist policy with regard to the overseas territories, and the desire of both colonial administrators and African politicians for a greater degree of political and administrative decentralisation. France and her overseas territories, forming 'la république une et indivisible,' together with the associated territories, comprised the French Union *librement consentie*. Contrary to the recommendations of the Brazzaville Conference, African deputies were to retain their seats in the National Assembly. Local assemblies were to be set up in the overseas territories, and these, together with the *conseils généraux* of the French departments, would elect the *Conseil de l'Union*.

Although the constitution had important decentralised features, it was ultimately integrationist in character, clearly defining legislative power for the overseas territories as the province of the National Assembly and not of the *Conseil de l'Union*, as the Brazzaville administrators had hoped it would. Nor was anything like autonomy conceded in the creation of the local assemblies, whose powers were much closer to those of the *conseils généraux* of the French departments than they ever were to embryonic local national assemblies. However, they were to be elected by universal suffrage and, more important still, nearly one-fifth of the seats in the National Assembly were to be allocated to overseas deputies. Furthermore, the two federations of West Africa (A.O.F.) and Equatorial Africa (A.E.F.) were to be headed not by administrative officials but by secretaries of state responsible to the Assembly. This constitution, associated as it was with the reforms concerning the *corvée* and the *indigénat*, had the support of all the West African deputies, but it was repudiated by the referendum of June 1946.

The African Deputies who had participated in the First Constituent Assembly joined the Second Constituent Assembly in August

1946, bitterly disappointed that the Metropolitan majority had rejected a constitution of which they had warmly approved and which, despite the opposition of French citizens originating from France, had gained a majority of votes in the overseas territories. They were also very concerned at the growing influence of colonial interests hostile to the reforms of the First Constituent Assembly. Yacine Diallo summed up this sense of frustration in the debate on the constitution of the French Union on 18 September 1946:

> I take the liberty of declaring in my turn that the African peoples have become anxious since the rejection of the Constitution .... As far as Black Africa is concerned, I must tell you that the texts which were voted upon on 19 April gave complete satisfaction to all the people. Since the newspapers and radio announced the intention of certain groups to withdraw the rights given to the overseas territories by the first *Constituante*, an immense uneasiness reigns in the territories which we represent.

The powers devolved on African politicians and on the African electorate by the constitution produced by the First Constituent Assembly had been a matter of concern both to the *colons* and the colonial business houses. To protect their interests in the Second Constituent Assembly, they formed the States General for Colonisation. The African deputies retaliated by forming a separate parliamentary intergroup, whereas in the First Constituent Assembly they had, on the whole, worked individually with the French parties to which they were affiliated. The new constitution threatened not only to reduce what little powers the local assemblies had but to introduce the principle of the dual electoral college to ensure sufficient seats for French colonists. This then meant the introduction of a double standard of French citizenship. Their sense of frustration even led the West African deputies as members of the Intergroup to subscribe to a remarkable set of constitutional proposals that bore the stamp of Ferhat Abbas, who proclaimed: 'I do not wish to take my seat here [in the Assembly], I want an Algerian state, an Algerian parliament.'

The constitutional project presented by the Intergroup was accepted by the Commission for Overseas Territories by a majority of one, and was presented to the Constitutional Commission on 24 July 1946.[11] Its important features were the official renunciation by France of all ideas of 'unilateral sovereignty over her colonised people'; the recognition of their *'liberté'* to govern themselves and to run their own affairs democratically; the postulate that the French *Union* was composed of nations and peoples who had freely consented to come together; and a stipulation that those states not enjoying the status of *'Etat libre'* could assume it within a twenty-year period. There would be local assemblies empowered to establish their own constitutions, and representation in the Constituent Assembly of the Union would be proportional to population. The project was, of course, not accepted, and its rejection evoked considerable anger among some of the African deputies, led by the Malagasies and the Algerians. Its ideas were to remain the most radical espoused by West African politicians for another decade.

The West Africans, however, with the exception of Sourou Mignan Apithy in Dahomey, seem to have been ultimately lukewarm in their support. Apithy, in a speech made during the final debate on the French Union, was the only West African deputy to pursue the idea of autonomy and possible secession from France. Alluding presumably to President Herriot's speech and the general fears of France's being dominated by the colonies, he declared:

> For those who fear the subjection of the mother country by the overseas peoples . . . we must simply but firmly say that our ideal is not to become French citizens. We simply want to enjoy in our countries the same rights and the same liberties as Frenchmen in your country. I should equally like to say that our ideal is not to sit on the banks of the Seine nor to impose ourselves in what are essentially metropolitan affairs, but to regulate the affairs of our own country on the banks of the Congo or of the Niger, free to discuss with the people of France matters interesting the *ensemble* which we form with them.[12]

Houphouet-Boigny calmed any fears France may have had that the West African deputies were being seduced by Ferhat Abbas' secessionist ideas by declaring: 'There are no secessionists on these benches'.[13]

Although it is very difficult at times to see just what the political objectives of the African deputies were, it does become clear that they all ultimately wanted, as Lamine Guèye of Senegal put it, a 'French Union founded not on disunion, but on the loyal support of the French Republicans that we are, with the same rights without distinction as to colour, religion or race'.[14]

The main concern of the deputies then was to attack the proposal that there should be a dual electoral college not only for the local assemblies but also for the elections to the National Assembly. As it was, there were only forty seats set aside for the overseas territories, and with the introduction of the dual electoral college, this would mean that only half that number would be indigenous to the territories they represented. They also attacked the idea of a double-standard citizenship, one for Frenchmen, one for Africans, which would exclude many of them from the franchise. In short, what they were asking of France was an honest application of her *politique d'assimilation*. Only Apithy and Senghor showed major concern that the political devolution promised by the First Constituent Assembly was being seriously whittled away. Most of the speeches were expressions of disappointment that France seemed to be turning her back on her universalist tradition. Since the Africans who were deputies in that Constituent Assembly are, with two exceptions, important political figures in their countries today and since all played crucial roles in French African politics up to the time of the *Loi Cadre*, it is worth recording those parts of their speeches in which they·declare their feelings for France and their ideas on their future association with her. Senghor said:

> I think that, in order for there to be a real federation — that is to say, a union of equal Socialist French Republics — it is necessary, first of all, that there be active assimilation on all sides. It is thus that together we shall create a new civilisation whose centre will be Paris, a new humanism which will be 'à la mesure de l'univers et de l'homme au même temps'.[15] . . . If the French Union is to endure, and here I am . . . reiterating the thesis of the Socialist Party, it is essential for it to be founded on liberty and equality, conditions of human brotherhood and of French brotherhood.[16]

Lamine Guèye said:

> It is as if we were being obliged to prove by our actions in the future that we are as French, as Republican, as anyone else, while we have shown this by our present and past actions.[17]

Yacine Diallo spoke as follows:

> What are the aspirations of the populations that I represent in this Assembly? They demand to be integrated into the French family.[18] . . . We must hope that this French Union will be realised and the French overseas territories will one day become French provinces.[19]

Fily Dabo Sissoko said:

> All this proves that when we ask you for pure and simple integration into the French nation, we do not use vague formulae; it is our deep conviction which makes us want to remain French until the end of time.[20]

And Houphouet-Boigny said:

> We are not attached to France by its money, by the franc, this poor franc which has lost so much of its value; this essentially material

bond would be too fragile. But there remains a powerful bond, capable of resisting all tests, a moral bond which unites us: It is the ideal of liberty, of equality and of brotherhood for whose triumph France has never hesitated to sacrifice its most noble blood. It doesn't seem to us rash to say that the French Union will be one day, with the inevitable evolution of the peoples who compose it, a multinational state which will lose none of its cohesion if one can retain within it the sacred love of liberty and equality.[21]

The constitution produced by the Second Constituent Assembly was approved by the referendum of 5 May 1946, and was then implemented as the Constitution of the Fourth Republic. Insofar as it concerned the overseas territories, it was much less liberal than that proposed by the First Constituent Assembly, though in fact all the West African deputies voted for it. The double-college system was retained for elections to the local assemblies. Franchise was extended only to a limited number of citizens within the Union. First, there were to be French citizens who could vote for the first college. (This category included those Africans who already had citizenship under the old law.) Second, there were to be Union citizens with the vote. And, third, there were to be Union citizens without the vote. Representation in the National Assembly was reduced, and the power of the federal and territorial assemblies was restricted, so that the most important focus for African politicians became the National Assembly. The federations of A.O.F. and A.E.F. were headed by a civil servant or governor general rather than by a secretary of state responsible to Parliament. Against this background, the Preamble of the Constitution sounded a little hollow: 'France, together with the peoples of its overseas territories, forms a union based on the equality of rights and duties without distinction of race or religion....'

The greatest defect of the Constitution was its failure to create a strong federal assembly. Though an Assembly of the Union was established, it was weak, with few powers, and was certainly not the federal assembly envisaged by the Brazzaville administrators. Moreover, it was situated at Versailles, and was thus removed – some would say significantly – from the main arena of French politics, Paris. Failure to establish a strong assembly where matters concerning the Union could be debated, and the accompanying restriction of African participation in local assemblies (which anyway had almost no power), meant that the demands for political *decentralisation* made by the Brazzaville administrators, and by Senghor and Apithy in the Second Constituent Assembly, were completely frustrated. There was now no way in which such demands could be contained in the future without constitutional revision. As it was, the only place where legislative decisions affecting the overseas territories could be made was in the Metropolitan Assembly of France.

The immediate problem for the African deputies was to organise themselves for the elections to the National Assembly as well as to the local assemblies. Should they continue to ally themselves with the Metropolitan parties or should they form specifically African parties? Lamine Guèye had united Senegalese political groups into the Bloc Africain to elect representatives to the Constituents, but in fact he remained faithful to the S.F.I.O., of which he merely headed the Senegalese branch. On the other hand, Félix Houphouet-Boigny felt there was urgent need for the establishment of an African-based party and to this end invited political leaders, including Senghor and Lamine Guèye, to attend a Congress at Bamako to discuss the question. In any case, neither of them did, at the request of the Metropolitan S.F.I.O., which feared that the new party would be dominated by the French Communist Party. Even Fily Dabo Sissoko, President of the new Congress, seems to have been torn between the desire to establish a purely African party and the need to be affiliated to one of the metropolitan parties for effective operation in the National Assembly. The other main preoccupation of the conference was over the question of local assemblies. One commission even proposed the establishment of sovereign assemblies with responsible government. The questions of the programme and structure of the party and of its relationship with the P.C.F. were referred to a commission that gave its report in Abidjan in early 1947 when the Rassemblement Démocratique Africain (R.D.A.) formally came into being.

The R.D.A. proclaimed itself a specifically African party, but decided to retain its affiliation with the P.C.F., and its party organisation was greatly influenced by Communist theory. Despite the recommendation of the earlier commission that the party demand the establishment of sovereign assemblies with responsible government, the party did not seek further territorial autonomy. It was quite explicit that it did not see its political future outside the framework of the Constitution of the French Union, as Mahjemout Diop stresses in his *Contribution à l'Etude des Problèmes Politiques en Afrique Noire.* He describes the party as the 'only anti-imperialist mass movement of consequence which has seen the light of day in this country', but he emphasises that the main objective of the party was the 'struggle for the political, economic, and social emancipation of Africa within the framework of the French Union founded on the equality of rights and obligations (duties)'. This faithfulness to the French Union and the proclaimed alliance between the French and African proletariat remained strong right up until 1958, as Diop points out, and was even retained by those who broke with Houphouet-Boigny over his decision to dissolve the alliance with the Communist Party in 1950.[22]

Indeed, the main preoccupation of the R.D.A. from its formation in 1947 until 1951 was its affiliation with the Communist Party rather than with its proclaimed Africanness. For, though official Stalinist policy with regard to the colonies tended to be one of encouraging revolt against the Metropolitan 'oppressors', this was far from the attitude adopted by the P.C.F., which was essentially assimilationist in outlook.[23] From 1934 onward, the P.C.F. was very silent about colonial questions, and, as the largest single party in both the First and Second Constituent Assemblies, it showed no enthusiasm for demands for autonomy on the part of the overseas territories. The Communist deputy, Florimonde Bonte, told the First Constituent Assembly that 'France is and ought to remain a great African power'.[24] It was opposed to Algerian nationalism, supported repression in Indo-China, and, as David Caute points out, five Communists held ministerial posts in the government in power at the time of the Malagasy massacres. Thus, Communist influence on the R.D.A. was hardly likely to be directed toward encouraging ideas of independence or indeed even of increased devolution of power. Rather, it tried to keep its ambitions within the orbit of the French. Union, where, at least in the early postwar years, it had some hopes of playing a dominant role, and laid emphasis on the international role of the proletariat.

Thus, the R.D.A. never proclaimed itself publicly for greater autonomy, let alone eventual independence for the African territories. At its Second Congress, in Treichville in 1949, at the height of Communist influence, it declared (somewhat bizarrely in view of the trend politics were taking over the border in Ghana) that it 'expresses its faith in the alliance with the great people of France, who, with the working class and the Communist party at their head, struggle with courage and confidence against American imperialism for their national independence'.

The break with the Communist Party, supported by the majority of the R.D.A., and conveniently justified as in accordance with its declared intention of being a purely African party, came about largely because the party was tired of the persecution it was receiving at the hands of the French colonial administration and saw little further advantage in association in Parliament with the P.C.F., which, by this time, seemed to have no prospects of acceding to power either in coalition or on its own.

What would be interesting to know is how much the R.D.A. leaders discussed the question of independence in private during the years of their Communist association. After all, this was a time of considerable anti-colonial agitation throughout the world and the R.D.A. was itself a self-declared anti-imperialist party. Gabriel d'Arboussier, Secretary-General of the Party in its pro-Communist days, has recently written that the period 1949-50 was the first time in which some members of the Party talked in terms of independence and over this question he was separated from his companions.[25] Mahjemout Diop, an early member of the R.D.A. and subsequently leader of the *Parti Africain de l'Indépendence*, a Marxist-oriented party, also writes that within the Party there was much discussion as to why the African territories did not claim their separation from the French Union.[26]

It was left to the more moderate deputies to make the next move toward what retrospectively can be seen to have been independence. In 1948, Senghor broke with Lamine Guèye and the S.F.I.O. to form a new party, both because he resented the domination of the Senegalese branch of the S.F.I.O. by the Metropolitan mother party, a domination in which Guèye acquiesced,[27] and because he felt the need for a specifically African party, declaring that 'assimilation was an illusion in a world where people have become aware of their own personality'.[28] In the National Assembly, Senghor and a group of deputies who shared his views formed an interparliamentary group known as the Indépendants d'Outre Mer (I.O.M.), whose aim was to remain independent of any metropolitan group. After the elections of 1951, which were based on a substantially wider franchise, there were enough I.O.M. members to form a separate Parliamentary group. The R.D.A. on the other hand, allied itself with Mitterand's *Union Démocratique des Socialistes Républicaines* (U.S.D.R.).

The I.O.M. failed in its attempt to transform its parliamentary unity into the basis of a new political party, but, at its conference at Bobo-Dioulasso in 1953, some revolutionary ideas about the future structure of the Union were introduced. While stressing that they had no separatist ambitions and that their goal was a 'symbiose Franco-Africaine', I.O.M. members insisted that the future of the French Union was a federal one in which there would have to be increasing devolution of powers onto the individual territorial assemblies, which should also have responsible governments.[29] This theme was taken up by Senghor, who became the chief advocate of the idea of a federal republic, and it took shape finally in the thesis that only through the federation with France of the two primary federations of French West and French Equatorial Africa could the African voters have any feeling of equality with voters of the mother country. This federal formula was taken up by the R.D.A., but there was no precision over the structure of the federation, for, although there were those like Sékou Touré who supported Senghor's thesis, the leader of the R.D.A., Houphouet-Boigny, favoured direct federation between the individual territories and France.

The federal formula was revolutionary because it raised the whole question of the unity of the French Republic. The Brazzaville administrators had advocated a federal solution in the form of a Federal Assembly in which France would be dominant; at the same time, they had preserved the unity of the Republic by emphasising that there should be political devolution, but not self-government. The local assemblies were to be, and in fact did become, merely advisory bodies.

What Senghor was advocating was a true federal formula for the French Union, that is, he was advancing the idea of a *république une et divisible*. He had already raised the possibility of a federation of autonomous republics in the debates on the Constitution of the Union and the distinctness of African culture, but, as we have seen, the Assembly of the Union was a 'chimera' and certainly not federal in structure. In it, seventy-six seats were reserved for France and the same number for the overseas territories, which had 20 million more inhabitants than France. The High Council of the Union, which did not even meet until 1951, had as its President by right the French President. The federal formula, which, in retrospect, seems to have been the only one that could have satisfied France's desire to retain the integrity of Greater France and given sufficient rein to the Africans' desires to regulate their own affairs, was assiduously avoided by France, particularly at the very time when it might have worked. In introducing the *Loi Cadre* in March 1956, France took into account the demand for some form of local responsibility in the overseas territories but did nothing to bring them into a federation, since this would have involved revising the Constitution of the Fourth Republic.

As early as 1954, the Mendès-France government had planned reforms for the overseas territories, but they were not put into effect until 1956, with the passage of the *Loi Cadre*, because of the instability of French governments. The *Loi Cadre*, which allowed for a considerable measure of political decentralisation, owed its introduction to the French Minister for the Overseas Territories, Gaston Defferre. In its final shape, however, it was much influenced by Houphouet-Boigny, who had become a Minister without portfolio in the French Government as a result of the great success of the R.D.A. in the January elections to the National Assembly.

The *Loi Cadre* was introduced in response to the changing international situation and the breaking up of a large part of the French Empire. Indo-China had become independent after a bloody war, Morocco and Tunisia had just gained independence, and Algeria was fighting for hers. Ghana's imminent independence had already forced France to concede the principle of autonomy to Togo to satisfy increasing nationalist demands there for self-government. If France was prepared to concede autonomy to Togo, why should she not also be prepared to concede it to the other West African territories?[30] Defferre in his speech on the *Loi Cadre* to the National Assembly made it quite clear that France did not believe that she could isolate her African territories from developments in the world at large. He then went on to record the constitutional progress made by Ghana and Nigeria toward self-government and ultimate independence:

> It is not a question for us of plagiarising the British, but the fact that they have transformed the political and administrative regime of their territories has certainly contributed to the growth of impatience among the peoples of French West and French Equatorial Africa.

The proposed reforms, as Defferre made quite clear, were designed 'to maintain and reinforce for many years to come the necessary union between Metropolitan France and the peoples of the overseas territories' [31] The only revolutionary aspect of the *Loi Cadre* was its introduction of the concept of responsible self-government at the local territorial level within the framework of the French Union. Otherwise, it merely effected reforms that had been demanded of France in the Second Constituent Assembly and that were also compatible with a true policy of assimilation. The double electoral college was abolished, and universal suffrage was introduced. The integrity of the Republic was preserved in the person of the respective Governors of the overseas territories. The Governor was also President of the territorial Council of Ministers and had a large number of reserve powers. The effective Prime Minister of the territory was to be the Vice-President, who in turn was to be the political leader commanding a majority in the Assembly. Thus it was clear from the start that a Vice-President with strong electoral support, such as Sékou Touré, would soon push the Governor into the background. It was for this reason that the quip that the 'Loi Cadre est déjà dépassée' was current only three months after its application.

The logical corollary to the granting of autonomy to the overseas territories would have seemed to have been the conversion of the French Union into the federation which the I.O.M., followed less enthusiastically by the R.D.A., was demanding. But this could not have been introduced without a revision of the Constitution, even if the Government had wanted it. One of the reasons put forward by Defferre for introducing the reforms in the guise of a *Loi Cadre* was the great delay that had been experienced in the passage of formal laws affecting the overseas territories, particularly the Labour Code, which had taken four years to enact. Since the *Loi Cadre* also had to make provision for Togo, there was particular urgency for its passage in order that Togo might have autonomy before Ghana became independent. However, it may very well have suited both the French Government and Houphouet, as we shall see, to bring in reforms concerning local self-government, before dealing with the question of federation, about which France had always been reluctant, particularly if it were to be in the form proposed by Senghor. Nevertheless, on 6 May 1956, René Pleven declared at Copenhagen:

> The Constitution of France will have to be amended within the next twelve months to allow the adoption of statutes for the union with greater flexibility than those which insist on the traditional conception of the Republic as one and indivisible. We must clear the way toward the conception of a federal republic or of a federation of republics.[32]

For a while the whole issue of federation with France was dominated by the question of what structure the federation would take. It was fundamental to Senghor's thesis of a French Federal Republic that the overseas territories enter into federation with France not as individual territories but in the regional groupings that obtained at the time. It was with considerable bitterness that he denounced France for failing to democratise the *Grand Conseils* of French West and French Equatorial Africa and endow them with responsible governments. It was clear that in this he was supported by the majority of R.D.A. leaders, in particular by Sékou Touré. However, Houphouet-Boigny wanted direct association with France for two reasons: he wanted to avoid the Ivory Coast's having to subsidise a political federation as she was subsidising the administrative federation; and he feared that a federation with responsible government would be dominated by radicals, who would become increasingly hostile to the more conservative policies he and the Ivory Coast section of the R.D.A. were following.[33]

Senghor accused Houphouet of being the instrument of France in Balkanising Africa. There was certainly no reason why France could not have extended the principle of responsible self-government to the federal level. There were no constitutional obstacles. France was well aware of the hostility she evoked from Senghor, but it was clearly in her own interest to adopt Houphouet's thesis, for there was more chance of maintaining her control over twelve weak states, economically very dependent on her, than over two large federations. Indeed, the French had every reason to believe that the federal formula put forward by Senghor might lead rapidly to demands for independence and national sovereignty. It had, after all, been suggested within the I.O.M. that the federal formula would permit the adhesion of Tunisia and Morocco, both of which were now independent states.

The question of establishing federal executives came into open discussion at the now famous R.D.A. Congress at Bamako in September 1957. Here it became clear that Houphouet and the Ivory Coast delegation were isolated from the rest of the party in their opinions about the future relationship of the African territories and France. The only support given to his thesis of direct association came from Gabon, whose political and economic position in Equatorial Africa was not dissimilar from that of Ivory Coast in West Africa. So strong was the desire to establish federal executives that the Congress very nearly voted in favour of them, and it was only in deference to their leader, who had sat for three days in a huff in the palace of the Governor (where his status as a French Minister entitled him to stay),[34] that they passed a compromise resolution:

> Conscious of the indissoluble economic, political and cultural ties which unite all the territories, and anxious to preserve the destinies of the French Community, the Congress gives a mandate to its elected members to submit the outline of a law tending towards a democratisation of the existing federal executive.

Just as important as the discussion of the federal executives was the R.D.A.'s attitude toward independence. The other parties, the newly formed Convention Africaine led by Senghor, and the Mouvement Socialiste Africain (M.S.A.), formed from the old S.F.I.O., both set the question of independence to one side and were concentrating on securing the creation of federal executives. The whole problem of independence could not be far from any politician's mind since Ghana had become independent in March 1957. But there was a tendency, at least in public conversation, to dismiss it as a problem, and by way of justification to point to the internal difficulties Ghana was experiencing.[35] The Convention Africaine, however, at its inaugural meeting in January 1957, had been quite willing to ask that France acknowledge Algeria's right to independence. In the *Loi Cadre* elections in Senegal, the Socialists actually denounced independence for Senegal as illusory; and Senghor in his campaign seems to have been entirely preoccupied with the threat of Balkanisation.[36]

However, there was one politician whom a number of observers in France and Great Britain suspected of having as his ultimate goal the independence not only of his own country, but of French West Africa as a whole. Sékou Touré was rapidly acquiring the reputation of the *enfant terrible* of West African politics.[37] The gulf between Houphouet and Nkrumah over the question of independence had appeared quite unbridgeable at their meeting in Abidjan shortly after Ghana's independence, but it was clear when Nkrumah visited Conakry immediately afterward that Sékou Touré was watching the Ghana experiment with close interest.[38]

At the R.D.A. Congress at Bamako, the whole question of independence burst rudely on the participants from the lips of one M. Papiebo, who represented the African students in Paris: 'The slogans of Franco-African Community and federalism have been made to deceive the real faithful of Africa. We the students of Black Africa, leaders of tomorrow, who represent five thousand in France, demand independence'. This bold demand was received rather coldly by the Africans at the Congress who for the past decade had made it a point of policy to work within the framework of the Constitution of the French Union. A somewhat warmer reception was given the representative of the French West African students in Dakar, M. Ly Baidi, who declared: 'No student is *a priori* opposed to the idea of the community of peoples. We want a Franco-African Community founded upon friendship and upon the recognition that the African peoples have the right to make their own decisions about their future, that is, the right to independence'.

This thesis of the right to independence was to become common during the coming year. Its enunciation not only by students but by politicians during 1957 really marks the turning point in the march to independence, for many apparently so reluctantly undertaken.

For long, independence had not been considered either a possible or indeed a legitimate goal. But now in 1957 it was becoming recognised as a real alternative to the French Union or what was now being called the Franco-African community. This became clear in the neat formula produced on the subject in the final resolution of the Congress:

> The Congress considers that the independence of peoples is an inalienable right permitting them to dispose of their possessions and sovereignty according to the interests of the masses.
>
> The Congress considers that interdependence is the golden rule in the life of a people and manifests itself in the twentieth century by the establishment of large political and economic groupings.
>
> The Congress, believing that the conditions of Black Africa's participation in a large economic and political grouping is a factor for strength and real independence for all members of this grouping, proposes the realisation and strengthening of a democratic Franco-African Community based on equality.

For the next nine months political leaders from all the major parties were to side-step the problem of independence with the convenient answer that they wanted to participate in the Franco-African community, provided that their right to independence was recognised. Most of them laid stress on the economic problems involved in independence, particularly if their countries were to take it up individually. In addition, they were all aware that France had, at that time, no intention of granting independence to her overseas territories.

The collapse of the Fourth Republic and the accession to power of General de Gaulle, who promised to undertake the preparation of a new constitution, added urgency to the discussions centring around the question of the establishment of federal executives and the prospects for independence. In the three months during which negotiations over the constitution of the Franco-African community took place, African leaders made hundreds of pronouncements about their political goals, some of which they elaborated, some of which they withdrew or contradicted; indeed, so obscure are some of the arguments that one is almost tempted to suggest that they did not really know what they wanted. Perhaps the moderate Malagasy leader Philibert Tsirinana summed up the dilemma most of his contemporaries faced by declaring, on 21 August 1958, at a press conference connected with De Gaulle's visit to Tananarive: 'When I let my heart talk, I am partisan of total and immediate independence; when I make my reason speak, I realise that it is impossible'.[39]

This was certainly the dilemma of Sékou Touré and Djibo Bakary of Niger, both of whom were clearly interested in independence. It was the dilemma faced by Modibo Keita of Sudan and Apithy of Dahomey. Some would also say that at that time Ouezzin Goulibaly would have liked to opt for independence. But for Senghor and Houphouet, the problem was not so straightforward. It was not just a question of economic realities. Both, in very different ways, believed in the Franco-African Community, so that their hearts too were divided on the question of total independence.

The only open partisans of independence at the time of De Gaulle's accession to power were student organisations; the important federal trade union organisation, U.G.T.A.N., whose President was Sékou Touré; and the small Senegalese-based, Marxist-oriented *Parti Africain de l'Indépendance.* However, at the Cotonou Conference of the *Parti du Regroupement Africain* (P.R.A.), formed from the Convention Africaine and the M.S.A., the demand for immediate and total independence was carried by the Congress, and even acclaimed by conservative leaders like Lamine Guèye, who was either carried away by the enthusiasm of the moment, or, perhaps, wanted to place his cautious colleague and former rival, Senghor, in an embarrassing position. Only Senghor, with considerable courage, in view of the conservative nature of his views on the subject, sounded a note of warning at the close of the conference. Soon, however, other members of the P.R.A. were beginning to question the wisdom of their decision, and during the next two months they indulged in a great deal of verbal acrobatics to make the word independence sound as though it did not in fact mean independence.

Ultimately, the theses put forward during these months were four. The first was for a community that would link France directly with the individual African territories, now transformed into autonomous republics. This was the thesis upheld by Houphouet and the one effectively promulgated by De Gaulle in the final draft of the constitution. The second thesis, upheld by Senghor and the P.R.A. and given open support by Sékou Touré and tacit support by other members of the R.D.A., was that France should join in a federation or confederation with the two African federations. Each would be endowed with an Executive Council and all would enjoy full autonomy. Some partisans of this thesis envisaged a third and more radical formula whereby the two African federations should declare their independence first and then join the confederation with all the attributes of national sovereignty. This thesis attracted Djibo Bakary of Niger and at times Senghor, who toyed with the possibility of the Maghreb joining in such a Community. This, of course, was coming very close to the Commonwealth idea.

The French were certainly not prepared to contemplate any federal (or confederal) solution to the problem of the Community and were hostile to the idea of establishing primary federations on the grounds that these would almost certainly quickly find themselves strong enough to demand independence. In either a federal or confederal community, unless special position was given to her in the institutions, France would find herself dominated by her former colonies, whose leaders, it was clear, for the most part only wanted to join with her for the economic benefits they would derive. The fourth thesis was, of course, independence, which France rejected as a goal that could be attained in continued friendship with her.

In the face of French intransigence over any solution to the shape of the community other than the one she favoured (an intransigence that became only too apparent to those African politicians who had sat on the Constitutional Consultative Committee), most of the African leaders decided to vote for the constitution after two important concessions had been made. First, after much pressure, De Gaulle included the 'right to independence' in the final draft of the constitution. He had already made it clear at Brazzaville on 24 August 1958, when confronted by banners demanding immediate independence, that anyone who wanted it could take it. Later, he was to add the threat that it could be taken 'with all its consequences'.[40] The second major concession was to include a clause that would permit member-states to regroup themselves within the community, so that the hoped-for West African federation could still be realised.

Both the P.R.A. and R.D.A. gave their territorial sections the right to decide for themselves how they would vote in the constitutional referendum. There was no question about Houphouet's decision in Ivory Coast. Nor was there any doubt that Mauretania, who was out of the mainstream of French West African politics, would vote for the constitution, since she depended on France's military aid to deal with her Moroccan-allied rebels. All the other leaders, with the exception of Djibo Bakary, were uncertain about their stand for a long time. For all of them the economic problems of independence were the gravest they had to face.[41] France gave vast economic aid to the overseas territories. For Senegal, who was dependent on France for the subsidy she paid on the groundnut crop, the choice was particularly difficult, especially since it involved alienating the radical wing of the governing party if a decision was made to vote 'Yes'. Senghor, although he emotionally resisted the idea of separating from France, was pressured by the conservative groundnut-producing countryside, led by the *marabouts* or religious leaders, into voting for the Constitution.

Senghor — like Modibo Keita in Sudan — felt that to take independence separately from the other territories would make federation impossible to achieve. It is reported that Houphouet had promised that, if his fellow R.D.A. members voted for the constitution in its present form, he would agree to come together in a federation afterwards — a promise that would have weighed seriously with Modibo Keita.[42] But there were other influences on Modibo's decision. Although his party had done well at the last election, securing a substantial majority over the P.S.S., it was just possible that with French electoral interference he might not be able to secure a majority for a 'No' vote.[43] This consideration certainly was cardinal in Apithy's decision to vote 'Yes' in Dahomey.

Guinea economically had a better basis for independence than any territory other than Ivory Coast, though she did depend on continued French assistance for the construction of the promised Konkoure Dam, which would provide her with enough electricity to process her own aluminium. It seems clear that emotionally Sékou Touré was very deeply attracted by the prospect of independence, but was more hesitant about the consequences than was Djibo Bakary of Niger, who was the first to declare his intention of voting against the constitution. Indeed, Sékou Touré had said that, provided the right to independence was included in the constitution, he would vote for it. However, a day after Djibo Bakary announced his decision to vote 'No', Sékou Touré followed suit. The reasons put forward for this decision have been many. Clearly, he was extremely annoyed at the arrogant treatment he received from De Gaulle on the latter's visit to Conakry.[44] Certainly, he was disillusioned by the terms of the referendum and the consequences threatened by France for voting 'No'. But probably as important were internal pressures on him. The students and many of the schoolmasters in Guinea favoured independence. The trade unionists, members of Sékou Touré's own U.G.T.A.N., had for long declared themselves for independence. Furthermore, the conservative opposition party, affiliated to the P.R.A., had declared for independence, which made the radical R.D.A. look somewhat foolish in the eyes of those who wanted independence. Finally, it is doubtful whether Sékou Touré ever realised the extent to which De Gaulle would go in demonstrating his anger at Guinea's decision. After all, Sékou Touré's first step was to send De Gaulle telegrams in the warmest of terms asking for the closest association between Guinea and France.[45]

It was with some relief that the other leaders saw one of their number take the plunge. Now they could sit back and watch the Guinean experiment, while those whose internal position was not very secure could be thankful that they had not followed Djibo Bakary's example and incurred the full force of French electoral interference.

De Gaulle's ruthless treatment of Guinea was motivated both by pique and by a desire to demonstrate to the other members of the community that they had been wise to vote 'Yes'. Houphouet was a champion of this approach. If Guinea continued to receive aid, the radical elements in all those states who voted 'Yes' would place their leaders in a most embarrassing position. If Guinea collapsed, as seemed likely, then the lesson would be driven home to all.

In fact, Guinea held together remarkably well. Russia, hoping to gain a foothold in Black Africa, immediately offered assistance, as did a number of other Communist powers. Suddenly Guinea became known all over the world and Sékou Touré became an African hero — young men as far afield as Nigeria wore 'Sékou Touré' hats. By December, given moral support by Ghana and the promise of a $28 million loan, it had become clear that Sékou Touré had complete control of his country. Though life in Guinea was difficult, there seemed to be something to his argument: 'Better freedom in poverty than slavery in riches'. Guinea became like the bad conscience of all those who had voted 'Yes'. In Dakar, it was not Senghor but Sékou Touré for whom the people cheered when his face appeared on cinema screens. What is more, Guinea realised her vantage point in the new African situation and Sékou Touré set out deliberately to persuade other African leaders to opt for independence.

The first efforts of those leaders who had voted 'Yes' was not to discuss the question of independence but to try and salvage what they could of the old federation. One of the regrets expressed by several leaders was that Guinea had effectively broken up the federation by going it alone on the question of independence. Had Sékou Touré been more patient, perhaps they could have forced Houphouet to go along with federation and thus gained 'real' independence together. Indeed, it appears that there had been many efforts to persuade Sékou Touré to change his mind, and it is probable that, had Ouezzin-Coulabaly lived, he would have been able to persuade the Guinean leader to stay within the community on the grounds that a more effective group-independence could be achieved at a later date.

As it was, the question of creating a federal executive was quickly raised and studied both within the R.D.A. and in the Grand Conseil before its dismantlement in accordance with the new structure of the community. It became quickly clear that Houphouet was not going to keep his promise about joining a federation — if indeed he had ever made such a promise — and that he was as hostile as ever to it. In this, he was supported by France, who clearly saw that her only hope of maintaining the community — which, like the *Loi Cadre* before it, was beginning to show signs of being 'déjà dépassée' before it was even promulgated — was by ensuring the continued Balkanisation of Africa.

Nevertheless, federalists from Senegal, Sudan, Upper Volta, and Dahomey, with observers from Mauritania, met at Bamako on 29 and 30 December and agreed that they would seek the necessary authority from their individual legislatures to participate in the proposed constituent assembly in Dakar on 14 January, which would draw up the constitution for the Federation of Mali. In due course, this constitution was drawn up with the approval of the four countries, and it was agreed that it would be submitted to referendum in each country for approval. Both Upper Volta and Dahomey rejected it, however, and the Federation of Mali finally comprised only Senegal and Sudan. During the federalist deliberations, both France and Ivory Coast brought pressure on Upper Volta and Dahomey to withdraw from the federation.[46] In Upper Volta, it was a question of taking advantage of a very fluid political situation and playing on the differences between the West, traditionally closer to Sudan, and the Mossi-dominated East. France had as its High Commissioner in Upper Volta, the newly appointed M. Masson, who enjoyed a notoriety similar to that of Gouverneur Colombani in Niger when it came to interfering in politics. From his side, Houphouet could play on Upper Volta's heavy dependence on Ivory Coast both for access to the sea and for employment of her migrant labour. The case of Dahomey was equally complex politically, and it is clear that she had genuine fears that she would be cartographically out on a limb in a federation based on Dakar. Most important of all, however, was the threat that France might not finance the projected deep-water port at Cotonou.

Houphouet had succeeded in staving off the federation he detested so much, but he had to come to terms with the fact that desperately poor countries like Upper Volta and Dahomey would find it very difficult to manage on their own and would feel more secure in some kind of alliance. Apithy himself had talked in terms of allying with Togo and forming a Union of Benin States. So, partly in response to this need, partly as a snub to the federalists, and probably also because he wanted to maintain his dominant position in West African politics, Houphouet formed the *Conseil de l'Entente*, a loose economic grouping consisting of Ivory Coast, Dahomey, Niger, and Upper Volta.

Once the political groupings had been settled, the question of independence, never far from the minds of the more radical political leaders, came to the fore. At the inaugural meeting of the new Parti de la Fédération Africain, formed from the governing parties of Sudan and Senegal, with members from federalist parties from other West African states, it became clear that independence was now the paramount issue in French African politics. The meeting, held in Dakar on 1-3 July 1959, declared that Mali would seek independence and join with France in a confederation. The young federation would thus hope to take advantage of that clause in the constitution of the community that allowed states to become independent and still remain associated with the community. From then on the community was split between those who saw it as a rather more tightly organised French-style commonwealth and those who wanted to retain it in its existing form. The proponents of a commonwealth-type arrangement were led by Modibo Keita and Senghor of the Mali Federation and Tsiranana of the Malagasy Republic, who had an active pro-independence opposition to contend with. Ranged against them were Houphouet-Boigny and the other leaders of the *Conseil de l'Entente*. Houphouet was quite explicit in his rejection of a French-style commonwealth and in his desire to establish a tight community with federal institutions. He was also scathing about independence. When interviewed about the All-African People's Conference held in Accra in December 1958, he described it as destined only to produce idle talk and demands for illusory independence.[47]

As far as France was concerned, her last chance to save the

community came when Mali demanded its transformation into a tightly organised commonwealth.⁽⁴⁸⁾ Even had she been willing to do this, she still would have had a hostile Houphouet to deal with, and right up until the last he was adamant that the only type of community that he was interested in was the one for which he and the Ivory Coast had voted.

France refused to recognise Mali's existence, and, when De Gaulle eventually came round to the fact that Houphouet's position was no longer tenable in a continent whose wind of change had been recognised so clearly by the British Prime Minister, it was too late. France finally yielded to the fact of African independence at the sixth meeting of the Executive Council of the Community at St. Louis on 11-12 December 1959. There, the Council of the Community recognised the existence of the Federation of Mali and conceded that it could take independence and remain associated with the community.⁽⁴⁹⁾ De Gaulle, not caring to repeat the experience with Guinea, then journeyed to Dakar, the capital of the Mali Federation. There, before the Federal Assembly, he made his historic speech acknowledging what he preferred to call Mali's impending 'accession to international sovereignty'. Houphouet, meanwhile, in pique, had left for Abidjan.

The Mali Federation became independent on 10 June 1960, after protracted bargaining with France over the terms of continued aid and in particular the concession to France of the right to retain her military bases in Dakar and Thies, as well as some troops in Sudan. Independence was adopted more enthusiastically by the Sudanese than by the Senegalese, who were becoming increasingly fearful of Sudanese domination.

Perhaps the most dramatic effect of Mali's decision to become independent was that Houphouet was forced to rethink his position. In one sense he had already made this more than clear. Once the community had decided at St. Louis to transform itself into a commonwealth, he lost interest in it. So, as if to spite the Maliens, and indeed to humiliate them, on the eve of Mali independence he announced that the four members of the *Conseil de l'Entente* would take independence without prior accords with France, such as Mali had had to negotiate. Any accord would be negotiated after international sovereignty had been assumed. Furthermore, they would take independence outside the community. Thus the *coup de grâce* to the community was delivered by the very man who had tried so hard to make it a reality.

The belatedness of a demand for independence among French West African politicians is only too easy to explain in economic terms. French West Africa, generally poor in resources, was receiving aid in the postwar period on a scale such as no other colonial dependency received from a metropolitan country. Export crop prices were stabilised by subsidies from France at a level well above that of the world market price. A substantial part of the administrative costs of the colonies was borne by the metropolitan budget.[50] The only economically viable unit among the territories of French West Africa was Ivory Coast, which alone had long-term income prospects of the order that could support a full-scale independent government, an army, and diplomatic representation. Guinea, despite her large mineral resources, could only become economically viable by intensive short-run capital investment, particularly in the financing of the proposed Konkouré Dam.

As it was, all the French-speaking West African states had become accustomed in the postwar period to living well above their income, and this was more true of Senegal than of any other state. In such circumstances, any abrupt break with France, involving loss of aid, technical assistance, and price subsidies, was impossible to contemplate for any leader without political control over his people as firm as that of Sékou Touré, who was able to persuade his people to accept economic sacrifices for the sake of independence. The extent and intricacy of France's aid to French West Africa, both before and since independence, is brought out clearly in *A.O.F. 1957* and in a series of Senate and National Assembly reports on 'cooperation'.[51] It is easy to understand the reluctance with which political leaders undertook a programme of independence that they had every good reason to believe would result in the loss of French aid and possibly even the loss of the political support of their people.

France, in addition to binding her overseas territories economically to her, also made it clear that independence was not a legitimate goal for the African political leaders. Indeed, even after Guinea's independence, De Gaulle refused to accept the fact that other African states would soon be asking for independence. As we have seen, when the newly formed Federation of Mali asked for independence within the community, he refused to acknowledge its existence right up until the Sixth Meeting of the Executive Council of the Community at St. Louis in December 1959, which marked France's final but reluctant acceptance of the political facts of life in Africa.[52]

It is difficult at this stage to assess the different effects of French and British colonial policy on the political attitudes of the West African leaders. For Kwame Nkrumah of Ghana and *Nnamdi Azikiwe of Nigeria*, independence was always a legitimate, if long-term goal. The main problem was to persuade the British Government that they represented 'the people' and that they were ready for self-government. Close to hand was the example of the Commonwealth, a successful organisation composed of former colonies, and, even, since the war, non-white members — Ceylon, India and Pakistan. The British West African territories were administered as political and economic units entirely separate from Britain so that the prospect of rupture was not the problem for them that it was for the French African states. French African leaders, however, were constantly being reminded of, and indeed themselves subscribed to, the idea of the unity and integrity of Greater France. They were acutely aware that independence was a difficult, often bloody path to choose. Close to hand were the examples of Indo-China and the Maghreb states, which anyway were only associated states and not parts of the republic one and indivisible. The ruthless suppression of the Malagasy 'rebels' and the war in Algeria served as reminders of what might happen to parts of the Republic that sought to hive off. They remembered also the persecution of the R.D.A. in its pro-Communist days, administrative interference in elections, economic blackmail, and finally the Balkanisation of French West Africa into small economically unviable autonomous states, whose independence it seemed could at best be only formal if ever attained. Against such a background it is hardly surprising that overt ambitions for independence were not so intense in French West Africa as in British West Africa.

But it takes more than the economic and political policies of France to explain why French West Africa remained so long isolated from the current ideas in the colonial world, from the spirit of Bandoeng, from the example of their fellow English-speaking African leaders. After all, even if France did not consider independence a legitimate goal, the rest of the world did, and the French West African leaders, because of their participation in the debates of the National Assembly, were usually much more sophisticated in their understanding of international affairs than their English-speaking counterparts. Even the Catholic Bishops of French West Africa had recognised the 'legitimacy of the aspiration to independence as well as all constructive efforts to achieve it' as far back as 1953.[53] What must not be forgotten, however, is the very deep affection and respect most of the African leaders had for France and for her universalist ideas. The concept of a French Union, of a Greater France, of a Franco-African community in which men of different races and colour, drawn together by French culture, would cooperate on the basis of 'liberté, égalité et fraternité', had a very great appeal for the African leaders.[54] The speeches of leaders at the 1946 Constituent Assembly are not explicable simply in terms of economic benefit. They were, after all, made against a background of forty years of economic neglect, and in an Assembly where the forces of colonial reaction were making themselves all too apparent.

It is difficult to exaggerate the impression made on French African leaders by their participation in the French National Assembly and in the other institutions of the Republic, where they became ministers, or presidents and secretaries of important commissions. Fily Dabo Sissoko made it clear at the Second Constituent Assembly how privileged he felt to be able to participate in it.

And even after the *Loi Cadre* and the political decentralisation it involved, one was more likely to meet the Vice-Presidents of the Conseil in Paris than in the territories they ruled. Paris had an enormous attraction for the leadership. They had in many cases spent student days there, and now as political leaders and members of Parliament they were treated not so much as honoured guests, but rather as special members of the family. 'Je vais en métropole' is an expression that still comes easily to the lips of the independent French-speaking African.

France was more than the metropolitan country that welcomed its leaders warmly. She was also symbol of a culture into which, as a result of her assimilation policy, most of the African leaders had been indoctrinated. If Britain exported her parliamentary and legal institutions to the colonies, France exported her culture, and if the one thing that worries the British about their former colonies is deviation from the standards of democracy and law that she established, then it is the possible rejection of French culture that concerns the French. Even the most violently politically anti-French politicians, like Doudou Guèye of Senegal, can say unashamedly: 'Nous sommes de culture française' before a mixed audience of English- and French-speaking Africans. In Guinea, Sékou Touré has insisted that the schools teach in French from the start and not in the indigenous languages. Even those Africans who symbolically rejected the domination of French culture and substituted for it negritude are often those like Senghor and Alioune Diop of Senegal who are most at home in French culture.

This feeling that French culture belonged not only to the Metropolitan French but to all those who accepted it acted, as did participation in the political institutions of France, as an effective brake on the demand for independence, a brake that is as important as the political and economic considerations involved.

NOTES

1. See Gil Dugué, *Vers les Etats Unis d'Afrique* (Dakar, 1960), for a detailed account of the Cotonou Congress.
2. Gordon Wright, *The Reshaping of French Democracy* (New York), 1948.

INDEPENDENCE AS A GOAL   311

3. It is significant that in the French text the word "self-governments" is used for want, apparently, of a French equivalent.
4. Félix Eboué, among the very few Negroes present at the conference, though himself not African-born, was one of the few champions at the conference of the need to recognise the values and the distinctiveness of African culture.
5. René Viard, *La Fin de L'Empire Colonial Français* (Paris, 1963), p.25, cited from Louis Merat, *Fictions et Réalités Coloniales* (Paris, 1947).
6. In the recommendations for a federal assembly, the Conference made it clear that such an assembly would be expected to "affirm the indissoluble unity of... the Franco-Colonial whole." See Bernard Brown and Roy Macridis, *The De Gaulle Republic* (Chicago, Illinois, 1960), p.192.
7. The French West African members of the First Constituent Assembly numbered six: Lamine Guèye (Senegal, 1st College, SFIO); Léopold Sédar Senghor' (Senegal, 2nd College, SFIO); Félix Houphouet-Boigny (Ivory Coast, 2nd College, PCF); Fily Dabo Sissoko (Sudan, 2nd College, PCF); Yacine Diallo (Guinea, 2nd College, SFIO); and Sourou Migan Apithy (Togo-Dahomey, 2nd College, PCF). In Ivory Coast, for instance, a Frenchman, Reste, was elected by the citizens with 1,821 out of 2,774 votes on the second count, while Houphouet-Boigny was elected by the noncitizens with 12,980 out of 28,835 votes on the second count. One African with French citizenship, Abdoulaye N'Diaye, stood for the 1st College but gained no votes.
8. Ernest Milcent, *L AOF entre en Scène* (Paris, 1958), p.27.
9. Thomas Hodgkin and Ruth Schachter, *French-Speaking West Africa in Transition* (New York, 1960).
10. 'While there were deep divisions among the major political parties and schools of thought in postwar France a negative consensus existed: all firmly rejected African self-government or independence as a legitimate end of policy'. Hodgkin and Schachter *ibid.*
11. Daniel Boisdon, *Les Institutions de l'Union Française* (Paris, 1949). See, in particular, pp.41-42.
12. *Journal Officiel*, Debates of the Second Constituent Assembly, 2nd Session, 18 September 1946, p.3,802.
13. *Ibid.*, 19 September, p.3,849. Houphouet added significantly: 'Certainly some of my colleagues ask for independence within the framework of the French Union for the countries which they represent. But that is not contrary to the principles that you yourselves have accepted and often affirmed.'
14. *Journal Officiel, op. cit.*, 18 September, p.3,801.
15. *Journal Officiel, op. cit.*, 1st Session, 18 September, p.3,791.
16. *Ibid.*, p.3,792.
17. *Ibid.*, p.3,798.
18. *Ibid.*, p.3,813.
19. *Ibid.*, p.3,814.
20. *Ibid.*, p.3,820.
21. *Ibid.*, 2nd Session, 19 September, p.3,850.
22. Majhemout Diop, *Contribution à l'Etude des Problèmes Politiques en Afrique Noire* (Paris, 1959), pp.134-35.
23. Aimé Césaire, *Lettre Ouverte à Maurice Thorez* (Paris, 1956).
24. David Caute, *Communism and the French Intellectuals* (New York, 1964), p.208. Algerian resentment of the Communist Party today is partly the result of the hostile position taken by the PCF with regard to Algerian independence.
25. Gabriel d'Arboussier, *Vers l'Unité Africaine* (Paris, 1961), Introduction.
26. Diop, *op. cit.*
27. Even when the SFIO took what were in fact positions hostile to the Overseas

Territories in the Assembly.
28. Michael Crowder, *Senegal: A Study in French Assimilation Policy* (London, 1962), p.36.
29. See Milcent, *op. cit.*, pp.75-76, where he quotes M. Aujoulat (Cameroun) as saying in his report: 'All our efforts are oriented towards the realisation of a Franco-African symbiosis which we judge as useful to Africa as to France. You will not find any separatists amongst us ... A movement of emancipation is showing itself throughout the world. To want to stem it would be to risk grave catastrophes.'
30. James Coleman, *Togoland, International Conciliation,* No. 509 (September, 1956).
31. *Journal Officiel, op. cit.,* 1st Session, 21 March 1956, pp.1108-12. (Speech of the Minister for Overseas France, M. Gaston Defferre).
32. Cited in Viard, *op. cit.,* p.71.
33. An excellent analysis of the economic motives behind Houphouet's stand is contained in Elliot J. Berg, 'The Economic Base of Political Choice in French West Africa,' *American Political Science Review,* LIV, No. 2 (June 1960).
34. André Blanchet, *L'Itineraire des Partis Politiques depuis Bamako* (Paris, 1958).
35. These difficulties were played up by the French administration at that time. (Personal conversations with French administrators and African leaders, September 1957-March 1958).
36. Kenneth Robinson, 'Polling Day in Senegal,' *West Africa,* 10 May 1957.
37. Blanchet, *op. cit.,* and 'Africa's Youngest Premier — Portrait of Sékou Touré,' *West Africa,* 25 May 1957.
38. Blanchet, *L'Itinéraire,* pp.113-17.
39. Cited in Viard, *op. cit.*
40. Viard, *op. cit.,* De Gaulle was reported by *Paris-Presse* as having appeared before the Constitutional Consultative Committee on 10 August, and saying: 'One cannot conceive of both an independent territory and a France which continues to aid it.' Cited in Marcel Merle, 'La Constitution et les Problèmes d'Outre-Mer,' *Revue Française de Science Politique,* March 1959, p.148.
41. For a full and very useful discussion of this, see Berg, *op. cit.*
42. Immanuel Wallerstein, 'How Seven States Were Born in Former French West Africa,' *Africa Report,* March 1961, pp.3-4, 7, 12, 15.
43. Wallerstein, *ibid.*
44. See Diabate Boubacar, *Porte Ouverte sur la Communauté Franco-Africaine* (Brussels, 1961), where De Gaulle's speech as well as that of Sékou Touré are published in full.
45. See Diabate Boubacar, *ibid.,* for the text of these telegrams. Sékou Touré declared in his speech to the Constituent National Assembly on Independence Day, 2 October 1958: 'The Republic of Guinea, in accordance with the terms of Article 88 of the French Constitution, will negotiate the bases of an association with the Republic of France.'
46. For a detailed account of the complex manoeuvres in Upper Volta and Dahomey, see Dugué, *op. cit.*
47. John Marcum, 'French-Speaking Africa at Accra,' *Africa Report,* February 1959.
48. There was very real enthusiasm on the part of Malian leaders from mid-1959 to mid-1960 on the whole possibility of establishing a French-style Commonwealth.
49. Jean Debay, *Evolutions en Afrique Noire* (Paris, 1962), has suggested that France agreed to the Federation of Mali's independence within the framework of the Community and did not cut her off as she had done Guinea, for fear that

50. she might join with Guinea and form a bloc hostile to France.
50. See Berg, *op. cit.*
51. Haut Commissariat de la République en Afrique Occidentale Française, *AOF 1957* (Dakar, 1957); and Assemblée Nationale, Constitution du 4 Octobre 1958, Première Législature, Première Session Ordinaire de 1961-62, *Rapport*, Annexe No. 10, *Coopération*, No. 1445; and *Avis*, Tome II, *Coopération*, No. 1459; Sénat, Première Session Ordinaire de 1961-62, *Rapport Général*, Tome III, Examen des Crédits et des Dispositions Spéciales, Annexe No. 8, *Coopération*. Most aid nowadays is channelled through the Ministry of Cooperation, but individual ministries can in fact make provision for aid to the independent French-speaking African states.
52. Today the official French version of the events following Guinea's independence is that De Gaulle foresaw that the other states would want independence and made provision for it in the Constitution of the Fifth Republic. 'The Constitution of the Fifth Republic established the procedure for accession to independence on the basis of self-determination. It offered the Overseas Territories, by means of a referendum, the free [sic] choice between immediate independence or membership in the institutional Community,' *France Aid and Cooperation* (New York: French Embassy Press and Information Service, 1962), p.13.
53. Jean Erhard, *Communauté ou Sécession?* (Paris, 1959).
54. *West Africa*, 12 October 1957, reported Houphouet as telling a press conference shortly after the Bamako Congress of the RDA that 'if we had been colonised by the Anglo-Saxons, there is no doubt that we would have chosen independence even at the cost of economic disadvantages. But in France we think we catch a note of human fraternity ... We need France, but we believe that France likewise needs the advantages of a Franco-African Community of free peoples founded on an absolute equality of rights and duties.' Senghor was reported in *West Africa* of 7 September 1957, in a review of *Une Nouvelle Afrique* by Paul-Henri Siriex (Paris, 1957), as telling the National Assembly: 'In Africa, when children have grown up, they leave the parents' hut, and build a hut of their own by its side. Believe me, we don't want to leave the French compound. We have grown up in it and it is good to be alive in it. We want simply to build our own huts.'

XV

COLONIAL RULE IN WEST AFRICA: FACTOR FOR DIVISION OR UNITY?*
(1965/1971)

Nearly a decade ago I wrote:

Nowadays it has become almost a platitude to say that the Channel divides West Africa. How true is it today that when one crosses from Nigeria into Dahomey or Niger, or from Gambia to Senegal, the main impression one has is that of crossing the twenty miles of water that separate England from France?[1]

The impressions formed from seemingly irrelevant details are still there: the long sticks of bread offered the traveller instead of the oblong blocks of wrapped bread: the change of road from one side to the other, though this is a difference that will soon be eliminated; the uniform and equipment of the ordinary policeman, especially the revolver in the gendarme's holster; the cut of the young dandy's clothes; the type of cloth used by the women; and lastly, but still probably most important, the ubiquitous presence of white Frenchmen in jobs that are a monopoly of Africans in the English-speaking territories. However irrelevant these details may seem, they are sufficiently marked for the Senegalese driver in Lagos to have 'French-boy' shouted after him, and conversely the Senegalese student will talk of the Nigerian student in Dakar as 'l'Anglais'. These differences are still not superficial, even ten years after independence. Anyone who has attended international Congresses in which both French- and English-speaking Africans have participated, knows the tendency of the two groups to separate, sometimes into hostile groups as was the case at the Conference on the Press held in Dakar in 1960. Indeed the division in such conferences is more frequently on linguistic than racial lines. I remember one Conference in which tension

*Adapted, July 1971, from the article of the same title published in *Civilisations*, 3, 1965, for a lecture at Makerere University, and reprinted by permission of L'Institut International des Civilisations Différentes.

between Anglophones and Francophones was running high. A would-be wit helped relieve tension by jocularly referring to the Anglophones as 'Vous les Saxophones' to which the quick reply of a rival wit was 'Et vous les Cacophones.'

I think that even today, ten years after independence, despite all the conscious attempts by African heads of state to cross this African Channel, the imprint of France and Britain in West Africa is still strong and that this difference lies not only in language but in the respective attitudes to such fundamental matters as law, political organisation and culture. The educated Yoruba from Dahomey, in his Parisian-cut suit, may have an indigenous language and social heritage in common with his cousin from Nigeria, probably wearing *agbada*; but when it comes to talking in terms of their respective present-day judicial systems and their ideas about politics, administration, or university education, then the gulf that is the heritage of colonial rule becomes apparent. The gulf is one that modern leaders of Africa are aware of and which many are trying to bridge as rapidly as possible, whether it is through demonstrations, albeit fleeting, of political solidarity, such as the Ghana-Guinea-Mali Union, the introduction of French or English into the curricula of secondary schools where in the colonial era they were never taught at all; through state visits, sports or student exchanges. Yet the legacy of difference — economic, political and cultural — still persists so that despite its *African* cultural homogeneity with Senegal, and despite the obvious long-term political and economic advantages of union with Senegal, tiny Gambia, with a population of only 360,000, maintains its Anglophone independence. There has only been one example of union between a state with an Anglophone heritage and one with a Francophone heritage: the Cameroons' amalgamation discussed later. Meanwhile let us assume that the gulf between the two is as apparently great as we have described and defer further discussion as to its character and how real or superficial it is in historical terms until certain other questions have been asked, which will, we hope, give some understanding of the nature of this division.

TO WHAT EXTENT DID THE FRENCH AND BRITISH BRING INTERNAL UNITY TO THE POLITICAL ENTITIES THEY CREATED IN WEST AFRICA?

Given that none of the colonies created by the French and British in West Africa was ethnically or culturally homogeneous, and indeed in many cases colonial frontiers cut across pre-colonial boundaries, how far did colonial rule contribute to the internal unity of the now independent states of West Africa? Clearly the greatest unifying factor brought by the colonial powers to their colonies was the introduction of a lingua franca though this was of course less important in an area like Northern Nigeria, where they already had a lingua franca in Hausa, than in areas like Ivory Coast where there was a multiplicity of tribal groups and consequently of languages. But the spread of the new lingua franca was dependent largely on the amount of education the colonial power was prepared to make available. In the case of most of the former French African colonies, although the quality of education was nearly always higher than in the British West African colonies, it was nevertheless thinly spread. In Guinea, for instance, just before independence the proportion of children of school age attending primary school was less than 10%.[2] There was a much better record in British West Africa, with the notable exception of Northern Nigeria, where English education was scant and Hausa remained dominant. The former Northern Region of Nigeria, for instance, had the only bi-lingual legislature in West Africa. The French on the other hand, even in schools for Muslim chiefs where Koranic law and Arabic were taught, used French as the language of instruction.

The second major contribution to the unity of these new political units was the introduction of common legal, political and administrative institutions. Here clearly the French did much more, not only for unity at the level of the individual colony but also for unity within the bloc of French colonies, for with the exception of Senegal, where the Four Communes had special status, each territory was administered in the same way under the same law and, after 1946, under the same representative institutions. The French system of administration, though based on chiefs like the British system, used them in such a way as largely to destroy their traditional political authority. The chief became a mere agent of the administration, a sort of civil servant, appointed on grounds of his potential efficiency rather than with regard to his traditional claim to chieftaincy. In so far as chiefs are the repositories of tradition and therefore major continuing factors for ethnic differentiation in the state, the French may be said to have done the modern African nation a great service in thus reducing their powers. The British, however, under their system of indirect rule, did much to preserve traditional political institutions, so that the system of native administration in Nigeria differed greatly in its application not only from one region to another, but within regions. In French Africa, the only aspects of traditional law to survive after 1944 were those affecting inheritance, property, marriage and divorce. In some parts of what was British West Africa, customary penal law, involving even the death sentence, was maintained till the eve of independence. The French-speaking states inherited a uniform pattern of administration, with emphasis on the powers of the central government, whilst the former British states

COLONIAL RULE: FACTOR FOR DIVISION 317

inherited patterns of administration whose original emphasis was primarily on local government institutions, sharply differentiated according to ethnic orgin, and resulting, in many cases, in strong centrifugal tendencies. This does not of course mean that the French states have escaped problems of regionalism and tribalism, as recent events in Dahomey and Chad have shown. However, traditional political institutions and ethnic differences are not nearly such great barriers to national unity in the French-speaking African states as in the former British Colonies. Indeed the French were on the whole much less conscious of the tribal origin of their colonial peoples than the British seemed to be. An African to the Frenchman was a Dahomeyan rather than a Gun, a Senegalese rather than a Wollof. This was certainly not the case with the British, who invariably asked which tribe a man came from.[3] The army in the colonial period in Nigeria, for instance, had definite preferences for particular ethnic groups as sources of recruitment. Indeed up until the 2nd World War there was a group of scheduled 'martial' tribes among whom alone recruitment could be conducted, and these were bounded by a southern line drawn from Ilesha in Borgu to Ibi on the Benue. Thus all ethnic groups in Southern Nigeria were excluded. An interesting result of this attitude is the frequency with which Nigerians filling in application forms for jobs write down their tribal origin in answer to the question as to their nationality.

The new sense of nationality was further aided by the demarcation of rigid boundaries between the political units created by the colonial powers.[4] These frontiers, often cutting across traditional political divisions, may have been of marginal significance to the Fulani herdsman, except as far as tax evasion was concerned, but for the trader carrying his goods from one colony to another, particularly if it was from a French to a British colony or vice versa, the frontier further promoted the process of national self-identification. At school, children were taught to recognise on a map the shape of the colony to which they belonged. Boundaries, then, had two important functions in the fostering of a sense of national unity: first they provided a physical barrier, albeit weak, between one colony and another; second they aided in the conceptualisation of the state, separating it clearly from other colonies.

Another major factor creating conditions for national unity was of course economic development.[5] This cut across traditional divisions in the country; and, through the building of railways and roads, opened up trade between groups that had previously had little contact with each other bringing them into vast new areas of exchange. Economic development has led to a noticeable redistribution of population through labour migration and through the growth of major cities. Whilst ethnic groups may have tried to maintain their identity in cities through tribal unions, it is there that tribal barriers are breaking down. For instance in Dakar it is now increasingly common for Lebou and Toucouleur, Wollof and Serer to inter-marry.[6] Economic development has led to the creation of new classes, with new social goals, in which ethnic differentiation is increasingly less important as a factor. It has provided a new social structure in which educational attainments are more important than status in the tribe, and in which, keeping up with the Joneses in the matter of Mercedes Benz, refrigerators and radiograms is becoming much more important than the achievement of traditional status. The emergence of a new Westernised elite was actively encouraged by the French but was to a considerable extent frustrated by the British especially before the Second World War. The British for long hoped to direct its educated elite into service in the native administration rather than the Central Government, whilst the French (though somewhat halfheartedly in the interwar period) had as their goal the creation of an educated elite that could work in the central administration.

We come now to that thorny question of 'divide and rule'. To what extent did the colonial powers deliberately adopt a policy of divide and rule in their African colonies so as to avert or delay independence? This is of course very difficult to assess. One could insist that the British through their system of indirect rule tried to emphasise and prolong existing differences, and with their concomitant reluctance to allow Africans to participate in the central administration, were doing this to maintain their position as overlords. On the other hand a French Administrator like Delavignette is full of admiration for the fact that Lugard brought Northern and Southern Nigeria together, and in view of the fact that none of the great Sudanese kingdoms managed to extend its hegemony over both savanna and forest,[7] he may be justified in calling this Lugard's greatest achievement. On the other hand the fact that from a political and administrative point of view amalgamation was largely nominal, with the North and South retaining their separate administrative identities, has been one of the stumbling blocks of Nigerian unity. In the political history of both Ghana and Nigeria, it seemed to nationalist leaders that Britain had an almost obsessive preoccupation with the rights of minorities immediately before independence. And in the case of Ghana there was certainly strong feeling that the British were behind the opposition moves for a regional constitution in the days immediately before independence. It is safe to say that there was among the British a tendency to emphasise potential differences rather than similarities, and a concern with safeguarding the position of minorities before they would agree to set the seal on independence. This contrasts radically with French willingness to give overnight, as in the case of the *Loi Cadre*, a standard constitution for each of its territories from Mauretania to Gabon. Nevertheless as will shortly be seen, it is France against whom the accusation that she deliberately divided in order to rule is more justified. It is difficult to maintain an argument that Britain had, at least after 1948, any ambitions to perpetuate her rule in West Africa. The question was not *whether* she should grant independence but *when*. Her preoccupation with the position of minorities and the resultant delaying tactics were inspired by a concern, which may have been misguided, that it was her duty to provide for the differences in the country to which she was giving independence — differences which of course her policy of indirect rule was not a little responsible for consolidating.

HOW FAR WAS COLONIAL RULE RESPONSIBLE FOR UNITING DIFFERENT TERRITORIES UNDER THE SAME ADMINISTRATION.

In the first place it must be remembered that France was in a better position than Britain for doing this in West Africa since all her possessions were geographically contiguous. But, in addition, the underlying philosophy of France in matters concerning her colonial empire militated in favour of close contact between her various colonial possessions in Africa. First her logical approach to all questions pertaining to government, whether at home or abroad, insisted that the African empire must be administered in the same way throughout. Despite the fact that men like Lyautey and Harmand advocated a colonial policy for France similar to Lugardian indirect rule, in practice France in Black Africa paid little attention to traditional institutions. The basic model for the administrator was French law, French institutions and French culture. Nor did France attribute to any of her territories, with the exception of Senegal, a particular character. Whereas the British administrator served most of his career in the same territory, or in the case of Northern Nigeria in the same region, the French administrator rotated between colonies as different as Mauritania and Gabon. Indeed it was a principle that no French administrator should serve more than two consecutive tours in the same colony to prevent corruption. This was known as the turn-table policy (*rouage*). Pierre Alexandre records that on his first tour in Cameroon he served in three stations in thirty months; on his second tour in Cameroons two stations in twenty-four months; on his third tour in Togo, four stations in twenty-eight months.[8] The African civil servant also did tours of duty in territories other than the one from which he originated. The French African colonies were organised into two federations with a large number of common services, such as higher and secondary education, health, transport and communications. The budget of the federation was always more important than that of the constituent territories which, after the Second World War, were heavily subsidised from Paris through the Federal Budget. The existence of a single monetary system, a single customs system, an inter-regional civil service, and federal schools like the William Ponty School in Dakar where a great number of the present-day elite of French-speaking Africans received its training, created a background for African unity. These prospects were further improved by the establishment of a Great Council in each federation, composed of representatives of the territorial assemblies, which were brought into being by the Constitution of 1946. Not surprisingly, then, African politics developed on a pan-French-African scale, with men like Léon Mba of Gabon and Modibo Keita of Sudan both working together as members of the same political party — in this case the R.D.A. (Rassemblement Démocratique Africain). For further example, Gabriel d'Arboussier, a Mulatto born in Mali, has served as a politician in the following countries because of his connection with R.D.A.: French Equatorial Africa, Ivory Coast, Niger, Federation of Mali and Senegal and is now an Ambassador of Senegal. Thus at all levels in French West Africa the situation was ideal for the development of pan-African or at least pan-West African politics.

It was therefore a serious reversal of policy when in 1956, as a result of increasing pressure on France to extend democratic self-government in some form or other to her Black African territories, she passed the *Loi Cadre* (or Outline Law) which gave autonomy to the individual territories, but gave no executive power to them at the federal level. Hitherto, at both the territorial and federal level, Africans had had only legislative powers. The executive still lay in the hands of the administration. This law elicited from Senghor[9] angry outbursts against this allegedly deliberate attempt at Balkanisation of Africa, and later at the 1957 Congress of the R.D.A. at Bamako from Sékou Touré of Guinea also. The French could of course reply with some justification that they were merely acting in response to the known wishes of the leader of the most powerful political party in French Black Africa, Felix Houphouet-Boigny, leader of the R.D.A. He had been insistent that Ivory Coast be taken out of any federation that would involve her, as the richest territory in the federation, subsidising the others, that is, supporting the budget of a political federal executive as she had hitherto the administrative federal executive.[10]

Behind this dispute there lay the growing rivalry between Ivory Coast and Senegal, and more specifically between Abidjan, prosperous territorial capital of Ivory Coast and Dakar, the federal capital of

French West Africa: the latter was being developed not only as a political but also as an industrial centre, a destiny for which Ivory Coast could legitimately feel Abidjan was more suited in view of the spectacular industrial development that had in fact taken place there since independence. It was thus clearly in the interest of Senegal to stand as champion of federation, and for Ivory Coast to oppose it. This jealousy in retrospect can also be seen as symptomatic of the growth of local nationalism within the administrative units that made up French West Africa.

However, in 1957 as far as French West Africa was concerned Houphouët-Boigny was alone in his stand of loyalty to his territory as against a wider loyalty to the Federation, as the Congress of his party at Bamako so clearly showed. Léon Mba, the R.D.A. leader from Gabon in French Equatorial Africa, took up a similar stand on the grounds that he did not want his small but rich territory to subsidise the other three members of the Equatorial federation. In the Grand Conseil of French West Africa too, unanimous resolutions in favour of the creation of a federal executive were passed. Did France then deliberately break up the federation? Clearly, to give self-government at the territorial level with no executive authority at the federal level diverted the attention of politicians from federal to regional politics. It is known that the High Commissioner for French West Africa, Gaston Cusin, was against the creation of a federal executive, whilst his counterpart in French Equatorial Africa was in favour of it. It was further whispered in the corridors at the Bamako Congress that the then Premier of France, M. Bourgès-Manoury, of whose cabinet Houphouët-Boigny was a member, was hostile to a federal executive.[11] It was said in some quarters in France that the projected Franco-African Community would have a greater chance of survival if it consisted of a series of small economically unviable states rather than of the two large federations, which Senghor had always insisted were the only media through which Africa could negotiate with France on anything like terms of equality. Certainly France was right in thinking that a Balkanised Africa would be more dependent on her in the post-independence era, as subsequent events have proved. In the light of her scarcely-veiled hostility to the creation of the Mali Federation two years later, the evidence seems to favour the view that France conceived the *Loi Cadre* largely as a means of prolonging her domination over her African territories and was not motivated by any concern for acknowledging existing differences within these federations. As Nkrumah asked, in a wider context, 'Can we seriously believe that the colonial powers meant these countries to be independent viable states?'[12] On the other hand at the meeting of the Monrovia powers' experts in Dakar in 1961 the then Senegalese

Foreign Minister Doudou Thiam blamed African politicians for failing to maintain the federation that France had created:

> But here, we must admit, we have not yet made much progress; in some cases, we have indeed fallen behind. To take, as but one example, the countries of the former French West Africa, we are surprised to note how, since our accession to autonomy, and then to independence, our internal legislations have become diversified, how indeed our economic systems have sometimes taken opposite directions. Before, we had the same economic legislation, the same labour legislation, the same laws concerning rent, housing and commercial rents, the same fiscal legislation, the same customs legislation and the same judicial organisation, the same system of public freedoms. Today we consider all that with nostalgic feelings somewhat tempered by our accession to independence.[13]

Azikiwe made similar complaint with respect to the lack of cooperation between the former colonies of British West Africa and their dismantling of such common services as Britain did set up. Here, of course, Nkrumah must bear much responsibility. Ghana, as the first of the British West African colonies to gain independence, could have seized the initiative in retaining these common services. Instead Nkrumah quite deliberately withdrew Ghana from them on the grounds that regional groupings would prove a stumbling block to the achievement of continental unity. Even if Britain abandoned any attempts at common administration once her colonies ceased to be mere coastal footholds, she did at least maintain a common currency service and encouraged cooperation through a number of inter-territorial institutions such as research organisations, or the West African Airways Corporation. Fourah Bay and Achimota College served as meeting grounds for the young members of the elite of West Africa. But it is difficult to see how any serious attempt at a Pakistan-type administration between even two of the four states, such as Gambia and Sierra Leone, as was frequently advocated, could have been effective in the long run. Even if the problems of lack of contiguity had been overcome, there was still the imbalance of size, with the giant Nigeria at one extreme and the geographically and economically absurd Gambia at the other. Even so, had Britain given the African politicans in the post-war period the opportunity of frequent meetings such as the French Africans had, not only in the Grand Conseil but also in the corridors of the metropolitan assemblies in Paris, perhaps there would have been a possibility of the development of a pan-British West African party. There was however a precedent in the 1910s and 1920s in the National Congress of British West Africa which received no encouragement from the British Colonial authorities. On the other hand there is a good case for considering that the African unity represented by the R.D.A. and other pan-French African parties was an artificial unity. Paris-bred. André Blanchet has described the R.D.A. as a gift of Paris to Africa.

HOW FAR DID FRANCE AND BRITAIN TRY TO ENCOURAGE COOPERATION BETWEEN THEIR RESPECTIVE SETS OF COLONIES?

The answer is they made almost no effort at all. There were almost no institutions for common consultation over colonial problems whether these were political, cultural or economic — with the exceptions of the Anglo-French Standing Consultative Commission for Togo which was forced on both powers by the United Nations, and the short-lived agreement on common economic policies during the early months of the Second World War made between Georges Mandel and Malcolm Macdonald, respectively Colonial Minister of France and Colonial Secretary of Britain. As R. J. Harrison Church complained in 1957, 'many problems result from the quite incredible ignorance of what is going on across the artificial boundaries. Despite the work of the Trusteeship Council, of Anglo-French cooperation, of the Scientific Council for Africa, and many other bodies, much research is pursued in ignorance of similar work across the boundary'.[14]

Economically there was a marginal amount of inter-territorial trade, and most of what did take place was of a pre-colonial pattern such as the export of cattle from Niger to Nigeria or of kola-nuts from Nigeria to Niger. One of the obvious exceptions to this was labour migration, particularly of Mossi to the mines and cocoa farms of Southern Ghana. A glance at the map will show how communications were developed by each power as though the other's territories did not exist. Roads stop short of the international boundaries; railways run parallel to each other. The most fantastic examples are the Gambia river, one of the finest water ways in Africa but denied its natural hinterland by the French, and the so-called 'Opération Hirondelle' in Niger and Dahomey. In order to prevent groundnuts and other produce in Niger from being exported through Nigeria, most of Niger's natural outlet to the sea, the French built a superb road up through Dahomey, bridged the Niger at Gaya-Malanville, to join up with a road that ran across Niger parallel to the Nigerian border. All this to export groundnuts through the port of Cotonou rather than down to the Kano railhead. The excuse for this at the time of the plan's conception was the frequency of hold-ups at the Kano railhead, but by the time the scheme got into operation, the Nigerian *railways were in* fact capable of dealing with Niger's produce. And this all took place before Cotonou's new port was built.

In the field of education, the situation was the same. The schools of Nigeria and Ghana, with very rare exceptions, never included French in their curricula.[15] The French Lycées did teach English, but not with a view to increasing possibilities of contact with English-speaking neighbours, only because the schools were based directly on the French system of education, and for the baccalauréat the student had to take a second language to French, and this could be English, German or Spanish. Indeed such was the distance between the two groups, that one can say without much exaggeration that contact between them was at the level of the Fulani herdsman and the Hausa trader.

I. A. Asiwaju, in a fascinating study of the differing impact of French and British administration on a coherent cultural group, the Yoruba, has shown that while uneducated Yoruba on both sides of the frontier maintain contact with each other this is not the case with the educated elite. An educated Dahomeyan Yoruba would prefer to spend his vacation in Ivory Coast or Senegal rather than Lagos, while the educated Nigerian Yoruba from near the Dahomeyan frontier would prefer to vacation in Ghana rather than Dahomey.[16]

The French tried to bring their colonies into the orbit of a greater France in which naturally the British colonies could play no part. As Thomas Hodgkin wrote in 1954: 'In British West Africa everyone who is politically conscious is a nationalist of some kind. In French West Africa there are Catholics and Anti-Clericals, Communists and Gaullists, Socialists, Syndicalists and Existentialists'.[17] Even Sékou Touré, for all his political revolt against France, is leader of a country that is still culturally very much dependent on her. And it is this heavy French orientation, with Paris still a glittering Metropole even after independence, that has led to considerable suspicion of the French-speaking African on the part of his English-speaking brother, even ten years after independence. Such suspicions are not allayed by the spectacle of President Bokassa of the Central African Republic weeping at the funeral of de Gaulle, his 'father'; or by Houphouët-Boigny's championing 'dialogue' with South Africa to whom France sells arms.

This orientation is given further emphasis by the economic dependence of the former French African colonies on France. Whilst it is true that the former British colonies were heavily oriented in their trade patterns towards Britain and the Commonwealth, Britain never adopted a policy of protection of her West African colonial market against other European countries such as France did. This means that consumer habits in post-independence French-speaking Africa are still heavily biased towards French goods, and the membership of France in the E.E.C. has as yet made relatively little inroad into the preponderance of French goods in the shops of Dakar and Abidjan. Such dependence is further emphasised by the heavy reliance on French aid by nearly all the French-speaking states. Indeed it is almost impossible to assess French aid to her former African colonies as a report by a French Senatorial Commission, charged with this task, has emphasised. Aid was given in many different forms, one of which was through individual French Ministers![18]

In 1967 for instance Ivory Coast imported 42,644 million C.F.A. worth of goods from France and the franc zone as against 15,805 million C.F.A. from the rest of the world. Nigeria's imports give a very different picture of her relationship with her former colonial master: only £64,574,000 worth of goods were imported from the United Kingdom as against £150,055,000 from the rest of the world in that same year. Membership of the franc zone is much more restricting than the sterling zone.

HOW DEEP ARE THE DIFFERENCES THAT WERE ENGENDERED BY COLONIAL RULE AND HOW EASILY WILL THEY BE OVERCOME?

There is a tendency on the part of the pessimistic outsider to exaggerate these differences and a reverse tendency on the part of the pan-Africanist to try and dismiss them on the grounds that 'we are all Africans after all'. Most people will agree that the colonial experience, though it covered such a short period in Africa's history, was one in which the changes and innovations brought about by its subjection to European colonial rule have been disproportionate in their importance to the length of time in which they took place. And the cynic will point to the difference in the impact of the French and British experience as one of the basic causes of the break-up of the Ghana-Guinea-Mali union; though close to hand is the failure of the Mali Federation, which from many points of view — the shared colonial experience of the two component states, their contiguity, their common adherence to Islam — should have succeeded. And the only example in West Africa today of two political units created by the two different colonial powers coming together in political union is that of the Southern Cameroons and the Cameroun Republic, respectively English- and French-speaking, to form the Cameroun Federation. In this experiment we can see some of the sort of difficulties that will be faced in any future attempts to bring English- and French-speaking Africa together.[19] But before attempting to diagnose these, I would like to point to two major problems that are general rather than particular ones. The first is the language barrier, which can of course be broken down if there are sufficient funds and teachers available. But behind any language, it must be remembered, lies a whole philosophy of life, a system of thinking, particular attitudes to such basic questions as liberty, democracy, justice, and the place and nature of culture, understanding of which comes only after really intensive study of the language. The second problem is the continued dependence of many of the French-speaking territories on France, not only economically but also culturally. This has led to a certain clannishness among the French African states in the contemporary African scene. O.C.A.M. and the *Conseil de l'Entente* provided obvious examples of this, having, apart from explicit economic and political aims, something of the atmosphere of old boys' clubs about them.

In 1964, when I originally wrote this article, it was, perhaps, too early to draw satisfactory conclusions about the Cameroun experiment. Claude Welch Junior seemed to me to have been more optimistic then, in his series of articles in *West Africa*[20], about the federal experiment than the reports of other recent visitors, both European and Camerounian, would justify. He considered that 'Because of the flexible policy of the federal and state governments, most problems of reunification have been solved satisfactorily'. He pointed to the successful changeover of the side of the road on which people drove in West Cameroun, and further examples such as the introduction of uniform currency, and changeover of weights and measures. But at that time it still remained a fact that there were customs posts and check-points between the West and East; that contact across the inter-state border was infrequent; that the federal radio had only one hour of English a day; that economically the West Cameroun was hard hit by the changeover to the franc zone, particularly as far as the sale of her banana crop was concerned. There were still immense problems of legal and administrative harmonisation to be overcome.[21] But these were to be expected. I concluded then, however, that a superficial impression indicated that the difficulties that the Cameroun federation was experiencing at that time were a legacy of colonial rule rather than what one might call African differences – and they were of the same order that Gambia and Senegal or any French-speaking and English-speaking territory would experience in uniting.[22]

Time has, however, justified Dr. Welch's optimism about the Cameroun experiment. Between 1966 and 1971 most of the services of the two states were progressively federalised. Indeed the main area of residual jurisdiction for the English-speaking West Cameroun state were local administration and chieftaincy affairs. In 1966 the two regional parties were merged into one national party and two years later S. T. Muna, a federalist supporter of President Ahidjo, took over from Mr. J. N. Foncha, who had strongly regionalist inclinations, as Prime Minister of West Cameroun. Indeed, by 1972 Ahidjo was able to create a unitary state in which the West Cameroun and East Cameroun states disappeared.[23] Let it be said, however, that the success of this experiment was in part due to the overwhelmingly dominant position of the French-speaking East Cameroun and the effective repression of opposition to President Ahidjo's views. The official languages of the state may be French and English, but it is undoubtedly the former which will prevail, as did French and English over German years before. Such a solution would certainly not have been so easy in a unification of English- and French-speaking states of roughly equal size and population. In such a case the differing legacies of colonial rule would have proved a much greater obstacle to effective unification.

In this sense colonial rule has been a very definite factor for division in Africa. But on the other hand I do not think we should underestimate the factor for unity that colonial rule has been at the national level, in this case overcoming many of these African differences. It could also have been a factor for unity in the case of former French West and Equatorial Africa at the inter-territorial level, if France had not chosen to rend asunder federations she had built up in order to perpetuate if not her rule, at least her political influence and cultural and economic domination in Africa.

NOTES

1. Michael Crowder, 'Colonial Rule in West Africa: Factor for Division or Unity *Civilisations*, 3, 1965.
2. *A.O.F. 1957* published by the Haut Commissariat de la République en Afrique Occidentale Français, Dakar, 1957.
3. Forms for recommendation for scholarships in Kano State ask the referee to answer the following four questions.
   (1) From which tribe do you believe the candidate comes?
   (2) From which tribe do you believe his father comes?
   (3) From which tribe does his mother come?
   (4) Give grounds for your belief.
4. The concept of a boundary as a line drawn on a map was of course unknown in pre-colonial Africa.
5. See L. P. Mair, 'Social change in Africa', *International Affairs*, vol. 36, No. 4, October 1960, for an interesting discussion of this topic.
6. Michael Crowder, *Senegal – A Study in French Assimilation Policy*, London, 1962.
7. A point emphasised by Professor J. F. Ade Ajayi in his paper to the seminar on the Problems of Pan Africanism held at Ibadan University entitled 'The Relevance of Pre-colonial Africa', 22 January 1964.
8. Pierre Alexandre, 'Chiefs, Commandants and Clerks' in Michael Crowder and Obaro Ikime (eds), *West African Chiefs: Their Changing Status under Colonial Rule and Independence*, Ife and New York, 1970.
9. Senghor's bitterness is well brought out in his intervention in the debate in the French National Assembly 1 February 1957 cited in *Présence Africaine*, No.

17-18 of 1958 'Nous ne sommes plus les grands enfants qu'on s'est plu à voir en nous, et c'est pourquoi les joujoux et sucettes ne nous interessent pas'.
10. André Blanchet *L'Itinéraire des Partis Africains depuis Bamako*, Paris 1958, also Gil Dugué *Les Etats-Unis d'Afrique*, Dakar, 1959.
Blanchet, *op. cit.*, pp 71-72 quotes M. Ouezzin Coulibaly, late Premier of Upper Volta and Secretary of the R.D.A. at the Bamako Congress of 1957, as blaming the politicians for dividing Africans against themselves. M. Blanchet himself suggests that much of the division in French African politics of that period was fostered by the fissiparous nature of French politics:
> Mais, en mettant en relief la part que prennent dans la vie africaine les considérations purement partisanes, elles amènent l'observateur à se demander si le système parlementaire français, si les préoccupations électorales des partis politiques et leur transposition sur le plan local, ne sont pas responsables d'une grande partie des divisions constatées dans chaque térritoire. Sans qu'il y ait nécéssairement, de la part des factions politiques françaises, volonté systématique de désunir les Africains, l'association de leurs pays à un régime aussi politisé que le nôtre n'aurait-elle pas contaminé les élites africaines au point de leur faire prendre aux jeux purement politiques un plaisir immoderé et — il faut bien le dire — merveilleusement accordé à leur tempérament? On peut se poser la question avec quelque remords. M. Ouezzin Coulibaly avait beau ne pas incriminer spécialement la métropole, on ne pouvait pas ne pas se sentir un peu honteux à l'entendre déclarer au congrès constitutif de la Convention auquel il apportait le salut du R.D.A. 'Les Africains ne sont pas divisés, voyez-les au village. Ce sont les hommes politiques qui les divisent par le mensonge, la surenchère et la démagogie'.

11. Blanchet (*op. cit.*, pp. 88-89) makes the following points concerning Ivory Coast's economic reasons for rejecting federation. She considered herself the 'vache à lait' of the Federation. With 1/7th of the population she had in 1956 (the year before the R.D.A. Bamako Congress) accounted for 38% of the exports and accounted for 88% of its revenue in dollars. It did not have its cocoa and coffee prices buttressed against the fluctuations of the world market as Senegal and other members of the Federation did for their ground-nuts and palm-oil. Ivory Coast therefore felt itself justified in considering itself different from the other territories of the federation. The Ivory Coast did of course enjoy some of the fruits of French price stabilisation policy, but it was economically of less advantage to her than to Senegal. See *Commodity Stabilisation Funds* published by F.A.O. (E/CN/13/51. C.C.P. 62/22 of 6 April 1962) for details of subsidies to crops in French-speaking Africa. There is an excellent discussion of Ivory Coast's economic position in the former A.O.F. in Elliot J. Berg, 'Economic Basis of Political Choice in French West Africa', *American Political Science Review*, June 1960, pp. 391-405.
12. Kwame Nkrumah, *I Speak of Freedom*, Preface, p. 11, New York, 1961.
13. Only the rather poor English translation of this speech was available to me.
14. R. J. Harrison Church, *West Africa*, London, 1957.
15. It was however easier for a Yoruba child from Dahomey, for instance, to transfer to a primary school in the Yoruba West of Nigeria, where the first years of education was conducted in the vernacular, than vice versa, *since all primary education in French territories was in French*; and no concession was made either to teaching of or in the vernacular.
16. I. A. Asiwaju, *Western Yorubaland under European Rule 1889-1945: A Comparative Analysis of French and British Colonialism*, London 1976.

17. Thomas Hodgkin in *West Africa*, pp. 5-6, 9 January 1954.
18. Senate paper no. 53, 1 re Session Ordinaire de 1961-1962 'Rapport Général etc. sur le projet de loi des finances pour 1962'... by Senator Marcel Pellenc, Tôme III, Examen des Credits et des Dispositions Spéciales, Annexe No. 8, Coopération (Rapporteur-spécial: M. André Armengaud).
19. It has been objected that the Cameroun experiment in bringing together French- and English-speaking Africa will not be very instructive for other such experiments since the common German experience of the two participating members of the Federation makes this a 'special case'. But this argument can be reduced to absurdity for we can argue that the proposed union of Gambia and Senegal will be a special case, since they have identical ethnic composition; or should Niger and Northern Nigeria wish to federate they have not only many ethnic groups in common, but both formed part of the Fulani Empire, etc....
20. Claude Welch Jr., 'Cameroon since Reunification', *West Africa*, October 19, 26, November 2, 9, 1963.
21. Victor T. Le Vine in his chapter on 'Cameroun' in Gwendolen Carter (ed), *Five African States — Responses to Diversity*, New York 1963, was much less optimistic than Welch about the federal experiment and wrote: 'There is even some question whether in some respects the Camerouns had not moved farther apart rather than closer together'. Le Vine cited the lack of institutional unity as provided by the constitution, the lack of political unity in the federation, where 'political activity remains primarily state activity', and the lack of progress towards economic integration though this is one field in which the prospects for integration seemed initially favourable. He also referred to the quite understandable reluctance of the West Cameroun to change over its educational system. He concluded: 'Thus national unity is still rather far away. The complexity and magnitude of the problems facing the states considered both individually and together must temper the most qualified optimism about the Camerounian future.' For an interesting discussion of the ideology of unification see Mr. Le Vine's recent paper, 'The Politics of Partition in Africa: The Cameroons and the Myth of Unification', *Journal of International Affairs*, XVIII, 2, 1964, pp. 198-210.
22. A striking illustration of this is the rivalry that will ensue between the river ports of Kaolack and Ziguinchor in Senegal and Bathurst in the Gambia, if the two countries federate. Had Senegambia been created in the first place it is likely that Bathurst would have become the most important city rather than Dakar. As it is, Bathurst, at the head of the Gambia river, but cut off from its natural hinterland, is only a small port of 20,000 population. The ports of Kaolack and Ziguinchor have been developed in order to handle the trade which but for the colonial boundary would have flowed down the Gambia river to Bathurst. If the two countries federate and adjust their economies to the same scale (many goods on sale in Bathurst cost twice as much in Dakar at present!) then the natural tendency will be for trade to be directed towards the Gambia river again to the profit of Bathurst and to the detriment of Kaolack and to a lesser extent Ziguinchor, both important political centres.
23. Victor T. E. Le Vine 'Recent History in "Cameroon" ', *Africa South of the Sahara 1973*, London, 1973, pp. 206-207.

INDEX

Abbas, Ferhat, 287, 289, 290
Abdullahi Abershi, Sarkin Yauri, 154
Abidjan (Ivory Coast), 325; rivalry between Dakar and, 320-1
Aborigines Rights Protection Society, 21
Act of Abolition (1807), 8
Administration, colonial administrative services: role of colonial administrators, 122-50: African context, 123-5; educational background, 125-6; transferability of officers, 127-8; study of African languages, 128; differing functions of officers, 128-30; distribution of administrators, 130; relations with native chiefs, 131; Portuguese in Angola, 131-2; European and African hierarchy, 133; French in West Africa, 134-5, 180, 235-9, 316-17; British in West Africa, 135-7, 138-41, 239-41, 316-17; in Belgian Congo, 137-8; judicial powers, 141-3; socio-economic roles, 143-7; Native Authority system in Bussa, 151-2, 156, 160-75; civilian administration in Borgu, 155-9; in Dahomeyan Borgu, 180-3; Indirect Rule — French and British style, 198-208, 209; role of West African Chiefs, 209-30; policies of colonial powers, 233-5; in Portuguese Africa, 241-4; in Gambia, 260-1; French post-war decentralisation, 286-7; colonial role in uniting different territories under same administration, 319-23
A.E.F. see French Equatorial Africa
Affonso, King of Kongo, 5, 6
African Association, British, 9
African responses and initiatives (to colonialism), 250-7
Agriculture, 18, 19, 123, 244, 245-7; cash crops, 18, 19-20, 112, 123, 144, 237, 244, 245-7, 248, 277; in French West Africa, 112, 237, 238, 275-6; forced labour, 145-6, 147; subsistence crops, 247; in Gambia, 259-60, 262, 263-6

Ahidjo, President of Cameroun, 326-7
Ahmadou of Segou, 48, 53, 56, 58
Ajayi, J. F. Ade, 15
Ajia Umoru, District Head of South Bussa, 162, 164, 165
Alagoa, E. A., 7
Alexandre, Pierre, 234, 319
Algeria, 108, 132, 272, 274, 284, 287, 289, 290, 294, 296, 299, 309
Ali Bachabi, 184, 185, 186
Aliu Wakil Sarkin Yauri (later Sarkin Yamma), 160, 162-3, 164, 166
Aliyara, District Head of West Bussa, 162, 164, 165, 166
Al-Maghali, *The Obligations of Princes* by, 4, 5
Anglo-French Agreement on partition of Borgu (1898), 180
Anglo-French Standing Consultative Commission for Togo, 323
Angola, 35-6; Portuguese colonial administration in, 122, 128, 131-3, 243; education, 124; legal administration, 141; forced labour, 145-6, 147
Angoulvant, Lieutenant-Governor, 110, 112, 115, 116, 117, 186-7, 193, 194
A.O.F. see French West Africa
Apithy, Sourou Mignan, 290, 291, 292, 301, 303, 306
Arabs, 2, 3, 4, 6, 10-11
d'Arboussier, Gabriel, Secretary-General of R.D.A., 295, 320
Ashanti (Asante), 4, 16, 26, 29, 30, 31, 45, 49-50, 55, 56, 219, 240, 255
Ashanti War (1874), 50, 59
Asiwaju, I. A., 324
Assimilation policy, 11, 12-16, 108, 134, 203-7, 233, 254, 284, 285-7, 288, 291, 295, 310
Assinie trading post, 26
Atacora revolt, 186-7, 192-3
Attahiru Amadu, Sultan of Sokoto, 46, 58
Azikiwe, Nnamdi, 308, 322

Baguene, Chief, 183-5
Bai Bureh (Kebalai), 46, 47, 49, 50, 53, 54, 57, 58, 59, 217; revolt against British

332 COLONIAL WEST AFRICA

in Sierra Leone and, 61-97; early years (the warrior), 72-7; as chief of Kasseh, 77-83; and war of, 83-95
Bai Inga, 76, 77-8, 80
Bakary, Djibo, 228, 301, 302, 303, 304
Bamako, 41, 116, 293, 305; R.D.A. Congress at (1957), 299, 300, 320, 321, 328
Bambara, 56, 57, 270
Bambey Groundnut Research Station, Senegal, 262
Bantaba (Mandinka palaver house), 259, 260
Bariba (French Borgu) Revolt (1916-17), 180-95: origins, 183-6; deterioration of situation, 187-90; and campaign against, 190-3; consequences and causes of rebellion, 193-5
Barje Bello, 155
Barreto, Honorio Pereira, 233
Barros, Joao de, 4-5
Barth, Heinrich, 28, 36, 246
Bathurst, 26, 30, 260, 261, 262, 266
Becou incident (French Borgu), 183-6, 190-1, 192, 193, 194
Belgians, 36, 40, 104; administrators in the Congo, 122, 125-6; legal system, 142; forced labour, 145, 146, 147
Benin, 6-7, 26, 306; Portuguese in, 4-5; Chiefs (Oba), 211-12, 214
Benue valley, Nigeria, 48
Berlin Conference (1884-5), 29, 30, 31, 33, 35, 40, 41-2
Bimbereke French post (Borgu), 183, 184, 185, 186, 187-9, 190-2, 193, 194
Bio Guera, Chief of Becou, 183-5, 188, 192, 193, 194
Bismarck, Count Otto von, 38, 39, 40-1, 44n
Blanchet, André, 323, 328n
Bloc African, Senegal, 293
Blyden, E. W., 47, 69
Bobo-Dioulasso, I.O.M. conference at (1953), 295
Boisson, Pierre, Vichy High Commissioner for Black Africa, 272, 273-5 276, 278
Bokari Bamp, Chief of Port Loko, 83-4
Bokassa, President of Central African Republic, 324
Bokhari, Muslim chief, 74, 75, 76, 77
Bonte, Florimonde, 294
Bordeaux Pact (1923), 104, 118-19

Borgu (Kontagora Province, Nigeria), 57; 180, 241, 246; British administration in, 151-2, 156; pre-colonial, 152-5; early civilian administration (1902-12), 155-9; Native Authority system in Bussa, 160-75; Bussa Revolt (1915), 163-7, 183, 194-5; and aftermath, 167-73; made part of Ilorin Province (1923), 170, 173; partitioned between Britain and France (1898), 180, 183; role of chiefs, 212-13
Borgu (French Dahomey): Bariba revolt against French (1916-17), 57, 167, 179-85: French administration, 180-3; Becou incident, 183-6; deterioration of situation, 187-90; and campaign against Bariba, 190-3; consequences and causes of rebellion, 193-5
Bosworth, Colonel Arthur, 88, 91-2
Bourgès-Manoury, M., 321
Brazzaville Conference (1944), 279-80, 284, 285-6, 287, 288, 292, 296, 302
Brevié, Jules, Governor-General of French West Africa, 237
British in West Africa: abolition of slave trade by, 3, 8-9; and trade, 8-9, 11, 28-31, 33, 260; nineteenth-century attitudes to Africans, 9, 11, 14-15; and cultural assimilation, 11, 12, 13-15; colonial rule, 16-19, 26, 34, 38-9, 231-2; location of interests (1850-80), 26, 27-31; and 'Bonds' with Gold Coast states, 26, 29; British government hostility to West African colonisation, 27-8, 31, 34, 38; protectionism, 38; occupation of Egypt by, 39-40, 41; Makoko Treaties and, 40; Anglo-Portuguese treaty, 40, 41; and Berlin Conference, 41, 42; African resistance to colonialism, 47-59 *passim*; Bai Bureh and Hut Tax Wars in Sierra Leone against, 61-103; recruitment of African troops for First World War and, 110-11, 113, 115, 117; colonial administrators, 122, 125, 126-7, 128-30, 131, 133, 135-7, 138-41, 142-3, 147-9, 240-1; legal system, 142-3; taxation, 139, 140, 141, 144, 146, 249; and forced labour, 144-5, 146-7; imposition of

INDEX

Native Authority system in Bussa and 1915 Rebellion, 151-75, 194-5; partition of Borgu between France and Britain, 180, 183; Indirect Rule, 198-208, 209, 220-4, 234; role of chiefs in local administration, 209-30; administrative policies, 233-5; and administrative structures, 239-41, 316-17; Colonial Development Fund, 248; social welfare, 249; Christian cultural influence, 253-4; in Gambia, 260-6; colonial policy during Second World War, 268, 270-1, 272, 273, 274, 275, 277, 278, 279, 280-1; and decolonisation, 308-9; Francophones v. Anglophones, 314-15; contribution to internal unity of West African states, 315-19; 'divide and rule' policy, 318-19; administrative unification of different territories under, 322-3; cooperation with French West Africa, 323-5
British Colonial Development Fund, 248
Bussa (Nigeria), 151-78, 180; 1915 Rebellion, 59, 151, 152, 163-7; British Native Authority in, 152, 156, 160-75; pre-colonial, 152-5; early civilian administration, 155-9; removal of Turak, 168-9; Kiwotede Kijibrim installed as Emir, 169-70; restoration of Kitoro Gani, 170-1; restoration of lost lands to, 171-2; subjection of Kaiama to, 172, 213

Cacheu, Portuguese, 233
Caldwell, T., 68
Cameron, Sir Donald, Governor of Nigeria, 199
Cameroun (Cameroons), 21, 41, 42, 130, 203, 231, 315, 319; during Second World War, 269-70, 273; formation of Federation, 325, 326-7, 329n
Campbell, D. G., 107, 132n
Cape Verde Island, Portuguese, 231, 243
Cardew, Sir Frederick, Governor of Sierra Leone, 61, 64-8, 70-1, 73, 81-2, 83, 86-7, 88-9, 91, 92, 93-4, 95, 96
Carpot, François, 104, 106, 107, 108, 109, 118
Cary, Joyce, D. O., Borgu, 171, 172-3
cash crops, 18, 19-20, 112, 123, 144, 237, 244, 245-7, 248, 251, 262, 264, 277

Caute, David, 284
Cayla, Governor-General Léon, 271, 272, 275
Chabi Prouka, King of Nikki, 183, 184, 185, 188, 189, 191, 192, 193, 194, 195
Chad, 272, 273, 317
Chalmers Commission (Sir Donald Chalmers), 66, 67, 68, 70, 94, 95
Chamberlain, Joseph, 54, 61, 65, 66, 67, 68, 92
Christianity, 251, 263; influence in West Africa, 1, 3-6, 253-7; colonial regimes' attitude to, 253-4; *see also* missionaries
Church, R. J. Harrison, 323
Clarke, J. C. O., Resident Bussa, 156, 157, 159-62, 163-5, 166, 167, 169, 173
Clifford, Sir Hugh, 19, 151, 170, 205, 240
Clozel, Governor-General, 111
cocoa, 11, 18, 19, 20, 123, 144, 146, 237, 244, 245, 246, 323
coffee, 11, 18, 147, 244, 245, 246; *arabica*, 123
Communists, French (P.C.F.), 278, 287, 293, 294-5
Congo (Kongo), 42; Portuguese in, 5-6, 10; Belgian colonial administrators in, 36, 122, 126, 127, 129, 130, 131, 133, 137-8, 142, 148; Makoko Treaties granting territory to French, 40, 41; wage-earners, 124; and education, 124; and legal system, 138, 142; and forced labour, 145, 146, 147
Congo-Brazzaville, 273
Congo river, 36, 38, 40, 41, 42
Conseil de l'Entente, 306, 307, 326
Conseil de l'Union, 288
Convention Africaine, 288, 301
Coppet, Governor-General de, 237
Cotonou, 29, 193, 306, 323; P.R.A. inaugural meeting at (1958), 283, 301
cotton cultivation, 8, 11, 123, 237, 238, 244, 250
Coumba, Yaro, 13, 51
Cowan, L. Gray, 206
Creoles, 13, 14, 30, 67, 69, 70, 71, 256
Crowther, Samuel Ajayi, 10, 13-14, 15, 47
Crozier, Brigadier F.C., 59
culture: European v. Arab influence, 3-7; assimilation policy, 11, 12-16, 108, 134, 203-7, 233, 254, 284, 285-7, 288, 291, 295, 310; African v. European, 253-5

currency, 20, 244
Cusin, Gaston, High Commission for French West Africa, 321

Dabou trading post, 26
Dahomey, 11, 13, 32, 45, 49, 51, 56, 111, 317; French colonial rule, 33, 42, 55, 233, 235; and African resistance, 50, 59; recruitment of African troops, 110, 111, 115, 116, 179, 180; Borgu revolt (1916), 57, 167, 179-95; and French 'police operations' against rebels, 186-7; French Indirect Rule, 201; economic development, 245; post-Second World War, 290, 301, 303, 305, 306; joins *Conseil de l'Entente*, 306, 307; 'Opération Hirondelle', 323
Dakar, 33, 37, 114, 115, 118-19, 186, 249, 256, 304, 306, 325; as administrative capital of French West Africa, 235-7; during Second World War, 271, 272-4, 277, 278; inaugural meeting of Parti de la Fédération Africain at, 306; as capital of independent Mali, 307; Conference on the Press (1960) at, 314; tribal inter-marriage, 318; William Ponty School, 320; rivalry between Abidjan and, 320-1
Dakar Jeunes (pro-Vichy journal), 278
Dangaladima Abershi, Sarkin Yauri, 155
Dantoro, Sarkin Bussa, 153, 154, 155
de Gaulle, General Charles, 269, 270, 271, 272, 273, 274-5, 279, 284, 301, 302, 304, 307, 308, 313n, 324
Decolonisation, 20-1; the chief during period of, 224-8; effect of Second World War on, 268, 277-81; *see also* Independence
Defferre, Gaston, 296, 297
Delavignette, Robert, 201, 203, 206-7, 238, 318
Deschamps, Gouverneur Hubert, 198, 200, 203, 276
Diagne, Blaise, 13, 104-8, 113-19, 179-80, 236
Diallo, Yacine, 289, 291
Diop, Alioune, 310
Diop, Mahjemout, 293, 295
Diori, Hamani, 228
Diouf, Galandou, 108
Dipoko, Mbella Sonne, 269-70

District Officers *see under* Administration
Dodds, General, 13, 46, 50, 51, 233
Dowda, Alikali of Forikaria, 76, 78
Duffy, James, 129
Durand-Valentin, Deputy, 233
Dutch, 27, 260
Dwyer, Fergus, Acting Resident of Kontagora, 158, 161, 165, 166

Eboué, Felix, Governor-General of French Equatorial federation, 273, 284
Ecole Nationale de la France d'Outre-Mer (E.N.F.O.M.), 125, 128, 214
economy, economic developments, under colonial rule, 19-20, 21, 244-50; impact of First World War in French West Africa on, 111-12; socio-economic roles of the bush administrator, 143-7; in French West Africa, 136-8, 245-6, 247, 248, 268, 269, 275-7, 280, 286, 307-8, 324, 326; in Gambia, 261-6; as major factor in creation of national unity, 317-18; Anglo-French cooperation, 323
education, 123, 124, 249, 254, 318; missionary, 10, 15; in Sierra Leone, 13, 149; European colonial, 17-18, 20, 21; in French West Africa, 112, 114, 124, 204-5, 236, 249, 269, 280, 286, 310, 316, 320, 324; in Nigeria, 124, 316; in Angola, 124; in Belgian Congo, 124; in Gambia, 261; Anglo-French lack of contact, 324
Egba, 45, 59
Egypt, British occupation of, 39-40, 41
Ellis, Colonel Alfred Burden, 81

Faidherbe, General, 9, 10, 11, 26, 31, 33-4, 37, 50
Fante, 10, 14, 56
Ferlus, *Commandant de Cercle* of Borgou, 184-6, 187, 194, 195
Ferry, Jules, 37, 38, 39
F.I.D.E.S. *(Fonds pour l'Investissement et Developpement Economiques et Sociales)*, 280
First World War (1914-18), 16, 19, 47, 250; French recruitment of African troops for, 105-19, 179-80, 238
Flegel, Joseph, 42

INDEX

Flint, J. E., 47, 56
forced labour (*corvée*), 144-7; in French West Africa, 104, 105, 134, 145, 146, 147, 179, 183, 194, 195, 235, 238, 246, 269, 280, 285, 287; in Angola, 132, 145, 147; in Nigeria, 144-5, 146; in Kenya, 145, 146-7; in Belgian Congo, 145, 146, 147; in Portuguese Guinea, 246
Fourah Bay College, 10
Free French régime in French West Africa, 237, 268-82, 284-5
Freetown, Sierra Leone, 13, 26, 50, 61; British in, 62, 75, 233; Hut Tax War and, 65, 67, 69, 70-1, 77, 78, 79, 80, 95; press, 69, 70-1; Christians and Muslims in, 256; in Second World War, 271
Franco-African Community (post-Second World War), 283-4, 300, 301, 305, 309, 321; 6th Meeting of (1959), 307, 308; *see also* French Union
French Constituent Assembly, 1st (1945): 286, 287, 288, 289, 292; 2nd : 285, 288-90, 291, 292, 294, 297, 309, 310
French Equatorial Africa, 108, 113, 115, 127, 146, 321; native administration in, 201-2, 203; during Second World War, 269, 273, 279, 284; and postwar, 288, 292, 295, 298
French National Assembly, West African representation in (after Second World War), 286, 290, 292, 293, 309-10
French Union, 284, 288-92, 293, 295, 296, 297, 300, 309
French in West Africa, 62, 76; assimilation policy, 11, 12-13, 15, 108, 134, 203-7; trade, 11, 30, 32, 75, 104, 105, 111, 112, 260; colonialism, 16-18, 37, 38, 39-40, 231-2; location of interests (1850-80), 26-7, 29, 30, 31-5; Protectionist policy, 38; Makoko Treaties, 40, 41; Berlin Conference, 41, 42; African resistance to, 47-59 *passim*, 180; and Borgu rebellion in Dahomey, 57, 167, 179-95; Blaise Diagne and recruitment of African troops for 1914-18 war, 104-21, 145, 179-80; forced labour, 104, 105, 134, 145, 146, 147, 180, 238, 246, 269, 280, 285, 287; and *indigénat,* 107, 114, 135, 142, 202, 236, 239, 269, 279, 280, 285, 287; economy, 111-12, 236-8, 245-6, 247, 248, 269, 275-7, 280, 286, 307-8, 323, 324-5, 326; wartime training of Africans for administration, 112; colonial administrators, 122, 125, 126, 127, 128-9, 130, 131, 133, 134-5, 141-2, 146, 148, 236-8; wage-earners, 124; *rouage* policy, 127, 214, 239; legal system, 107, 114, 135, 141-2, 239, 316; partition of Borgu between British and (1898), 180, 183; 'police operations' against Dahomeyan rebels, 186-7; Indirect Rule, 198-208, 209, 220-4; African élite, 205; role of African chiefs in local administration, 209-30, 335, 238-9; administrative policies, 233-5: and administrative structure, 235-9, 216-17; Mandate in Togo, 235; social welfare, 249; Christian cultural influence, 253-4; Vichy and Free France in, 268-82; formation of G.E.C.s, 278-9; Brazzaville Conference (1944), 279-80, 284, 285-6; Independence as a goal (1944-60), 283-313; formation of French Union, 288-92, 293; and R.D.A., 293-5; Anglophones v. Francophones, 314-15; contribution to internal unity of African states, 315-19; and 'divide and rule' policy, 318-19; administrative unification of different territories in, 319-23; and co-operation with British West Africa, 323-5
Frontier Police, British, 62, 69, 70, 81-2, 83, 86, 88
Fulani *see* Hausa-Fulani
Furse, Sir Ralph, 125
Futa Jallon, 200, 208n, 228
Fyfe, Christopher, 7, 9, 73

Gabon, 299, 319, 320, 321
Gallo of Yauri, 154, 155
Gambia, 7, 33, 110, 115, 259-67, 315, 322; British in, 12, 13, 31, 260-6; groundnuts production, 34, 247, 260, 262, 276; Indirect Rule, 221, 234; taxation, 238, 261; administration, 240, 260-1; migration of labour, 246, 259-60; Senegal and, 260, 263, 315, 329n; public works, 261-2; rice

revolution, 263-6; in Second World War, 271, 276, 278
Gambia Minerals Ltd, 262
Gambia river, 323, 329n
Gamble, D. P., 259, 264, 266
Garba-Jahumpa, 263
Gbelegbuwa II, Awujale of Ijebuland, 214
Géay, *Commandant de Cercle* of Moyen-Niger, 188, 189, 190, 191, 194
Geismar, Governor of Senegal, 278
Germans, 34; traders, 37, 111; colonialism, 16, 38, 39, 40-1, 42, 231, 235
Ghana, 11, 123, 283, 304, 318, 323, 324; Independence, 296-7, 298, 300, 308, 322; *see also* Gold Coast
Ghana-Guinea-Mali Union, 315, 325
Gide, André, *Voyage au Congo* by, 105
Gold Coast, 27, 50, 51, 110; European trade, 1-3, 7, 129-30; and British assimilation policy, 12, 13, 14; and colonial rule, 19, 20, 21, 26, 29, 30, 31; cocoa production, 19, 20; administrative service, 126, 240; and taxation, 144, 238; Indirect Rule, 221, 222, 234; peasant migration, 238, 246, 269; economic development, 245; *see also* Ghana
gold trade, 1-3, 11, 20, 49, 246
Goldie, Sir George Taubman, 30, 33, 37, 41
Gorée island, 26
Gorer, Geoffrey, 203
Goulibaly, Ouezzin, 301
Grand Bassam trading post, 26
Great Empire Loan (French West Africa), 248
groundnuts and oil, 11, 29, 30, 33, 34, 105, 144, 237, 244, 245, 246, 247, 250, 260, 262, 264, 265, 275-6, 277, 303, 323
Groupes d'Etudes Communistes (G.E.C.s), 278-9
Guemou, battle of (1859), 50
Guèye, Lamine, 18, 25n, 107, 290, 291, 293, 295, 301
Guinea, French, 33, 47, 64, 108, 235, 276, 307, 308, 310; recruitment of African troops, 109, 110, 111, 115, 116; revolts against French, 179; native administration, 202, 260; and chiefs, 225, 228; Independence (1958), 284, 303, 304-5, 308, 313n;

education, 316
Guinea, Portuguese (Guinea-Bissau), 27, 113, 128, 132, 231, 233, 243, 254, 261
gum trade, 32, 34
guns (firearms), 3, 16, 46, 48, 51-5, 59; development of machine guns, 51-2; European superiority in, 51-3; African supplies of, 54-5; *see also* military forces

Hailey, Lord, 237, 263
Haliru, Emir of Kaiama, 172
Hamilton-Browne, W., Resident, Kontagora, 159-60, 161, 162-5, 169, 170, 173
Hargreaves, J. D., 27, 32
Harmand, Jules, 204, 319
Hausa-Fulani, 4, 42, 55, 59, 128, 139, 152, 154, 157, 160, 175, 182, 200, 202-3
Haut-Sénégal-Niger, recruitment of African troops in, 109, 110, 111, 116, 117, 179; *see also* Senegal
Havelock, Governor Arthur Edward, 75
Hay, Governor Sir James Shaw, 77-8, 79
Hermon-Hodge, Hon. H., Resident Ilorin, 170, 172, 173
Herriot, President, 285, 290
Hirst, Elizabeth, 73, 74, 96
Hodgkin, Thomas, 324
Holle, Paul, 13, 51
Horton, James Africanus Beale, 14
Hoskyns-Abrahall, T., D.O., Borgu, 170, 171, 172
Houphouët-Boigny, Félix, 283-4, 290-307 *passim*, 313n, 320, 321, 324
Hut Tax Wars *see under* Sierra Leone
Huxley, Elspeth, 259

Ibadan, 30, 53, 56, 210
Ife, 6-7
Ife University: seminar on West African Chiefs (1968), 209-11
Ijebu, 49, 50, 52, 53, 54, 56, 59; Awujale (chiefs), 211, 214, 216-17
Indépendants d'Outre Mer (I.O.M.), 295, 299
Independence, as a goal in French West African politics (1944-60), 283-313
Indigénat (code of administrative justice in French West Africa), 107, 114, 135, 142, 202, 236, 239, 269, 279, 280, 285, 287

Indirect Rule: French v. British, 198-208; in Nigeria, 138-41, 199-200, 234; role of chiefs in local administration, 209-30; definition, 220-4; in Gold Coast, 221, 222, 234; in Sierra Leone, 221, 222, 234; in Gambia, 221, 234; *see also* Native authority
Ingham, Kenneth, 136-7
International Labour Conference (1930), Diagne's declaration at, 104-5
Ivory Coast, 21, 27, 32, 33, 45, 58, 144, 235; resistance to colonial rule, 47, 48, 179; recruitment of African troops, 110, 111, 116; forced labour, 146; Angoulvant's 'pacification' of, 186; native administration, 203; and economy, 245, 308, 325, 328n; seasonal migration of labour to, 246; during Second World War, 273, 277; and post-war decolonisation, 283, 298, 299, 303, 307; joins *Conseil de l'Entente*, 306, 307; lingua franca as unifying factor, 316; rivalry between Senegal and, 320-1

James Island, 260
Jihad(s) (Muslim holy wars), 4, 7, 8, 10-11, 74, 75, 154
Jobson, Richard, 259
John Holt Company, 248
Johnson, I. T. A. Wallace, 18
Johnston, Sir Harry, 15
Jones, Captain A. T., 45
Jones, Dr G. I, 210, 212

Kaiama (southern Borgu), 153, 155, 156-7, 159, 160, 162, 163, 164, 165, 166, 172, 212-13
Kamara, Issa, 73, 74, 96
Kamberri, 153, 154-5
Kandi province (French Borgu), 180, 182, 183, 188, 190, 191, 194
Kano, 4, 140, 201, 246, 323; Emir of, 211-12, 216, 219
Karene district (Sierra Leone), 64, 66, 67, 71, 73, 83-95 *passim*
Karimu (Susu chief), 78, 79, 80
Kasseh state (Sierra Leone), 49, 61, 64, 69-70
Keita, Modibo, 301, 303, 306, 320
Kenya: role of British administrators, 122, 126, 127, 128, 129, 130, 131, 133, 135-7, 148; wage-earners, 124; legal system, 142-3; forced labour, 145, 146-7
Kimble, David, 29
Kingsley, Mary, 68
Kitoro Gani, Sarkin Bussa, 156, 157, 158-9, 160, 161, 164, 166-7, 168, 172, 174-5; deposed by British (1915), 151-2, 162-3, 165, 166; and restoration of (1923), 170-1, 173; deposed again (1935), 171
Kiwotede Kijibrim, Emir of Bussa, 169-70, 174-5
kola-nuts, 49, 323
Konkouré Dam, Guinea, 303, 308
Kontagora Province *see* Borgu

labour *see* forced labour; migration; wage labour
Labour Code, French (1952), 287, 297
Lagos, 7, 12, 13, 29, 32, 33, 34, 45, 50, 233, 256
Laird, Macgregor, 28
Lamine, Mahmadou, 13, 50, 51, 53, 56
languages, 324, 325; colonial administrators' study of African, 127, 128, 205, 214; lingua franca as unifying factor, 315-16
Laval, Pierre, 270
law, legal system: *Sharia* (Islamic law), 4, 5, 7, 143; in Fante States, 10; in French West Africa, 12, 107, 114, 135, 141-2, 202, 235, 239, 316; in Kenya, 136-7, 142-3; in Belgian Congo, 138, 142; in Nigeria, 139, 141, 142-3, 199; judicial powers of colonial administrators, 141-3; in Angola, 141; judicial authority of chiefs, 217
Lebanese middlemen/traders, 20, 112, 245
Le Clerc, Colonel, 273
Lefilliâtre, *Administrateur-en-chef*, 188, 189
Légion Française de Combattants (pro-Vichy), 278
Lendy, Captain Edward Augustus, 80-1
Leopold, King of the Belgians, 36, 40, 42
Le Vine, Victor T., 329n
Lewis, M. D., 204
Lewis, Captain P. E., D. O. Borgu, 172
Lewis, Samuel, 13
Liberia, 36, 109, 110
Limba, 78, 79, 80; chiefs, 211-12, 216, 222

Livingstone, David, 40
Loi Cadre (1956; in French West Africa), 236, 291, 296-7, 299, 310, 319, 320, 321
Loi Lamine Guèye (1st and 2nd), 287
Lokko, 73, 74, 78, 80, 96
Louveau, Ernest, 273
Lugard, Lord, 46, 47, 59, 110, 115, 138-9, 156, 163, 167, 173, 198, 199, 221-2, 234, 246, 253, 318

Macdonald, Malcolm, 323
Maclean, George, 10
Mcphee, Alan, 20
Madagascar (Malagasy Republic), 108, 127, 279, 287, 290, 301, 306, 309
Mair, Lucy, 205
Maji Maji rising, Tanganyika (1905-6), 47
Makoko Treaties (1882), 40, 41
Mali, 45, 109; formation of Federation, 305, 321, 325; and Independence (1960), 306-7, 308; see also Soudan; Haut-Sénégal-Niger
Mandel, Georges, 323
Mandinkas (Mandingos), 49, 50, 74, 259-60
Mangin, General, 108-9
manufactured goods, 244-5, 247-8, 276
Margne, M. Jules, 38
Marshall, Lieutenant-Colonel John Willoughby Astell, 92-3
Mashi, Sarkin Yashikera, 160, 162, 163
Mauretania, 45, 231, 235, 303, 305, 319
Mba, Léon, 320, 321
Mende rebellion (Sierra Leone), 61, 68-9, 93, 94
Mendès-France, Pierre, 296
Merlin, Governor-General Martial, of Senegal, 117, 118, 236
Mers-el Kébir, destruction of French fleet at, 272
Meyer, Jean Daniel, 205-6
migration, labour, 237-8, 246, 252-3, 260, 269, 276, 317, 323
military forces: African resistance to European invaders, 45-60; European superiority in weapons and discipline, 51-3; guerilla tactics adopted by Africans, 54, 57-9; recruitment of African troops in First World War, 105, 106, 107-19, 179-80, 183, 194, 238, 270; and in Second World War, 270, 274, 275, 279
missionaries, Christian, 1, 4-6, 8-10, 23n, 28-9, 30, 69, 249, 254
Mitchell, Sir Philip, 207-8n
Mitterand, François, 295
Moçambique (Mozambique), 132, 243
Mohamman Sani (Babakki), Emir of Bussa, 171, 175
Mohammed Korau, King of Katsina, 4
Mohammed Rumfa, King of Kano, 4, 5
Mora Tasude, Emir of Kaiama, 153, 155, 156, 159, 160
Mossi, 109, 202-3, 216, 225, 275, 323
Mouvement Socialiste Africain (M.S.A.), 299, 301
Moyen-Niger, cercle (Borgu), 180, 182, 188, 189, 191, 193
Muhammad Bello, Caliph, 4
mulattoes (métis), 9, 12-13, 104, 105, 106, 118, 127, 233, 243
Muna, S. T., 326
Muslims (Islam), 1, 50, 58, 316; cultural influence in West Africa, 4, 5, 255-6; nineteenth-century jihads, 7, 10-11; in Sierra Leone, 69, 73-4, 75; in Senegal, 106, 107; in Portuguese West Africa, 243; in Gambia, 263

Nana Olumu (of Ebrohimie), 46, 49, 54, 56, 58
Nathan, Sir Matthew, 95
Native Administration/Authority: in Nigeria, 139-41; and in Bussa, 151-2, 156, 160-75, 195; French v. British, 198-208, 234; role of West African chiefs, 209-30; in Gambia, 261; educated élite in, 318
Native chiefs: relations with colonial administrators, 131, 133; in Angola (regulos), 131-2, 243; in French West Africa, 134-5, 179, 200-2, 203, 235, 236, 238-9; in Kenya (headmen), 135-7; in Belgian Congo, 137-8; in Borgu, 180, 182; in French Equatorial Africa, 201-2, 203; role in local administration, 209-30: definition, 211-13; legitimacy in colonial period, 213-16; nature of change of authority, 216-18; functions under colonial rule, 218-20; during period of decolonisation,

INDEX

224-8; under African governments, 228-9
Ndebele rising (1896-7), 47
Newbury, C. W., 38
Newton, T. C., 156, 158, 159
Niger, 45, 272; French colonial rule, 33, 179, 203, 235; seasonal migration of labour, 237-8, 246; Independence as a goal, 283, 301; joins *Conseil de l'Entente*, 306, 307; trade with Nigeria, 323; *see also* Haut-Sénégal-Niger
Niger Delta, 29, 30, 31, 33, 37, 41, 42
Niger River, 33, 36, 37, 38, 40, 41, 42
Nigeria, 30, 45, 48, 59, 110, 115, 316, 318, 322; British colonial administrators, 122, 126-7, 128, 129, 130, 131, 133, 135-6, 138-41, 147-8; wage-earners, 123-4; and education, 124, 316, 324; Indirect Rule, 138-41, 199-200, 202, 205, 221-2, 234; taxation, 139, 140, 141, 144, 152, 199, 200, 222, 229, 238; legal system, 142-3, 199; forced labour, 144-5, 146; imposition of Native Authority system in Bussa and the 1915 Rebellion, 151-75; role of chiefs in local administration, 210, 211, 212, 227, 228, 229; administrative structure, 240-1; economy, 245, 250, 323, 325; Independence, 297, 308; trade with Niger, 323
Nikki (French Borgu), 152-4, 156, 157, 158, 180, 182-6, 190-1; *see also* Borgu
Nkrumah, Kwame, 227, 229, 300, 308, 321, 322
Norris, Major Richard Joseph, 86, 87-9, 91
Noufflard, Lieutenant-Governor of Dahomey, 183, 184, 187-8, 189, 190, 192, 194

Ohori revolt (Dahomey), 186
Old Calabar, 11, 22n
'Opération Hirondelle', 323
Osei Kojo, Asantehene, 4
Ouezzin-Coulibaly (Prime Minister of Upper Volta), 207, 228, 305
Ouidah, Dahomey, 32
Oyo, 29, 49, 180; Alafin of, 211, 216, 228

Paden, John, 222-3
Palmerston, Viscount, 27

palm-oil and produce, 8, 11, 20, 26, 29, 33, 237, 244, 245, 250, 262
Pan-African Congress: Second (1919), 104; Third (1921), 104
Parakou (French Borgu), 180, 182, 183, 184, 187, 188
Parkes, J. C. E., 14, 65, 66, 70, 78, 79, 82, 233
Parti Africain de l'Indépendence, 195, 301
Parti de la Fédération Africain, 306
Parti du Regroupement Africain (P.R.A.), 283, 301, 302, 303, 304
Partridge, D. P., 210
P.C.F. *see* Communists, French
Perham, Margery, 205
Pétain, Marshal, 269, 270, 271, 273, 278
Phérivong Mission of Inspection (Borgu, 1919), 184, 185, 194, 195
Pila Pila revolt (Dahomey), 186-7
Pittendrigh, W. M., 70
Pleven, René, 284, 298
Politique d'association, 203, 204, 207
Ponty, Governor-General William, 182, 215
Pope-Hennessy, Governor Sir John, 13, 14, 64
Porto Novo, 29, 32
Portuguese, 23n, 27, 113, 247, 260; on Gold Coast, 1-2; in Benin, 4-5; in Kongo, 5-6, 10, 40; colonialism, 16, 38-9, 42, 231; abolition of slave trade by, 36; Treaty between Britain and, 40, 41; colonial administrators in Angola, 122, 126, 127, 128-9, 130, 131-3, 141; and forced labour, 132, 145-6, 246, 249; colonial administrative policy, 233; and structure, 241-4; under Republican Regime, 242; and under *Estado Novo*, 242-4; social welfare, 249; Christian cultural influence, 253-4
Price, Rev. J. A. L., 66, 68

Quaque, Rev. Philip, 3, 23n
Quatre Communes, Senegal, 105, 106-8, 111, 118, 235, 269, 284, 316; *see also* Senegal
quinine, 16, 28, 51

racist theories, European, 9, 14, 15-16, 38
railways and roads, 36-7, 236, 246-7, 248, 261-2, 275, 317, 323

Ramaswami, Indian rice expert, 265, 267n
Ranger, T. O. 46-7
Rassemblement Démocratique Africain (R.D.A.), 47, 279, 293-5, 298, 302, 303, 304, 305, 309, 320, 322; Bamako Congress (1957), 299, 300, 320, 321, 328n
Régis, Ainé, 32
Regulos (Angolan chiefs), 131-2
Renard, Commandant, 187-8, 189, 190, 182
Republican Socialist Party (Senegal), 118
rice production, 260, 262, 263-6, 276
Rodney, Walter, 7
Rogers, Sir Fredric, 27
rouage (French 'turn-table' policy), 127, 214, 239, 319
Ruanda-Urundi, 127
rubber, 244, 250

Sabukki, Prince: Bussa Rebellion led by, 151, 161, 163-5, 167, 168, 169; granted amnesty (1924), 171
Saint Louis de Sénégal, 7, 10, 12, 26, 32, 33, 34, 37, 50, 54, 118
Salisbury, Lord, 34, 35
Samori, Almami, 3, 16, 46, 47, 48-9, 50, 52, 53, 54, 55, 57, 58, 96
Sanda, Sierra Leone, 79-80, 93
Sansanding Dam Project, Soudan, 238, 269, 280
Sarraut, Albert, 206
Schachter-Morgenthau, Ruth, 47
Scramble for Africa, 9, 13, 36-44; location of European interests (1850-80), 26-35; beginnings of, (1880-85), 35-41; Berlin Conference, 41-2; West African resistance, 45-60
Second World War, 20, 237; Vichy and Free France in West Africa during, 268-82
Senegal, 7, 9, 10, 11, 37, 144, 201, 261, 308; French assimilation policy, 12-13, 15, 134, 204, 225, 233, 285; and colonial rule, 18, 26, 27, 31, 33-4, 38, 39, 41, 233, 235-7; African resistance to French, 50, 51; Blaise Diagne and recruitment of African troops for 1914-18 war, 104-19; citizens' rights of *originaires* in *Quatre Communes*, 106-8, 118, 233; agriculture, 245-6, 250, 262; seasonal migration of labour, 246, 262; Gambia and, 260, 263, 315, 329n; during Second World War, 270, 272-4, 276, 277, 278; and post-war, 283, 293, 299, 303, 304, 305; joins Federation of Mali, 305, 306; rivalry between Ivory Coast and, 320-1
Senghor, Léopold Sedar, 18, 283, 291, 292, 293, 295, 296, 298, 299, 301-2, 303, 304, 306, 310, 320, 321
Senna Bunde, Almami, 70
Senoussi (Senussi) rebels, 192, 195
S.F.I.O., 293, 295, 299
Sharp, Granville, 8
Sharpe, Captain Wilfred Stanley, D. C. Karene, 65, 72, 73, 81, 83-5, 86, 87, 91
Sierra Leone, 9, 33, 34, 57, 109, 115, 263; Christian Community for Freed Blacks, 8; British assimilation policy, 12, 13-14, 233; and colonial rule, 29, 31; and trade, 30; resistance to colonialism, 49; Bai Bureh and Hut Tax War, 61-103: the building up of resentment against British, 62-72; the early years: Bai Bureh the warrior, 72-7; Bai Bureh as chief of Kasseh, 77-83; and war, 83-95; Indirect Rule, 221, 222, 234; and taxation, 238; administrative structure, 240; economic development, 248; peasant migration to, 269
Sissoko, Fily Dabo, 280, 286, 291, 293, 310
slave trade, slavery, 11, 22n, 32, 49; Atlantic, 3, 6-7, 8-9, 10; Portuguese, 2, 6; Arab, 6, 35-6; abolition of, 8-9, 11-12, 19, 28, 35-6, 64, 69-70, 182
Smith, Captain Carr, 91
social classes, creation of new, 318
social welfare, 249, 269, 280
socio-economic roles of bush administrators, 143-7
Sokoto Caliphate, 5, 30, 36, 47, 50, 53, 161; British treaties with, 41-2; and conquest of, 58, 59
Sorie Bunki, Chief, Port Loko, 84, 86, 94
Soudan, French, 31, 33, 34, 41, 47, 56-7, 58, 59, 144, 202, 205-6, 235; seasonal migration of labour, 238, 246, 276; and forced labour, 238; Sansanding Dam project, 238, 269; joins Federation of Mali, 305, 306; *see also* Mali

INDEX

Southern Rhodesia, 47, 123, 126, 127, 136
Stern, Jacques, 275
Stevens, Lt, Resident, Bussa, 155-6
Suret-Canale, Jean, 34, 208n
Susu, 73, 74, 75, 76-7, 78, 79, 81
Syrian middlemen/traders, 20, 112

Tamba Janneh, 264
Tambi expedition, Sierra Leone, 79-81
Tanganyika, 47, 123, 126, 199
Tarbet, Major Alexander, 81, 84-6, 87
taxation, 18, 19-20, 32, 143-4, 244, 246; in Sierra Leone, 61, 64-8, 69, 83-4, 91, 238; in French West Africa, 64, 97n, 179; 183-4, 195, 202, 235, 237, 238, 249; in Belgian Congo, 138; in Nigeria, 139, 140, 141, 144, 152, 199, 200, 222, 229, 238; in Kenya, 146; in Bussa, 157, 161, 167; prestation (labour tax), 238; in Gold Coast, 144, 238, 246; in Gambia, 238, 261; in Portuguese Africa, 132, 243, 249
technology, technical aid, 5, 6, 10; military, 51-2
Temne (Sierra Leone), 49, 61, 65-6, 68-9, 71-96 *passim*
Temple, Sir Charles, 147-8, 149
Thiam, Doudou, 322
Thomson, Graeme, Governor of Nigeria, 241
Tieba of Sikasso, 53, 57
Tirailleurs Sénégalais, 50, 109, 189, 190, 191-3
Togo, 54, 297, 298, 306, 319, 323; Germans in, 41, 42, 231; French Mandate, 235
Touré, Sekou, 47, 202, 227, 228, 284, 295, 297, 298, 299-300, 301, 302, 303-5, 308, 310, 320, 324
Townsend, Henry, 15
trade and commerce, 7, 20, 244-5, 247-8; European, 1-3, 6-7, 10, 11-12, 21, 22n, 35, 37; trans-Saharan, 3, 4, 11, 12, 21; Arab, 1, 2, 3, 4; British, 8-9, 26, 28-31, 37, 67-8, 75; French, 30, 32-5, 37, 75, 104, 105, 111, 112; in Sierra Leone, 67-8, 70, 71, 74-5; in Senegal, 104; in Borgu, 183; in Gambia, 260; Anglo-French interterritorial, 323; *see also* economy; slave trade
Treichville, R.D.A. 2nd Congress at (1949), 294

Tsirinana, Philibert, 301, 306
Tukolor, 48, 50, 56
Turaki, District Head of Bussa, 160, 162, 164, 165, 166, 167, 168-9, 214

Uganda, 126, 202
U.G.T.A.N., 301, 304
Umar (Omar), Al-Hajj, 12, 27, 33, 47, 50, 51, 57
Union Démocratique des Socialistes Republicaines (U.S.D.R.), 295
United Africa Company, 148
United Nations, 287, 323
Upper Volta, 109, 228, 269, 273; French colonial rule, 33, 144, 235; and native administration, 202-3; seasonal migration of labour, 237-8, 246; post-war decolonisation, 305-6; joins *Conseil de l'Entente*, 306, 307; *see also* Haut-Sénégal-Niger
Usman dan Fodio, Shehu, 4, 5, 7

Valentin, Durand, 12
Van der Plas, C.O., 266
Venn, Henry, 14-15
Vichy regime, 237, 268-82
Vollenhoven, Joost van, Governor-General of French West Africa, 111, 113-14, 117, 179-80, 208n

wage labour, 123-4
Wasangari (rulers of Borgu), 180, 182, 183, 193-4
Welch, Claude, Jr, 326
West Africa Frontier Force (W.A.F.F.), 164-5, 167, 239, 271
West African Shipping Conference, 245
West India Regiment, 81, 82, 86-7, 89
Wilks, Ivor, 29
Williams, F. R. A., 211
Wolseley, General Garnet, 46, 51, 53
Wyn-Harris, Sir Percy, 265, 266

Yameogo, Maurice, 228
Yauri (Nigeria), 152, 154-5, 157-8, 160, 161, 162-3, 165, 166, 167, 169-70, 171-2, 173
Yoruba, Yorubaland, 30, 31, 32, 49, 56, 140, 175, 180, 191, 201, 255, 315, 324

Milton Keynes UK
Ingram Content Group UK Ltd.
UKHW022334141123
432589UK00010B/60